SERMONS OF ST. ALPHONSUS LIGUORI

For All the Sundays of the Year

by

St. Alphonsus de Liguori

Bishop of St. Agatha, Founder of the Redemptorists, and Doctor of the Church

FOURTH EDITION

E P B M
ECHO POINT BOOKS & MEDIA, LLC
Brattleboro, Vermont

This book was originally published in 1852
by James Duffy, Dublin, Ireland.

Published in 2021 by Echo Point Books & Media
Brattleboro, Vermont
www.EchoPointBooks.com

The Sermons of St. Alphonsus Liguori
for All the Sundays of the Year
ISBN: 978-1-63561-979-9 (casebound)
978-1-63561-980-5 (paperback)

Cover design by Kaitlyn Whitaker

Cover image: Saint Alphonsus Liguori (1696-1787),
artist unknown, courtesy of Pinterest

ST. ALPHONSUS LIGUORI

An Inspirational Life

Born in 1696, to an Italian family of noble status, Alphonsus Liguori was a true Renaissance scholar. Though his family was not considered wealthy, the young Alphonsus received an extraordinarily broad education. His father had been a naval officer, and although the emerging Liguori had learned to ride, fence, and shoot, his myopic vision precluded following in his father's footsteps.

Alphonsus studied and excelled at music, painting, poetry, and writing. His first chosen profession became law, which he practiced successfully for eight years. Upon losing his first case at age 27, he reconsidered his career path and chose to answer a higher calling.

Despite the reluctance of his father, Alphonsus studied for the priesthood and was ordained at the age of 30. From the beginning he served the homeless and less fortunate, and his sermons became well known for their simple clarity. He said, "I have never preached a sermon which the poorest old woman in the congregation could not understand." Indeed, his discourses were known to have a strong beneficent influence on many who had wandered astray.

Continuing his lifelong compassion and caring for the poor and downtrodden, Father Alphonsus founded the Congregation of the Most Holy Redeemer in 1732. One of the major missions was to preach in the city slums of the region. Often converting heretics who had willfully rejected church doctrine, Liguori believed in forgiveness and redemption rather than punishment.

A talented musician, he wrote many hymns, the most well-known, originally written in Latin as *Quanno Nascetti Ninno,* which Pope Pius IX later translated into the Italian *Tu Scendi Dalle Stelle,* and which we know in English as "From Starry Skies Descending." He wrote several books and articles, along with countless sermons throughout his life of devotion.

Though he protested and tried to refuse, he was appointed Bishop of Sant'Agata dei Goti in 1762. From this position he observed widespread abuses of power and worked to reform the seminary. Also, as an exemplary act of charity, he sold his coach and gold ring in order to make a donation to the poor. These acts of reformation and benevolence did nothing in the eyes of many fellow priests, who persecuted him mercilessly in his old age. He was dismissed from the very congregation he had founded. Retiring in 1775, he lived in Pagani, Italy until his death in 1787.

Alphonsus Liguori was beatified in 1816 by Pope Pius VII, and canonized in 1839 by Pope Gregory XVI. The legacy of Saint Alphonsus continues to thrive, as he is to this day one of the most widely read Catholic authors in the world.

The 52 sermons presented here are a small yet very significant part of his gift. Written to be thorough, yet concise, these humble discourses are perfect for anyone wishing to observe Christian virtue, and to ponder the value of his or her own soul. Those seeking salvation and spiritual guidance will find pure inspiration in the compelling work of Saint Alphonsus.

PROTESTATION.

In obedience to the decrees of Urban VIII., I protest that, of the miraculous works and gifts ascribed in this work to certain servants of God, and not already approved by the Holy See, I claim no other belief than that which is ordinarily given to history resting on mere human authority; and that, in bestowing the title of Saint, or of Blessed, on any person not canonized or beatified by the Church, I only intend to do it according to the usage and opinion of men.

BULL

OF

THE CANONIZATION

OF

SAINT ALPHONSUS MARIA LIGUORI,

FOUNDER OF THE CONGREGATION OF THE MOST HOLY REDEEMER, AND BISHOP OF ST. AGATHA OF THE GOTHS.

GREGORY, BISHOP,

SERVANT OF THE SERVANTS OF GOD,

FOR A PERPETUAL REMEMBRANCE OF THE THING.

The Proemium.

ACCORDING to the Apostle of Nations, sanctity and learning should so adorn a Bishop, to whose trust is committed the salvation of souls, that he may, by the most exemplary manner of life, serve as a light to guide his flock without stumbling on the road to eternal happiness, and also be able to exhort them in sound doctrine, and to convince the gainsayers. We learn from the history of every age, that there have been Bishops eminently entitled to this twofold praise, who, reflecting the image of the Good Pastor, and being made the pattern of the flock from the heart, devoted their exertions and wisdom to the promotion of its salvation; and who, like a candle placed upon a candlestick, shed a lustre over the Church of God, not less by the example of a most perfect life, than by the singular excellence of their doctrine.

A general commendation of the virtues & merits of Alphonsus.

2. For the purpose of furnishing his Church with a new example of such worthy Bishops in the last century, the Almighty appears to have given ALPHONSUS MARIA LIGUORI, who, having, from his tenderest years, carefully cultivated the Christian virtues, and having acquired a wonderful knowledge especially of sacred literature, was called to the very arduous office of the Episcopacy, that, in the field of the Lord, in which he had long since received the Priesthood and proved himself a laborious husbandman, he might labour with greater effect and advantage. Not content that his zeal

for the increase of the glory of God should be confined within the narrow limits of his own life, he, in order to transmit to the remotest ages a series of successors in such a salutary work, instituted a society of Priests, who, inflamed with like charity, should devote to the salvation of souls all their care and exertions. It having been ascertained, after the eminent virtues of ALPHONSUS were examined with the wonted severity of judgment, that they had reached the highest summit of Christian perfection, and that no doubt could be entertained of the miracles by which God—the Author of all good—had attested the sanctity of his servant, we, in virtue of the Apostolical authority with which, though unworthy, we are invested by God, and with the advice not only of the Cardinals of the holy Roman Church, but of the Patriarchs, Archbishops, and Bishops, of whom a very great number were present in the city, decree and declare, by the present letters, that the honours of the Heavenly citizens are to be paid to the blessed ALPHONSUS LIGUORI by the universal Church, and that his intercession with God is to be implored.

The birth and early education of Alphonsus.

3. ALPHONSUS, descended of an illustrious race, was born in Naples on the 5th of the Kalends of October, 1696. Being endowed with wonderful activity of mind, he, on the termination of his childhood, applied himself successively to the study of the classics, of the more severe sciences, and of the law. He possessed such felicitous aptitude for learning, that he scarcely had entered on his sixteenth year, when, after a rigorous examination, he obtained, with distinguished applause, his degrees both in civil and canon law. Yielding to the wishes of his father, he applied all his attention to the study and practice of the profession of the law. Though he preserved his chastity and integrity in that avocation, nevertheless, the troubles and dangers by which it was beset induced him to abandon it and enter into the service of the Church. Wherefore, declining an offer of a high matrimonial connexion, and spontaneously and cheerfully transferring to his brother the paternal property, which descended to him as the eldest son, he cast away all care of human things.

He receives the Priesthood. The preservation of chastity his study. His wonderful love of God and of his neighbour.

4. Having received holy orders, and being raised to the dignity of the Priesthood, he began to apply all his energy to extend on every side the glory of God, to sow the seeds of virtue in the minds of men, and to pluck up the roots of vice. Persuaded that the apostolical labours of no man can be productive of abundant fruit, unless he support his teaching by his example, it became a principal object of his care to exhibit himself by the practice of every description of virtue, "as a minister of God" and a "dispenser of His mysteries". Of chastity, which he had long since consecrated by vow to God, he was always the most faithful guardian, incessantly exerting all the powers of his mind and employing every movement of his body for the sole purpose of preserving it free from the slightest stain. To attain this object with perfect security, he confidently consigned that virtue to the care of the Mother of God. He was carried towards God with so vehement an impulse of love, that his attention was perpetually fixed upon Him; and nothing appears to have afforded him

delight, but to think and speak of God. From the great fervour of his love for God, it is easy to conclude how ardent must have been the charity with which he burned for his neighbour. Hence, to recall men involved in vice and wickedness to the bosom and embraces of God, he never spared either toil or trouble. Hence it became his constant occupation to visit the hospitals for the purpose of assisting the sick, and of aiding by his presence those in particular who were in immediate danger of death. Hence it was that he accustomed himself to hear confessions with the greatest patience, and to spend in the performance of that function, not only whole days, but a considerable part of the night. Hence, too, was he in the habit of addressing from the pulpit his crowded audience in strains of such fervid language as to conquer and break down the obstinacy of abandoned sinners, and, by exhibiting to them the turpitude of the crimes which had hardened their hearts, to excite in the minds of his hearers such a lively sense of sorrow, as to move them to tears, and to fill, on various occasions, the sacred edifice with weeping and lamentations. Allowing himself, by day or by night, no intermission of the vast exertions, both of mind and body, which he made to procure the salvation of souls, he naturally became enfeebled and exhausted by incessant toil, and fell into a mortal malady, from which he was no sooner released by the Divine Power, than he immediately resumed with increased alacrity the performance of works of charity.

He institues a congregation, which takes its name from the most holy Redeemer.

5. As soon as he had learned that, in the designs of the Supreme Being, he was called to establish a religious society for the purpose of preventing a want of laborious husbandmen while the harvest was so abundant, he was deterred by no accumulation of difficulties from pressing forward the completion of a work which would redound so much to the advantage of the Church. Wherefore, relying on the Divine assistance, he commenced the undertaking, and happily eluded the designs and artifices of the infernal enemy, who strove to impede the furtherance of this new work. Having associated with him twelve men of eminent piety, he laid the foundation of a religious sodality, which received its name from the most holy Redeemer. His leading object in the institution of the society was, to reform as much as possible, both by word and example, the profligate and abandoned morals particularly of the peasantry, who were scattered through the rural districts. In a short time the society became wonderfully propagated through the towns and provinces of Italy: he then procured from Benedict the Fourteenth, our predecessor, its confirmation by Apostolical authority. On being appointed its superior by that Pontiff, the extent to which he incited the brotherhood by his example to the practice of every virtue, is truly astonishing.

Remarkable for humility and penitential spirit, he is inflamed with an incredible love for the sacrament of the most holy Eucharist, and for the Virgin Mother of God.

6. For the virtue of humility he was particularly distinguished; for, though the highest opinion of his great sanctity universally prevailed, and though he was respected and honoured by the most exalted dignitaries, he perpetually entertained the lowliest sentiments of himself, and esteemed himself unworthy of any mark of honour or respect. Towards the Blessed Virgin, whom he regarded

as a mother, he cherished the most singular piety. For the most holy Sacrament of the Eucharist he was penetrated with the deepest sentiments of love and veneration: and filled with extraordinary delight, he used to spend in adoring it several consecutive hours. That he might, in imitation of the Apostle, bring his body into subjection to the spirit, he kept it as a domestic enemy, under continual restraint, and subjected it to every species of torment. It was allowed by him as much meat and drink as would scarcely seem sufficient to renew its strength, or to support life: and the more effectually to extinguish every sense of pleasure, he was accustomed to sprinkle the very coarse food which he used with juices of the bitterest description. His side was constantly girded with a very rough horse-hair cloth; and he never omitted to attach small iron chains to the members of his body. He was in the habit of exercising on himself, by means of sharp-pointed disciplines, such a degree of severity, that the floor and walls were sprinkled with the blood which gushed from his mangled flesh; and to prevent the discovery of the mortifications which he practised, he took particular care to efface these stains of blood.

Though nearly exhausted by his apostolical labours he applies closely to the study of sacred literature, and publishes a great number of works for the good of the Church.

7. Perpetually occupied, as he was, in the discharge of his Apostolical functions, and enfeebling his body by every species of torture, it must excite wonder to find, notwithstanding, that he applied with so much energy, and devoted so much time, to the study of sacred literature, as to be able to render, by the publication of works equally learned and elaborate, the most important services to the cause of Christianity. In order that he might consecrate himself and all his actions to the service of God, he bound himself by an arduous and almost novel description of vow, not to waste the smallest portion of his time in idleness, but to be perpetually engaged in some profitable occupation. He composed a great number of books with the view of supporting the doctrine of morals, of fully elucidating the nature and duties of the clerical order, of confirming the truth of the Catholic religion, of asserting the rights of this Apostolic See, and of exciting sentiments of piety in the minds of Christians. They are wonderfully remarkable for unusual force, for extent and variety of learning, and for the singular proofs they afford of his great solicitude for the Church, and his ardent zeal for religion. But what deserves to be particularly noticed is, that after a careful examination of his works, it has been ascertained that they all, notwithstanding their number and extent, may be perused by the faithful with the most perfect safety *(inoffenso prorsus pede percurri a fidelibus posse)*.

He is appointed Bishop of St. Agatha by Clement the Thirteenth.

8. In consequence of so high a reputation for sanctity and erudition, Alphonsus was promoted by the authority of Clement the Thirteenth, to the Episcopal See of St. Agatha of the Goths. The holy man dreaded the weight of so great a burden, and employed every means to decline it. But having discovered the will of God in the designs of the Pontiff, he considered it to be his duty to acquiesce, and, with confidence in the Divine protection, to undertake with cheerfulness and courage a task to which, through humility, he deemed himself unequal.

9. It is difficult to describe the laborious attention and zeal with which he sought to discharge all the duties of a Pastor. He watched unceasingly over the flock committed to his care, and laboured to the utmost of his ability to prevent the loss of even one of the sheep entrusted to him. Nor did the acquisition of his new dignity cause any abatement of the rigorous mortification of his life: he avoided all daintiness of food and all costliness of dress: there was nothing superfluous, nothing splendid in his palace or furniture. His charity to the poor was truly astonishing: they were liberally supplied by him with food, clothes, and money; and to relieve their necessities he sometimes did not hesitate to sell even his golden cross and the episcopal ring. From his own revenue he was accustomed to give young females the portion necessary to enable them to enter the marriage state, and to support, at his own expense, young ecclesiastics of poor and humble parents, while pursuing their course of studies. To holy virgins he opened the cloister; and for such females as might stand exposed to the danger of losing their chastity, he established houses of refuge. In the visitation of his diocess, retarded neither by the badness of the roads nor by the inclemency of the season, he visited the villages on the summits of the mountains, and the people scattered through the country, and, in language full of ardour, enkindled in them the love of virtue, and deterred them from the turpitude of sin. To priests, and to young men who had commenced their preparation for the ecclesiastical state, he paid peculiar attention. Great indeed were the exertions he made, that, in the very flower of life, they should grow up in piety, and be imbued especially with sacred science, in order that they might at length become fit for the due administration of sacred things, and for the proper direction of the Christian people. It must be acknowledged, that the life of the excellent prelate acted upon their minds as a powerful stimulus; for, beholding his mode of life, they had before their eyes the brightest example of continency, of religion, of piety,—in fine, of all the virtues with which a priest, if he wish to contribute any thing toward the common advantage of the Church, should be furnished and adorned.

His eminent virtues in the discharge of the pastoral duties.

10. After having, for the space of thirteen years, governed the church committed to his care with all pastoral zeal and the most exemplary vigilance, bending under the united weight of old age and sickness, he, after repeated applications to our predecessor, Pius the Sixth, at length obtained leave to resign his burdensome charge. Released from the duties of the episcopacy, he rejoined his congregation; but, instead of devoting the remainder of his life to innocent repose, he, even in extreme old age, engaged in other laborious occupations. He was constantly employed in committing to writing something which might be productive of advantage to the faithful; and continued to preach, in order that he might reform the morals of men, and inflame them as much as possible with the love of virtue.

He resigns the bishopric, and returns to his congregation.

11. At length when he had reached the ninety-first year of his life, now hastening to its close, he was com-

Full of years and merits, he dies in the peace of Christ.

pelled, pressed down as he was by the weight of years, and seized by serious illness, to keep his bed. Having endured with incredible patience the excruciating pains of his illness, and having strongly exhorted the brethren of the religious society he had established to the practice of every virtue, he was refreshed by the Viaticum of the most holy Eucharist, and fortified by the sacrament of extreme unction. After he had received these sacraments of the Church most religiously, his soul, which longed for nothing more ardently than to be delivered from the prison of the body, and to be with Christ, full of joy and gladness, most placidly flew into the bosom of God.

The prevailing opinion of his sanctity confirmed by miracles. The drawing up of the juridical account of his virtues and miracles.

12. As soon as the intelligence of ALPHONSUS' death had obtained circulation, a great concourse of the faithful collected round his remains, lamenting the loss of so great a man, and evincing their respect and veneration for him by their efforts to procure something which he had used during life. Nor was fame silent regarding the miracles by which God publicly declared to all the extraordinary sanctity of the Bishop. A report of these miracles being spread far and wide, the opinion of his virtues, which had long since prevailed, became confirmed in a surprising degree; and several princes and other high personages, together with very many of the religious orders, earnestly besought the supreme Pontiff, Pius the Sixth, to order a juridical account of the most holy life of ALPHONSUS to be drawn up. This having been done in the usual manner, and weighed with the greatest nicety—the works also which he published, having been most attentively perused and examined—our predecessor, Pius the Seventh, with the advice of the Congregation of Rites, issued, on the Nones of May, 1807, a decree declaring that it was proved beyond doubt, that the venerable ALPHONSUS MARIA DE LIGUORI possessed in a heroic degree the theological and cardinal virtues, together with those connected with them.

Two miracles approved of by the Holy See for his beatification, are related.

13. Afterwards, in the same sacred council, an investigation took place of the miracles which were alleged to have been performed by Almighty God in favour of the venerable ALPHONSUS. Of these miracles, two in particular, of the second order, were pronounced to be most undoubtedly certain. The first was the sudden cure of Magdalen de Nuncio, who was brought to the point of death by a gangrenous ulcer, on account of which a great part of one side of her breast had been cut away. She implored the intercession of ALPHONSUS; her breast was made whole, and she was restored to health, contrary to the expectation of all. The second was likewise the perfect and instantaneous cure of Francis ab Octavino, of the order of the Reformed Minors of St. Francis. He was so grievously afflicted with a pulmonary phthisis and confirmed marasmus, that no hopes were entertained of his recovery. After having poured forth his supplications to the venerable ALPHONSUS for several days, he was suddenly restored to health, and not a single trace of consumption remained. But, in a matter of such serious importance, Pius the Seventh, of sacred memory, thought it proper to refrain from pronouncing his judgment until he should more earnestly have implored light from on high. At length, on

the 16th of the Kalends of October, 1815, the festival of the Dolours of the Mother of God, the memory of whose sorrows, ALPHONSUS, during his mortal career, had piously and religiously cherished, our said predecessor was pleased to declare his opinion, and published a decree, in which the two cures above mentioned were pronounced to be true miracles. At last, after taking the opinion of the Sacred Congregation, he issued pontifical letters, on the 12th of the Kalends of January, 1816, declaring that the honours of the blessed should, at some time, be paid to the venerable ALPHONSUS MARIA LIGUORI. The ceremony of the beatification was performed with solemn pomp and splendour in the Basilica of the Vatican, on the 16th of the Kalends of September, 1816.

Miracles ratified by the Holy See for his Canonization, and declared to be most true.

14. After the honours of public worship had been paid to the venerable ALPHONSUS, many others in actual danger experienced his aid, manifestly in order that all might know that in proportion to the labours and exertions of this most pious Bishop for the advancement of the glory of the Divine name, God, of his great bounty, wished to accumulate honours in this world on the faithful dispenser of his house. Moved by the celebrity of these miracles, Ferdinand the First, the most pious King of the Two Sicilies, and other Princes, besides most of the Cardinals of the Holy Roman Church, of the Archbishops and Bishops, together with the religious orders, and especially the sodality of the Most Holy Redeemer, which justly boasts of ALPHONSUS as its founder, again and again besought Pius the Seventh to refer as speedily as possible to the Sacred Congregation of Rites, the question of the propriety of enrolling the blessed ALPHONSUS in the catologue of the saints. The same Pontiff most graciously yielded to their prayers: an accurate inquiry into the truth of the recent miracles was commenced; and, after a long deliberation, two miracles were ascertained to be placed beyond all doubt. The first of these was the sudden and perfect cure of Antonia Tarsia, who was reduced to the last extremity by a mortal contusion in the abdomen, and most severe internal injuries, which she received by falling headlong from a considerable height while she was carrying a heavy load. She implored in the most earnest manner the aid of ALPHONSUS; and to the great amazement of all present, she suddenly bounded forth perfectly restored. The second was the cure of Brother Peter Canali, a professed lay brother of the congregation of the Camaldolese. He suffered under a most horrible ulcer in the breast, which had become fistulous, callous, and carious, and which appeared to be more and more exasperated by every attempt to effect its cure; so that, abandoning all hopes of recovery, he was in hourly expectation of death. He for some days implored ALPHONSUS to be propitious to him, and to avert from him the certain danger of death. His prayers were heard; for every vestige of the ulcer was effaced, and he forthwith recovered that health for which he sighed so long.

Secret, public, and semi-public consistories held before his Canonization.

15. The truly wonderful cures which we have mentioned being juridically proved, Pius the Eighth, our predecessor, published a decree declaratory of their truth, on the 3rd of the Nones of December, 1829. Afterwards,

when, in the Sacred Congregation of Rites, the usual question was proposed, whether the solemn canonization might be safely proceeded with, and whether all those steps had been taken, which the usages of the Apostolic See necessarily require, the same Pontiff, Pius the Eighth, on the fifth Sunday after the Paschal solemnity, after having celebrated Mass in the Quirinal palace, on the 17th of the Kalends of June, 1830, announced his judgment, that it was safe to proceed to the said canonization. Now, desirous to execute this decree, and gladly yielding to the wishes of the sodality of the most holy Redeemer, we, in the first instance, in a secret consistory held on the 4th of the Ides of December, 1838, communicated on the subject with the entire college of our venerable brethren the Cardinals of the holy Roman Church; all of whom were of one opinion—that the honours of the saints should be paid to blessed ALPHONSUS MARIA DE LIGUORI. Soon after, we summoned to a consultation on so important a measure, a great number of our venerable brethren the Archbishops and Bishops, and submitted to their judgment the series of all the acts which comprised the virtues and miracles of the blessed ALPHONSUS, both orally in the public consistory, where our beloved son Anthony Maria Cagiano de Azevedo, the advocate of our Consistorial Court, pleaded the cause of the blessed Bishop; and in a written statement containing an accurate relation of these acts, taken from the authentic records of the same sacred council. After these proceedings, we called to a semi-public consistory, held in our presence on the 8th of the Ides of May, not only our venerable brethren the Cardinals of the holy Roman Church, but also our venerable brethren the Patriarchs, Archbishops, and Bishops, who were present in the city, and asked their opinion on the subject of the canonization of the blessed ALPHONSUS. When all had unanimously expressed their opinion in favour of the measure, and even professed the greatest desire that this honour should be conferred on the blessed ALPHONSUS, we gave directions to our beloved sons the Notaries of the Apostolic See, to draw up the necessary public documents; and we ordered that the written votes of our venerable brethren, signed by each, should be preserved in the archives of the Roman Church.

Notwithstanding the foregoing precautions, we deemed it proper, in a case of such momentous importance, to delay the peremptory sentence, until we should have ordered days of solemn fast to be observed in the city, and appoint churches for supplication to God, that we might obtain from the Heavenly Father of Light a more copious effusion of the rays of his wisdom.

On the feast of the most holy Trinity, the solemn ceremony of the canonization is celebrated with great pomp.

16. The 7th of the Kalends of June being at last fixed for the aforesaid solemn canonization of blessed ALPHONSUS, as well as for that of the other blessed individuals, namely—Francis de Hieronymo, of the Society of Jesus; John Joseph of the Cross, of the order of the Discalced Minors of St. Peter of Alcantara; Pacificus a S. Severino, of the order of Reformed Minors de Observantia; and Veronica de Julianis, Abbess of the Capuchin Nuns—we proceeded in festive pomp to the Vatican Basilick, attended by the several orders of the secular and regular clergy, by the nobles and officers of the Roman Court and of our Palace, and by our venerable brethren the Cardinals of the holy Roman Church, together with the Patriarchs, Archbishops, and Bishops. Before

we approached the altar for the celebration of the sacred mysteries, our beloved son Aloysius Lambruschini, Cardinal Priest of the holy Roman Church, of the title of S. Callistus, presented again, through the Advocate of our Consistorial Court, the most humble prayers of Christian Princes, of Bishops, and of the people, that the blessed ALPHONSUS should be raised to the rank of the saints; and we ourselves, falling on our knees, besought the choirs of angels, and all the saints in Heaven, to be propitious to us, and then, with reiterated importunity, implored the Holy Ghost in the most earnest manner, to strengthen, by his power, our mind, now about to pronounce the definite sentence. At last, taking into consideration the most humble prayers of the Postulator in the cause, and also the wishes of the universal Church, the searching investigation to which this important affair had been subjected, and the votes which the Bishops, aided by God, had given; we, by virtue of the Apostolic authority which, though unworthy, we possess, as the successor of St. Peter, the Prince of the Apostles, in the supreme government of the Church, in honour of the Holy and Undivided Trinity, for the splendour and glory of the Catholic Faith and Religion, announced our solemn and decretorial judgment, and placed in the catalogue of holy Bishops and Confessors, the blessed ALPHONSUS MARIA DE LIGUORI, refulgent with the light of Christian virtues, and most celebrated for miracles, and ordained that his memory should be venerated by the universal Church, on the 4th of the Nones of August. On those who should, on the said day, visit the tomb of SAINT ALPHONSUS, and on the days appointed, honour the remains of the other saints, we graciously bestowed an indulgence of seven years and of seven 40 days.

Public indulgences granted on the occasion of the canonization.

17. Afterwards, on the great altar of the Basilick of the Vatican, we reverently offered up the Immaculate Lamb to God the Father. Lastly, from the gallery of the upper hall of the Vatican Basilick, we most lovingly gave to a crowded congregation a solemn benediction, and bestowed a plenary indulgence, not only upon such of the faithful as assisted at this benediction, but upon all those who were present at the sacred ceremony of the canonization.

The faithful are incited to virtue by the bright example of Alphonsus.

18. Let us now, therefore, rejoice exceedingly, as we justly may, and return due thanks to Almighty God, who never fails to supply his Church with new examples of virtue, that we may be more powerfully incited to walk with cheerfulness in the way of salvation. Besides, beset as we are with so many and such great dangers, and surrounded by the arms of so many bitter foes, let us have recourse to the intercession of SAINT ALPHONSUS, that, strengthened by the Divine aid, we may one day obtain the reward of victory, and a crown of never-fading glory in Heaven.

The authority of the copies.

19. And that no length of time might ever obliterate the memory of this most auspicious event, we wished that it should be committed to writing, and confirmed by Apostolical letters, and ordained that such copies as should be signed by a Notary Public, and bear the seal of an Ecclesiastical Dignitary, should have as much authority as these the originals, if shown or exhibited.

20. Let no man, therefore, infringe or, with daring temerity, contravene this instrument of our will and decree. If any should presume to make such an attempt, be it known to him, that he shall incur the indignation of the Omnipotent God, and of the blessed Apostles Peter and Paul. Penal sanction.

21. Given at Rome, at St. Peter's, on the 7th of the Kalends of June, in the year 1839 of our Lord's Incarnation, and in the ninth year of our pontificate.

✠ GREGORY, Bishop of the Catholic Church.

✠ B. Pacca, Cardinal Bishop of Ostia and Veletri; Dean of the Sacred College.
✠ E. De Gregorio, Cardinal Bishop of Porto, St. Ruphina, and Civita Vecchia; Major Penitentiary.
✠ J. F. Falzacappa, Cardinal Bishop of Albano.
✠ C. M. Pedicini, Cardinal Bishop of Præneste; Vice-Chancellor.
✠ F. Micara, Cardinal Bishop of Tusculum.
✠ A. D. Gamberini, Cardinal Bishop of Sabina.
✠ C. Opizzoni, Cardinal Priest of the title of St. Bernard ad Thermas.
✠
✠
✠ H. Dandini, Cardinal Priest of the title of St. Balbina.
✠
✠
✠
✠ J. B. Bussi, Cardinal Priest of the title of St. Pancratius.

✠ J. Giustiniani, Cardinal Priest of the title of St. Peter and St. Marcellinus.

✠ J. Ph. Franzoni, Cardinal Priest of the title of St. Mary in Aracœli.

✠ B. Barberini, Cardinal Priest of the title of St. Mary beyond the Tiber.

✠

✠ A. Lambruschini, Cardinal Priest of the title of St. Callistus.

✠

✠ F. Serra Cassano, Cardinal Priest of the title of the Twelve Apostles.

✠

✠

✠

✠

✠ A. Del Drago, Cardinal Priest of the title of St. Laurence in Pane et Perna.

✠ C. Castracane De Antelminellis, Cardinal Priest of the title of St. Peter ad Vincula.

✠

✠

✠ J. A. Brignole, Cardinal Priest of the title of St. Cecily.

✠ J. Della Porta Rodiani, Cardinal Priest of the title of St. Susanna.

✠ C. Patrizi, Cardinal Priest of the title of St. Sylvester in Capite.

✠ J. Alberghini, Cardinal Priest of the title of St. Prisca.

✠ P. Polidori, Cardinal Priest of the title of St. Eusebius.

✠ P. M. Tadini, Cardinal Priest of the title of St. Mary in Transpontina.

✠

✠

✠ A. Mai, Cardinal Priest of the title of St. Anastasia.

✠

✠ C. Falconieri, Cardinal Priest of the title of St. Marcellus.

✠ A. Tosti, Cardinal Priest of the title of St. Peter in Monte Aureo.

✠

✠ J. Mezzofante, Cardinal Priest of the title of St. Onuphrius.

✠

✠ A. S. Rivarola, (Prior) Cardinal Deacon of St. Mary ad Martyres.

✠

✠ Th. Bernetti, Cardinal Deacon of St. Cæsareus.

✠ J. F. S. Marco-y-Catalan, Cardinal Deacon of St. Agatha ad Suburram.

✠ L. S. Gazzoli, Cardinal Deacon of St. Eustachius.

✠ M. S. Mattei, Cardinal Deacon of St. Mary ad Aquiria.

✠

✠ A. S. Spada, Cardinal Deacon of St. Mary in Cosmedin.

✠ A. S. De Flisco, Cardinal Deacon of St. Mary in Porticu.

✠ A. S. Ciacchi, Cardinal Deacon of St. Angelo in Pescaria.

✠

✠

✠

B. Cardinal Pacca Pro Datarius.
Place of ✠ Seal

E. Cardinal de Gregorio.
Seen at the Court
J. M. Vespignani, Archbishop of Tyana.

OBJECT OF THE WORK.

THE present Work is entitled ABRIDGED SERMONS FOR ALL THE SUNDAYS OF THE YEAR. They are called *Abridged Sermons*, because, although each contains abundant matter for a sermon, the sentiments are briefly expressed—not, however, so briefly as to render the sense obscure. Hence the work may be used for spiritual lectures. Diffuseness has been purposely avoided, that the preacher may extend the subject treated, in the way which may appear best to him. A preacher will scarce ever deliver with zeal and warmth, sentiments which he has not made in some manner his own. Hence the matter of each sermon has been condensed into a small compass, that the preacher may extend it according to his pleasure, and thus make it his own.

In each sermon there are many passages from the Scriptures and Holy Fathers, and a variety of reflections—perhaps too many for a single discourse—that the reader may select what will be most pleasing to him. The style is easy and simple, and therefore calculated to render the preaching of the Divine Word conducive to the salvation of souls.

INSTRUCTIONS TO PREACHERS.

1. In the first place, the preacher, if he wishes that his preaching shall produce abundant fruit, should propose to himself the proper end—that is, to preach, not with a view to obtain honour, or applause, or any temporal advantage, but solely to gain souls to God; and hence it is necessary, that when he enters upon his exalted office of divine ambassador, he should pray to God fervently to inflame his heart with His holy love; because it is by this means that his preaching will be productive of much fruit. The venerable Father John D'Avila being once asked, what was most conducive towards preaching well, replied in those short but expressive words—"*To love Jesus Christ well*". It has been therefore found by experience, that preachers who love Jesus Christ have often effected more by a single discourse, than others by several.

2. St. Thomas of Villanova said, that the words of a sermon should be like so many darts of fire, which would wound and inflame the hearers with divine love. "But how", he subjoined, "can the heart be set on fire by those sermons which, though long and elaborate, issue, notwithstanding, from a frozen heart?" St. Francis de Sales observes, that the tongue speaks to the ear, but the heart speaks to the heart. He proceeds to say, that when the sentiments do not spring from the heart of the preacher, it is with difficulty they draw the hearts of others to divine love: he must himself be first inflamed with it. "Lampades ejus lampades ignis, atque flammarum"—*Cant.*, viii. 6. He must be first a fire to burn, and afterwards a flame to set others on fire. St. Bernard explained this in other terms, when he said, that he must be first a cistern, and then a canal: first a cistern—that is, full of the fervour and zeal which are collected in mental prayer; and then a canal, to communicate it to others.

3. With regard to the subject matter of sermons. Those

subjects should be selected which move most powerfully to detest sin and to love God; whence the preacher should often speak of the last things—of death, of judgment, of Hell, of Heaven, and of eternity. According to the advice of the Holy Spirit, "Memorare novissima tua, et in æternum non peccabis"—*Eccl.*, vii. 40, it is particularly useful often to make mention of death, by delivering several discourses on that subject during the year, speaking at one time on the uncertainty of death, which terminates all the pleasures, as well as all the afflictions of this life; at another, on the uncertainty of the time at which death may arrive; now on the unhappy death of the sinner; and again, on the happy death of the just.

4. The preacher should often speak of the love which Jesus Christ bears towards us, of the love which we should bear to Jesus Christ, and of the confidence we should have in His mercy whenever we are resolved to amend our lives. It would appear that some preachers do not know how to speak of anything but the justice of God, terrors, threats, and chastisements. There is no doubt but that terrifying discourses are of use to arouse sinners from the sleep of sin; but we should be persuaded at the same time, that those who abstain from sin solely through the fear of punishment, will with difficulty persevere for a long time. Love is that golden link which binds the soul to God, and makes it faithful in repelling temptation and practising virtue. St. Augustine said: "Ama et fac quod vis". He who truly loves God, flies from everything displeasing to Him, and seeks to please Him to the utmost of his power. And here let us cite that remarkable saying of St. Francis de Sales: "The love that does not spring from the passion of Christ is weak". By this the saint gives us to understand, that the passion of Christ moves us most effectually to love Him.

5. Thus it is very useful, and most conducive to inspire the love of God, to speak to sinners of the confidence which we should have in Jesus Christ if we abandon sin. "Viam mandatorum, tuorum cucurri, cum dilatasti cor meum"—*Ps.*, cxviii. 32. When the heart is dilated with confidence, it easily runs in the way of the Lord. In like manner, the preacher should often speak of the confidence which we should have in the intercession of the Mother of God. Besides the discourses delivered

during the course of the year, on the principal festivals of the Blessed Virgin Mary, — as the Annunciation, the Assumption, her Patronage, and her Dolours, — let him oftentimes, in his addresses to the people, inculcate upon the minds of his auditors, devotion to the Mother of God. Some preachers have a very laudable custom of introducing into every sermon something regarding the Blessed Virgin, either by relating some example of graces bestowed on her clients, or of some act of homage performed by her votaries, or some prayer which we should offer to her.

6. Moreover, the preacher should often speak of the means by which we are preserved in the grace of God; such as, flying dangerous occasions and wicked companions, frequenting the sacraments, and especially recommending ourselves often to God and the Virgin Mother, in order to obtain the graces necessary for salvation, and principally the graces of perseverance and of the love of Jesus Christ, without which we cannot be saved.

7. The preacher should likewise often speak against bad confessions, in which sins are concealed through shame. This is an evil not of rare occurrence, but frequent, especially in small country districts, which consigns innumerable souls to Hell. Hence it is very useful to mention, from time to time, some example of souls that were damned by wilfully concealing sins in confession.

8. We shall now speak briefly of the parts of a discourse, which are nine: — the exordium, the proposition, the division, the introduction, the proof, the confutation, the amplification, the peroration or conclusion, the epilogue, and the appeal to the passions. These are again reduced to three principal divisions: 1. the exordium; 2. the proof, which comprises the introduction, that precedes, and the confutation of the opposite arguments, that follows it; 3. the peroration or conclusion, which comprises the epilogue, the moral exhortation, and the appeal to the passions. To the exordium rhetoricians assign seven parts: — the introduction, general proposition, confirmation, repetition of the proposition, connection, particular proposition, and division. But, commonly speaking, the substantial parts of the exordium are three: — 1. the general proposition; 2. the connection, or the link by which it is connected with the parti-

cular proposition; 3. the particular proposition, or the principal one of the discourse, which includes the division of the points. For example: 1. "We must work out our salvation, because there is no alternative: whosoever is not saved is damned": that is the general proposition. 2. "But, to be saved, we must die a happy death": that is the connection or application. 3. "But it is exceedingly difficult to die a happy death after a wicked life": and that is the particular proposition, or principal one of the discourse, which ought to be clear, concise, and simple, and, at the same time, one; otherwise, if unity be not observed in the proposition, it would not be one sermon, but several; and, therefore, the points into which the discourse is divided ought all tend to prove one single proposition. For example: "The person who is addicted to a bad habit is with difficulty saved, because the bad habit (1.) darkens the understanding, (2.) hardens the heart": and these will be the two points of the discourse. Let the points be short and few, not exceeding two, or, at most, three; and sometimes a single point will be sufficient. For example: "Mortal sin is a great evil, because it is an injury done to God"; or, "He who abuses too much the mercy of God will be abandoned by Him".

9. With regard to the body of the discourse, and, in the first place, the proof, it ought to be a perfect syllogism, but without appearing to be so. The major proposition should be proved before we pass to the minor; and the minor before we pass to the conclusion. This, however, is to be understood when the major or minor proposition requires proof: otherwise, when they express truths already known and certain, it is sufficient to amplify, without proving them.

10. As far as regards the order of the proofs, generally speaking, the authority of the Scriptures and of the Holy Fathers should be first adduced; then the arguments from reason; and afterwards the illustrations and examples. The texts of Scripture should be cited in an impressive and emphatic manner. It is better then to dwell on the exposition of one or two texts of Scripture, than to cite many at once, without considering well their import. The citations from the Fathers should be few and brief, and containing some sentiment that is strong and animated, and not trivial. After the citations, the arguments from reason

should be adduced; concerning which, some assert that the weaker reasons should be advanced in the first place, and then the stronger; but I am disposed to adopt the opinion of others, who think it better that the strong arguments should be adduced in the last place, but that in the first place a strong argument should be advanced; and that the weaker ones should occupy the middle place; because, were a weak argument adduced in the commencement, it might make a bad impression on the minds of the auditors. After the arguments from reason come the examples and illustrations. I have said that this arrangement should be observed *ordinarily;* but, occasionally, it will be of use to give some one of the forementioned proofs precedence of the others: this must be left to the discretion of the preacher.

11. Care should be taken that the transition from one point to the other be made naturally, without passing from one thing to another that has no relation to it. The most ordinary and easiest modes are these: "Let us proceed to the other point", etc.; or, "Thus, after having seen", etc. And passing from one argument to another, you may say: "Besides, we should consider", etc., taking care, as far as it is possible, that the last part of the preceding argument has some connection with the following point or argument.

12. We have spoken of proofs. As far as regards the amplification of proofs, one is verbal, which consists in words; another is real, which may consist either in climax — for example, "It is a virtue to suffer tribulations with patience — a greater virtue to desire them: it is a greater still to take delight in them": or it may be borrowed from the circumstances of the subject, or from comparison with another subject of equal or lesser consideration. The morals have their proper place, as we shall remark in the peroration. It is, however, occasionally allowed, after a satisfactory proof has been adduced, to address a short exhortation; and this is particularly the case in the sermons of the Mission, in which the audience is generally composed of rude, uneducated persons, on whom moral exhortation makes more impression; but these moral exhortations that are incidentally introduced, should not be too long or too frequent, so as to render the discourse tedious or languid.

13. The peroration contains three parts — the epilogue, the moral exhortation, and the appeal to the passions. The epilogue

is a recapitulation of the discourse, in which the most convincing arguments that have been already advanced are repeated, but which must be handled with a view to the movement of the passions which is to follow; whence the preacher, in this recapitulation, should commence to move the passions.

14. As to the moral exhortation, it may be observed, that oftentimes the principal fruit of the sermon consists, especially in discourses addressed to the people, in explaining the moral truths suitable to the subject of the discourse, with propriety and earnestness. The preacher, therefore, should take care to speak against the most prevalent vices; viz., hatred, impurity, blasphemy; against evil occasions, wicked companions; against parents who allow their children to hold intercourse with persons of different sex; and especially against mothers who invite young men into their houses to converse with their daughters. Let him also exhort the heads of families to remove from their houses bad books, and particularly novels, which insinuate a secret poison that corrupts youth. Let him speak against games of hazard, which are the ruin of families and of souls.

15. In a word, let the preacher endeavour, in his sermons, always to insinuate whatever he can that is practical,—that is, the remedies of the different vices; the means of persevering in a virtuous life; such as to fly dangerous occasions and bad company; to offer violence to one's self in motions of anger, so as not to break out into injurious actions or words; by suggesting to the hearers some form of expression, to avoid blasphemies or imprecations: for example, "Lord, give me patience!" "Virgin Mary, assist me!" and the like. Let him recommend the people to hear Mass every morning; to read every day some spiritual book; every morning to renew the resolution of not offending God, and to ask the divine assistance in order to persevere; to make each day a visit to the most holy sacrament and the Blessed Virgin, in some representation of her; each evening to make the examination of conscience, with an act of sorrow; after having committed a sin, immediately to make an act of contrition, and to confess it as soon as possible: above all, let him recommend his hearers to have recourse to God and to the Blessed Virgin in the time of temptation, by repeating oftentimes the names of Jesus and Mary, and continuing to invoke their aid until the temptation ceases. Those

means and remedies should be often repeated by the preacher, and recommended frequently in the course of his sermons; and he must not be deterred by the apprehension of being criticised by some learned person, who may remark that the preacher repeated the same things. In preaching we must not seek the applause of the learned, but the divine approbation, and the advantage of souls, and particularly of poor ignorant persons, who do not profit so much by thoughts and arguments, as by those easy practices which are suggested and repeated to them. I say repeated, since those rude and unlettered persons will easily forget what they hear, unless it is oftentimes repeated to them.

16. Let young preachers also take care to develope, and to commit to memory, their sermons, before they deliver them from the pulpit. To preach extempore is useful, inasmuch as the discourse becomes thus more natural and familiar; this, however, is not the case with young men, but only with those who have been in the habit of preaching for many years; otherwise, young men would contract a habit of speaking without preparation, and of preaching at random, saying whatever occurred to them, without any order or arrangement. However, young preachers should take care to develope their sermons, not in the florid style of elaborate expression, lofty thoughts, and sounding periods. Read the golden treatise on popular eloquence by the celebrated scholar, Louis Muratori; in which he proves that all sermons addressed to an audience composed of learned and unlearned, ought to be not only familiar, but also popular; composed in an easy and simple style, such as the people are in the habit of using; avoiding, however, all low and vulgar expressions, which are not suited to the dignity of the pulpit. "The people", says Muratori, "are composed for the most part of the ignorant; if you address to them abstruse doctrines and reflections, and use words and phrases that are not adapted to ordinary comprehensions, what fruit do you hope for from persons who do not understand you? Wherefore, the practice of those preachers will never be conformable to the rules of the art, or the principles of genuine eloquence, who, instead of accommodating themselves to the limited capacity of so many of their hearers, appear to study to make themselves intelligible to the learned only; as if they were ashamed to make themselves understood by the poor, who have

as good a right to the word of God as the learned. Nay more, a Christian preacher is bound to each one of his auditory in particular, as if there were no other who heard him. He who employs lofty reasoning, and is not careful to make himself understood by all, betrays the cause of God and his own duty, and disregards the spiritual necessities of a great portion of his audience". Hence the Council of Trent prescribes to all parish priests, to compose their discourses in a manner adapted to the capacity of their audience: "Archipresbyteri et parochi per se, vel alios idoneos, plebes sibi commissas pro earum capacitate pascant salutaribus verbis"—*sess.* v. *cap.* i., *de Reform.*

17. St. Francis de Sales said, that select language and sounding periods are the bane of sacred eloquence; and the principal reason of this is, that sermons composed in this style have not the divine sanction and concurrence. They may be of use to the learned, but not to the illiterate, who generally constitute the principal part of every audience. On the other hand, sermons composed in a familiar style are useful to the illiterate as well as to the learned. Muratori adds, that when the preacher addresses the humbler classes alone, or country people, he ought to make use of the most popular and familiar style possible, in order to accommodate himself to the gross understanding of such ignorant persons. He says, that the preacher, when speaking to those rude people, should imagine himself to be one of them, who was desirous to persuade a companion of something; that, on this account also, the periods of sermons addressed to the common people, should be concise and broken, so that whoever has not caught the meaning of the first sentence, may be able to comprehend the second; which cannot be done when the sentences are long and connected; for then, whoever does not understand the first period, will not understand the second nor the third.

18. Muratori also observes, that, in preaching to the people, it is very useful to make frequent use of the figure called *antiphora;* by which a question is asked, and replied to by the speaker. For example: "Tell me why so many sinners relapse, after confession, into the same sins? I will tell you: because they do not remove the dangerous occasions of sins". It is also useful oftentimes to call on the auditory to attend to what is said, and especially to certain things that are more important. For example: "O good

God! you come to us in order to save us, and we fly from you to destroy ourselves". It is useful likewise to repeat with emphasis some striking maxim of religion; as, for example: "There is no alternative: sooner or later we must die;—sooner or later we must die"; or, "My brethren, it is certain that, after this life, we must be eternally happy or eternally miserable".

19. I do not enlarge more on this subject, which I deem most important, as I have found it necessary to write more at length on it in a letter of apology which I published in reply to a religious who censured me for approving of sermons composed in a simple and popular style. I there premised in a succinct manner whatever Muratori has observed on this subject, and subjoined what the Holy Fathers have written on it, as far as I was able to discover. I pray the reader not to omit to read this letter: it is an uncommon little treatise, which contains matter not treated by any preceding writer.*

20. I do not, however, deem it right to omit to say something on the modulation of the voice, and on the gesture which should be used in preaching. As far as regards the voice, the preacher should avoid speaking in an inflated tone, or in a monotonous and invariably loud tone of voice. What moves and engages the attention of the hearers is, to speak at one time in a strong, at another time in a middle voice, and at another in a low voice, according as it suits the sentiment that is expressed, but without any sudden or violent fall or elevation; now to exclaim; now to pause; and now to resume with a sigh. This variety of tone and manner keeps the audience always attentive.

21. The preacher should avoid gesture that is affected, or oftentimes repeated in the same form, or too vehement, with much agitation of the body. The arms should be moved with moderation; ordinarily the right hand should be used; the left but seldom. The hands should not be raised above the head, nor too much extended sideways, nor held too confined. In delivering the exordium, the preacher should remain stationary, and should not move from a middle position in the pulpit: in delivering the first sentence he should not use gesture; in the second, he should only

* The translation of this Letter, which St. Alphonsus endeavoured to circulate as widely as possible through Italy, will be found in St. Liguori's *Instructions to Preachers*, published by the publisher of this volume.

commence to move the right hand, keeping the left resting on the pulpit or the breast. Let him take care not to keep the arms attached close to the sides, or to raise them both at same time in form of a cross, or throw them behind the shoulders. He must rarely strike them against each other or against the pulpit: to stamp the feet is very unbecoming. The motion of the head should correspond with that of the hand, accompanying it in the direction in which it moves. It is a fault to twist the head, or move it too often or too violently, or to hold it always raised, or always inclined upon the breast. The eyes ought to accompany the motion of the head; whence it is a fault to keep them always closed or cast downwards, or fixed immoveably in one direction. It may be permitted sometimes to sit down, but it should be seldom. The same may be said of moving back and forward: but the preacher should never run from one side of the pulpit to the other. He should, for the most part, speak from a middle position, so as to be seen equally from either side; but it is useful to incline occasionally to the right or left, without, however, turning the back to the opposite direction. Finally, as far as regards the length of the sermon. The Lent sermon should not exceed an hour; and the Sunday discourse should not occupy more than three quarters of an hour; but the parochial instructions should not be longer than a half hour, including the act of contrition, to which, ordinarily, it is advisable to accustom the common people, making them, at the close of the sermon, have recourse to the Mother of God, to ask of her some particular grace,—as, holy perseverance, a happy death, the love of Jesus Christ, and the like. Nor does it signify, that in order to make room for the act of contrition, the time of the sermon must be shortened; for these acts are the most precious fruit to be derived from it.

It were well that the preacher should sometimes exhort the audience to relate to others what they have heard in the sermon; as by this means it may be made useful even to those who have not heard it.

SERMONS

OF

SAINT ALPHONSUS LIGUORI.

SERMON I.

FOR THE FIRST SUNDAY OF ADVENT.

On the General Judgment.

"And they shall see the Son of Man coming in the clouds of Heaven with much power and majesty"—*Matt.*, xxiv. 30.

AT present God is not known, and therefore he is as much despised by sinners, as if he could not avenge, whenever he pleases, the injuries offered to him. The wicked "looketh upon the Almighty as if he could do nothing"—*Job*, xxii. 17. But the Lord has fixed a day, called in the Scriptures "the day of the Lord", on which the Eternal Judge will make known his power and majesty. "The Lord", says the Psalmist, "shall be known when he executeth judgment"—*Ps.*, ix. 17. On this text St. Bernard writes: "The Lord, who is now unknown while he seeks mercy, shall be known when he executes justice"—*Lib. de* xii. *Rad.* The prophet Sophonias calls the day of the Lord "a day of wrath—a day of tribulation and distress—a day of calamity and misery"—i. 15.

Let us now consider, in the first point, the different appearance of the just and the unjust; in the second, the scrutiny of consciences; and in the third, the sentence pronounced on the elect and on the reprobate.

First point. On the different appearance of the just and of sinners in the valley of Josaphat.

1. This day shall commence with fire from Heaven, which will burn the Earth, all men then living, and all things upon the Earth. "And the Earth and the works which are in it shall be burnt up" — II. *Pet.*, iii. 10. All shall become one heap of ashes.

2. After the death of all men, "the trumpet shall sound, and the dead shall rise again"—I. *Cor.*, xv. 52. St. Jerome used to say: "As often as I consider the day of judgment, I tremble. Whether I eat, or drink, or whatever else I do, that terrible trumpet appears to sound in my ears, 'arise, ye dead, and come to judgment'"—*in Matt.*, *c.* v.; and St. Augustine declared, that nothing banished from him Earthly thoughts so effectually as the fear of judgment.

3. At the sound of that trumpet the souls of the blessed shall descend from Heaven to be united to the bodies with which they served God on Earth; and the unhappy souls of the damned shall come up from Hell to take possession again of those bodies with which they have offended God. Oh! how different the appearance of the former, compared with that of the latter! The damned shall appear deformed and black, like so many firebrands of Hell; but "the just shall shine as the sun" — *Matt.*, xiii. 43. Oh! how great shall then be the happiness of those who have mortified their bodies by works of penance! We may estimate their felicity from the words addressed by St. Peter of Alcantara, after death, to St. Teresa: "O happy penance! which merited for me such glory".

4. After their resurrection, they shall be summoned by the angels to appear in the valley of Josaphat. "Nations, nations, in the valley of destruction, for the day of the Lord is near"—*Joel*, iii. 14. Then the angels shall come and separate the reprobate from the elect, placing the latter on the right, and the former on the left. "The angels shall go out, and shall separate the wicked from among the just" — *Matt.*, xiii. 49. Oh! how great will then be the confusion which the unhappy damned shall suffer! "What think you", says the author of the Imperfect Work, "must be the confusion of the impious, when, being separated from the just, they shall be abandoned?"—*hom.* liv. This

punishment alone, says St. Chrysostom, would be sufficient to constitute a hell for the wicked. "Et si nihil ulterius paterentur, ista sola verecundia sufficeret eis ad pœnam"—*in Matt.*, *c.* xxiv. The brother shall be separated from the brother, the husband from his wife, the son from the father, etc.

5. But, behold! the heavens are opened—the angels come to assist at the general judgment, carrying, as St. Thomas says, the sign of the cross and of the other instruments of the passion of the Redeemer. "Veniente Domino ad judicium signum crucis, et alia passionis indicia demonstrabunt"—*Opusc.*, ii. 244. The same may be inferred from the twenty-fourth chapter of St. Matthew: "And then shall appear the sign of the Son of Man in Heaven; and then shall all the tribes of the Earth mourn"—xxiv. 30. Sinners shall weep at the sign of the cross; for, as St. Chrysostom says, the nails will complain of them—the wounds and the cross of Jesus Christ will speak against them. "Clavi de te conquerentur, cicatrices contra te loquentur, crux Christi contra te perorabit"—*hom.* xx., *in Matt.*

6. Most holy Mary, the queen of saints and angels, shall come to assist at the last judgment; and lastly, the Eternal Judge shall appear in the clouds, full of splendour and majesty. "And they shall see the Son of Man coming in the clouds of Heaven with much power and majesty"—*Matt.*, xxiv. 30. Oh! how great shall be the agony of the reprobate at the sight of the Judge! "At their presence", says the prophet Joel, "the people shall be in grievous pains"—*Joel*, ii. 6. According to St. Jerome, the presence of Jesus Christ will give the reprobate more pain than Hell itself. "It would", he says, "be easier for the damned to bear the torments of Hell than the presence of the Lord". Hence, on that day, the wicked shall, according to St. John, call on the mountains to fall on them and to hide them from the sight of the Judge. "And they shall say to the mountains and the rocks: Fall upon us, and hide us from the face of Him that sitteth on the throne, and from the wrath of the Lamb"—*Apoc.*, vi. 16.

Second point. The scrutiny of conscience.

7. "The judgment sat, and the books were opened"—*Dan.*, vii. 10. The books of conscience are opened, and the judg-

ment commences. The Apostle says, that the Lord "will bring to light the hidden things of darkness"—I. *Cor.*, iv. 5. And, by the mouth of his prophet, Jesus Christ has said: "I will search Jerusalem with lamps"—*Soph.*, i. 12. The light of the lamp reveals all that is hidden.

8. "A judgment", says St. Chrysostom, "terrible to sinners, but desirable and sweet to the just"—*hom.* iii., *de Dav.* The last judgment shall fill sinners with terror, but will be a source of joy and sweetness to the elect; for God will then give praise to each one according to his works (I. *Cor.*, iv. 5). The Apostle tells us that on that day the just will be raised above the clouds, to be united to the angels, and to increase the number of those who pay homage to the Lord. "We shall be taken up together with them in the clouds to meet Christ, into the air"—I. *Thess.*, iv. 16.

9. Worldlings now regard as fools the saints, who led mortified and humble lives; but then they shall confess their own folly, and say: "We fools esteemed their life madness, and their end without honour. Behold how they are numbered among the children of God, and their lot is among the saints"—*Wis.*, v. 4, 5. In this world, the rich and the noble are called happy; but true happiness consists in a life of sanctity. Rejoice, ye souls who live in tribulation; "your sorrow shall be turned into joy"—*John*, xvi. 20. In the valley of Josaphat you shall be seated on thrones of glory.

10. But the reprobate, like goats destined for the slaughter, shall be placed on the left, to await their last condemnation. "Judicii tempus", says St. Chrysostom, "misericordiam non recipit". On the day of judgment, there is no hope of mercy for poor sinners. "Magna", says St. Augustine, "jam est pœna peccati, metum et memoriam divini perdidisse judicii"—*serm.* xx., *de Temp.* The greatest punishment of sin in those who live in enmity with God, is to lose the fear and remembrance of the divine judgment. Continue, continue, says the Apostle, to live obstinately in sin; but in proportion to your obstinacy, you shall have accumulated for the day of judgment a treasure of the wrath of God. "But according to thy hardness and impenitent heart, thou treasurest up to thyself wrath against the day of wrath"—*Rom.*, ii. 5.

11. Then sinners will not be able to hide themselves; but,

with insufferable pain, they shall be compelled to appear in judgment. "To lie hid", says St. Anselm, "will be impossible —to appear will be intolerable". The devils will perform their office of accusers, and, as St. Augustine says, will say to the Judge: "Most just God, declare him to be mine, who was unwilling to be yours". The witnesses against the wicked shall be, first, their own conscience—"Their conscience bearing witness to them"—*Rom.*, ii. 15; secondly, the very walls of the house in which they sinned shall cry out against them — "The stone shall cry out of the wall" — *Hab.*, ii. 11; thirdly, the Judge himself will say—"I am the judge and the witness, saith the Lord"—*Jer.*, xxix. 23. Hence, according to St. Augustine, "He who is now the witness of your life, shall be the judge of your cause"—*lib.* x. *de Chord.*, *c.* ii. To Christians particularly he will say: "Wo to thee Corozain, wo to thee Bethsaida; for if in Tyre and Sidon had been wrought the miracles that have been wrought in you, they had long ago done penance in sackcloth and ashes"—*Matt.*, xi. 21. Christians, he will say, if the graces which I have bestowed on you had been given to the Turks or to the Pagans, they would have done penance for their sins; but you have ceased to sin only with your death. He shall then manifest to all men their most hidden crimes. "I will discover thy shame to thy face" — *Nahum.*, iii. 5. He will expose to view all their secret impurities, injustices, and cruelties. "I will set all thy abominations against thee" — *Ezech.*, vii. 3. Each of the damned shall carry his sins written on his forehead.

12. What excuses can save the wicked on that day? Ah! they can offer no excuses. "All iniquity shall stop her mouth" —*Ps.*, cvi. 42. Their very sins shall close the mouth of the reprobate, so that they will not have courage to excuse themselves. They shall pronounce their own condemnation.

Third point. Sentence of the elect, and of the reprobate.

13. St. Bernard says, that the sentence of the elect, and their destiny to eternal glory, shall be first declared, that the pains of the reprobate may be increased by the sight of what they lost. "Prius pronunciabitur sententia electis, ut acrius (reprobi) doleant videntes quid amiserint"—*ser.* viii., *in Ps.* xc. Jesus Christ, then, shall first turn to the elect, and with a serene countenance shall

say: "Come, ye blessed of my Father, possess the kingdom prepared for you from the foundation of the world"—*Matt.*, xxv. 34. He will then bless all the tears shed through sorrow for their sins, and all their good works, their prayers, mortifications, and communions; above all, he will bless for them the pains of his passion, and the blood shed for their salvation. And, after these benedictions, the elect, singing alleluias, shall enter Paradise to praise and love God for all eternity.

14. The Judge shall then turn to the reprobate, and shall pronounce the sentence of their condemnation in these words: "Depart from me, you cursed, into everlasting fire"—*Matt.*, xxv. 41. They shall then be for ever accursed, separated from God, and sent to burn for ever in the fire of Hell. "And these shall go into everlasting punishment: but the just into life everlasting"—*Matt.*, xxv. 46.

15. After this sentence, the wicked shall, according to St. Ephrem, be compelled to take leave for ever of their relatives, of Paradise, of the saints, and of Mary the divine mother. "Farewell, ye just! farewell, O cross! farewell, O Paradise! farewell, fathers and brothers: we shall never see you again! farewell, O Mary, mother of God!"—*S. Eph. de variis serm. inf.* Then a great pit shall be opened in the middle of the valley: the unhappy damned shall be cast into it, and shall see those doors shut which shall never again be opened. O accursed sin! to what a miserable end will you one day conduct so many souls redeemed by the blood of Jesus Christ! O unhappy souls! for whom is prepared such a melancholy end. But, brethren, have confidence. Jesus Christ is now a father, and not a judge. He is ready to pardon all who repent. Let us then instantly ask pardon from him.

[*Let the preacher here propose for the people an act of sorrow, a purpose of amendment, and a prayer to Jesus and to Mary for the gift of holy perseverance. Let him repeat the same at the end of every sermon.*]

SERMON II.

FOR THE SECOND SUNDAY OF ADVENT.

On the advantages of tribulations.

"Now when John had heard in prison the wonderful works of Christ", etc.—*Mat.*, xi. 2.

In tribulations God enriches his beloved souls with the greatest graces. Behold, St. John in his chains comes to the knowledge of the works of Jesus Christ: "When John had heard in prison the works of Christ". Great indeed are the advantages of tribulations. The Lord sends them to us, not because he wishes our misfortune, but because he desires our welfare. Hence, when they come upon us, we must embrace them with thanksgiving, and must not only resign ourselves to the divine will, but must also rejoice that God treats us as he treated his Son Jesus Christ, whose life upon this Earth was always full of tribulation. I shall now show, in the first point, the advantages we derive from tribulations; and in the second I shall point out the manner in which we ought to bear them.

First point. On the great advantages we derive from tribulations.

1. "What doth he know, that hath not been tried? A man that hath much experience shall think of many things, and he that hath learned many things shall show forth understanding" —*Eccl.*, xxxiv. 9. They who live in prosperity, and have no experience of adversity, know nothing of the state of their souls. In the first place, tribulation opens the eyes which prosperity had kept shut. St. Paul remained blind after Jesus Christ appeared to him, and, during his blindness, he perceived the errors in which he had lived. During his imprisonment in Babylon, King Manasses had recourse to God, was convinced of the malice of his sins, and did penance for them. "And after that he was in distress, he prayed to the Lord his God, and did penance exceedingly before the God of his fathers"—

II. *Paral.*, xxxiii. 12. The prodigal, when he found himself under the necessity of feeding swine, and afflicted with hunger, exclaimed: "I will arise and go to my father"—*Luke*, xv. 18.

Secondly, tribulation takes from our hearts all affections to Earthly things. When a mother wishes to wean her infant, she puts gall on the paps, to excite his disgust and induce him to take better food. God treats us in a similar manner: to detach us from temporal goods, he mingles them with gall, that by tasting their bitterness, we may conceive a dislike for them, and place our affections on the things of Heaven. "God", says St. Augustine, "mingles bitterness with Earthly pleasures, that we may seek another felicity, whose sweetness does not deceive"—*ser.* xxix., *de Verb. Dom.*

Thirdly, they who live in prosperity are molested by many temptations of pride, of vain-glory, of desires of acquiring greater wealth, greater honours, and greater pleasures. Tribulations free us from these temptations, and make us humble and content in the state in which the Lord places us. Hence the Apostle says: "We are chastised by the Lord, that we may not be condemned with this world"—I. *Cor.*, xi. 32.

2. Fourthly, by tribulations we atone for the sins we have committed, much better than by voluntary works of penance. "Be assured", says St. Augustine, "that God is a physician, and that tribulation is a salutary medicine". Oh! how great is the efficacy of tribulation in healing the wounds caused by our sins! Hence, the same saint rebukes the sinner who complains of God for sending him tribulations. "Why", he says, "do you complain? What you suffer is a remedy, not a punishment"—*in Ps.* lv. Job called those happy whom God corrects by tribulations; because he heals them with the very hands with which he strikes and wounds them. "Blessed is the man whom God correcteth......For he woundeth and cureth. He striketh, and his hand shall heal"—*Job*, v. 17, 18. Hence, St. Paul gloried in his tribulations: "Gloriamur in tribulationibus"—*Rom.*, v. 3.

3. Fifthly, by convincing us that God alone is able and willing to relieve us in our miseries, tribulations remind us of him, and compel us to have recourse to his mercy. "In their affliction they will rise early to me"—*Osee*, vi. 1. Hence, addressing the afflicted, the Lord said: "Come to me, all you

that labour and are burdened, and I will refresh you"—*Matt.*, xi. 28. Hence he is called "a helper in troubles"—*Ps.*, xlv. 1. "When", says David, "he slew them, then they sought him, and they returned"—*Ps.*, lxxvii. 34. When the Jews were afflicted, and were slain by their enemies, they remembered the Lord, and returned to him.

4. Sixthly, tribulations enable us to acquire great merits before God, by giving us opportunities of exercising the virtues of humility, of patience, and of resignation to the divine will. The venerable John d'Avila used to say, that a single *blessed be God*, in adversity, is worth more than a thousand acts of thanksgiving in prosperity. "Take away", says St. Ambrose, "the contests of the martyrs, and you have taken away their crowns"—*in Luc.*, *c.* iv. Oh! what a treasure of merits is acquired by patiently bearing insults, poverty, and sickness. Insults from men were the great objects of the desires of the saints, who sought to be despised for the love of Jesus Christ, and thus to be made like unto him.

5. How great is the merit gained by bearing with the inconvenience of poverty. "My God and my all", says St. Francis of Assisium: in expressing this sentiment, he enjoyed more of true riches than all the princes of the Earth. How truly has St. Teresa said, that "the less we have here, the more we shall enjoy hereafter"! Oh! how happy is the man who can say from his heart: My Jesus, thou alone art sufficient for me! If, says St. Chrysostom, you esteem yourself unhappy because you are poor, you are indeed miserable and deserving of tears; not because you are poor, but because, being poor, you do not embrace your poverty, and esteem yourself happy. "Sane dignus es lachrymis ob hoc, quod miserum te existimas, non ideo quod pauper es"—*serm.* II. *Epis. ad Phil.*

6. By bearing patiently with the pains of sickness, a great, and perhaps the greater, part of the crown which is prepared for us in Heaven, is completed. The sick sometimes complain that in sickness they can do nothing; but they err; for, in their infirmities they can do all things, by accepting their sufferings with peace and resignation. "The cross of Christ", says St. Chrysostom, "is the key of Paradise"—*hom. in Luc. de vir.*

7. St. Francis de Sales used to say: "To suffer constantly for Jesus is the science of the saints; we shall thus soon become

saints". It is by sufferings that God proves his servants, and finds them worthy of himself. "Deus tentavit es, et invenit eos dignos se"—*Wis.*, iii. 5. "Whom", says St. Paul, "the Lord loveth, he chastiseth; and he scourgeth every son whom he receiveth"—*Heb.*, xii. 6. Hence Jesus Christ once said to St. Teresa: "Be assured that the souls dearest to my Father are those who suffer the greatest afflictions". Hence Job said: "If we have received good things at the hand of God, why should we not receive evil?"—*Job*, ii. 10. If we have gladly received from God the goods of this Earth, why should we not receive more cheerfully tribulations, which are far more useful to us than worldly prosperity? St. Gregory informs us, that, as flame fanned by the wind increases, so the soul is made perfect when she is oppressed by tribulations. "Ignis flatu premitur, ut crescat"—*Ep.*, xxv.

8. To holy souls the most severe afflictions are the temptations by which the Devil impels them to offend God: but they who bear these temptations with patience, and banish them by turning to God for help, shall acquire great merit. "And", says St. Paul, "God is faithful, who will not suffer you to be tempted above that which you are able, but will also make issue with the temptation that you may be able to bear it"—I. *Cor.*, x. 13. God permits us to be molested by temptations, that, by banishing them, we may gain greater merit. "Blessed", says the Lord, "are they that mourn, for they shall be comforted"—*Mat.*, v. 5. They are blessed, because, according to the Apostle, our tribulations are momentary and very light, compared with the greatness of the glory which they shall obtain for us for eternity in Heaven. "For that which is at present momentary and light of our tribulation, worketh for us above measure exceedingly an eternal weight of glory"—II. *Cor.*, iv. 17.

9. It is necessary, then, says St. Chrysostom, to bear tribulations in peace; for, if you accept them with resignation, you shall gain great merit; but if you submit to them with reluctance, you shall increase, instead of diminishing, your misery. "Si vero ægre feras, neque calamitatem minorem facies, et majorem reddes procellam"—*hom.* lxiv., *ad Pop.* If we wish to be saved, we must submit to trials. "Through many tribulations we must enter into the kingdom of God"—*Acts*, xiv. 21. A great servant

of God used to say, that Paradise is the place of the poor, of the persecuted, of the humble and afflicted. Hence St. Paul says: "Patience is necessary for you, that, doing the will of God, you may receive the promise"—*Heb.*, x. 36. Speaking of the tribulations of the saints, St. Cyprian asks: "What are they to the servants of God, whom Paradise invites?"—*Ep. ad Demetr.* Is it much for those to whom the eternal goods of Heaven are promised, to embrace the short afflictions of this life?

10. In fine, the scourges of Heaven are sent not for our injury, but for our good. "Let us believe that these scourges of the Lord, with which, like servants, we are chastised, have happened for our amendment, and not for our destruction"—*Judith*, viii. 27. "God", says St. Augustine, "is angry when he does not scourge the sinner"—*in Ps.*, lxxxix. When we see a sinner in tribulation in this life, we may infer that God wishes to have mercy on him in the next, and that he exchanges eternal for temporal chastisement. But miserable the sinner whom the Lord does not punish in this life! For those whom he does not chastise here, he treasures up his wrath, and for them he reserves eternal chastisement.

11. "Why", asks the Prophet Jeremy, "doth the way of the wicked prosper?"—xii. 1. Why, O Lord, do sinners prosper? To this the same prophet answers: "Gather them together as sheep for a sacrifice, and prepare them for the day of slaughter"—*ib.*, *v.* 3. As on the day of sacrifice the sheep intended for slaughter are gathered together, so the impious, as victims of divine wrath, are destined to eternal death. "Destine them", says Du Hamel, in his commentary on this passage, "as victims of thy anger on the day of sacrifice".

12. When, then, God sends us tribulations, let us say with Job: "I have sinned, and indeed I have offended, and I have not received what I have deserved"—*Job*, xxxiii. 27. O Lord, my sins merit far greater chastisement than that which thou hast inflicted on me. We should even pray with St. Augustine, "Burn—cut—spare not in this life, that thou mayst spare for eternity". How frightful is the chastisement of the sinner of whom the Lord says: "Let us have pity on the wicked, but he will not learn justice"—*Is.*, xxvi. 10. Let us abstain from chastising the impious: as long as they remain in this life, they will continue to live in

sin, and shall thus be punished with eternal torments. On this passage St. Bernard says: "Misericordiam hanc nolo, super omnem iram miseratio ista"—*serm.* xlii., *in Cant.* Lord, I do not wish for such mercy, which is a chastisement that surpasses all chastisements.

13. The man whom the Lord afflicts in this life has a certain proof that he is dear to God. "And", said the angel to Tobias, "because thou wast acceptable to God, it was necessary that temptation should prove thee"—*Tob.*, xii. 13. Hence St. James pronounces blessed the man who is afflicted; because after he shall have been proved by tribulation, he will receive the crown of eternal life. "Blessed is the man that endureth temptation; for when he hath been proved, he shall receive the crown of life"—*Jam.*, i. 12.

14. He who wishes to share in the glory of the saints, must suffer in this life as the saints have suffered. None of the saints has been esteemed or treated well by the world—all of them have been despised and persecuted. In them have been verified the words of the Apostle, "All that will live godly in Christ Jesus, shall suffer persecution"—II. *Tim.*, iii. 12. Hence St. Augustine said, that they who are unwilling to suffer persecutions, have not as yet begun to be Christians. "Si putas non habere persecutiones, nondum cœpisti esse Christianus"—*in Ps.*, lv. When we are in tribulation, let us be satisfied with the consolation of knowing that the Lord is then near us, and in our company. "The Lord is nigh unto them that are of a contrite heart"—*Ps.*, xxxiii. 19. "I am with him in tribulation"—*Ps.*, xc. 15.

Second point. On the manner in which we should bear tribulations.

15. He who suffers tribulations in this world, should, in the first place, abandon sin, and endeavour to recover the grace of God; for, as long as he remains in sin, the merit of all his sufferings is lost. "If", says St. Paul, "I should deliver my body to be burned, and have not charity, it profiteth me nothing"—I. *Cor.*, xiii. 3. If you suffered all the torments of the martyrs, or bore to be burned alive, and were not in the state of grace, it would profit you nothing.

16. But, to those who can suffer with God, and with resig-

nation for God's sake, all their tribulations shall be a source of comfort and gladness. "Your sorrow shall be turned into joy"—*John*, xvi. 20. Hence, after having been insulted and beaten by the Jews, the apostles departed from the council full of joy because they had been maltreated for the love of Jesus Christ. "And they indeed went from the presence of the council, rejoicing that they were accounted worthy to suffer reproach for the name of Jesus"—*Acts*, v. 41. Hence, when God visits us with any tribulations, we must say with Jesus Christ: "The chalice which my Father hath given me, shall I not drink it?"—*John*, xviii. 11. It is necessary to know that every tribulation, though it may come from men, is sent to us by God.

17. When we are surrounded on all sides with tribulations, and know not what to do, we must turn to God, who alone can console us. Thus King Josaphat, in his distress, said to the Lord: "As we know not what to do, we can only turn our eyes to thee"—II. *Par.*, xx. 12. Thus David also in his tribulation had recourse to God, and God consoled him: "In my trouble I cried to the Lord, and he heard me"—*Ps.*, cxix. 1. We should turn to God, and pray to him, and never cease to pray till he hears us. "As the eyes of the handmaid are on the hands of her mistress, so are our eyes unto the Lord our God, until he have mercy on us"—*Ps.*, cxxii. 2. We must keep our eyes continually raised to God, and must continue to implore his aid, until he is moved to compassion for our miseries. We must have great confidence in the heart of Jesus Christ, and ought not to imitate certain persons, who instantly lose courage because they do not feel that they are heard as soon as they begin to pray. To them may be applied the words of the Saviour to St. Peter: "O thou of little faith! why didst thou doubt?"—*Mat.*, xiv. 31. When the favours which we ask are spiritual, or can be profitable to our souls, we should be certain of being heard, provided we persevere in prayer, and do not lose confidence. "All things, whatsoever you ask when ye pray, believe that you shall receive, and they shall come unto you"—*Mark*, xi. 24. In tribulations, then, we should never cease to hope with confidence that the divine mercy will console us; and if our afflictions continue, we must say with Job: "Although he should kill me, I will trust in him"—xiii. 15.

18. Souls of little faith, instead of turning to God in their tribulations, have recourse to human means, and thus provoke God's anger, and remain in their miseries. "Unless the Lord build the house, they labour in vain that build it. Unless the Lord keep the city, he watcheth in vain that keepeth it"—*Ps.*, cxxvi. 1. On this passage St. Augustine writes: "Ipse ædificat, ipse intellectum aperit, ipse ad finem applicat sensum vestrum: et tamen laboramus et nos tanquam operarii, sed nisi Dominus custodierit civitatem", etc. All good—all help must come from the Lord. Without him, creatures can give us no assistance.

19. Of this the Lord complains by the mouth of his prophet: "Is not", he says, "the Lord in Sion?...Why then have they provoked me to wrath with their idols?...Is there no balm in Galaad? or is there no physician there? Why then is not the wound of the daughter of my people closed?"—*Jer.*, viii. 19, 22. Am I not in Sion? Why then do men provoke me to anger by recurring to creatures, which they convert into idols by placing in them all their hopes? Do they seek a remedy for their miseries? Why do they not seek it in Galaad, a mountain full of balsamic ointments, which signify the divine mercy? There they can find the physician and the remedy of all their evils. Why then, says the Lord, do your wounds remain open? Why are they not healed? It is because you have recourse not to me, but to creatures, and because you confide in them, and not in me.

20. In another place the Lord says: "Am I become a wilderness to Israel, or a lateward springing land? Why then have my people said: We are revolted; we will come to thee no more?...But my people have forgotten me days without number"—*Jer.*, ii. 31, 32. God complains, and says: Why, my children, do you say that you will have recourse to me no more? Am I become to you a barren land, which gives no fruit, or gives it too late? Is it for this reason that you have so long forgotten me? By these words he manifests to us his desire that we pray to him, in order that he may be able to give us his graces; and he also gives us to understand that when we pray to him, he is not slow, but instantly begins to assist us.

21. The Lord, says David, is not asleep when we turn to

his goodness, and ask the graces which are profitable to our souls: he hears us immediately, because he is anxious for our welfare. "Behold, he shall neither slumber nor sleep that keepeth Israel" —*Ps.*, cxx. 4. When we pray for temporal favours, St. Bernard says that God "will give what we ask, or something more useful". He will grant us the grace which we desire, whenever it is profitable to our souls; or he will give us a more useful grace, such as the grace to resign ourselves to the divine will, and to suffer with patience our tribulations, which shall merit a great increase of glory in Heaven.

[*Act of sorrow and amendment, prayer to Jesus and Mary.*]

SERMON III.

FOR THE THIRD SUNDAY OF ADVENT.

On the means necessary for salvation.

"I am the voice of one crying in the wilderness: Make straight the way of the Lord"—*John*, i. 23.

All would wish to be saved and to enjoy the glory of Paradise; but to gain Heaven, it is necessary to walk in the straight road that leads to eternal bliss. This road is the observance of the divine commands. Hence, in his preaching, the Baptist exclaimed: "Make straight the way of the Lord". In order to be able to walk always in the way of the Lord, without turning to the right or to the left, it is necessary to adopt the proper means. These means are, first, diffidence in ourselves; secondly, confidence in God; thirdly, resistance to temptations.

First means. Diffidence in ourselves.

1. "With fear and trembling", says the Apostle, "work out your salvation"—*Phil.*, ii. 12. To secure eternal life, we must be always penetrated with fear, we must be always afraid

of ourselves *(with fear and trembling)*, and distrust altogether our own strength; for, without the divine grace we can do nothing. "Without me", says Jesus Christ, "you can do nothing". We can do nothing for the salvation of our own souls. St. Paul tells us, that of ourselves we are not capable of even a good thought. "Not that we are sufficient to think anything of ourselves, as of ourselves, but our sufficiency is from God"—II. *Cor.*, iii. 5. Without the aid of the Holy Ghost, we cannot even pronounce the name of Jesus so as to deserve a reward. "And no one can say the Lord Jesus, but by the Holy Ghost"—I. *Cor.*, xii. 3.

2. Miserable the man who trusts to himself in the way of God. St. Peter experienced the sad effects of self-confidence. Jesus Christ said to him: "In this night, before cock-crow, thou wilt deny me thrice"—*Mat.*, xxvi. 34. Trusting in his own strength and in his good will, the Apostle replied: "Yea, though I should die with thee, I will not deny thee"—*v.* 35. What was the result? On the night on which Jesus Christ had been taken, Peter was reproached in the court of Caiphas with being one of the disciples of the Saviour. The reproach filled him with fear: he thrice denied his Master, and swore that he had never known him. Humility and diffidence in ourselves are so necessary for us, that God permits us sometimes to fall into sin, that, by our fall, we may acquire humility and a knowledge of our own weakness. Through want of humility David also fell: hence, after his sin, he said: "Before I was humbled, I offended"—*Ps.*, cxviii. 67.

3. Hence the Holy Ghost pronounces blessed the man who is always in fear: "Blessed is the man who is always fearful"—*Prov.*, xxviii. 14. He who is afraid of falling, distrusts his own strength, avoids as much as possible all dangerous occasions, and recommends himself often to God, and thus preserves his soul from sin. But the man who is not fearful, but full of self-confidence, easily exposes himself to the danger of sin: he seldom recommends himself to God, and thus he falls. Let us imagine a person suspended over a great precipice by a cord held by another. Surely he would constantly cry out to the person who supports him: *Hold fast, hold fast; for God's sake, do not let go.* We are all in danger of falling into the abyss of all crime, if God does not support us. Hence we

should constantly beseech him to keep his hands over us, and to succour us in all dangers.

4. In rising from bed, St. Philip Neri used to say every morning: O Lord, keep thy hand this day over Philip; if thou do not, Philip will betray thee. And one day, as he walked through the city, reflecting on his own misery, he frequently said, *I despair*, *I despair*. A certain religious who heard him, believing that the saint was really tempted to despair, corrected him, and encouraged him to hope in the divine mercy. But the saint replied: "I despair of myself, but I trust in God". Hence, during this life, in which we are exposed to so many dangers of losing God, it is necessary for us to live always in great diffidence of ourselves, and full of confidence in God.

Second means. Confidence in God.

5. St. Francis de Sales says, that the mere attention to self-diffidence on account of our own weakness, would only render us pusillanimous, and expose us to great danger of abandoning ourselves to a tepid life, or even to despair. The more we distrust our own strength, the more we should confide in the divine mercy. This is a balance, says the same saint, in which the more the scale of confidence in God is raised, the more the scale of diffidence in ourselves descends.

6. Listen to me, O sinners who have had the misfortune of having hitherto offended God, and of being condemned to Hell: if the Devil tells you that but little hope remains of your eternal salvation, answer him in the words of the Scripture: "No one hath hoped in the Lord, and hath been confounded"—*Eccl.*, ii. 11. No sinner has ever trusted in God, and has been lost. Make, then, a firm purpose to sin no more; abandon yourselves into the arms of the divine goodness; and rest assured that God will have mercy on you, and save you from Hell. "Cast thy care upon the Lord, and he shall sustain thee"—*Ps.*, liv. 23. The Lord, as we read in Blosius, one day said to St. Gertrude: "He who confides in me, does me such violence that I cannot but hear all his petitions".

7. "But", says the Prophet Isaias, "they that hope in the Lord shall renew their strength; they shall take wings as eagles; they shall run, and not be weary; they shall walk, and

not faint"—xl. 31. They who place their confidence in God shall renew their strength; they shall lay aside their own weakness, and shall acquire the strength of God; they shall fly like eagles in the way of the Lord, without fatigue and without ever failing. David says, that "mercy shall encompass him that hopeth in the Lord"—*Ps.*, xxxi. 10. He that hopes in the Lord shall be encompassed by his mercy, so that he shall never be abandoned by it.

8. St. Cyprian says, that the divine mercy is an inexhaustible fountain. They who bring vessels of the greatest confidence, draw from it the greatest graces. Hence, the Royal Prophet has said: "Let thy mercy, O Lord, be upon us, as we have hoped in thee" —*Ps.*, xxxii. 22. Whenever the Devil terrifies us by placing before our eyes the great difficulty of persevering in the grace of God in spite of all the dangers and sinful occasions of this life, let us, without answering him, raise our eyes to God, and hope that in his goodness he will certainly send us help to resist every attack. "I have lifted up my eyes to the mountains, from whence help shall come to me"—*Ps.*, cxx. 1. And when the enemy represents to us our weakness, let us say with the Apostle: "I can do all things in him who strengtheneth me"—*Phil.*, iv. 13. Of myself I can do nothing; but I trust in God, that, by his grace, I shall be able to do all things.

9. Hence, in the midst of the greatest dangers of perdition to which we are exposed, we should continually turn to Jesus Christ, and, throwing ourselves into the hands of him who redeemed us by his death, should say: "Into thy hands I commend my spirit: thou hast redeemed me, O Lord, the God of truth"—*Ps.*, xxx. 6. This prayer should be said with great confidence of obtaining eternal life, and to it we should add: "In thee, O Lord, I have hoped; let me not be confounded for ever" —*Ps.*, xxx. 1.

Third means. Resistance to temptations.

10. It is true that when we have recourse to God with confidence in dangerous temptations, he assists us; but, in certain very urgent occasions, the Lord sometimes wishes that we coöperate, and do violence to ourselves, to resist temptations. On such occasions, it will not be enough to have recourse to

God once or twice; it will be necessary to multiply prayers, and frequently to prostrate ourselves, and send up our sighs before the image of the Blessed Virgin and the crucifix, crying out with tears: Mary, my mother, assist me; Jesus, my Saviour, save me; for thy mercy's sake, do not abandon me — do not permit me to lose thee.

11. Let us keep in mind the words of the Gospel: "How narrow is the gate and strait is the way that leadeth to life: and few there are that find it"—*Mat.*, vii. 14. The way to Heaven is strait and narrow: they who wish to arrive at that place of bliss by walking in the paths of pleasure shall be disappointed; and therefore few reach it, because few are willing to use violence to themselves in resisting temptations. "The kingdom of Heaven suffereth violence, and the violent bear it away"—*Matt.*, xi. 12. In explaining this passage, a certain writer says: "Vi queritur, invaditur, occupatur". It must be sought and obtained by violence: he who wishes to obtain it without inconvenience, or by leading a soft and irregular life, shall not acquire it — he shall be excluded from it.

12. To save their souls, some of the saints have retired into the cloister; some have confined themselves in a cave; others have embraced torments and death. "The violent bear it away". Some complain of their want of confidence in God; but they do not perceive that their diffidence arises from the weakness of their resolution to serve God. St. Teresa used to say: "Of irresolute souls the Devil has no fear". And the Wise Man has declared, that "desires kill the slothful"—*Prov.*, xxi. 25. Some would wish to be saved and to become saints, but never resolve to adopt the means of salvation, such as meditation, the frequentation of the sacraments, detachment from creatures; or, if they adopt these means, they soon give them up. In a word, they are satisfied with fruitless desires, and thus continue to live in enmity with God, or at least in tepidity, which, in the end, leads them to the loss of God. Thus in them are verified the words of the Holy Ghost, "desires kill the slothful".

13. If, then, we wish to save our souls, and to become saints, we must make a strong resolution, not only in general to give ourselves to God, but also in particular to adopt the proper means, and never to abandon them after having once taken them up.

Hence we must never cease to pray to Jesus Christ, and to his holy mother, for holy perseverance.

SERMON IV.

FOR THE FOURTH SUNDAY OF ADVENT.

On the love of Jesus Christ for us, and on our obligations to love him.

"And all flesh shall see the salvation of God"—*Luke*, iii. 6.

THE Saviour of the world, whom, according to the prediction of the Prophet Isaias, men were one day to see on this Earth ("and all flesh shall see the salvation of God"), has already come. We have not only seen him conversing among men, but we have also seen him suffering and dying for the love of us. Let us, then, this morning consider the love which we owe to Jesus Christ at least through gratitude for the love which he bears to us. In the first point we shall consider the greatness of the love which Jesus Christ has shown to us; and in the second we shall see the greatness of our obligations to love him.

First point. On the great love which Jesus Christ has shown to us.

1. "Christ", says St. Augustine, "came on Earth that men might know how much God loves them". He has come, and, to show the immense love which this God bears us, he has given himself entirely to us, by abandoning himself to all the pains of this life, and afterwards to the scourges, to the thorns, and to all the sorrows and insults which he suffered in his passion, and by offering himself to die, abandoned by all, on the infamous tree of the cross. "Who loved me, and delivered himself for me"—*Gal.*, ii. 20.

2. Jesus Christ could save us without dying on the cross, and without suffering. One drop of his blood would be suffi-

cient for our redemption. Even a prayer offered to his Eternal Father would be sufficient; because, on account of his divinity, his prayer would be of infinite value, and would therefore be sufficient for the salvation of the world, and of a thousand worlds. "But", says St. Chrysostom, or another ancient author, "what was sufficient for redemption, was not sufficient for love". To show how much he loved us, he wished to shed not only a part of his blood, but the entire of it by dint of torments. This may be inferred from the words which he used on the night before his death: "This is my blood of the new testament, which shall be shed for many"—*Matt.*, xxvi. 28. The words *shall be shed* show that, in his passion, the blood of Jesus Christ was poured forth even to the last drop. Hence, when after death his side was opened with a spear, blood and water came forth, as if what then flowed was all that remained of his blood. Jesus Christ, then, though he could save us without suffering, wished to embrace a life of continual pain, and to suffer the cruel and ignominious death of the cross. "He humbled himself, becoming obedient unto death, even the death of the cross"—*Phil.*, ii. 8.

3. "Greater love than this no man hath, that a man lay down his life for his friends"—*John*, xv. 13. To show his love for us, what more could the Son of God do than die for us? What more can one man do for another than give his life for him? "Greater love than this no man hath". Tell me, my brother, if one of your servants—if the vilest man on this Earth had done for you what Jesus Christ has done in dying through pain on a cross, could you remember his love for you, and not love him?

4. St. Francis of Assisium appeared to be unable to think of anything but the passion of Jesus Christ; and, in thinking of it, he continually shed tears, so that by his constant weeping he became nearly blind. Being found one day weeping and groaning at the foot of the crucifix, he was asked the cause of his tears and lamentations. He replied: "I weep over the sorrows and ignominies of my Lord. And what makes me weep still more, is, that the men for whom he has suffered so much, live in forgetfulness of him".

5. O Christian, should a doubt ever enter your mind that Jesus Christ loves you, raise your eyes and look at him hang-

ing on the cross. Ah! says St. Thomas of Villanova, the cross to which he is nailed, the internal and external sorrows which he endures, and the cruel death which he suffers for you, are convincing proofs of the love which he bears you. "Testis crux, testes dolores, testis amara mors quam pro te sustinuit"—*Conc.* 3. Do you not, says St. Bernard, hear the voice of that cross, and of those wounds, crying out to make you feel that he truly loves you? "Clamat crux, clamat vulnus, quod vere dilexit".

6. St. Paul says that the love which Jesus Christ has shown in condescending to suffer so much for our salvation, should excite us to his love more powerfully than the scourging, the crowning with thorns, the painful journey to Calvary, the agony of three hours on the cross, the buffets, the spitting in his face, and all the other injuries which the Saviour endured. According to the Apostle, the love which Jesus has shown us not only obliges, but in a certain manner forces and constrains us, to love a God who has loved us so much. "For the charity of Christ presseth us"—II. *Cor.*, v. 14. On this text St. Francis de Sales says: "We know that Jesus the true God has loved us so as to suffer death, and even the death of the cross, for our salvation. Does not such love put our hearts as it were under a press, to force from them love by a violence which is stronger in proportion as it is more amiable?"

7. So great was the love which inflamed the enamoured heart of Jesus, that he not only wished to die for our redemption, but during his whole life, he sighed ardently for the day on which he should suffer death for the love of us. Hence, during his life, Jesus used to say: "I have a baptism wherewith I am to be baptized; and how am I straitened until it be accomplished"—*Luke*, xii. 50. In my passion I am to be baptized with the baptism of my own blood, to wash away the sins of men. "And how am I straitened!" How, says St. Ambrose, explaining this passage, am I straitened by the desire of the speedy arrival of the day of my death. Hence, on the night before his passion he said: "With desire I have desired to eat this pasch with you before I suffer"—*Luke*, xxii. 15.

8. "We have", says St. Lawrence Justinian, "seen wisdom become foolish through an excess of love". We have, he says, seen the Son of God become as it were a fool, through

the excessive love which he bore to men. Such, too, was the language of the Gentiles, when they heard the apostles preaching that Jesus Christ suffered death for the love of men. "But we", says St. Paul, "preach Christ crucified, unto the Jews indeed a stumbling block, unto the Gentiles foolishness"—I. *Cor.*, i. 23. Who, they exclaimed, can believe that a God, most happy in himself, and who stands in need of no one, should take human flesh and die for the love of men, who are his creatures? This would be to believe that a God became foolish for the love of men. "It appears folly", says St. Gregory, "that the Author of Life should die for men"—*hom.* vi. But, whatever infidels may say or think, it is of faith that the Son of God has shed all his blood for the love of us, to wash away the sins of our souls. "Who hath loved us, and washed us from our sins in his own blood"—*Apoc.*, i. 5. Hence, the saints were struck dumb with astonishment at the consideration of the love of Jesus Christ. At the sight of the crucifix, St. Francis of Paul could do nothing but exclaim, *O love! O love! O love!*

9. "Having loved his own who were in the world, he loved them unto the end"—*John*, xiii. 1. This loving Lord was not content with showing us his love by dying on the cross for our salvation; but, at the end of his life, he wished to leave us his own very flesh for the food of our souls, that thus he might unite himself entirely to us. "Take ye and eat, this is my body"—*Mat.*, xxvi. 26. But of this gift and this excess of love we shall speak at another time, in treating of the most holy sacrament of the altar. Let us pass to the second point.

Second point. On the greatness of our obligation to love Jesus Christ.

10. He who loves wishes to be loved. "When", says St. Bernard, "God loves, he desires nothing else than to be loved"—*ser.* lxxxiii. *in Cant.* The Redeemer said: "I am come to cast fire on the Earth, and what will I but that it be kindled?"—*Luke*, xii. 49. I, says Jesus Christ, came on Earth to light up the fire of divine love in the hearts of men, "and what will I but that it be kindled?" God wishes nothing else from us than to be loved. Hence the holy Church prays in the following words: "We beseech thee, O Lord, that the Spirit may inflame us with that fire

which Jesus Christ cast upon the Earth, and which he vehemently wished to be kindled". Ah! what have not the saints, inflamed with this fire, accomplished! They have abandoned all things—delights, honours, the purple and the sceptre—that they might burn with this holy fire. But you will ask what are you to do, that you too may be inflamed with the love of Jesus Christ. Imitate David: "In my meditation a fire shall flame out"—*Ps.*, xxxviii. Meditation is the blessed furnace in which the holy fire of divine love is kindled. Make mental prayer every day, meditate on the passion of Jesus Christ, and doubt not but you too shall burn with this blessed flame.

11. St. Paul says, that Jesus Christ died for us to make himself the master of the hearts of all. "To this end Christ died and rose again, that he might be Lord both of the dead and of the living"—*Rom.*, xiv. 9. He wished, says the Apostle, to give his life for all men, without a single exception, that not even one should live any longer for himself, but that all might live only to that God who condescended to die for them. "And Christ died for all, that they also who live may not now live to themselves, but unto him who died for them"—II. *Cor.*, v. 15.

12. Ah! to correspond to the love of this God, it would be necessary that another God should die for him, as Jesus Christ died for us. O ingratitude of men! A God has condescended to give his life for their salvation, and they will not even think on what he has done for them! Ah! if each of you thought frequently on the sufferings of the Redeemer, and on the love which he has shown to us in his passion, how could you but love him with your whole hearts? To him who sees with a lively faith the Son of God suspended by three nails on an infamous gibbet, every wound of Jesus speaks and says: "Thou shalt love the Lord thy God". Love, O man, thy Lord and thy God, who has loved thee so intensely. Who can resist such tender expressions! "The wounds of Jesus Christ", says St. Bonaventure, "wound the hardest hearts, and inflame frozen souls".

13. "Oh! if you knew the mystery of the cross!" said St. Andrew the Apostle to the tyrant by whom he was tempted to deny Jesus Christ. O tyrant, if you knew the love which your

Saviour has shown you by dying on the cross for your salvation, instead of tempting me, you would abandon all the goods of this Earth to give yourself to the love of Jesus Christ.

14. I conclude, my most beloved brethren, by recommending you henceforth to meditate every day on the passion of Jesus Christ. I shall be content, if you daily devote to this meditation a quarter of an hour. Let each at least procure a crucifix: let him keep it in his room, and from time to time give a glance at it, saying: Ah! my Jesus, thou hast died for me, and I do not love thee! Had a person suffered for a friend, injuries, buffets, and prisons, he would be greatly pleased to find that they were remembered and spoken of with gratitude. But he should be greatly displeased if the friend for whom they had been borne, were unwilling to think or to hear of his sufferings. Thus frequent meditation on his passion is very pleasing to our Redeemer; but the neglect of it greatly provokes his displeasure. Oh! how great will be the consolation which we shall receive in our last moments from the sorrows and death of Jesus Christ, if, during life, we shall have frequently meditated on them with love! Let us not wait till others, at the hour of death, place in our hands the crucifix; let us not wait till they remind us of all that Jesus Christ suffered for us. Let us, during life, embrace Jesus Christ crucified; let us keep ourselves always united to him, that we may live and die with him. He who practises devotion to the passion of our Lord, cannot but be devoted to the dolours of Mary, the remembrance of which will be to us a source of great consolation at the hour of death. Oh! how profitable and sweet the meditation of Jesus on the cross! Oh! how happy the death of him who dies in the embraces of Jesus crucified, accepting death with cheerfulness for the love of that God who has died for the love of us!

SERMON V.

FOR THE SUNDAY WITHIN THE OCTAVE OF THE NATIVITY.

In what true wisdom consists.

"Behold, this CHILD is set for the fall and for the resurrection of many in Israel"—*Luke*, ii. 34.

SUCH was the language of holy Simeon when he had the consolation to hold in his hands the infant Jesus. Among other things which he then foretold, he declared that "this child was set for the fall and for the resurrection of many in Israel". In these words he extols the lot of the saints, who, after this life, shall rise to a life of immortality in the kingdom of bliss, and he deplores the misfortune of sinners, who, for the transitory and miserable pleasures of this world, bring upon themselves eternal ruin and perdition. But, notwithstanding the greatness of his own misery, the unhappy sinner, reflecting only on the enjoyment of present goods, calls the saints fools, because they seek to live in poverty, in humiliation, and self-denial. But a day will come when sinners shall see their errors, and shall say: "We fools esteemed their life madness, and their end without honour"—*Wis.*, v. 4. *We fools:* behold how they shall confess that they themselves have been truly fools. Let us examine in what true wisdom consists, and we shall see, in the first point, that sinners are truly foolish, and, in the second, that the saints are truly wise.

First point. Sinners are truly foolish.

1. What greater folly can be conceived than to have the power of being the friends of God, and to wish to be his enemies? Their living in enmity with God makes the life of sinners unhappy in this world, and purchases for them an eternity of misery hereafter. St. Augustine relates that two courtiers of the emperor entered a monastery of hermits, and that one of them began to read the life of St. Anthony. "He read", says the

saint, "and his heart was divested of the world". He read, and in reading, his affections were detached from the Earth. Turning to his companion, he exclaimed: "What do we seek? The friendship of the emperor is the most we can hope for. And through how many perils shall we arrive at still greater danger? Should we obtain his friendship, how long shall it last?" Friend, said he, fools that we are, what do we seek? Can we expect more in this life, by serving the emperor, than to gain his friendship? And should we, after many dangers, succeed in making him our friend, we shall expose ourselves to greater danger of eternal perdition. What difficulties must we encounter in order to become the friends of Cæsar. "But, if I wish, I can in a moment become the friend of God". I can acquire his friendship by endeavouring to recover his grace. His divine grace is that infinite treasure which makes us worthy of his friendship. "For she is an infinite treasure to men, which they that use become the friends of God"— *Wis.*, vii. 14.

2. The Gentiles believed it impossible for a creature to become the friend of God; for, as St. Jerome says, friendship makes friends equal. "Amicitia pares accipit, aut pares facit". But Jesus Christ has declared, that if we observe his commands, we shall be his friends. "You are my friends if you do the things that I command"—*John*, xv. 14.

3. How great then is the folly of sinners, who, though they have it in their power to enjoy the friendship of God, wish to live in enmity with him! The Lord does not hate any of his creatures: he does not hate the tiger, the viper, or the toad. "For thou lovest all things that are, and hatest none of the things which thou hast made"—*Wis.*, xi. 25. But he necessarily hates sinners. "Thou hatest all the workers of iniquity" —*Ps.*, v. 7. God cannot but hate sin, which is his enemy and diametrically opposed to his will; and therefore, in hating sin, he necessarily hates the sinner who is united with his sin. "But to God the wicked and his wickedness are hateful alike" —*Wis.*, xiv. 9.

4. The sinner is guilty of folly in leading a life opposed to the end for which he was created. God has not created us, nor does he preserve our lives, that we may labour to acquire riches or Earthly honours, or that we may indulge in amusements: but

that we may love and serve him in this world, in order to love and enjoy him for eternity in the next. " And the end life everlasting"—*Rom.*, vi. 22. Thus the present life, as St. Gregory says, is the way by which we must reach Paradise, our true country. " In the present life we are as it were on the road by which we journey to our country"—*S. Greg. hom.* xi. *in Evan.*

5. But the misfortune of the greater part of mankind is, that, instead of following the way of salvation, they foolishly walk in the road to perdition. Some have a passion for Earthly riches, and, for a vile interest, they lose the immense goods of Paradise: others have a passion for honours, and, for a momentary applause, they lose their right to be kings in Heaven: others have a passion for sensual pleasures, and, for transitory delights, they lose the grace of God, and are condemned to burn for ever in a prison of fire. Miserable souls! if, in punishment of a certain sin, their hand was to be burned with a red hot iron, or if they were to be shut up for ten years in a dark prison, they certainly would abstain from it. And do they not know that, in chastisement of their sins, they shall be condemned to remain for ever in Hell, where their bodies, buried in fire, shall burn for all eternity? Some, says St. John Chrysostom *(hom. de recup. laps.)*, to save the body, choose to destroy the soul; but, do they not know that, in losing the soul, their bodies shall be condemned to eternal torments? " *If we neglect the soul, we cannot save the body*".

6. In a word, sinners lose their reason, and imitate brute animals, that follow the instinct of nature, and seek carnal pleasures without ever reflecting on their lawfulness or unlawfulness. But to act in this manner is, according to St. Chrysostom, to act not like a man, but like a beast. *Hominem illum dicimus*", says the saint " *qui imaginem hominis salvam retinet: quæ autem est imago hominis? Rationalem esse*". To be men we must be rational; that is we must act, not according to the sensual appetite, but according to the dictates of reason. If God gave to beasts the use of reason, and if they acted according to its rules, we should say that they acted like men. And it must, on the other hand, be said, that the man whose conduct is agreeable to the senses, but contrary to reason, acts like a beast. He who follows the dictates of

reason, provides for the future. "Oh! that they would be wise and would understand, and would provide for their last end"—*Deuter.*, xxii. 29. He looks to the future—that is, to the account he must render at the hour of death, after which he shall be doomed to Hell or to Heaven, according to his merits. "Non est sapiens", says St. Bernard, "qui sibi non est"—*lib. de consid.*

7. Sinners think only of the present, but regard not the end for which they were created. But what will it profit them to gain all things, if they lose their last end, which alone can make them happy? "But one thing is necessary"—*Luke*, x. 42. To attain our end is the only thing necessary for us: if we lose it, all is lost. What is this end? It is eternal life. "Finem vero vitam æternam". During life, sinners care but little for the attainment of their end. Each day brings them nearer to death and to eternity; but they know not their destination. Should a pilot who is asked whither he is going, answer that he did not know, would not all, says St. Augustine, cry out, that he was bringing the vessel to destruction? "Fac hominem perdidisse quo tendit, et dicatur ei: quo is? et dicat, nescio; nonne iste navem ad naufragium perducet?" The saint then adds: "Talis est qui currit præter viam". Such are the wise of the world, who know how to acquire wealth and honours, and to indulge in every kind of amusement; but know not how to save their souls. How miserable the rich glutton, who, though able to lay up riches, and to live splendidly, was, after death, buried in Hell! How miserable Alexander the Great, who, after gaining so many kingdoms, was condemned to eternal torments! How great the folly of Henry the Eighth, who rebelled against the Church, but seeing at the hour of death that his soul should be lost, cried out in despair: "Friends, we have lost all"! O God, how many others now weep in Hell, and exclaim: "What hath pride profited us? or what advantage hath the boasting of riches brought us? All those things are passed away like a shadow"—*Wis.*, v. 8. In the world we made a great figure—we enjoyed abundant riches and honours; but now all is passed away like a shadow, and nothing remains for us but to suffer and weep for eternity. St. Augustine says, that the happiness which sinners enjoy in this life, is their greatest misfortune. "Nothing is more calamitous than the felicity of sinners, by which their perverse

will, like an internal enemy, is strengthened"—*Ep.*, v. *ad Marcellin.*

8. In fine, the words of Solomon are fulfilled, with regard to all who neglect their salvation: "Mourning taketh hold of the end of joy"—*Prov.*, xiv. 13. All their pleasures, honours, and greatness end in eternal sorrow and wailing. "Whilst I was yet beginning, he cut me off"—*Is.*, xxxviii. 12. Whilst they are laying the foundation of their hopes of realizing a fortune, death comes, and, cutting the thread of life, deprives them of all their possessions, and sends them to Hell to burn for ever in a pit of fire. What greater folly can be conceived, than to wish to be transformed from the friend of God into the slave of Lucifer, and from the heir of Paradise to become, by sin, doomed to Hell? For, the moment a Christian commits a mortal sin, his name is written among the number of the damned. St. Francis de Sales said, that, if the angels were capable of weeping, they would do nothing else than shed tears at the sight of the destruction which a Christian who commits mortal sin brings upon himself.

9. Oh! how great is the folly of sinners, who, by living in sin, lead a life of misery and discontent! All the goods of this world cannot content the heart of man, which has been created to love God, and can find no peace out of God. What are all the grandeurs and all the pleasures of this world, but "*vanity of vanities*"?—*Eccl.*, i. 2. What are they but "*vanity and vexation of spirit*"?—*ibid.*, iv. 16. Earthly goods are, according to Solomon, who had experience of them, vanity of vanities; that is, mere vanities, lies, and deceits. They are also a "*a vexation of spirit*": they not only do not content, but they even afflict the soul; and the more abundantly they are possessed, the greater the anguish which they produce. Sinners hope to find peace in their sins; but what peace can they enjoy? "There is no peace to the wicked, saith the Lord"—*Is.*, xlviii. 22. I abstain from saying more at present on the unhappy life of sinners: I shall speak of it in another place. At present, it is enough for you to know that God gives peace to the souls who love him, and not to those who despise him. Instead of seeking to be the friends of God, sinners wish to be the slaves of Satan, who is a cruel and merciless tyrant to all who submit to his yoke. "Crudelis est et

non miserebitur"—*Jer.*, vi. 23. And if he promises delights, he does it, as St. Cyprian says, not for our welfare, but that we may be the companions of his torments in Hell: "Ut habeat socios pœnæ, socios gehennæ".

Second point. The saints are truly wise.

10. Let us be persuaded that the truly wise are those who know how to love God, and to gain Heaven. Happy the man to whom God has given the science of the saints. "Dedit illi scientiam sanctorum"—*Wisd.*, x. 10. Oh! how sublime the science which teaches us to know how to love God and to save our souls! Happy, says St. Augustine, is the man "*who knows God, although he is ignorant of other things*". They who know God, the love which he merits, and how to love him, stand not in need of any other knowledge. They are wiser than those who are masters of many sciences, but know not how to love God. Brother Egidius, of the order of St. Francis, once said to St. Bonaventure: Happy you, O Father Bonaventure, who are so learned, and who, by your learning, can become more holy than I can, who am a poor, ignorant man. Listen, replied the saint: if an old woman knows how to love God better than I do, she is more learned and more holy than I am. At hearing this, Brother Egidius exclaimed: O poor old woman! poor old woman! Father Bonaventure says, that, if you love God more than he does, you can surpass him in sanctity.

11. This excited the envy of St. Augustine, and made him ashamed of himself. "Surgunt indocti", he exclaimed, "et rapiunt cœlum". Alas! the ignorant rise up, and bear away the kingdom of Heaven; and what are we, the learned of this world, doing? Oh! how many of the rude and illiterate are saved, because, though unable to read, they know how to love God; and how many of the wise of the world are damned! Oh! truly wise were St. John of God, St. Felix of the order of St. Capuchins, and St. Paschal, who were poor lay Franciscans, and unacquainted with human sciences, but learned in the science of the saints. But the wonder is, that, though worldlings themselves are fully persuaded of this truth, and constantly extol the merit of those who retire from the world to live only to God, still they act as if they believed it not.

12. Tell me, brethren, to which class do you wish to

belong—to the wise of the world, or to the wise of God? Before you make a chcice, St. Chrysostom advises you to go to the graves of the dead. "*Proficiscamur ad sepulchra*". Oh! how eloquently do the sepulchres of the dead teach us the science of the saints, and the vanity of all Earthly goods! For my part, said the saint, "I see nothing but rottenness, bones, and worms". As if he said: Among these skeletons, I cannot distinguish the noble, the rich, or the learned; I see that they have all become dust and rottenness: thus all their greatness and glory have passed away like a dream.

13. What then must we do? Behold the advice of St. Paul. "This, therefore, I say, brethren: the time is short: it remaineth that...they that use this world BE as if they used it not; for the fashion of this world passeth away"—I. *Cor.*, vii. 29, 31. This world is a scene which shall pass away and end very soon: "The time is short". During the days of life that remain, let us endeavour to live like men who are wise, not according to the world, but according to God, by attending to the sanctification of our souls, and by adopting the means of salvation; by flying dangerous occasions; by practising prayer; joining some pious sodality; frequenting the sacraments; reading every day a spiritual book; and by daily hearing Mass, if it be in our power; or, at least, by visiting Jesus in the holy sacrament of the altar, and some image of the most holy Mary. Thus we shall be truly wise, and shall be happy for time and eternity.

SERMON VI.

On the malice of mortal sin.

"Behold, thy father and I have sought thee sorrowing"—*Luke*, ii. 48.

MOST holy Mary lost her Son for three days: during that time she wept continually for having lost sight of Jesus, and did not cease to seek after him till she found him. How then does it happen that so many sinners not only lose sight of Jesus, but even lose his divine grace; and instead of weeping for so great a loss, sleep in peace, and make no effort to recover so great a blessing? This arises from their not feeling what it is to lose God by sin. Some say; I commit this sin, not to lose God, but to enjoy this pleasure, to possess the property of another, or to take revenge of an enemy They who speak such language show that they do not understand the malice of mortal sin. What is mortal sin?

First point. It is a great contempt shown to God.
Second point. It is a great offence offered to God.

First point. Mortal sin is a great contempt shown to God.

1. The Lord calls upon Heaven and Earth to detest the ingratitude of those who commit mortal sin, after they had been created by him, nourished with his blood, and exalted to the dignity of his adopted children. "Hear, O ye Heavens, and give ear, O Earth; for the Lord hath spoken. I have brought up children and exalted them; but they have despised me"—*Isa.*, i. 2. Who is this God whom sinners despise? He is a God of infinite majesty, before whom all the kings of the Earth and all the blessed in Heaven are less than a drop of water or a grain of sand. "As a drop of a bucket,......as a little dust"—*Isa.*, xl. 15. In a word, such is the majesty of God, that, in his presence, all creatures are as if they did not exist. "All nations are before him as if they had no being at all"—*ibid.*, xl. 17. And what is man, who insults him? St. Bernard answers: "Saccus vermium, cibus vermium". A heap of worms, the food of worms, by which he shall be devoured in the grave. "Thou art wretched and miserable and poor and blind and naked"—*Apoc.*, iii. 17. He is so miserable that he can do nothing, so blind that he knows nothing, and so poor that he possesses nothing. And this worm dares to despise a God, and to provoke his wrath. "Vile dust", says the same saint, "dares to irritate such tremendous majesty". Justly then has St. Thomas asserted, that the malice of mortal sin is, as it were, infinite. "Peccatum habet quandam infinitatem malitiæ ex infinitate divinæ majestatis"—*par.* 3, *q.* 2, *a.* 2, *ad.* 2. And St. Augustine calls it *an infinite evil.* Hence Hell and a thousand Hells are not a sufficient chastisement for a single mortal sin.

2. Mortal sin is commonly defined by theologians to be "a turning away from the immutable good"—*St. Thom., par.* 1, *q.* 24, *a.* 4; a turning one's back on the sovereign good. Of this God complains by his prophet, saying: "Thou hast forsaken me, saith the Lord; thou art gone backward"—*Jer.*, xv. 6. Ungrateful man, he says to the sinner, I would never have separated myself from thee; thou hast been the first to abandon me: *thou art gone backward;* thou hast turned thy back upon me.

3. He who contemns the divine law, despises God; because he knows that, by despising the law, he loses the divine grace: "By transgression of the law, thou dishonourest God"—*Rom.*, ii. 23. God is the Lord of all things, because he has created them. "All things are in thy power...Thou hast made Heaven and Earth"—*Esth.*, xiii. 9. Hence all irrational creatures—the winds, the sea, fire, and rain—obey God. "The winds and the sea obey him"—*Matt.*, viii. 27. "Fire, hail, snow, ice, stormy winds, which fulfil his word"—*Ps.*, cxlviii. 8. But man, when he sins, says to God: Lord, thou dost command me, but I will not obey; thou dost command me to pardon such an injury, but I will resent it; thou dost command me to give up the property of others, but I will retain it; thou dost wish that I should abstain from such a forbidden pleasure, but I will indulge in it. "Thou hast broken my yoke, thou hast burst my bands, and thou saidst: 'I will not serve'"—*Jer.*, ii. 20. In fine, the sinner, when he breaks the command, says to God: I do not acknowledge thee for my Lord. Like Pharaoh, when Moses, on the part of God, commanded him in the name of the Lord to allow the people to go into the desert, the sinner answers: "Who is the Lord, that I should hear his voice, and let Israel go?"—*Exod.*, v. 2.

4. The insult offered to God by sin is heightened by the vileness of the goods for which sinners offend him. "Wherefore hath the wicked provoked God?"—*Ps.*, x. 13. For what do so many offend the Lord? For a little vanity; for the indulgence of anger; or for a beastly pleasure. "They violate me among my people for a handful of barley and a piece of bread"—*Ezec.*, xiii. 19. God is insulted for a handful of barley—for a morsel of bread! O God! why do we allow ourselves to be so easily deceived by the Devil? "There is", says the

Prophet Osee, "a deceitful balance in his hand"—xii. 7. We do not weigh things in the balance of God, which cannot deceive, but in the balance of Satan, who seeks only to deceive us, that he may bring us with himself into Hell. "Lord", said David, "who is like to thee?"—*Ps.*, xxxiv. 10. God is an infinite good; and when he sees sinners put him on a level with some Earthly trifle or with a miserable gratification, he justly complains in the language of the prophet: "To whom have you likened me or made me equal? saith the Holy One"—*Isa.*, xl. 25. In your estimation, a vile pleasure is more valuable than my grace. Is it a momentary satisfaction you have preferred before me? "Thou hast cast me off behind thy back"—*Ezec.*, xxiii. 35. Then, adds Salvian, "There is no one for whom men have less esteem than for God"—*lib.* v., *Adv. Avar.* Is the Lord so contemptible in your eyes as to deserve to have the miserable things of the Earth preferred before him?

5. The tyrant placed before St. Clement a heap of gold, of silver, and of gems, and promised to give them to the holy martyr if he would renounce the faith of Christ. The saint heaved a sigh of sorrow at the sight of the blindness of men, who put Earthly riches in comparison with God. But many sinners exchange the divine grace for things of far less value: they seek after certain miserable goods, and abandon that God who is an infinite good, and who alone can make them happy. Of this the Lord complains, and calls on the Heavens to be astonished, and on its gates to be struck with horror: "Be astonished, O ye Heavens, at this; and ye gates thereof, be very desolate, saith the Lord". He then adds: "For my people have done two evils: they have forsaken me, the fountain of living water, and have digged to themselves cisterns—broken cisterns—that can hold no water"—*Jer.*, ii. 12 *and* 13. We regard with wonder and amazement the injustice of the Jews, who, when Pilate offered to deliver Jesus or Barabbas, answered: "Not this man, but Barabbas"—*John*, xviii. 40. The conduct of sinners is still worse; for, when the Devil proposes to them to choose between the satisfaction of revenge — a miserable pleasure — and Jesus Christ, they answer: "Not this man, but Barabbas". That is, not the Lord Jesus, but sin.

6. "There shall be no new God in thee", says the Lord, *Ps.*, lxxx. 10. You shall not abandon me, your true God, and make

for yourself a new god, whom you shall serve. St. Cyprian teaches that men make their god whatever they prefer before God, by making it their last end; for God is the only last end of all: "Quidquid homo Deo anteponit, Deum sibi facit". And St. Jerome says: "Unusquisque quod cupit, si veneratur, hoc illi Deus est. Vitium in corde, est idolum in altari"—*in Ps.* lxxx. The creature which a person prefers to God, becomes his god. Hence, the holy doctor adds, that as the Gentiles adored idols on their altars, so sinners worship sin in their hearts. When King Jeroboam rebelled against God, he endeavoured to make the people imitate him in the adoration of idols. He one day placed the idols before them, and said: "Behold thy gods, O Israel!"—III. *Kings*, xii. 28. The Devil acts in a similar manner towards sinners; he places before them such a gratification, and says: Make this your god. Behold! this pleasure, this money, this revenge is your god: adhere to these, and forsake the Lord. When the sinner consents to sin, he abandons his Creator, and in his heart adores as his god the pleasure which he indulges. "Vitium in corde est idolum in altari".

7. The contempt which the sinner offers to God is increased by sinning in God's presence. According to St. Cyril of Jerusalem, some adored the sun as their god, that during the night they might, in the absence of the sun, do what they pleased, without fear of divine chastisement. "Some regarded the sun as their god, that, after the setting of the sun, they might be without a god"—*Catech.* iv. The conduct of these miserable dupes was very criminal; but they were careful not to sin in presence of their god. But Christians know that God is present in all places, and that he sees all things: "Do I not fill Heaven and Earth? saith the Lord"—*Jer.*, xxiii. 24; and still they do not abstain from insulting him and from provoking his wrath in his very presence: "A people that continually provoke me to anger before my face"—*Isa.*, lxv. 3. Hence, by sinning before him who is their judge, they even make God a witness of their iniquities: "I am the judge and the witness, saith the Lord"—*Jer.*, xxix. 23. St. Peter Chrysologus says, that "the man who commits a crime in the presence of his judge, can offer no defence". The thought of having offended God in his divine presence, made David weep and exclaim: "To thee only have

I sinned, and have done evil before thee"—*Ps.*, l. 6. But let us pass to the second point, in which we shall see more clearly the enormity of the malice of mortal sin.

Second point. Mortal sin is a great offence offered to God.

8. There is nothing more galling than to see oneself despised by those who were most beloved and most highly favoured. Whom do sinners insult? They insult a God who bestowed so many benefits upon them, and who loved them so as to die on a cross for their sake; and by the commission of mortal sin they banish that God from their hearts. A soul that loves God is loved by him, and God himself comes to dwell within her. "If any one love me, he will keep my word, and my Father will love him, and we will come to him, and will make our abode with him"—*John*, xiv. 23. The Lord, then, never departs from a soul, unless he is driven away, even though he should know that she will soon banish him from her heart. According to the Council of Trent, "he deserts not the soul, unless he is deserted".

9. When the soul consents to mortal sin, she ungratefully says to God: Depart from me. "The wicked have said to God: Depart from us"—*Job*, xxi. 14. Sinners, as St. Gregory observes, say the same, not in words, but by their conduct. "Recede, non verbis, sed moribus". They know that God cannot remain with sin in the soul: and, in violating the divine commands, they feel that God must depart; and, by their acts, they say to him: Since you cannot remain any longer with us, depart—farewell. And through the very door by which God departs from the soul, the Devil enters to take possession of her. When the priest baptizes an infant, he commands the demon to depart from the soul. "*Go out from him, unclean spirit, and make room for the Holy Ghost*". But when a Christian consents to mortal sin, he says to God: *Depart from me; make room for the Devil, whom I wish to serve.*

10. St. Bernard says, that mortal sin is so opposed to God, that, if it were possible for God to die, sin would deprive him of life. "Peccatum quantum in se est Deum perimit". Hence, according to Job, in committing mortal sin, man rises up against God, and stretches forth his hand against him: "For

he hath stretched out his hand against God, and hath strengthened himself against the Almighty"—*Job.*, xv. 25.

11. According to the same St. Bernard, they who wilfully violate the divine law, seek to deprive God of life in proportion to the malice of their will. "Quantum in ipsa est Deum perimit propria voluntas"—*Serm.*, iii., *de Res.* Because, adds the saint, self-will "would wish God to see its own sins, and to be unable to take vengeance on them". Sinners know that the moment they consent to mortal sin, God condemns them to Hell. Hence, being firmly resolved to sin, they wish that there was no God, and, consequently, they would wish to take away his life, that he might not be able to avenge their crime. "He hath", continues Job, in his description of the wicked, "run against him with his neck raised up, and is armed with a fat neck"—xv. 26. The sinner raises his neck; that is, his pride swells up, and he runs to insult his God; and, because he contends with a powerful antagonist, "he is armed with a fat neck". "*A fat neck*" is the symbol of ignorance, of that ignorance which makes the sinner say: *This is not a great sin; God is merciful; we are flesh; the Lord will have pity on us.* O temerity! O illusion! which brings so many Christians to Hell.

12. Moreover, the man who commits a mortal sin, afflicts the heart of God. "But they provoked to wrath and afflicted the spirit of the Holy One"—*Isaias*, lxiii. 10. What pain and anguish would you not feel, if you knew that a person whom you tenderly loved, and on whom you bestowed great favours, had sought to take away your life! God is not capable of pain; but, were he capable of suffering, a single mortal sin would be sufficient to make him die through sorrow. "Mortal sin", says Father Medina, "if it were possible, would destroy God himself; because it would be the cause of infinite sadness to God". As often, then, as you committed mortal sin, you would, if it were possible, have caused God to die of sorrow; because you knew that by sin you insulted him and turned your back upon him, after he had bestowed so many favours upon you, and even after he had given all his blood and his life for your salvation.

[*An act of sorrow, etc.*]

SERMON VII.

FOR THE SECOND SUNDAY AFTER THE EPIPHANY.

*On the confidence with which we ought to recommend ourselves to the Mother of God.**

"And the wine failing, the Mother of Jesus saith to him: They have no wine"—*John*, ii. 3.

In the Gospel of this day we read that Jesus Christ, having been invited, went with his holy mother to a marriage in Cana of Galilee. "The wine failing", Mary said to her divine Son: "They have no wine". By these words she intended to ask her Son to console the spouses, who were afflicted because the wine had failed. Jesus answered: "Woman, what is it to me and to thee? my hour is not yet come"—*John*, ii. 4. He meant that the time destined for the performance of miracles was that of his preaching through Judea. But, though his answer appeared

* In a notice to the reader, prefixed to the *Glories of Mary*, St. Alphonsus explains the sense in which he wished his doctrine regarding the privileges of the Blessed Virgin to be understood. He concludes this explanation in the following words: "Then, to say all in a few words, the God of all holiness, in order to glorify the Mother of the Redeemer, has decreed and ordained, that her great charity should pray for all those for whom her Divine Son has paid and offered the most superabundant price of his precious blood, in which alone is '*our salvation, life, and resurrection*'. And on the foundation of this doctrine, and inasmuch as they accord with it, I have intended to lay down my propositions, which the saints, in their affectionate colloquies with Mary, and in their fervent discourses upon her, have not hesitated to assert"—*Glories of Mary, Monza Edition*, vol. i., pp. 11, 12.

In the third chapter of the first volume (pp. 123, 124), St. Alphonsus compares the hope which we place in the Blessed Virgin, to the confidence which a person has in a minister of state whom he asks to procure a favour from his sovereign.

"Whatsoever Mary obtains for us, she obtains it through the merits of Jesus Christ, and because she prays in the name of Jesus Christ"—*Glories of Mary*, vol. i., p. 188.

"Mary, then, is said to be omnipotent in the manner in which omnipotence can be understood of a creature; for a creature is incapable of a divine attribute. Thus she is omnipotent, inasmuch as she obtains by her prayers whatever she asks"—*ibid.*, p. 223.

To obtain favours through the intercession of Mary, by practising devout exercises in her honour, "the first condition is, that we perform our devotions with a soul free from sin, or, at least, with a desire to give up sin". "If a person wish to commit sin with the hope of being saved by the Blessed Virgin, he shall thus render himself unworthy and incapable of her protection"—*Glories of Mary*, vol. ii., pp. 325, 326.

to be a refusal of the request of Mary, the Son, says St. Chrysostom, resolved to yield to the desire of the mother. "Although he said, 'my hour is not yet come', he granted the petition of his mother"—*hom. in* ii. *Joan.* Mary said to the waiters: "Whatsoever he shall say to you, do ye". Jesus bid them fill the water pots with water—the water was changed into most excellent wine. Thus the bridegroom and the entire family were filled with gladness. From the fact related in this day's gospel, let us consider, in the first point, the greatness of Mary's power to obtain from God the graces which we stand in need of; and in the second, the tenderness of Mary's compassion, and her readiness to assist us in all our wants.

First point. The greatness of Mary's power to obtain from God for us all the graces we stand in need of.

1. So great is Mary's merit in the eyes of God, that, according to St. Bonaventure, her prayers are infallibly heard. "The merit of Mary is so great before God, that her petition cannot be rejected"—*de Virg.*, *c.* iii. But why are the prayers of Mary so powerful in the sight of God? It is, says St. Antonine, because she is his mother. "The petition of the mother of God partakes of the nature of a command, and therefore it is impossible that she should not be heard"—*par.* 4, *tit.* 13, *c.* xvii. § 4. The prayers of the saints are the prayers of servants; but the prayers of Mary are the prayers of a mother, and therefore, according to the holy doctor, they are regarded in a certain manner as commands by her Son, who loves her so tenderly. It is then impossible that the prayers of Mary should be rejected.

2. Hence, according to Cosmas of Jerusalem, the intercession of Mary is all-powerful. "Omnipotens auxilium tuum O Maria". It is right, as Richard of St. Lawrence teaches, that the son should impart his power to the mother. Jesus Christ, who is all-powerful, has made Mary omnipotent, as far as a creature is capable of omnipotence; that is, omnipotent in obtaining from him, her divine Son, whatever she asks. "Cum autem eadem sit potestas filii et matris ab omnipotente filio, omnipotens mater facta est"—*lib.* 4, *de Laud. Virg.*

3. St. Bridget heard our Saviour one day addressing the Virgin in the following words: "Ask from me whatever you wish, for your petition cannot be fruitless"—*Rev.*, *l.* 1, *cap.* iv. My mother, ask of me what you please; I cannot reject any

prayer which you present to me; "because since you refused me nothing on Earth, I will refuse you nothing in Heaven"—*ibid.* St. George, Archbishop of Nicomedia, says that Jesus Christ hears all the prayers of his mother, as if he wished thereby to discharge the obligation which he owes to her for having given to him his human nature, by consenting to accept him for her son. "Filius exolvens debitum petitiones tuas implet"—*Orat. de Exitu Mar.* Hence St. Methodius, martyr, used to say to Mary: "Euge, euge, quæ debitorum habes filium, Deo enim universi debemus, tibi autem ille debitor est"—*Orat. Hyp. Dom.* Rejoice, rejoice, O holy virgin; for thou hast for thy debtor that Son to whom we are all debtors; to thee he owes the human nature which he received from thee.

4. St. Gregory of Nicomedia encourages sinners by the assurance, that, if they have recourse to the virgin with a determination to amend their lives, she will save them by her intercession. Hence, turning to Mary, he exclaimed: "Thou hast insuperable strength, lest the multitude of our sins should overcome thy clemency". O mother of God, the sins of a Christian, however great they may be, cannot overcome thy mercy. "Nothing", adds the same saint, "resists thy power; for the Creator regards thy glory as his own". Nothing is impossible to thee, says St. Peter Damian: thou canst raise even those who are in despair to hopes of salvation. "Nihil tibi impossibile, quæ etiam desperatos in spem salutis potes relevare"—*ser.* i., *de Nat. B. V.*

5. Richard of St. Lawrence remarks, that, in announcing to the Virgin that God had chosen her for the mother of his Son, the Archangel Gabriel said to her; "Fear not, Mary; for thou hast found grace with God"—*Luke*, i. 30. From which words the same author concludes: "Cupientes invenire gratiam, quæramus inventricem gratiæ". If we wish to recover lost grace, let us seek Mary, by whom this grace has been found. She never lost the divine grace; she always possessed it. If the angel declared that she had found grace, he meant that she had found it not for herself, but for us miserable sinners, who have lost it. Hence Cardinal Hugo exhorts us to go to Mary, and say to her: O blessed lady, property should be restored to those who lost it: the grace which thou hast found is not thine—for thou hast never lost the grace of God—but it is ours; we have lost it through our own fault: to us, then, thou oughtest to restore it.

"Sinners who by your sins have forfeited the divine grace, run to the Virgin, and say to her with confidence: Restore to us our property, which thou hast found".

6. It was revealed to St. Gertrude, that all the graces which we ask of God through the intercession of Mary, shall be given to us. She heard Jesus saying to his divine mother: "Through thee all who ask mercy with a purpose of amending their lives, shall obtain grace". If all Paradise asked a favour of God, and Mary asked the opposite grace, the Lord would hear Mary, and would reject the petition of the rest of the celestial host. Because, says Father Suarez, "God loves the Virgin alone, more than all the other saints". Let us, then, conclude this first point in the words of St. Bernard: "Let us seek grace, and let us seek it through Mary; for she is a mother, and her petition cannot be rejected"—*serm. de Aquæd.* Let us seek through Mary all the graces we desire to receive from God, and we shall obtain them; for she is a mother, and her Son cannot refuse to hear her prayers, or to grant thegraces which she asks from him.

Second point. On the tender compassion of Mary, and her readiness to assist us in all our wants.

7. The tenderness of Mary's mercy may be inferred from the fact related in this day's Gospel. The wine fails—the spouses are troubled—no one speaks to Mary to ask her Son to console them in their necessity. But the tenderness of Mary's heart, which, according to St. Bernardine of Sienna, cannot but pity the afflicted, moved her to take the office of advocate, and, without being asked, to entreat her Son to work a miracle. "Unasked, she assumed the office of an advocate and a compassionate helper"—*tom.* III., *ser.* ix. Hence, adds the same saint, if, unasked, this good lady has done so much, what will she not do for those who invoke her intercession? "Si hoc non rogata perfecit, quid rogata perficiet?"

8. From the fact already related St. Bonaventure draws another argument, to show the great graces which we may hope to obtain through Mary, now that she reigns in Heaven. If she was so compassionate on Earth, how much greater must be her mercy now that she is in Paradise? "Great was the mercy of Mary while in exile on Earth; but it is much greater now that she is a queen in Heaven; because she now sees the misery of

men"—*St. Bona. in Spec. Virg., cap.* viii. Mary in Heaven enjoys the vision of God; and therefore she sees our wants far more clearly than when she was on Earth; hence, as her pity for us is increased, so also is her desire to assist us more ardent. How truly has Richard of St. Victor said to the Virgin: "So tender is thy heart, that thou canst not see misery, and not afford succour". It is impossible for this loving mother to behold a human being in distress without extending to him pity and relief.

9. St. Peter Damian says that the Virgin "loves us with an invincible love"—*ser.* i., *de Nat. Virg.* How ardently soever the saints may have loved this amiable queen, their affection fell far short of the love which Mary bore to them. It is this love that makes her so solicitous for our welfare. The saints in Heaven, says St. Augustine, have great power to obtain grace from God for those who recommend themselves to their prayers; but as Mary is of all the saints the most powerful, so she is of all the most desirous to procure for us the divine mercy. "Sicut omnibus sanctis potentior, sic omnibus est pro nobis sollicitior".

10. And as this our great advocate once said to St. Bridget, she regards not the iniquities of the sinner who has recourse to her, but the disposition with which he invokes her aid. If he comes to her with a firm purpose of amendment, she receives him, and by her intercession, heals his wounds, and brings him to salvation. "However great a man's sins may be, if he shall return to me, I am ready instantly to receive him. Nor do I regard the number or the enormity of his sins, but the will with which he comes to me; for I do not disdain to anoint and heal his wounds, because I am called, and I truly am, the mother of mercy".

11. The Blessed Virgin is called a "fair olive tree in the plains". "Quasi oliva speciosa in campis"—*Eccl.*, xxiv. 19. From the olive, oil only comes forth; and from the hands of Mary only graces and mercies flow. According to Cardinal Hugo, it is said that she remains in the plains, to show that she is ready to assist all who have recourse to her. "Speciosa in campis ut omnes ad eam confugiant". In the old law, there were five cities of refuge, in which not all, but only those who had committed certain crimes, could find an asylum; but in Mary, says St. John Damascene, all criminals, whatever may be their offences, may take refuge. Hence he calls her "the city of

refuge for all who have recourse to her". Why then, says St. Bernard, should we be afraid to approach Mary? She is all sweetness and clemency; in her there is nothing austere or terrible. "Quid ad Mariam accedere trepidat humana fragilitas? Nihil austerum in ea, nihil terribile, tota suavis est".

12. St. Bonaventure used to say, that, in turning to Mary, he saw mercy itself receiving him. "When I behold thee, O my lady, I see nothing but mercy". The Virgin said one day to St. Bridget: "Miser erit, qui ad misericordiam cum possit, non accedit". Miserable and miserable for eternity shall be the sinner who, though he has it in his power during life to come to me, who am able and willing to assist him, neglects to invoke my aid, and is lost. "The Devil", says St. Peter, "as a roaring lion goeth about seeking whom he may devour"—I. *Pet.*, v. 8. But, according to Bernardine a Bustis, this mother of mercy is constantly going about in search of sinners to save them. "She continually goes about seeking whom she may save"—*Maril.*, *par.* 3, *ser.* iii. This queen of clemency, says Richard of St. Victor, presents our petitions, and begins to assist us before we ask the assistance of her prayers. "Velocius occurrit ejus pietas quam invocetur, et causas miserorum anticipat"—*in Can.*, *c.* xxiii. Because, as the same author says, Mary's heart is so full of tenderness towards us, that she cannot behold our miseries without affording relief. "Nec possis miserias scire, et non subvenire".

13. Let us, then, in all our wants, be most careful to have recourse to this mother of mercy, who is always ready to assist those who invoke her aid. "Invenies semper paratam auxiliari", says Richard of St. Lawrence. She is always prepared to come to our help, and frequently prevents our supplications: but, ordinarily, she requires that we should pray to her, and is offended when we neglect to ask her assistance. "In te domina peccant", says St. Bonaventure, "non solum qui tibi injuriam irrogant, sed etiam qui te non rogant"—*in Spec. Virg.* Thou, O blessed lady, art displeased not only with those who commit an injury against thee, but also with those who do not ask favours from thee. Hence, as the same holy doctor teaches, it is not possible that Mary should neglect to succour any soul that flies to her for protection; for she cannot but pity and console the afflicted who have recourse to her. "Ipsa enim non misereri ignorat et miseris non satisfacere".

14. But, to obtain special favours from this good lady, we must perform in her honour certain devotions practised by her servants; such as, first, to recite every day at least five decades of the Rosary; secondly, to fast every Saturday in her honour. Many persons fast every Saturday on bread and water: you should fast in this manner at least on the vigils of her seven principal festivals. Thirdly, to say the three *Aves* when the bell rings for the *Angelus Domini;* and to salute her frequently during the day with an *Ave Maria*, particularly when you hear the clock strike, or when you see an image of the Virgin, and also when you leave or return to your house. Fourthly, to say every evening the Litany of the Blessed Virgin before you go to rest; and for this purpose procure an image of Mary, and keep it near your bed. Fifthly, to wear the scapular of Mary in sorrow, and of Mount Carmel. There are many other devotions practised by the servants of Mary; but the most useful of all is, to recommend yourself frequently to her prayers. Never omit to say three *Aves* in the morning, to beg of her to preserve you from sin during the day. In all temptations have immediate recourse to her, saying: "*Mary, assist me*". To resist every temptation, it is sufficient to pronounce the names of Jesus and Mary; and if the temptation continues, let us continue to invoke Jesus and Mary, and the Devil shall never be able to conquer us.

15. St. Bonaventure calls Mary the salvation of those who invoke her. "O salus te invocantium". And if a true servant of Mary were lost (I mean one truly devoted to her, who wishes to amend his life, and invoke with confidence this advocate of sinners), this should happen either because Mary would be unable or unwilling to assist him. But, says St. Bernard, this is impossible: being the mother of omnipotence and of mercy, Mary cannot want the power or the will to save her servants. Justly then is she called the salvation of all who invoke her aid. Of this truth there are numberless examples: that of St. Mary of Egypt will be sufficient. After leading for many years a sinful and dissolute life, she wished to enter the church of Jerusalem in which the festival of the holy cross was celebrated. To make her feel her miseries, God closed against her the door which was open to all others: as often as she endeavoured to enter, an invisible force drove her back. She instantly perceived her miserable condition,

and remained in sorrow outside the church. Fortunately for her, there was an image of most holy Mary over the porch of the church. As a poor sinner she recommended herself to the divine mother, and promised to change her life. After her prayer, she felt encouraged to go into the church, and, behold! the door which was before closed against her, she now finds open: she enters, and confesses her sins. She leaves the church, and, under the influence of divine inspiration, goes into the desert, where she lived for forty-seven years, and became a saint.

SERMON VIII.

FOR THE THIRD SUNDAY AFTER THE EPIPHANY.

On the remorse of the damned.

"But the children of the kingdom shall be cast out into the exterior darkness: there shall be weeping and gnashing of teeth"—*Matt.*, viii. 12.

In the gospel of this day it is related that, "*when Jesus Christ entered into Capharnaum, there came to him a centurion beseeching him*" to cure his servant, who lay sick of the palsy. Jesus answered: "I will come and heal him". No, replied the centurion: "I am not worthy that thou shouldst enter under my roof, but only say the word, and my servant shall be healed" —*v.* 8. Seeing the centurion's faith, the Redeemer instantly consoled him by restoring health to his servant; and, turning to his disciples, he said: "Many shall come from the east and the west, and shall sit down with Abraham and Isaac and Jacob in the kingdom of Heaven. But the children of the kingdom shall be cast out into the exterior darkness: there shall be weeping and gnashing of teeth". By these words our Lord wished to signify, that many persons born in infidelity shall be saved, and enjoy the society of the saints, and that many who are born in the bosom of the Church, shall be cast into Hell, where the worm of conscience, by its gnawing, shall make them weep bitterly for all eternity.

Let us examine the remorses of conscience which a damned

Christian shall suffer in Hell. First remorse, arising from the thought of the little which he required to do in order to save his soul. Second remorse, arising from the remembrance of the trifles for which he lost his soul. Third remorse, arising from the knowledge of the great good which he has lost through his own fault.

First remorse of the damned Christian, arising from the thought of the little which he required to do in order to save his soul.

1. A damned soul once appeared to St. Hubert, and said, that two remorses were her most cruel executioners in Hell:— the thought of the little which was necessary for her to have done in this life to secure her salvation; and the thought of the trifles for which she brought herself to eternal misery. The same thing has been said by St. Thomas. Speaking of the reprobate, he says: "They shall be in sorrow principally because they are damned for nothing, and because they could most easily have obtained eternal life". Let us stop to consider this first source of remorse; that is, how few and transitory are the pleasures for which all the damned are lost. Each of the reprobate will say for eternity: If I abstained from such a gratification; if, in certain circumstances, I overcame human respect; if I avoided such an occasion of sin—such a companion, I should not now be damned; if I had frequented some pious sodality; if I had gone to confession every week; if, in temptations, I had recommended myself to God, I would not have relapsed into sin. I have so often proposed to do these things, but I have not done them. I began to practise these means of salvation, but afterwards gave them up; and thus I am lost.

2. This torment of the damned will be increased by the remembrance of the good example given them by some young companions who led a chaste and pious life even in the midst of the world. It will be still more increased by the recollection of all the gifts which the Lord had bestowed upon them, that by their coöperation they might acquire eternal salvation; the gifts of nature—health, riches, respectability of family, talents; all gifts granted by God, not to be employed in the indulgence of pleasures and in the gratification of vanity, but in the sanctification of their souls, and in becoming saints. So many gifts of grace, so many divine lights, holy inspirations, loving calls,

and so many years of life to repair past disorders. But they shall for ever hear from the angel of the Lord that for them the time of salvation is past. "The angel whom I saw standing, swore by Him that liveth for ever and ever,......that time shall be no longer"—*Apoc.*, x. 6.

3. Alas! what cruel swords shall all these blessings received from God be to the heart of a poor damned Christian, when he shall see himself shut up in the prison of Hell, and that there is no more time to repair his eternal ruin. In despair he will say to his wretched companions: "The harvest is past; the summer is ended; and we are not saved"—*Jer.*, viii. 20. The time, he will say, of gathering fruits of eternal life is past; the summer, during which we could have saved our souls, is over, but we are not saved: the winter is come; but it is an eternal winter, in which we must live in misery and despair as long as God shall be God.

4. O fool, he will say, that I have been! If I had suffered for God the pains to which I have submitted for the indulgence of my passions—if the labours which I have endured for my own damnation, had been borne for my salvation, how happy should I now be! And what now remains of all past pleasures, but remorse and pain, which now torture, and shall torture me for eternity? Finally, he will say, I might be for ever happy, and now I must be for ever miserable. Ah! this thought will torture the damned more than the fire and all the other torments of Hell.

Second remorse of the damned, arising from the remembrance of the trifles for which they lost their souls.

5. Saul forbid the people, under pain of death, to taste food. His son Jonathan, who was then young, being hungry, tasted a little honey. Having discovered that Jonathan had violated the command, the king declared that he should die. Seeing himself condemned to death, Jonathan said with tears: "I did but taste a little honey,......and behold I must die"—I. *Kings*, xiv. 43. But the people, moved to pity for Jonathan, interposed with his father, and delivered him from death. For the unhappy damned there is no compassion; there is no one to intercede with God to deliver them from the eternal death of Hell. On the contrary, all rejoice at the just punishment which they suffer

for having wilfully lost God and Paradise for the sake of a transitory pleasure.

6. After having eaten the pottage of lentiles for which he sold his right of primogeniture, Esau was tortured with grief and remorse for what he had lost, and "roared out with a great cry"—*Gen.*, xxvii. 34. Oh! how great shall be the roaring and howling of the damned, at the thought of having lost, for a few poisonous and momentary pleasures, the everlasting kingdom of Paradise, and of being condemned for eternity to a continual death!

7. The unfortunate reprobate shall be continually employed in reflecting on the unhappy cause of their damnation. To us who live on Earth our past life appears but a moment—but a dream. Alas! what will the fifty or sixty years which they may have spent in this world appear to the damned, when they shall find themselves in the abyss of eternity, and when they shall have passed a hundred and a thousand millions of years in torments, and shall see that their miserable eternity is only beginning, and shall be for ever in its commencement? But, have the fifty years spent on this Earth been full of pleasures? Perhaps the sinner, living in enmity with God, enjoyed uninterrupted happiness in his sins? How long do the pleasures of sin last? Only for a few moments: the remaining part of the lives of those who live at a distance from God is full of anguish and pain. Oh! what will these moments of pleasure appear to a damned soul, when she shall find herself in a pit of fire?

8. "What hath pride profited us? or what advantage hath the boasting of riches brought us? All those things have passed away like a shadow"—*Wis.*, v. 8. Unhappy me! each of the damned shall say, I have lived on Earth according to my corrupt inclinations; I have indulged my pleasures; but what have they profited me? They have lasted but for a short time; they have made me lead a life of bitterness and disquietude; and now I must burn in this furnace for ever, in despair, and abandoned by all.

Third remorse of the damned, arising from the knowledge of the great good which they have lost by their own fault.

9. A certain queen, blinded by the ambition of being a sovereign, said one day: "*If the Lord gives me a reign of*

forty years, I will renounce Paradise". The unhappy queen reigned for forty years; but now that she is in another world, she cannot but be grieved at having made such a renunciation. Oh! how great must be her anguish, at the thought of having lost the kingdom of Paradise for the sake of a reign of forty years, full of troubles, of crosses, and of fears! "Plus cœlo torquetur, quam gehenna", says St. Peter Chrysologus. To the damned the voluntary loss of Paradise is a greater torment than the very pains of Hell.

10. The greatest pain in Hell is the loss of God, that sovereign good, who is the source of all the joys of Paradise. "Let torments", says St. Bruno, "be added to torments, and let them not be deprived of God"—*serm. de jud. fin.* The damned would be content to have a thousand Hells added to the Hell which they suffer, provided they were not deprived of God; but their Hell shall consist in seeing themselves deprived for ever of God through their own fault. St. Teresa used to say, that when a person loses, through his own fault, a trifle—a small sum of money, or a ring of little value—the thought of having lost it through his own neglect afflicts him and disturbs his peace. What then must be the anguish of the damned in reflecting that they have lost God, a good of infinite value, and have lost him through their own fault?

11. The damned shall see that God wished them to be saved, and had given them the choice of eternal life or of eternal death. "Before man is life and death,...that which he shall choose shall be given him"—*Eccles.*, xv. 18. They shall see that, if they wished, they might have acquired eternal happiness, and that, by their own choice, they are damned. On the day of judgment they shall see many of their companions among the elect; but, because they would not put a stop to their career of sin, they have gone to end it in Hell. "Therefore we have erred", they shall say to their unhappy associates in Hell; we have erred in losing Heaven and God through our own fault, and our error is irreparable. They shall continually exclaim: "There is no peace for my bones because of my sins"—*Ps.*, xxxvii. 4. The thought of having been the cause of their own damnation, produces an internal pain, which enters into the very bones of the damned, and prevents them from ever enjoying a moment's repose. Hence, each

of them shall be to himself an object of the greatest horror. Each shall suffer the pain threatened by the Lord: "I will set THEE before thy face"—*Ps.*, xlix. 21.

12. If, beloved brethren, you have hitherto been so foolish as to lose God for a miserable pleasure, do not persevere in your folly. Endeavour, now that you have it in your power, to repair your past error. Tremble! Perhaps, if you do not now resolve to change your life, you shall be abandoned by God, and be lost for ever. When the Devil tempts you, remember Hell;—the thought of Hell will preserve you from that land of misery. I say, remember Hell, and have recourse to Jesus Christ and to most holy Mary, and they will deliver you from sin, which is the gate of Hell.

SERMON IX.

FOR THE FOURTH SUNDAY AFTER THE EPIPHANY.

Dangers of eternal salvation.

"And when he entered into the boat, his disciples followed him; and, behold, a great tempest arose in the sea"—*Matt.*, viii. 23, 24.

On the greatness of the dangers to which our eternal salvation is exposed, and on the manner in which we ought to guard against them.

1. IN this day's Gospel we find that, when Jesus Christ entered the boat along with his disciples, a great tempest arose, so that the boat was agitated by the waves, and was on the point of being lost. During this storm the Saviour was asleep; but the disciples, terrified by the storm, ran to awake him, and said: "Lord, save us: we perish"—*v.* 25. Jesus gave them courage by saying: "Why are ye fearful, O ye of little faith? Then rising up, he commanded the winds and the sea, and there came a great calm". Let us examine what is meant by the boat in the midst of the sea, and by the tempest which agitated the sea.

2. The boat on the sea represents man in this world. As a

vessel on the sea is exposed to a thousand dangers—to pirates, to quicksands, to hidden rocks, and to tempests; so man in this life is encompassed with perils arising from the temptations of Hell—from the occasions of sin, from the scandals or bad counsels of men, from human respect, and, above all, from the bad passions of corrupt nature, represented by the winds that agitate the sea, and expose the vessel to great danger of being lost.

3. Thus, as St. Leo says, our life is full of dangers, of snares, and of enemies: "Plena omnia periculis, plena laqueis: incitant cupiditates, insidiantur illecebræ; blandiuntur lucra"—*S. Leo, serm.* v., *de Quad.* The first enemy of the salvation of every Christian is his own corruption. "*But every man is tempted by his own concupiscence, being drawn away and allured*"—*St. James*, i. 14. Along with the corrupt inclinations which live within us, and drag us to evil, we have many enemies from without that fight against us. We have the devils, with whom the contest is very difficult, because they are stronger than we are. "Bellum grave", says Cassiodorus, "quia cum fortiore"—*in Psal.* v. Hence, because we have to contend with powerful enemies, St. Paul exhorts us to arm ourselves with the divine aid: "Put you on the armour of God, that you may be able to stand against the deceits of the Devil. For our wrestling is not against flesh and blood, but against principalities and powers, against the rulers of the world of this darkness, against the spirits of wickedness in high places"—*Eph.*, vi. 11, 12. The Devil, according to St. Peter, is a lion who is continually going about roaring, through the rage and hunger which impel him to devour our souls. "Your adversary, the Devil, like a roaring lion, goeth about seeking whom he may devour"—I. *Peter*, v. 8. St. Cyprian says that Satan is continually lying in wait for us, in order to make us his slaves. "Circuit demon nos singulos, et tanquam hostis clausos obsidens muros explorat et tentat num sit pars aliqua minus stabilis, cujus aditu ad interiora penetretur"—*S. Cyp.*, *lib. de zelo*, *etc.*

4. Even the men with whom we must converse endanger our salvation. They persecute or betray us, or deceive us by their flattery and bad counsels. St. Augustine says that, among the faithful, there are in every profession hollow and deceitful men. "Omnis professio in ecclesia habet fictos"—*in Ps.*, xcix. Now if a fortress were full of rebels within, and encompassed by

enemies from without, who is there that would not regard it as lost? Such is the condition of each of us as long as we live in this world. Who shall be able to deliver us from so many powerful enemies? Only God: "Unless the Lord keep the city, he watcheth in vain that keepeth it"—*Ps.*, cxxvi. 2.

5. What then is the means by which we can save our souls in the midst of so many dangers? It is to imitate the holy disciples —to have recourse to our Divine Master, and say to him: "Save us; we perish". Save us, O Lord; if thou do not, we are lost. When the tempest is violent, the pilot never takes his eyes from the light which guides him to the port. In like manner we should keep our eyes always turned to God, who alone can deliver us from the many dangers to which we are exposed. It was thus David acted when he found himself assailed by the dangers of sin. "I have lifted up my eyes to the mountains, from whence help shall come to me"—*Ps.*, cxx. 1. To teach us to recommend ourselves continually to him who alone can save us by his grace, the Lord has ordained that, as long as we remain on this Earth, we should live in the midst of a continual tempest, and should be surrounded by enemies. The temptations of the Devil, the persecutions of men, the adversity which we suffer in this world, are not evils: they are, on the contrary, advantages, if we know how to make of them the use which God wishes, who sends or permits them for our welfare. They detach our affections from this Earth, and inspire a disgust for this world, by making us feel bitterness and thorns even in its honours, its riches, its delights, and amusements. The Lord permits all these apparent evils, that we may take away our affections from fading goods, in which we meet with so many dangers of perdition, and that we may seek to unite ourselves with him who alone can make us happy.

6. Our error and mistake is, that when we find ourselves harassed by infirmities, by poverty, by persecutions, and by such tribulations, instead of having recourse to the Lord, we turn to men, and place our confidence in their assistance, and thus draw upon ourselves the malediction of God, who says: "Cursed be the man who trusteth in man"—*Jer.*, xvii. 5. The Lord does not forbid us, in our afflictions and dangers, to have recourse to human means; but he curses those who place their whole trust in them. He wishes us to have recourse to himself before all others,

and to place our only hope in him, that we may also centre in him all our love.

7. As long as we live on this Earth, we must, according to St. Paul, work out our salvation with fear and trembling, in the midst of the dangers by which we are beset. "Cum metu et tremore vestram salutem operamini"—*Phil.*, ii. 12. Whilst a certain vessel was in the open sea, a great tempest arose, which made the captain tremble. In the hold of the vessel there was an animal eating with as much tranquillity as if the sea were perfectly calm. The captain being asked why he was so much afraid, replied: If I had a soul like the soul of this brute, I too would be tranquil and without fear; but because I have a rational and an immortal soul, I am afraid of death, after which I must appear before the judgment-seat of God; and therefore I tremble through fear. Let us also tremble, beloved brethren. The salvation of our immortal souls is at stake. They who do not tremble are, as St. Paul says, in great danger of being lost; because they who fear not, seldom recommend themselves to God, and labour but little to adopt the means of salvation. Let us beware: we are, says St. Cyprian, still in battle array, and still combat for eternal salvation. "Adhuc in acie constituti de vita nostra dimicamus" —*S. Cypr.*, *lib.* I., *cap.* i.

8. The first means of salvation, then, is, to recommend ourselves continually to God, that he may keep his hands over us, and preserve us from offending him. The next is, to cleanse the soul from all past sins by making a general confession. A general confession is a powerful help to a change of life. When the tempest is violent the burden of the vessel is diminished, and each person on board throws his goods into the sea in order to save his life. O folly of sinners, who, in the midst of such great dangers of eternal perdition, instead of diminishing the burden of the vessel—that is, instead of unburdening the soul of her sins—load her with a greater weight. Instead of flying from the dangers of sin, they fearlessly continue to put themselves voluntarily into dangerous occasions; and, instead of having recourse to God's mercy for the pardon of their offences, they offend him still more, and compel him to abandon them.

9. Another means is, to labour strenuously not to allow ourselves to become the slaves of irregular passions. "Give

me not over to a shameless and foolish mind"—*Eccl.*, xxiii. 6. Do not, O Lord, deliver me up to a mind blinded by passion. He who is blind sees not what he is doing, and therefore he is in danger of falling into every crime. Thus so many are lost by submitting to the tyranny of their passions. Some are slaves to the passion of avarice. A person who is now in the other world, said: Alas! I perceive that a desire of riches is beginning to rule over me. So said the unhappy man; but he applied no remedy. He did not resist the passion in the beginning, but fomented it till death, and thus at his last moments left but little reason to hope for his salvation. Others are slaves to sensual pleasures. They are not content with lawful gratifications, and therefore they pass to the indulgence of those that are forbidden. Others are subject to anger; and because they are not careful to check the fire at its commencement, when it is small, it increases and grows into a spirit of revenge.

10. "Hi hostes cavendi", says St. Ambrose, "hi graviores tyranni. Multi in persecutione publica coronati, in hac persecutione ceciderunt"—*in Ps.* cxviii., *serm.* 20. Disorderly affections, if they are not beaten down in the beginning, become our greatest tyrants. Many, says St. Ambrose, after having victoriously resisted the persecutions of the enemies of the faith, were afterwards lost because they did not resist the first assaults of some Earthly passion. Of this, Origen was a miserable example. He fought for, and was prepared to give his life in defence of the faith; but, by afterwards yielding to human respect, he was led to deny it (*Natalis Alexander*, *His. Eccl.*, *tom.* 7, *dis.* xv., *q.* 2, *a.* 1). We have still a more miserable example in Solomon, who, after having received so many gifts from God, and after being inspired by the Holy Ghost, was, by indulging a passion for certain pagan women, induced to offer incense to idols. The unhappy man who submits to the slavery of his wicked passions, resembles the ox that is sent to the slaughter after a life of constant labour. During their whole lives worldlings groan under the weight of their sins, and, at the end of their days, fall into Hell.

11. Let us conclude. When the winds are strong and violent, the pilot lowers the sails and casts anchor. So, when we find ourselves assailed by any bad passion, we should always lower the sails; that is, we should avoid all the occasions which may increase

the passion, and should cast anchor by uniting ourselves to God, and by begging of him to give us strength not to offend him.

12. But some of you will say, What am I to do? I live in the midst of the world, where my passions continually assail me even against my will. I will answer in the words of Origen: "Donec quis in tenebris sæcularibus manet et in negotiorum obscuritate versatur, non potest servire Domino. Exeundum est ergo de Egypto, relinquendus est mundus, non loco sed animo"—*hom.* iii., *in Exod.* The man who lives in the darkness of the world, and in the midst of secular business, can with difficulty serve God. Whoever then wishes to insure his eternal salvation, let him retire from the world, and take refuge in one of those exact religious communities which are the secure harbours in the sea of this world. If he cannot actually leave the world, let him leave it at least in affection, by detaching his heart from the things of this world, and from his own evil inclinations: "Go not after thy lusts, says the Holy Ghost, but turn away from thy own will"—*Eccl.*, xviii. 30. Follow not your own concupiscence; and when your will impels you to evil, you must not indulge, but must resist its inclinations.

14. "The time is short: it remaineth that they also who have wives be as if they had none; and they that weep, as though they wept not; and they that rejoice, as if they rejoiced not; and they that buy, as if they possessed not; and they that use this world, as if they used it not: for the fashion of this world passeth away"—I. *Cor.*, vii. 29, *etc.* The time of life is short; we should then prepare for death, which is rapidly approaching; and to prepare for that awful moment, let us reflect that everything in this world shall soon end. Hence, the Apostle tells those who suffer in this life to be as if they suffered not, because the miseries of this life shall soon pass away, and they who save their souls shall be happy for eternity; and he exhorts those who enjoy the goods of this Earth to be as if they enjoyed them not, because they must one day leave all things; and if they lose their souls, they shall be miserable for ever.

SERMON X.

FOR THE FIFTH SUNDAY AFTER THE EPIPHANY.

On the pains of Hell.

"Gather up first the cockle, and bind into bundles to burn"—*Matt.*, xiii. 30.

I shall first speak of the fire, which is the principal pain that torments the senses of the damned, and afterwards of the other pains of Hell.

1. BEHOLD! the final doom of sinners who abuse the divine mercy is, to burn in the fire of Hell. God threatens Hell, not to send us there, but to deliver us from that place of torments. "Minatur Deus gehennam", says St. Chrysostom, "ut a gehenna liberet, et ut firmi ac stabiles evitemus minas"—*hom.* v., *de Pœnit.* Remember, then, brethren, that God gives you to-day the opportunity of hearing this sermon, that you may be preserved from Hell, and that you may give up sin, which alone can lead you to Hell.

2. My brethren, it is certain and of faith that there is a Hell. After judgment, the just shall enjoy the eternal glory of Paradise, and sinners shall be condemned to suffer the everlasting chastisement reserved for them in Hell. "And these shall go into everlasting punishment, but the just into life everlasting"—*Mat.*, xxv. 46. Let us examine in what Hell consists. It is what the rich glutton called it—a place of torments. "In hunc locum tormentorum"—*Luc.*, xvi. 28. It is a place of suffering, where each of the senses and powers of the damned has its proper torment, and in which the torments of each person will be increased in proportion to the forbidden pleasures in which he indulged. "As much as she hath glorified herself and lived in delicacies, so much torment and sorrow give ye to her"—*Apoc.*, xviii. 7.

3. In offending God the sinner does two evils: he abandons God, the sovereign good, who is able to make him happy, and turns to creatures, who are incapable of giving any real happiness

to the soul. Of this injury which men commit against him, the Lord complains by his prophet Jeremy: "For my people have done two evils. They have forsaken me, the fountain of living waters, and have digged to themselves cisterns—broken cisterns—that can hold no water"—*Jer.*, ii. 13. Since, then, the sinner turns his back on God, he shall be tormented in Hell by the pain arising from the loss of God, of which I shall speak on another occasion (*see the Sermon for the nineteenth Sunday after Pentecost, p.* 361); and since, in offending God, he turns to creatures, he shall be justly tormented by the same creatures, and principally by fire.

4. "The vengeance on the flesh of the ungodly is fire and worms"—*Eccl.*, vii. 19. Fire and the remorses of conscience are the principal means by which God takes vengeance on the flesh of the wicked. Hence, in condemning the reprobate to Hell, Jesus Christ commands them to go into eternal fire. "Depart from me, you cursed, into everlasting fire"—*Matt.*, xxv. 41. This fire, then, shall be one of the most cruel executioners of the damned.

5. Even in this life, the pain of fire is the most terrible of all torments. But St. Augustine says, that, in comparison of the fire of Hell, the fire of this Earth is no more than a picture compared with the reality. "In cujus comparatione noster hic ignus depictus est". St. Anselm teaches, that the fire of Hell as far surpasses the fire of this world, as the fire of the real, exceeds that of painted fire. The pain, then, produced by the fire of Hell is far greater than that which is produced by our fire; because God has made the fire of this Earth for the use of man, but he has created the fire of Hell purposely for the chastisement of sinners; and therefore, as Tertullian says, he has made it a minister of his justice. "Longe alius est ignis, qui usui humano, alius qui Dei justitiæ deservit". This avenging fire is always kept alive by the wrath of God. "A fire is kindled in my rage"—*Jer.*, xv. 14.

6. "And the rich man also died, and he was buried in Hell"—*Luke*, xvi. 22. The damned are buried in the fire of Hell; hence they have an abyss of fire below, an abyss of fire above, and an abyss of fire on every side. As a fish in the sea is surrounded by water, so the unhappy reprobate are encompassed by fire on every side. The sharpness of the pain of fire may

be inferred from the circumstance, that the rich glutton complained of no other torment. "I am tormented in this flame" —*ibid.*, *v.* 24.

7. The Prophet Isaias says that the Lord will punish the guilt of sinners with the spirit of fire. "If the Lord shall wash away the filth of the daughters of Sion......by the spirit of burning"—iv. 4. "*The spirit of burning*" is the pure essence of fire. All spirits or essences, though taken from simple herbs or flowers, are so penetrating, that they reach the very bones. Such is the fire of Hell. Its activity is so great, that a single spark of it would be sufficient to melt a mountain of bronze. *The disciple* relates, that a damned person, who appeared to a religious, dipped his hand into a vessel of water; the religious placed in the vessel a candlestick of bronze, which was instantly dissolved.

8. This fire shall torment the damned not only externally, but also internally. It will burn the bowels, the heart, the brains, the blood within the veins, and the marrow within the bones. The skin of the damned shall be like a caldron, in which their bowels, their flesh, and their bones shall be burned. David says, that the bodies of the damned shall be like so many furnaces of fire. "Thou shalt make them as an oven of fire in the time of thy anger"—*Ps.*, xx. 10.

9. O God! certain sinners cannot bear to walk under a strong sun, or to remain before a large fire in a close room; they cannot endure a spark from a candle; and they fear not the fire of Hell, which, according to the Prophet Isaias, not only burns, but devours the unhappy damned. "Which of you can dwell with devouring fire?"—*Isaias*, xxxiii. 14. As a lion devours a lamb, so the fire of Hell devours the reprobate; but it devours without destroying life, and thus tortures them with a continual death. Continue, says St. Peter Damian to the sinner who indulges in impurity, continue to satisfy your flesh; a day will come, or rather an eternal night, when your impurities, like pitch, shall nourish a fire within your very bowels. "Venit dies, imo nox, quando libido tua vertetur in picem qua se nutriet perpetuus ignis in visceribus tuis"—*Epist.* 6. And according to St. Cyprian, the impurities of the wicked shall boil in the very fat which will issue from their accursed bodies.

10. St. Jerome teaches, that, in this fire, sinners shall suffer

not only the pain of the fire, but also all the pains which men endure on this Earth. "In uno igne omnia supplicia sentient in inferno peccatores"—*Ep. ad Pam.* How manifold are the pains to which men are subject in this life. Pains in the sides, pains in the head, pains in the loins, pains in the bowels. All these together torture the damned.

11. The fire itself will bring with it the pain of darkness; for, by its smoke it will, according to St. John, produce a storm of darkness which shall blind the damned. "To whom the storm of darkness is reserved for ever"—*St. Jude*, 13. Hence, Hell is called a land of darkness covered with the shadow of death. "A land that is dark and covered with the mist of death: a land of misery and darkness, where the shadow of death, and no order but everlasting horror dwelleth"—*Job*, x. 21, 22. To hear that a criminal is shut up in a dungeon for ten or twenty years excites our compassion. Hell is a dungeon closed on every side, into which a ray of the sun or the light of a candle never enters. Thus the damned "shall never see light"—*Ps.*, xlviii. 20. The fire of this world gives light, but the fire of Hell is utter darkness. In explaining the words of David, "the voice of the Lord divideth the flame of fire"—*Ps.*, xxviii. 7,—St. Basil says, that in Hell the Lord separates the fire that burns from the flame which illuminates, and therefore this fire burns, but gives no light. B. Albertus Magnus explains this passage more concisely by saying that God "divides the heat from the light". St. Thomas teaches, that in Hell there is only as much light as is necessary to torment the damned by the sight of their associates and of the devils. "Quantum sufficit ad videndum illa quæ torquere possunt"—3 *p.*, *q.* 97, *art.* 5. And according to St. Augustine, the bare sight of these infernal monsters excites sufficient terror to cause the death of all the damned, if they were capable of dying. "Videbunt monstra, quorum visio postet illos occidere".

12. To suffer a parching thirst without having a drop of water to quench it, is intolerably painful. It has sometimes happened, that travellers who could procure no refreshment after a long journey, have fainted from the pain produced by thirst. So great is the thirst of the damned, that if one of them were offered all the water on this Earth, he would exclaim: All this water is not sufficient to extinguish the burning thirst which

I endure. But, alas! the unhappy damned shall never have a single drop of water to refresh their tongues. "He cried out and said: Father Abraham, have mercy on me, and send Lazarus, that he may dip the tip of his finger in water, to cool my tongue, for I am tormented in this flame"—*St. Luke*, xvi. 24. The rich glutton has not obtained, and shall never obtain, this drop of water, as long as God shall be God.

13. The reprobate shall be likewise tormented by the stench which pervades Hell. This stench shall arise from the very bodies of the damned. "Out of their carcasses shall arise a stink"—*Isa.*, xxxiv. 3. The bodies of the damned are called carcasses, not because they are dead (for they are living, and shall be for ever alive to pain), but on account of the stench which they exhale. Would it not be very painful to be shut up in a close room with a fetid corpse? St. Bonaventure says, that if the body of one of the damned were placed in the Earth, it would, by its stench, be sufficient to cause the death of all men. How intolerable, then, must it be to live for ever in the dungeons of Hell in the midst of the immense multitudes of the damned! Some foolish worldlings say: *If I go to Hell, I shall not be there alone.* Miserable fools! do you not see that the greater the number of your companions, the more insufferable shall be your torments? "There", says St. Thomas, "the society of the reprobate shall cause an increase and not a diminution of misery"—*Suppl.*, *q.* 86, *art.* 1. The society of the reprobate augments their misery, because each of the damned is a source of suffering to all the others. Hence, the greater their number, the more they shall mutually torment each other. "And the people", says the Prophet Isaias, "shall be as ashes after a fire, as a bundle of thorns they shall be burnt with fire"—*Isa.*, xxxiii. 12. Placed in the midst of the furnace of Hell, the damned are like so many grains reduced to ashes by that abyss of fire, and like so many thorns tied together and wounding each other.

14. They are tormented not only by the stench of their companions, but also by their shrieks and lamentations. How painful is it to a person longing for sleep to hear the groans of a sick man, the barking of a dog, or the screams of an infant. The damned must listen incessantly to the wailing and howling of their

associates, not for a night, nor for a thousand nights, but for all eternity without the interruption of a single moment.

15. The damned are also tormented by the narrowness of the place in which they are confined; for, although the dungeon of Hell is large, it will be too small for so many millions of the reprobate, who like sheep shall be heaped one over the other. "They are", says David, "laid in Hell like sheep"—*Ps.*, xlviii. 15. We learn from the Scriptures that they shall be pressed together like grapes in the winepress, by the vengeance of an angry God. "The winepress of the fierceness of the wrath of God the Almighty"—*Apoc.*, xix. 15. From this pressure shall arise the pain of immobility. "Let them become unmoveable as a stone"—*Exod.*, xvi. 16. In whatever position the damned shall fall into Hell after the general judgment, whether on the side, or on the back, or with the head downwards, in that they must remain for eternity, without being ever able to move foot or hand or finger, as long as God shall be God. In a word, St. Chrysostom says, that all the pains of this life, however great they may be, are scarcely a shadow of the torments of the damned. "Hæc omnia ludicra sunt et risus ad illa supplicia: pone ignem, ferrum, et bestias, attamen vix umbra sunt ad illa tormenta"—*hom.* xxxix., *ad pop. Ant.*

16. The reprobate, then, shall be tormented in all the senses of the body. They shall be also tormented in all the powers of the soul. Their memory shall be tormented by the remembrance of the years which they had received from God for the salvation of their souls, and which they spent in labouring for their own damnation; by the remembrance of so many graces and so many divine lights which they abused. Their understanding shall be tormented by the knowledge of the great happiness which they forfeited in losing their souls, Heaven, and God, and by a conviction that this loss is irreparable. Their will shall be tormented by seeing that whatsoever they ask or desire shall be refused. "The desire of the wicked shall perish"—*Ps.*, cxi. 10. They shall never have any of those things for which they wish, and must for ever suffer all that is repugnant to their will. They would wish to escape from these torments and to find peace; but in these torments they must for ever remain, and peace they shall never enjoy.

17. Perhaps they may sometimes receive a little comfort or

at least enjoy occasional repose? No, says Cyprian: "Nullum ibi refrigerium, nullum remedium, atque ita omni tormento atrocius desperatio"—*serm. de Ascens.* In this life, how great soever may be the tribulations which we suffer, there is always some relief or interruption. The damned must remain for ever in a pit of fire, always in torture, always weeping, without ever enjoying a moment's repose. But perhaps there is some one to pity their sufferings? At the very time that they are so much afflicted, the devils continually reproach them with the sins for which they are tormented, saying: Suffer, burn, live for ever in despair: you yourselves have been the cause of your destruction. And do not the saints, the divine mother, and God, who is called the Father of Mercies, take compassion on their miseries? No; "The sun shall be darkened, and the moon shall not give her light, and the stars shall fall from Heaven"—*Matt.*, xxvi. 29. The saints, represented by the stars, not only do not pity the damned, but they even rejoice in the vengeance inflicted on the injuries offered to their God. Neither can the divine mother pity them, because they hate her Son. And Jesus Christ, who died for the love of them, cannot pity them, because they have despised his love, and have voluntarily brought themselves to perdition.

SERMON XI.

FOR THE SIXTH SUNDAY AFTER THE EPIPHANY.

On the death of the just.

"The kingdom of Heaven is like unto leaven, which a woman took and hid in three measures of meal until the whole was leavened"—*Matt.*, xiii. 33.

In this day's gospel we find that a woman, after putting leaven in the dough, waits till the entire is fermented. Here the Lord gives us to understand that the kingdom of Heaven—that is, the attainment of eternal beatitude—is like the leaven. By the leaven is understood the divine grace, which makes the soul acquire merits for eternal life. But this eternal life is obtained only when "the whole is leavened"; that is, when the soul has arrived at the end of the present life and the completion of her merits. We shall, then, speak to-day of the death of the just, which we should not fear, but should desire with our whole souls. For, says St. Bonaventure, "Triplex in morte congratulatio, hominem ab omni labore, peccato, et periculo liberari". Man should rejoice at death, for three reasons: first, because death delivers him from labour—that is, from suffering the miseries of this life and the assaults of his enemies. Secondly, because it delivers him from actual sins. Thirdly, because it delivers him from the danger of falling into Hell, and opens Paradise to him.

First point. Death delivers us from the miseries of this life, and from the assaults of our enemies.

1. What is death? St. Eucherius answers, that "death is the end of miseries". Job said that our life, however short it may be, is full of miseries, of infirmities, of crosses, of persecutions, and fears. "Man born of a woman, living for a short time, is filled with many miseries"—*Job*, xiv. 1. What, says St. Augustine, do men who wish for a prolongation of life on this Earth desire but a prolongation of suffering? "Quid est diu vivere nisi diu torqueri"—*ser.* xvii. *de Verb. Dom.* Yes; for, as St. Ambrose remarks, the present life was given to us not for repose and enjoyment, but for labour and suffering, that by toils and pains we may merit Paradise. "Hæc vita homini non ad quietem data est, sed ad laborem"—*serm.* xliii. Hence the same holy doctor says, that, though death is the punishment of sin, still the miseries of this life are so great, that death appears to be a relief, rather than a chastisement. "Ut mors remedium videatur esse, non pœna".

2. To those who love God, the severest of all the crosses of this life, are the assaults of Hell to rob them of the divine grace. Hence St. Denis the Areopagite says, that they joyfully meet death, as the end of their combats, and embrace it with gladness, because they hope to die a good death, and to be thus freed from all fear of ever again falling into sin. "Divino gaudio et mortis terminum tanquam ad finem certaminum tendunt, non amplius metuentes perverti"—*de Hier. Eccl.*, *cap.* vii. The greatest con-

solation which a soul that loves God experiences at the approach of death, arises from the thought of being delivered from so many temptations, from so many remorses of conscience, and from so many dangers of offending God. Ah! says St. Ambrose, as long as we live, "we walk among snares". We walk continually in the midst of the snares of our enemies, who lie in wait to deprive us of the life of grace. It was the fear of falling into sin that made St. Peter of Alcantara, in his last moments, say to a lay brother who, in attending the saint, accidentally touched him: "*Brother, remove, remove from me, for I am still alive and in danger of being lost*". The thought of being freed from the danger of sin by death, consoled St. Teresa, and made her rejoice as often as she heard the clock strike, that an hour of the combat was past. Hence she used to say: "In each moment of life we may sin and lose God". Hence the news of approaching death filled the saints not with sorrow or regret, but with sentiments of joy; because they knew that their struggles and the dangers of losing the divine grace were soon to have an end.

3. "But the just man, if he be prevented with death, shall be in rest"—*Wis.*, iv. 7. He who is prepared to die, regards death as a relief. If, says St. Cyprian, you lived in a house whose walls and roof were tottering and threatening destruction, would you not fly from it as soon as possible? In this life everything menaces ruin to the poor soul;—the world, the devils, the flesh, the passions, all draw her to sin and to eternal death. It was this that made St. Paul exclaim: "Who shall deliver me from the body of this death?"—*Rom.*, vii. 24. Who shall deliver me from this body of mine, which lives continually in a dying state, on account of the assaults of my enemies? Hence he esteemed death as a great gain, because it brought to him the possession of Jesus Christ, his true life. Happy then are they who die in the Lord: because they escape from pains and toils, and go to rest. "Blessed are the dead who die in the Lord. From henceforth now, saith the spirit, that they may rest from their labours"—*Apoc.*, xiv. 13. It is related in the lives of the ancient fathers, that one of them who was very old, when dying, smiled, while the others wept. Being asked why he smiled, he said: *Why do you weep at seeing me go to rest? Ex labore ad requiem vado, et vos ploratis?* At the hour of death, St. Catherine of Sienna said to her sisters in religion:

Rejoice with me; for I leave this land of suffering, and am going to the kingdom of peace. The death of the saints is called a sleep;—that is, the repose which God gives to his servants as the reward of their toil. "When he shall give sleep to his beloved, behold the inheritance of the Lord"—*Ps.*, cxxvi. 2. Hence the soul that loves God neither weeps nor is troubled at the approach of death; but, embracing the crucifix, and burning with love, she says: "In peace in the self same I will sleep and I will rest"—*Ps.*, iv. 9.

4. That "*Proficiscere de hoc mundo*" *(Depart, Christian soul, from this world)*, which is so appalling to sinners at the hour of death, does not alarm the saints. "But the souls of the just are in the hands of God, and the torment of death shall not touch them"—*Wis.*, iii. 1. The saint is not afflicted, like worldlings, at the thought of being obliged to leave the goods of this Earth, because he has kept the soul detached from them. During life, he always regarded God as the Lord of his heart, and as the sole riches which he desired. "What have I in Heaven? and, besides thee, what do I desire upon Earth? Thou art the God of my heart, and the God that is my portion for ever"—*Ps.*, lxxii. 25, 26. He is not afflicted at leaving honours, because the only honour which he sought was, to love and to be loved by God. All the honours of this world he has justly esteemed as smoke and vanity. He is not afflicted at leaving his relatives, because he loved them only in God. In his last moments he recommends them to his Heavenly Father, who loves them more than he does. And having a secure confidence of salvation, he hopes to be better able to assist his relatives from Paradise, than on this Earth. In a word, what he frequently said during life, he continues to repeat with greater fervour at the hour of death—"My God and my all".

5. Besides, his peace is not disturbed by the pains of death; but, seeing that he is now at the end of his life, and that he has no more time to suffer for God, or to offer him other proofs of love, he accepts those pains with joy, and offers them to God as the last remains of life; and uniting his death with the death of Jesus Christ, he offers it to the Divine Majesty.

6. And although the remembrance of the sins which he has committed will afflict, it will not disturb him; for, since he is convinced that the Lord will forget the sins of all true peni-

tents, the very sorrow which he feels for his sins, gives him an assurance of pardon. "If the wicked do penance......I will not remember all his iniquities that he hath done"—*Ezec.*, xviii. 21 *and* 22. "How", asks St. Basil, "can any one be be certain that God has pardoned his sins? He may be certain of pardon if he say: I have hated and abhorred iniquity"—*in Reg.*, *inter.* 12. He who detests his sins, and offers to God his death in atonement for them, may rest secure that God has pardoned them. "Mors", says St. Augustine, "quæ in lege naturæ erat pœna peccati in lege gratiæ est hostia pro peccato"—*lib.* IV. *de Trin.*, *c.* xxii. Death, which was a chastisement of sin under the law of nature, has become, in the law of grace, a victim of penance, by which the pardon of sin is obtained.

7. The very love which a soul bears to God, assures her of his grace, and delivers her from the fear of being lost. "Charity casteth out fear"—I. *John*, iv. 18. If, at the hour of death, you are unwilling to pardon an enemy, or to restore what is not your own, or if you wish to keep up an improper friendship, then tremble for your eternal salvation; for you have great reason to be afraid of death: but if you seek to avoid sin, and to preserve in your heart a testimony that you love God, be assured that he is with you: and if the Lord is with you, what do you fear? And if you wish to be assured that you have within you the divine love, embrace death with peace, and offer it from your heart to God. He that offers to God his death, makes an act of love the most perfect that it is possible for him to perform; because, by cheerfully embracing death to please God, at the time and in the manner which God ordains, he becomes like the martyrs, the entire merit of whose martyrdom consisted in suffering and dying to please God.

Second point. Death frees us from actual sins.

8. It is impossible to live in this world without committing at least some slight faults. "A just man shall fall seven times" —*Prov.*, xxiv. 16. He who ceases to live, ceases to offend God. Hence St. Ambrose called death the burial of vices: by death they are buried, and never appear again. "Quid est mors nisi sepultura vitiorum?"—*De Bono Mort.*, *cap.* iv. The venerable Vincent Caraffa consoled himself at the hour of death by saying: Now that I cease to live, I cease for ever to offend my

God. He who dies in the grace of God, goes into that happy state in which he shall love God for ever, and shall never more offend him. "Mortuus", says the same holy doctor, "nescit peccare. Quid tantopere vitam istam desideramus, in qua quanto diutius quis fuerit, tanto majori oneratur sarcina peccatorum". How can we desire this life, in which, the longer we live, the greater shall be the load of our sins?

9. Hence the Lord praises the dead more than any man living: "I praised the dead rather than the living"—*Eccl.*, iv. 2. Because no man on this Earth, however holy he may be, is exempt from sins. A spiritual soul gave directions that the person who should bring to her the news of death, should say: "*Console yourself, for the time has arrived when you shall no longer offend God*".

10. St. Ambrose adds, that God permitted death to enter into the world, that, by dying, men should cease to sin: "Passus est Dominus subintrare mortem ut culpa cessaret"—*Loco cit.* It is, then, a great error to imagine that death is a chastisement for those who love God. It is a mark of the love which God bears to them; because he shortens their life to put an end to sin, from which they cannot be exempt as long as they remain on this Earth. "For his soul pleased God: therefore he hastened to bring him out of the midst of iniquities"—*Wis.*, iv. 14.

Third point. Death delivers us from the danger of falling into Hell, and opens Paradise to us.

11. "Precious in the sight of the Lord is the death of the saints"—*Ps.*, cxv. 15. Considered according to the senses, death excites fear and terror; but, viewed with the eyes of faith, it is consoling and desirable. To the saints it is as amiable and as precious, as it appears terrible to sinners. "It is precious", says St. Bernard, "as the end of labours, the consummation of victory, the gate of life". The joy of the cupbearer of Pharaoh, at hearing from Joseph that he should soon be released from prison, bears no comparison to that which a soul that loves God feels on hearing that she is to be liberated from the exile of this Earth, and to be transported to the enjoyment of God in her true country. The Apostle says, that, as long as we remain in the body, we wander at a distance from

our country, in a strange land, and far removed from the life of God: "While we are in the body, we are absent from the Lord"—II. *Cor.*, v. 6. Hence, St. Bruno teaches, that our death should not be called death, but the beginning of life. "Mors dicenda non est, sed vitæ principium". And St. Athanasius says: "Non est justis mors sed translatio". To the just death is but a passage from the miseries of this Earth to the eternal delights of Paradise. O desirable death! exclaimed St. Augustine; who is there that does not desire thee? For thou art the term of evils, the end of toils, and the beginning of everlasting repose! "O mors desirabilis, malorum finis, laboris clausula, quietis principium".

12. No one can enter into Heaven to see God without passing through the gate of death. "This is the gate of the Lord—the just shall enter into it"—*Ps.*, cxvii. 20. Hence, addressing death, St. Jerome said: "Aperi mihi soror mea". Death, my sister, if you do not open the gate to me, I cannot enter to enjoy my God. And St. Charles Borromeo seeing in his house a picture of death with a knife in the hand, sent for a painter to cancel the knife, and substitute for it a key of gold; because, said the saint, it is death that opens Paradise. Were a queen confined in a dark prison, how great would be her joy at hearing that the gates of the prison are opened, and that she is to return from the dungeon to her palace! It was to be liberated by death from the prison of this life that David asked, when he said: "Bring my soul out of prison"—*Ps.*, cxli. 8. This, too, was the favour which the venerable Simeon asked of the infant Jesus, when he held him in his arms: "Now thou dost dismiss thy servant"—*Luke*, ii. 29. "As if detained by force", says St. Ambrose, "he asked to be dismissed". Simeon sought to be delivered by death, as if he had been compelled by force to live on this Earth.

13. St. Cyprian says, that the sinner who shall pass from temporal to eternal death, has just reason to be afraid of death. "Mori timeat, qui ad secundum mortem de hac morte transibit". But he who is in the state of grace, and hopes to pass from death to eternal life—which is the true life—fears not death. It is related, that a certain rich man gave to St. John the Almoner a large sum of money to be dispensed in alms, for the purpose of obtaining from God a long life for his only son.

The son died in a short time. The father complained of the death of his son; but, to console him, the Lord sent an angel to say to him: "You have sought a long life for your son, and the Lord has heard your prayer; for your son is in Heaven, where he enjoys eternal life". This is the grace which, according to the promise of the prophet Osee, the Redeemer obtained for us. "O death, I will be thy death"—xiii. 14. By his redemption, Jesus Christ destroyed death, and changed it into a source of life to us. When St. Pionius, martyr, was asked how he could go to death with so much joy, he answered: You err, I go not to death but to life. "Erratis non ad mortem, sed ad vitam contendo"—*Apud. Euseb.*, *lib.* IV., *cap.* xiv. Thus also St. Symphorosa exhorted her son, St. Symphorian, to martyrdom: "My son", said she, "life is not taken away from you; it is only changed for a better one".

14. St. Augustine says, that they who love God desire to see him speedily, and that, therefore, to them life is a cause of suffering, and death an occasion of joy. "Patienter vivit, delectabiliter moritur"—*trac.* ix. *in Ep Joan.* St. Teresa used to say, that, to her, life was death. Hence she composed the celebrated hymn, "*I die because I do not die*". To that great servant of God, D. Sancia Carriglio—a penitent of Father M. Avila—it was one day revealed, that she had but a year to live; she answered: "Alas! must I remain another year at a distance from God? O sorrowful year, which will appear to me longer than an age". Such is the language of souls who love God from their heart. It is a mark of little love of God not to desire to see him speedily.

15. Some of you will say: I desire to go to God, but I fear death. I am afraid of the assaults which I shall then experience from Hell. I find that the saints have trembled at the hour of death; how much more ought I to tremble! I answer: It is true that Hell does not cease to assail even the saints at death, but it is also true that God does not cease to assist his servants at that moment; and when the dangers are increased, he multiplies his helps. "Ibi plus auxilii", says St. Ambrose, "ubi plus periculi"—*ad Jos.*, *cap.* v. The servant of Eliseus was struck with terror when he saw the city surrounded by enemies, but the saint inspired him with courage by showing to him a multitude of angels sent by God to defend it. Hence the prophet

afterwards said: "Fear not, for there are more with us than with them"—IV. *Kings*, vi. 16. The powers of Hell will assail the dying Christian; but his angel guardian will come to console him. His patrons, and St. Michael, who has been appointed by God to defend his faithful servants in their last combat with the devils, will come to his aid. The Mother of God will come to assist those who have been devoted to her. Jesus Christ shall come to defend from the assaults of Hell the souls for which he died on a cross: he will give them confidence and strength to resist every attack. Hence, filled with courage, they will say: "The Lord is my light and my salvation: whom shall I fear?"—*Is.*, xxvi. 1. Truly has Origen said, that the Lord is more desirous of our salvation, than the Devil is of our perdition, because God's love for us far surpasses the Devil's hatred of our souls. "Major illi cura est, ut nos ad veram pertrahat salutem, quam diabolo, ut nos ad æternam damnationem impellat"—*hom.* xx.

16. God is faithful: he will never permit us to be tempted above our strength: "Fidelis Deus non patietur vos tentari supra id quod potestis"—I. *Cor.*, x. 13. It is true that some saints have suffered great fear at the hour of death; but they have been few. The Lord, as Belluacensis says, has permitted this fear, to cleanse them at death from some defect. "Justi quandoque dure moriendo purgantur in hoc mundo". But we know that, generally speaking, the saints have died with a joyful countenance. Father Joseph Scamacca, a man of a holy life, being asked if, in dying, he felt confidence in God, answered: Have I served Mahomet, that I should now doubt of the goodness of my God, or of his wish to save me? Ah! the Lord knows well how to console his servants in their last moments. Even in the midst of the agony of death, he infuses into their souls a certain sweetness and a certain foretaste of that happiness which he will soon bestow upon them. As they who die in sin begin to experience from the bed of death a certain foretaste of Hell—certain extraordinary terrors, remorses, and fits of despair; so, on the other hand, the saints, by the fervent acts of divine love which they then make, and by the confidence and the desire which they feel of soon seeing God, taste, before death, that peace which they shall afterwards fully enjoy in Heaven.

17. Father Suarez died with so much peace, that in his last moments he said: "I could not have imagined that death was so sweet". Being advised by his physician not to fix his thoughts so constantly on death, Cardinal Baronius said: Is it lest the fear of death should shorten my life? I fear not; on the contrary, I love and desire death. Of the Cardinal Bishop of Rochester, Saunders relates, that, in preparing to die for the faith, he put on his best clothes, saying that he was going to a nuptial feast. When he came within view of the place of execution, he threw away his staff, and said: O my feet, walk fast; for we are not far from Paradise. "Ite pedes, parum a paradiso distamus". Before death, he wished to recite the TE DEUM, in thanksgiving to God for permitting him to die for the holy faith; and, full of joy, he laid his head on the block. St. Francis of Assisium began to sing at the hour of death. Brother Elias said to him: Father, at the hour of death, we ought rather to weep than to sing. But, replied the saint, I cannot abstain from singing at the thought of soon going to enjoy God. A nun of the order of St. Teresa, in her last moments, said to her sisters in religion, who were in tears: O God! why do you weep? I am going to possess my Jesus; if you love me, weep not, but rejoice with me.—*Dis. Parol.*, i. § 6.

18. Father Granada relates, that a certain sportsman found in a wood, a solitary singing in his last agony. How, said the sportsman, can you sing in such a state? The hermit replied: Brother, between me and God there is nothing but the wall of this body. I now see that, since my flesh is falling in pieces, the prison shall be destroyed, and I shall soon go to see God. It is for this reason that I rejoice and sing. Through the desire of seeing God, St. Ignatius, martyr, said, that if the wild beasts should spare him, he would provoke them to devour him. "Ego vim faciam, ut devorer". St. Catherine of Genoa was astonished that some persons regarded death as a misfortune, and said: "O beloved death, in what a mistaken light do men view you. Why do you not come to me? I call on you day and night"—*Vita.*, c. 7.

19. Oh! how peculiarly happy is the death of the servants of Mary! Father Binetti relates, that a person whom he assisted in his last moments, and who was devoted to the Blessed Virgin, said to him: "Father, you cannot conceive the

consolation which arises at death from the remembrance of having served Mary. Ah my father! if you knew what happiness I feel on account of having served this good mother! I cannot express it". What joy shall the lovers of Jesus Christ experience at his coming to them in the most holy viaticum! Happy the soul that can then address her Saviour in the words which St. Philip Neri used when the viaticum was brought to him: *Behold my love! behold my love! give me my love!* But, to entertain these sentiments at death, we must have ardently loved Jesus Christ during life.

SERMON XII.

FOR SEPTUAGESIMA SUNDAY.

On the importance of salvation.

"He sent them into his vineyard"—*Matthew*, xx. 2.

THE vines of the Lord are our souls, which he has given us to cultivate by good works, that we may be one day admitted into eternal glory. "How", says Salvian, "does it happen that a Christian believes, and still does not fear the future?" Christians believe death, judgment, Hell, and Paradise; but they live as if they believed them not—as if these truths of faith were fables or the inventions of human genius. Many live as if they were never to die, or as if they had not to give God an account of their life—as if there were neither a Hell nor a Heaven. Perhaps they do not believe in them? They believe, but do not reflect on them; and thus they are lost. They take all possible care of worldly affairs, but attend not to the salvation of their souls. I shall show you, this day, that the salvation of your souls is the most important of all affairs.

First point. Because, if the soul is lost, all is lost.
Second point. Because if the soul is lost once, it is lost for ever.

First point. If the soul is lost, all is lost.

1. "But", says St. Paul, "we entreat you......that you do your own business"—I. *Thess.*, iv. 10, 11. The greater part of worldlings are most attentive to the business of this world. What diligence do they not employ to gain a law-suit or a post of emolument! How many means are adopted—how many measures taken! They neither eat nor sleep. And what efforts do they make to save their souls? All blush at being told that they neglect the affairs of their families; and how few are ashamed to neglect the salvation of their souls. Brethren, says St. Paul, *I entreat you that you do your own business;* that is, the business of your eternal salvation.

2. "Nugæ puerorum", says St. Bernard, "nugæ vocantur, nugæ malorum negotia vocantur". The trifles of children are called trifles, but the trifles of men are called business; and for these many lose their souls. If in one worldly transaction you suffer a loss, you may repair it in another; but if you die in enmity with God, and lose your soul, how can you repair the loss? "What exchange shall a man give for his soul?"—*Mat.*, xvi. 26. To those who neglect the care of salvation, St. Euterius says: "Quam pretiosus sis O homo, si Creatori non credis, interroga Redemptorem"—*hom.* ii. *in Symb.* If, from being created by God to his own image, you do not comprehend the value of your soul, learn it from Jesus Christ, who has redeemed you with his own blood. "You were not redeemed with corruptible things, as gold or silver,......but with the precious blood of Christ, as of a lamb unspotted and undefiled"—I. *Pet.*, i. 18, 19.

3. God, then, sets so high a value on your soul; such, too, is its value in the estimation of Satan, that, to become master of it, he does not sleep night or day, but is continually going about to make it his own. Hence St. Augustine exclaims: "The enemy sleeps not, and you are asleep". The enemy is always awake to injure you, and you slumber. Pope Benedict the Twelfth being asked by a prince for a favour which he could not conscientiously grant, said to the ambassador: Tell the prince, that, if I had two souls, I might be able to lose one of them in order to please him; but, since I have but one, I cannot consent to lose it. Thus he refused the favour which the prince sought from him.

4. Brethren, remember that, if you save your souls, your failure in every worldly transaction will be but of little importance; for, if you are saved you shall enjoy complete happiness for all eternity. But, if you lose your souls, what will it profit you to have enjoyed all the riches, honours, and amusements of this world? If you lose your souls, all is lost. "What doth it profit a man, if he gain the whole world, and suffer the loss of his own soul?"—*Mat.*, xvi. 26. By this maxim St. Ignatius of Loyola drew many souls to God, and among them the soul of St. Francis Xavier, who was then at Paris, and devoted his attention to the acquirement of worldly goods. One day St. Ignatius said to him: "*Francis, whom do you serve? You serve the world, which is a traitor, that promises, but does not perform. And if it should fulfil all its promises, how long do its goods last? Can they last longer than this life? And, after death, what will they profit you if you shall not have saved your soul?*" He then reminded Francis of the maxims of the gospel: "What doth it profit a man, if he gain the whole world, and suffer the loss of his own soul?"; "But one thing is necessary"—*Luke*, x. 42. It is not necessary to become rich on this Earth—to acquire honours and dignities; but it is necessary to save our souls; because, unless we gain Heaven, we shall be condemned to Hell: there is no middle place; we must be either saved or damned. God has not created us for this Earth; neither does he preserve our lives that we may become rich, and enjoy amusements. "And the end life everlasting"—*Rom.*, vi. 22. He has created us, and preserves us, that we may acquire eternal glory.

5. St. Philip Neri used to say, that he who does not seek, above all things, the salvation of his soul, is a fool. If on this Earth there were two classes of men, one mortal, and the other immortal, and if the former saw the latter entirely devoted to the acquisition of Earthly goods, would they not exclaim: O fools that you are! you have it in your power to secure the immense and eternal goods of Paradise, and you lose your time in procuring the miserable goods of this Earth, which shall end at death. And for these you expose yourselves to the danger of the eternal torments of Hell. Leave to us, for whom all shall end at death, the care of these Earthly things. But, brethren, we are all immortal, and each of us shall be eternally happy or

eternally miserable in the other life. But the misfortune of the greater part of mankind is, that they are solicitous about the present, and never think of the future. "Oh! that they would be wise, and would understand, and would provide for their last end"—*Deut.*, xxxii. 29. Oh! that they knew how to detach themselves from present goods, which last but a short time, and to provide for what must happen after death—an eternal reign in Heaven, or everlasting slavery in Hell. St. Philip Neri, conversing one day with Francis Zazzera, a young man of talent who expected to make a fortune in the world, said to him: *You shall realize a great fortune; you shall be a prelate, afterwards a cardinal, and in the end perhaps pope. But what must follow? what must follow? Go, my son, think on these words.* The young man departed, and, after meditating on the words, *what must follow? what must follow?* he renounced his worldly prospects, and gave himself entirely to God; and, retiring from the world, he entered into the congregation of Saint Philip, and died a holy death.

6. "The fashion of this world passeth away"—I. *Cor.*, vii. 31. On this passage Cornelius a Lapide says, that "*the world is as it were a stage*". The present life is a comedy, which passes away. Happy the man who acts his part well in this comedy by saving his soul. But if he shall have spent his life in the acquisition of riches and worldly honours, he shall justly be called a fool; and at the hour of death he shall receive the reproach addressed to the rich man in the gospel: "Fool, this night do they require thy soul of thee; and whose shall these things be which thou hast provided?"—*Luke*, xii. 20. In explaining the words "*they require*", Toletus says, that the Lord has given us our souls to guard them against the assaults of our enemies; and that at death the angels shall come to require them of us, and shall present them at the tribunal of Jesus Christ. But, if we shall have lost our souls by attending only to the acquisition of Earthly possessions, these shall belong to us no longer—they shall pass to other hands: and what shall then become of our souls?

7. Poor worldlings! of all the riches which they acquired, of all the pomps which they displayed in this life, what shall they find at death? "They have slept their sleep: and all the

men of riches have found nothing in their hands"—*Ps.*, lxxv. 6. The dream of this present life shall be over at death, and they shall have acquired nothing for eternity. Ask of so many great men of this Earth — of the princes and emperors, who, during life, have abounded in riches, honours, and pleasures, and are at this moment in Hell,—what now remains of all the riches which they possessed in this world? They answer with tears: *Nothing, nothing.* And of so many honours enjoyed,—of so many past pleasures,—of so many pomps and triumphs, what now remains? They answer with howling: *Nothing, nothing.*

8. Justly, then, has St. Francis Xavier said, that, in the world there is but one good and one evil. The former consists in saving our souls; the latter in losing them. Hence, David said: "One thing I have asked of the Lord; this I will seek after,—that I may dwell in the house of the Lord"—*Ps.*, xxvi. 4. One thing only have I sought, and will for ever seek, from God,—that he may grant me the grace to save my soul; for, if I save my soul, all is safe; if I lose it, all is lost. And, what is more important, if my soul be once lost, it is lost for ever. Let us pass to the second point.

Second point. If the soul be once lost, it is lost for ever.

9. Men die but once. If a Christian died twice, he might lose his soul the first, and save it the second time. But we can die only once: if the soul be lost the first time, it is lost for ever. This truth St. Teresa frequently inculcated to her nuns: "*One soul*", she would say, "*one eternity*". As if she said: We have but one soul: if this be lost, all is lost. There is but *one eternity;* if the soul be once lost, it is lost for ever. *Periisse semel æternum est.*

10. St. Eucherius says, that there is no error so great as the neglect of eternal salvation. "Sane supra omnem errorem est dissimulare negotium æternæ salutis". It is an error which surpasses all errors, because it is irremediable. Other mistakes may be repaired: if a person loses property in one way, he may acquire it in another; if he loses a situation, a dignity, he may afterwards recover them; if he even loses his life, provided his soul be saved, all is safe. But he who loses his soul has no means of repairing the loss. The wailing of the damned arises from the thought, that

for them the time of salvation is over, and that there is no hope of remedy for their eternal ruin. "The summer is ended, and we are not saved"—*Jer.*, viii. 20. Hence they weep, and shall inconsolably weep for ever, saying: "Therefore we have erred from the way of truth, and the light of justice hath not shined unto us"—*Wis.*, v. 6. But what will it profit them to know the error they have committed, when it will be too late to repair it?

11. The greatest torment of the damned arises from the thought of having lost their souls, and of having lost them through their own fault. "Destruction is thy own, O Israel; thy help is only from me"—*Osee*, xiii. 9. O miserable being! God says to each of the damned; thy perdition is thine own; that is from thyself; by sin thou hast been the cause of thy damnation; for I was ready to save thee if thou hadst wished to attend to thy salvation. St. Teresa used to say, that, when a person loses a trifle through negligence, his peace is disturbed by the thought of having lost it through his own fault. O God! what shall be the pain which each of the damned shall feel on entering into Hell, at the thought of having lost his soul—his all,—and of having lost them through his own fault!

12. We must, then, from this day forward, devote all our attention to the salvation of our souls. There is not question, says St. John Chrysostom, of losing some Earthly good which we must one day relinquish. But there is question of losing Paradise, and of going to suffer for ever in Hell. "De immortalibus suppliciis, de cœlestis regni amissione res agitur". We must fear and tremble; it is thus we shall be able to secure eternal happiness. "With fear and trembling work out your salvation"—*Phil.*, ii. 12. Hence, if we wish to save our souls, we must labour strenuously to avoid dangerous occasions, to resist temptations, and to frequent the sacraments. Without labour we cannot obtain Heaven. "*The violent bear it away*". The saints trembled at the thought of eternity. St. Andrew Avellino exclaimed with tears: Who knows whether I shall be saved or damned? St. Lewis Bertrand said with trembling: What shall be my lot in the other world? And shall we not tremble? Let us pray to Jesus Christ and his most holy mother, to help us to save our souls. This is for us the most important of all affairs: if

we succeed in it, we shall be eternally happy; if we fail, we must be for ever miserable.

SERMON XIII.

FOR SEXAGESIMA SUNDAY.

On the unhappy life of sinners, and on the happy life of those who love God.

"And that which fell among the thorns, are they who have heard, and, going their way, are choked with the cares and riches of this life, and yield no fruit"—*Luke*, viii. 14.

In the parable of this day's gospel we are told that part of the seed which the sower had gone out to sow fell among thorns. The Saviour has declared that the seed represents the divine word, and the thorns the attachment of men to Earthly riches and pleasures, which are the thorns that prevent the fruit of the word of God, not only in the future, but even in the present life. O misery of poor sinners! By their sins they not only condemn themselves to eternal torments in the next, but to an unhappy life in this world. This is what I intend to demonstrate in the following discourse.

First point. The unhappy life of sinners.
Second point. Happy life of those who love God.

First point. Unhappy life of sinners.

1. The Devil deceives sinners, and makes them imagine that, by indulging their sensual appetites, they shall lead a life of happiness, and shall enjoy peace. But there is no peace for those who offend God. "There is no peace to the wicked, saith the Lord"—*Isa.*, xlviii. 22. God declares that all his enemies have led a life of misery, and that they have not even known the way of peace. "Destruction and unhappiness in their ways: and the way of peace they have not known"—*Ps.*, xiii. 3.

2. Brute animals that have been created for this world, enjoy

peace in sensual delights. Give to a dog a bone, and he is perfectly content; give to an ox a bundle of hay, and he desires nothing more. But man, who has been created for God, to love God, and to be united to him, can be made happy only by God, and not by the world, though it should enrich him with all its goods. What are worldly goods? They may be all reduced to pleasures of sense, to riches, and to honours. "All that is in the world", says St. John, "is the concupiscence of the flesh", *or sensual delights*, "and the concupiscence of the eyes", *or riches*, "and the pride of life"—that is, Earthly honours,—I. *John*, ii. 16. St. Bernard says, that a man may be puffed up with Earthly goods, but can never be made content or happy by them. "Inflari potest, satiari non potest". And how can earth and wind and dung satisfy the heart of man? In his comment on these words of St. Peter,—"behold, we have left all things",—the same saint says, that he saw in the world different classes of fools. All had a great desire of happiness. Some, such as the avaricious, were content with riches; others, ambitious of honours and of praise, were satisfied with wind; others, seated round a furnace, swallowed the sparks that were thrown from it,—these were the passionate and vindictive; others, in fine, drank fetid water from a stagnant pool,—and these were the voluptuous and unchaste. O fools! adds the saint, do you not perceive that all these things, from which you seek content, do not satisfy, but, on the contrary, increase the cravings of your heart? "Hæc potius famem provocant, quam extinguunt". Of this we have a striking example in Alexander the Great, who, after having conquered half the world, burst into tears, because he was not master of the whole Earth.

3. Many expect to find peace in accumulating riches; but how can these satisfy their desires? "Major pecunia", says St. Augustine, "avaritiæ fauces non claudit, sed extendit". A large quantity of money does not close, but rather extends, the jaws of avarice;—that is, the enjoyment of riches excites, rather than satiates, the desire of wealth. "Thou wast debased even to Hell; thou hast been wearied in the multitude of thy ways; yet thou saidst not, I will rest"—*Isa.*, lvii. 9, 10. Poor worldlings! they labour and toil to acquire an increase of wealth and property; but never enjoy repose: the more they

accumulate riches, the greater their disquietude and vexation. "The rich have wanted, and have suffered hunger; but they that seek the Lord shall not be deprived of any good"—*Ps.*, xxxiii. 11. The rich of this world are, of all men, the most miserable; because, the more they possess, the more they desire to possess. They never succeed in attaining all the objects of their wishes, and therefore they are far poorer than men who have but a competency, and seek God alone. These are truly rich; because they are content with their condition, and find in God every good. "They that seek the Lord shall not be deprived of any good". To the saints, because they possess God, nothing is wanting: to the worldly rich, who are deprived of God, all things are wanting, because they want peace. The appellation of fool was, therefore, justly given to the rich man in the gospel (*Luke*, xii. 19), who, because his land brought forth plenty of fruits, said to his soul: "Soul, thou hast much goods laid up for many years: take rest, eat, drink, make good cheer"—*Luke*, xii. 19. But this man was called a fool. "Thou fool, this night do they require thy soul of thee; and whose shall those things be which thou hast provided?"—*v.* 20. And why was he called a fool? Because he imagined, that by these goods—by eating and drinking—he should be content, and should enjoy peace. *Rest*, he said, *eat*, *drink*. "Numquid", says St. Basil of Seleucia, "animam porcinam habes?" Hast thou the soul of a brute, that thou expectest to make it happy by eating and drinking?

4. But, perhaps sinners who seek after and attain worldly honours, are content? All the honours of this Earth are but smoke and wind ("*Ephraim feedeth on the wind*"—*Osee*, xii. 1): and how can these content the heart of a Christian? "The pride of them", says David, "ascendeth continually"—*Ps.*, lxxiii. 23. The ambitious are not satisfied by the attainment of certain honours: their ambition and pride continually increase; and thus their inquietude, their envy, and their fears are multiplied.

5. They who live in the habit of sins of impurity, feed, as the Prophet Jeremiah says, on dung. "Qui voluptuose vescebantur, amplexati sunt stercora"—*Thren.*, iv. 5. How can dung content or give peace to the soul? Ah! what peace, what peace can sinners at a distance from God enjoy? They may possess the

riches, honours, and delights of this world; but they never shall have peace. No; the word of God cannot fail: he has declared that there is no peace for his enemies: "There is no peace to the wicked, saith the Lord"—*Isaias*, xlviii. 22. Poor sinners! they, as St. Chrysostom says, always carry about with them their own executioner—that is, a guilty conscience, which continually torments them. "Peccator conscientiam quasi carnificem circumgestat"—*serm.* x., *de Laz.* St. Isidore asserts, that there is no pain more excruciating than that of a guilty conscience. Hence he adds, that he who leads a good life is never sad. "Nulla pœna gravior pœna conscientiæ: vis nunquam esse tristis? bene vive" —*S. Isid., lib.* II., *Solit.*

6. In describing the deplorable state of sinners, the Holy Ghost compares them to a sea continually tossed by the tempest. "The wicked are like the raging sea, which cannot rest"—*Isa.*, lvii. 20. Waves come and go, but they are all waves of bitterness and rancour; for every cross and contradiction disturbs and agitates the wicked. If a person at a ball or musical exhibition, were obliged to remain suspended by a cord with his head downwards, could he feel happy at the entertainment? Such is the state of a Christian in enmity with God: his soul is as it were turned upside down; instead of being united with God, and detached from creatures, it is united with creatures, and separated from God. But creatures, says St. Vincent Ferrer, are without, and do not enter to content the heart, which God alone can make happy. "Non intrant ibi ubi est sitis". The sinner is like a man parched with thirst, and standing in the middle of a fountain: because the waters which surround him do not enter to satisfy his thirst, he remains in the midst of them more thirsty than before.

7. Speaking of the unhappy life which he led when he was in the state of sin, David said: "My tears have been my bread, day and night, whilst it is said to me daily: Where is thy God?"—*Ps.*, xli. 4. To relieve himself, he went to his villas, to his gardens, to musical entertainments, and to various other royal amusements, but they all said to him: "David, if thou expectest comfort from us, thou art deceived. Where is thy God? Go and seek thy God, whom thou hast lost; for he alone can restore thy peace". Hence David confessed, that, in the midst of his princely wealth, he enjoyed no repose, and that he

wept night and day. Let us now listen to his son Solomon, who acknowledged that he indulged his senses in whatsoever they desired. "Whatsoever my eyes desired, I refused them not"—*Eccles.*, ii. 10. But, after all his sensual enjoyments, he exclaimed: "Vanity of vanities:...behold all is vanity and affliction of spirit"—*Eccles.*, i. 2 *and* 14. Mark! he declares that all the pleasures of this Earth are not only vanity of vanities, but also affliction of spirit. And this sinners well know from experience; for sin brings with it the fear of divine vengeance. The man who is encompassed by powerful enemies, never sleeps in peace; and can the sinner, who has God for an enemy, enjoy tranquillity? "Fear to them that work evil"—*Prov.*, x. 29. The Christian who commits a mortal sin, feels himself oppressed with fear—every leaf that moves excites terror. "The sound of dread is always in his ears"—*Job*, xv. 21. He appears to be always flying away, although no one pursues him. "The wicked man fleeth when no man pursueth"—*Prov.*, xxviii. 1. He shall be persecuted, not by men, but by his own sin. It was thus with Cain, who, after having killed his brother Abel, was seized with fear, and said: "Every one, therefore, that findeth me shall kill me"—*Gen.*, iv. 14. The Lord assured him that no one should injure him: "The Lord said to him: No; it shall not be so"—*v.* 15. But, notwithstanding this assurance, Cain, pursued by his own sin, was, as the Scripture attests, always flying from one place to another. "He dwelt a fugitive on the Earth"—*v.* 16.

8. Moreover, sin brings with it remorse of conscience—that cruel worm that gnaws incessantly, and never dies. "Their worm shall not die"—*Isa.*, lxvi. 24. If the sinner goes to a festival, to a comedy, to a banquet, his conscience continually reproaches him, saying: Unhappy man! you have lost God; if you were now to die, what should become of you? The torture of remorse of conscience, even in the present life, is so great, that to free themselves from it, some persons have put an end to their lives. Judas, through despair, hanged himself. A certain man who had killed an infant, was so much tormented with remorse, that he could not rest. To rid himself of it, he entered into a monastery; but finding no peace even there, he went before a judge, acknowledged his crime, and got himself condemned to death.

9. God complains of the injustice of sinners in leaving him, who is the fountain of all consolation, to plunge themselves into fetid and broken cisterns, which can give no peace. "For my people have done two evils: they have forsaken me, the fountain of living water, and have digged to themselves cisterns—broken cisterns—that can hold no water"—*Jer.*, ii. 13. You have, the Lord says to sinners, refused to serve me, your God, in peace. Unhappy creatures! you shall serve your enemies in hunger, and thirst, and nakedness, and in want of every kind. "Because thou didst not serve the Lord thy God with joy and gladness,......thou shalt serve thy enemy in hunger, and thirst, and nakedness, and in want of all things"—*Deut.*, xxviii. 47, 48. This is what sinners experience every day. What do not the vindictive endure after they have satisfied their revenge by the murder of an enemy? They fly continually from the relations of their murdered foe, and from the minister of justice. They live as fugitives, poor, afflicted, and abandoned by all. What do not the voluptuous and unchaste suffer, in order to gratify their wicked desires? What do not the avaricious suffer, in order to acquire the possession of others? Ah! if they suffered for God what they suffer for sin, they would lay up great treasures for eternity, and would lead a life of peace and happiness: but, by living in sin, they lead of life of misery here, to lead a still more miserable life for eternity hereafter. Hence they weep continually in Hell, saying: "We wearied ourselves in the way of iniquity and destruction, and have walked through hard ways"—*Wis.*, v. 7. We have, they exclaim, walked through hard ways, through paths covered with thorns. We wearied ourselves in the way of iniquity: we have laboured hard: we have sweated blood: we have led a life full of misery, of gall, and of poison. And why? To bring ourselves to a still more wretched life in this pit of fire.

Second point. The happy life of those who love God.

10. "Justice and peace have kissed"—*Ps.*, lxxxiv. 11. Peace resides in every soul in which justice dwells. Hence David said: "Delight in the Lord, and he will give thee the requests of thy heart"—xxxvi. 4. To understand this text, we must consider that worldlings seek to satisfy the desires of their hearts with the goods of this Earth; but, because these

cannot make them happy, their hearts continually make fresh demands; and, how much soever they may acquire of these goods, they are not content. Hence the Prophet says: "Delight in the Lord, and he will give thee the requests of thy heart". Give up creatures, seek your delight in God, and he will satisfy all the cravings of your heart.

11. This is what happened to St. Augustine, who, as long as he sought happiness in creatures, never enjoyed peace; but, as soon as he renounced them, and gave to God all the affections of his heart, he exclaimed: "*All things are hard, O Lord, and thou alone art repose*". As if he said: Ah Lord, I now know my folly. I expected to find felicity in Earthly pleasures; but now I know that they are only vanity and affliction of spirit, and that thou alone art the peace and joy of our hearts.

12. The Apostle says, that the peace which God gives to those who love him, surpasses all the sensual delights which a man can enjoy on this Earth. "The peace of God, which surpasseth all understanding"—*Phil.*, iv. 7. St. Francis of Assisium, in saying "*My God and my all*", experienced on this Earth an anticipation of Paradise. St. Francis Xavier, in the midst of his labours in India for the glory of Jesus Christ, was so replenished with divine consolations, that he exclaimed: "*Enough, O Lord, enough*". Where, I ask, has any lover of this world been found, so satisfied with the possessions of worldly goods, as to say: Enough, O world, enough; no more riches, no more honours, no more applause, no more pleasures? Ah no! worldlings are constantly seeking after higher honours, greater riches, and new delights; but the more they have of them, the less are their desires satisfied, and the greater their disquietude.

13. It is necessary to persuade ourselves of this truth, that God alone can give content. Worldlings do not wish to be convinced of it, through an apprehension that, if they give themselves to God, they shall lead a life of bitterness and discontent. But, with the Royal Prophet, I say to them: "O taste, and see that the Lord is sweet"—*Ps.*, xxxiii. 9. Why, O sinners, will you despise and regard as miserable, that life which you have not as yet tried? "O taste and see". Begin to make a trial of it; hear Mass every day; practise mental prayer and the visitation of the most holy sacrament; go to

communion at least once a-week; fly from evil conversations; walk always with God; and you shall see that, by such a life, you will enjoy that sweetness and peace which the world, with all its delights, has not hitherto been able to give you.

SERMON XIV.

FOR QUINQUAGESIMA SUNDAY.

Delusions of sinners.

"Lord, that I may see"—*Luke*, xviii. 41.

1. The Devil brings sinners to Hell by closing their eyes to the dangers of perdition. He first blinds them, and then leads them with himself to eternal torments. If, then, we wish to be saved, we must continually pray to God in the words of the blind man in the gospel of this day, "Lord, that I may see". Give me light: make me see the way in which I must walk in order to save my soul, and to escape the deceits of the enemy of salvation, I shall, brethren, this day place before your eyes the delusions by which the Devil tempts men to sin and to persevere in sin, that you may know how to guard yourselves against his deceitful artifices.

2. To understand these delusions better, let us imagine the case of a young man who, seized by some passion, lives in sin, the slave of Satan, and never thinks of his eternal salvation. My son, I say to him, what sort of a life do you lead? If you continue to live in this manner, how will you be able to save your soul? But, behold! the Devil, on the other hand, says to him: Why should you be afraid of being lost? Indulge your passions for the present: you will afterwards confess your sins, and thus all shall be remedied. Behold the net by which the Devil drags so many souls into Hell. *Indulge your passions; you will hereafter make a good confession.* But, in reply, I, say, that in the mean time you lose your soul. Tell me: if you had a jewel worth a thousand pounds, would you throw it into

a river with the hope of afterwards finding it again? What if all your efforts to find it were fruitless? O God! you hold in your hand the invaluable jewel of your soul, which Jesus Christ has purchased with his own blood, and you cast it into Hell! Yes; you cast it into Hell; because, according to the present order of providence, for every mortal sin you commit, your name is written among the number of the damned. But you say: *I hope to recover God's grace by making a good confession.* And if you should not recover it, what shall be the consequences? To make a good confession, a true sorrow for sin is necessary, and this sorrow is the gift of God: if he does not give it, will you not be lost for ever?

3. You rejoin: *I am young;—God compassionates my youth: I will hereafter give myself to God.* Behold another delusion! You are young; but do you not know that God counts, not the years, but the sins of each individual? You are young; but how many sins have you committed? Perhaps there are many persons of a very advanced age, who have not been guilty of the fourth part of the sins which you have committed. And do you not know that God has fixed for each of us the number of sins which he will pardon? "The Lord patiently expecteth, that, when the day of judgment shall come, he may punish them in the fulness of their sins"—II. *Mach.*, vi. 14. God has patience, and waits for awhile; but, when the measure of the sins which he has determined to pardon is filled up, he pardons no more, but chastises the sinner by suddenly depriving him of life in the miserable state of sin, or by abandoning him in his sin, and executing the threat which he made by the prophet Isaias—"I shall take away the hedge thereof, and it shall be wasted"—*Isa.*, v. 5. If a person has cultivated land for many years, has encompassed it with a hedge for its protection, and expended a large sum of money on it, but finds that, after all, it produces no fruit, what will he do with it? He will pluck up the hedge, and abandon it to all men and beasts that may wish to enter. Tremble, then, lest God should treat you in a similar manner. If you do not give up sin, your remorse of conscience and your fear of divine chastisement shall daily decrease. Behold the hedge taken away, and your soul abandoned by God—a punishment worse than death itself.

4. You say: *I cannot at present resist this passion.* Behold the third delusion of the Devil, by which he makes you believe that at present you have not strength to overcome certain temptations. But St. Paul tells us, that God is faithful, and that he never permits us to be tempted above our strength. "And God is faithful, who will not permit you to be tempted above that which you are able"—I. *Cor.*, x. 13. I ask, if you are not now able to resist the temptation, how can you expect to resist it hereafter? If you yield to it, the Devil will become stronger, and you shall become weaker; and if you be not now able to extinguish this flame of passion, how can you hope to be able to extinguish it when it shall have grown more violent? You say: *God will give me his aid.* But this aid God is ready to give at present, if you ask it. Why then do you not implore his assistance? Perhaps you expect that, without now taking the trouble of invoking his aid, you will receive from him increased helps and graces, after you shall have multiplied the number of your sins? Perhaps you doubt the veracity of God, who has promised to give whatever we ask of him? "Ask", he says, "and it shall be given you"—*Mat.*, vii. 7. God cannot violate his promises. "God is not as man, that he should lie, nor as the son of man, that he should be changed. Hath he said, then, and will he not do?"—*Num.*, xxiii. 19. Have recourse to him, and he will give you the strength necessary to resist the temptation. God commands you to resist it, and you say: *I have not strength.* Does God, then, command impossibilities? No; the Council of Trent has declared that "God does not command impossibilities; but, by his commands, he admonishes you to do what you can, and to ask what you cannot do; and he assists, that you may be able to do it"—*sess.* 6, *c.* xiii. When you see that you have not sufficient strength to resist temptation with the ordinary assistance of God, ask of him the additional help which you require, and he will give it to you; and thus you shall be able to conquer all temptations, however violent they may be.

5. But you will not pray; and you say, that at present you will commit this sin, and will afterwards confess it. But, I ask, how do you know that God will give you time to confess it? You say: *I will go to confession before the lapse of a week.* And who has promised you this week? Well, then you say:

I will go to confession to-morrow. And who promises you to-morrow? "Crastinum Deus non promisit", says St. Augustine, "fortasse dabit, et fortasse non dabit". God has not promised you to-morrow. Perhaps he will give it, and perhaps he will refuse it to you, as he has to so many others. How many have gone to bed in good health, and have been found dead in the morning! How many, in the very act of sin, has the Lord struck dead and sent to Hell! Should this happen to you, how will you repair your eternal ruin? *Commit this sin, and confess it afterwards.* Behold the deceitful artifice by which the Devil has brought so many thousands of Christians to Hell. We scarcely ever find a Christian so sunk in despair as to intend to damn himself. All the wicked sin, with the hope of afterwards going to confession. But, by this illusion, how many have brought themselves to perdition! For them there is now no time for confession, no remedy for their damnation.

6. *But God is merciful.* Behold another common delusion, by which the Devil encourages sinners to persevere in a life of sin! A certain author has said, that more souls have been sent to Hell by the mercy of God, than by his justice. This is indeed the case; for men are induced by the deceits of the Devil to persevere in sin, through confidence in God's mercy; and thus they are lost. *God is merciful.* Who denies it? But, great as his mercy, how many does he every day send to Hell? God is merciful, but he is also just, and is therefore obliged to punish those who offend him. "And his mercy", says the divine mother, "to them that fear him"—*Luke*, i. 50. But with regard to those who abuse his mercy and despise him, he exercises justice. The Lord pardons sins; but he cannot pardon the determination to commit sin. St. Augustine says, that he who sins with the intention of repenting after his sin, is not a penitent but a scoffer. "Irrisor est non pœnitens". But the Apostle tells us that God will not be mocked. "Be not deceived: God is not mocked"—*Gal.*, vi. 7. It would be a mockery of God to insult him as often and as much as you pleased, and afterwards to expect eternal glory.

7. *But*, you say, *as God has shown me so many mercies hitherto, I hope he will continue to do so for the future.* Behold another delusion! Then, because God has not as yet chastised your sins, he will never punish them. On the contrary, the

greater have been his mercies, the more you should tremble, lest, if you offend him again, he should pardon you no more, and should take vengeance on your sins. Behold the advice of the Holy Ghost—"Say not: I have sinned, and what harm hath befallen me? for the Most High is a patient rewarder"—*Eccles.*, v. 4. Do not say: "*I have sinned, and no chastisement has fallen upon me*". God bears for a time, but not for ever. He waits for a certain time; but, when that arrives, he then chastises the sinner for all his past iniquities: and the longer he has waited for repentance, the more severe the chastisement. "Quos diutius expectat", says St. Gregory, "durius damnat". Then, my brother, since you know that you have frequently offended God, and that he has not sent you to Hell, you should exclaim: "The mercies of the Lord, that we are not consumed"—*Thren.*, iii. 22. Lord, I thank you for not having sent me to Hell, which I have so often so deserved. And therefore you ought to give yourself entirely to God, at least through gratitude, and should consider, that, for less sins than you have committed, many are now in that pit of fire, without the smallest hope of being ever released from it. The patience of God in bearing with you, should teach you not to despise him still more, but to love and serve him with greater fervour, and to atone, by penitential austerities and by other holy works, for the insults you have offered to him. You know that he has shown mercies to you, which he has not shown to others. "He hath not done in like manner to every nation"—*Ps.*, cxlvii. 20. Hence you should tremble, lest, if you commit a single additional mortal sin, God should abandon you, and cast you into Hell.

8. Let us come to the next illusion. *It is true that, by this sin, I lose the grace of God; but, even after committing this sin, I may be saved.* You may indeed be saved: but it cannot be denied, that, if, after having committed so many sins, and after having received so many graces from God, you again offend him, there is great reason to fear that you shall be lost. Attend to the words of the sacred Scripture—"A hard heart shall fare evil at the last"—*Eccles.*, iii. 27. The obstinate sinner shall die an unhappy death. "Evil doers shall be cut off"—*Ps.*, xxxvi. 9. The wicked shall be cut off by the divine justice. "For what things a man shall sow, those also shall he

reap"—*Gal.*, vi. 8. He that sows in sin, shall reap eternal torments. "Because I called and you refused,......I also will laugh in your destruction, and will mock when that shall come to you which you feared"—*Prov.*, i. 24, 26. I called, says the Lord, and you mocked me; but I will mock you at the hour of death. "Revenge is mine, and I will repay them in *due* time"—*Deut.*, xxxii. 35. The chastisement of sins belongs to me, and I will execute vengeance on them when the time of vengeance shall arrive. "The man that with a stiff neck despiseth him that reproveth him, shall suddenly be destroyed, and health shall not follow him"—*Prov.*, xxix. 1. The man who obstinately despises those who correct him, shall be punished with a sudden death, and for him there shall be no hope of salvation.

9. Now, brethren, what think you of these divine threats against sinners? Is it easy, or is it not very difficult, to save your souls, if, after so many divine calls, and after so many mercies, you continue to offend God? You say: *But after all, it may happen that I will save my soul.* I answer: What folly is it to trust your salvation to a perhaps? How many with this *Perhaps I may be saved*, are now in Hell? Do you wish to be one of their unhappy companions? Dearly beloved Christians, enter into yourselves, and tremble: for this sermon may be the last of God's mercies to you.

SERMON XV.

FOR THE FIRST SUNDAY OF LENT.

On the number of sins beyond which God pardons no more.

"Thou shalt not tempt the Lord thy God"—*Matt.*, iv. 7.

In this day's gospel we read, that, having gone into the desert, Jesus Christ permitted the Devil to *set him upon the pinnacle of the temple*, and say to him: "*If thou be the Son of God, cast thyself down*"; for the angels shall preserve thee from all injury. But the Lord answered, that, in the Sacred Scriptures it is written: *Thou shalt not tempt the Lord thy God.* The sinner who abandons himself to sin without striving to resist temptations, or without at least asking God's help to conquer them, and hopes that the Lord will one day draw him from the precipice, tempts God to work miracles, or rather to show to him an extraordinary mercy not extended to the generality of Christians. God, as the Apostle says, "will have all men to be saved"—I. *Tim.*, ii. 4; but he also wishes us all to labour for our own salvation, at least, by adopting the means of overcoming our enemies, and of obeying him when he calls us to repentance. Sinners hear the calls of God, but they forget them, and continue to offend him. But God does not forget them. He numbers the graces which he dispenses, as well as the sins which we commit. Hence, when the time which he has fixed arrives, God deprives us of his graces, and begins to inflict chastisement. I intend to show, in this discourse, that, when sins reach a certain number, God pardons no more. Be attentive.

I. St. Basil, St. Jerome, St. John Chrysostom, St. Augustine, and other fathers, teach, that, as God (according to the words of Scripture, "Thou hast ordered all things in measure, and number, and weight"—*Wis.*, xi. 21) has fixed for each person the number of the days of his life, and the degrees of health and talent which he will give him, so he has also determined for each the number of sins which he will pardon; and when this number is completed, he will pardon no more. "Illud sentire nos convenit", says St. Augustine, "tamdiu unumquemque a Dei patientia sustineri, quo consummato nullam illi veniam reservari"—*de Vita Christi*, *cap.* iii. Eusebius of Cesarea says: "Deus expectat usque ad certum numerum et postea deserit"—*lib.* VIII. *cap.* ii. The same doctrine is taught by the abovementioned fathers.

2. "The Lord hath sent me to heal the contrite of heart"—*Isa.*, lxi. 1. God is ready to heal those who sincerely wish to amend their lives, but cannot take pity on the obstinate sinner. The Lord pardons sins, but he cannot pardon those who are determined to offend him. Nor can we demand from God a reason why he pardons one a hundred sins, and takes others out of life, and sends them to Hell, after three or four sins. By

his Prophet Amos, God has said: "For three crimes of Damascus, and for four, I will not convert it"—i. 3. In this we must adore the judgments of God, and say with the Apostle: "O depth of the riches, of the wisdom, and of the knowledge of God! How incomprehensible are his judgments"—*Rom.*, xi. 33. He who receives pardon, says St. Augustine, is pardoned through the pure mercy of God; and they who are chastised, are justly punished. "Quibus datur misericordia, gratis datur: quibus non datur ex justitia non datur"—I. *de Corrept.* How many has God sent to Hell for the first offence? St. Gregory relates, that a child of five years, who had arrived at the use of reason, for having uttered a blasphemy, was seized by the Devil and carried to Hell. The divine mother revealed to that great servant of God, Benedicta of Florence, that a boy of twelve years was damned after the first sin. Another boy of eight years died after his first sin, and was lost. You say: I am young: there are many who have committed more sins than I have. But is God on that account obliged to wait for your repentance if you offend him? In the gospel of St. Matthew (xxi. 19), we read, that the Saviour cursed a fig tree the first time he saw it without fruit. "May no fruit grow on thee henceforward for ever. And immediately the fig tree withered away". You must, then, tremble at the thought of committing a single mortal sin, particularly if you have already been guilty of mortal sins.

3. "Be not without fear about sin forgiven, and add not sin to sin"—*Eccl.*, v. 5. Say not then, O sinner, As God has forgiven me other sins, so he will pardon me this one if I commit it. Say not this; for, if to the sin which has been forgiven, you add another, you have reason to fear that this new sin shall be united to your former guilt, and that thus the number will be completed, and that you shall be abandoned. Behold how the Scripture unfolds this truth more clearly in another place. "The Lord patiently expecteth, that when the day of judgment shall come, he may punish them in the fulness of sins"—II. *Mac.*, vi. 14. God waits with patience until a certain number of sins is committed; but, when the measure of guilt is filled up, he waits no longer, but chastises the sinner. "Thou hast sealed up my offences as it were in a bag"—*Job*, xiv. 17. Sinners multiply their sins without keeping any account of them; but

God numbers them, that, when the harvest is ripe, that is, when the number of sins is completed, he may take vengeance on them. "Put ye in the sickles, for the harvest is ripe"—*Joel*, iii. 13.

4. Of this there are many examples in the Scriptures. Speaking of the Hebrews, the Lord in one place says: "All the men that have tempted me now ten times......shall not see the land"—*Num.*, xiv. 22, 23. In another place, he says, that he restrained his vengeance against the Amorrhites, because the number of their sins was not completed. "For as yet the iniquities of the Amorrhites are not at the full"—*Gen.*, xv. 16. We have again the example of Saul, who, after having disobeyed God a second time, was abandoned. He entreated Samuel to interpose before the Lord in his behalf. "Bear, I beseech thee, my sin, and return with me, that I may adore the Lord"—I. *Kings*, xv. 25. But, knowing that God had abandoned Saul, Samuel answered: "I will not return with thee, because thou hast rejected the word of the Lord, and the Lord hath rejected thee", etc.—*v.* 26. Saul, you have abandoned God, and he has abandoned you. We have another example in Balthassar, who, after having profaned the vessels of the Temple, saw a hand writing on the wall, *Mane, Thecel, Phares.* Daniel was requested to expound the meaning of these words. In explaining the word Thecel, he said to the king: "Thou art weighed in the balance, and art found wanting"—*Dan.*, v. 27. By this explanation, he gave the king to understand that the weight of his sins in the balance of divine justice, had made the scale descend. "The same night Balthassar, the Chaldean king, was killed"—*Dan.*, v. 30. Oh! how many sinners have met with a similar fate! continuing to offend God till their sins amounted to a certain number, they have been struck dead and sent to Hell! "They spend their days in wealth, and in a moment they go down to Hell"—*Job*, xxi. 13. Tremble, brethren, lest, if you commit another mortal sin, God should cast you into Hell.

5. If God chastised sinners the moment they insult him, we should not see him so much despised. But, because he does not instantly punish their transgressions, and because, through mercy, he restrains his anger, and waits for their return, they are encouraged to continue to offend him. "For, because sentence

is not speedily pronounced against the evil, the children of men commit evil without any fear"—*Eccles.*, viii. 11. But it is necessary to be persuaded, that though God bears with us, he does not wait, nor bear with us for ever. Expecting, as on former occasions, to escape from the snares of the Philistines, Samson continued to allow himself to be deluded by Dalila. "I will go out as I did before, and shake myself"—*Judges*, xvi. 20. But "the Lord was departed from him". Samson was at length taken by his enemies, and lost his life. The Lord warns you not to say: I have committed so many sins, and God has not chastised me. "Say not: I have sinned, and what harm hath befallen me; for the Most High is a patient rewarder"—*Eccl.*, v. 4. God has patience for a certain term, after which he punishes the first and last sins. And the greater has been his patience, the more severe his vengeance.

6. Hence, according to St. Chrysostom, God is more to be feared when he bears with sinners, than when he instantly punishes their sin. "Plus timendum est, cum tolerat quam cum festinanter punit". And why? Because, says St. Gregory, they to whom God has shown most mercy, shall, if they do not cease to offend him, be chastised with the greatest rigour. "Quos diutius expectat durius damnat". The saint adds that God often punishes such sinners with a sudden death, and does not allow them time for repentance. "Sæpe qui diu tolerati sunt subita morte rapiuntur, ut nec flere ante mortem liceat". And the greater the light which God gives to certain sinners for their correction, the greater is their blindness and obstinacy in sin. "For it had been better for them not to have known the way of justice, than, after they had known it, to turn back"—II. *Pet.*, ii. 21. Miserable the sinners, who, after having been enlightened, return to the vomit. St. Paul says, that it is morally impossible for them to be again converted. "For it is impossible for those who were once illuminated—have tasted also the Heavenly gifts,...and are fallen away, to be renewed again to penance"—*Heb.*, vi. 4, 6.

7. Listen, then, O sinner, to the admonition of the Lord: "My son, hast thou sinned? do so no more, but for thy former sins pray that they may be forgiven thee"—*Eccl.*, xxi. 1. Son, add not sins to those which you have already committed, but be careful to pray for the pardon of your past transgressions; other-

wise, if you commit another mortal sin, the gates of the divine mercy may be closed against you, and your soul may be lost for ever. When, then, beloved brethren, the Devil tempts you again to yield to sin, say to yourself: If God pardons me no more, what shall become of me for all eternity? Should the Devil, in reply, say: *Fear not, God is merciful;* answer him by saying: What certainty or what probability have I, that, if I return again to sin, God will show me mercy or grant me pardon? Behold the threat of the Lord against all who despise his calls: "Because I have called and you refused,......I also will laugh in your destruction, and will mock when that shall come to you which you feared"—*Prov.*, i. 24, 26. Mark the words, *I also;* they mean that, as you have mocked the Lord by betraying him again after your confession and promises of amendment, so he will mock you at the hour of death. *I will laugh and will mock.* But, "God is not mocked"—*Gal.*, vi. 7. "As a dog", says the Wise Man, "that returneth to his vomit, so is the fool that repeateth his folly"—*Prov.*, xxvi, 11. B. Denis the Carthusian gives an excellent exposition of this text. He says, that, as a dog that eats what he has just vomited, is an object of disgust and abomination, so the sinner who returns to the sins which he has detested and confessed, becomes hateful in the sight of God. "Sicut id quod per vomitum est rejectum, resumere est valde abominabile ac turpe sic peccata deleta reiterari".

8. O folly of sinners! If you purchase a house, you spare no pains to get all the securities necessary to guard against the loss of your money; if you take medicine, you are careful to assure yourself that it cannot injure you; if you pass over a river, you cautiously avoid all danger of falling into it: and for a transitory enjoyment, for the gratification of revenge, for a beastly pleasure, which lasts but a moment, you risk your eternal salvation, saying: *I will go to confession after I commit this sin.* And when, I ask, are you to go to confession? You say: *On to-morrow.* But who promises you to-morrow? Who assures you that you shall have time for confession, and that God will not deprive you of life, as he has deprived so many others, in the act of sin? "Diem tenes", says St. Augustine, "qui horam non tenes". You cannot be certain of living for another hour, and you say: *I will go to confession to-morrow.* Listen to the words of St. Gregory: "He

who has promised pardon to penitents, has not promised to-morrow to sinners"—*hom.* xii., *in Evan.* God has promised pardon to all who repent; but he has not promised to wait till to-morrow for those who insult him. Perhaps God will give you time for repentance, perhaps he will not. But, should he not give it, what shall become of your soul? In the mean time, for the sake of a miserable pleasure, you lose the grace of God, and expose yourself to the danger of being lost for ever.

9. Would you, for such transient enjoyments, risk your money, your honour, your possessions, your liberty, and your life? No, you would not. How then does it happen, that, for a miserable gratification, you lose your soul, Heaven, and God? Tell me: do you believe that Heaven, Hell, eternity, are truths of faith? Do you believe, that, if you die in sin, you are lost for ever? Oh! what temerity, what folly is it, to condemn yourself voluntarily to an eternity of torments with the hope of afterwards reversing the sentence of your condemnation! "Nemo", says St. Augustine, "sub spe salutis vult ægrotare". No one can be found so foolish as to take poison with the hope of preventing its deadly effects by adopting the ordinary remedies. And you will condemn yourself to Hell, saying that you expect to be afterwards preserved from it. O folly! which, in conformity with the divine threats, has brought, and brings every day, so many to Hell. "Thou hast trusted in thy wickedness, and evil shall come upon thee, and thou shalt not know the rising thereof"—*Isa.*, xlvii. 10, 11. You have sinned, trusting rashly in the divine mercy: the punishment of your guilt shall fall suddenly upon you, and you shall not know from whence it comes. What do you say? What resolution do you make? If, after this sermon, you do not firmly resolve to give yourself to God, I weep over you, and regard you as lost.

SERMON XVI.

FOR THE SECOND SUNDAY OF LENT.

On Heaven.

"Lord, it is good for us to be here"—*Matt.*, xvii. 4.

In this day's gospel we read, that wishing to give his disciples a glimpse of the glory of Paradise, in order to animate them to labour for the divine honour, the Redeemer was transfigured, and allowed them to behold the splendour of his countenance. Ravished with joy and delight, St. Peter exclaimed: "Lord, it is good for us to be here". Lord, let us remain here; let us never more depart from this place; for, the sight of thy beauty consoles us more than all the delights of the Earth. Brethren, let us labour during the remainder of our lives to gain Heaven. Heaven is so great a good, that, to purchase it for us, Jesus Christ has sacrificed his life on the cross. Be assured, that the greatest of all the torments of the damned in Hell, arise from the thought of having lost Heaven through their own fault. The blessings, the delights, the joys, the sweetness of Paradise may be acquired; but they can be described and understood only by those blessed souls that enjoy them. But let us, with the aid of the holy Scripture, explain the little that can be said of them here below.

1. According to the Apostle, no man on this Earth can comprehend the infinite blessings which God has prepared for the souls that love him. "Eye hath not seen, nor ear heard, neither hath it entered into the heart of man, what things God hath prepared for them that love him"—I. *Cor.*, ii. 9. In this life, we cannot have an idea of any other pleasures than those which we enjoy by means of the senses. Perhaps we imagine that the beauty of Heaven resembles that of a wide extended plain covered with the verdure of spring, interspersed with trees in full bloom, and abounding in birds fluttering about and singing on every side; or, that it is like the beauty of a garden

full of fruits and flowers, and surrounded by fountains in continual play. *Oh! what a Paradise,* to behold such a plain, or such a garden! But, oh! how much greater are the beauties of Heaven! Speaking of Paradise, St. Bernard says: O man, if you wish to understand the blessings of Heaven, know that in that happy country there is nothing which can be disagreeable, and everything that you can desire. "Nihil est quod nolis, totum est quod velis". Although there are some things here below which are agreeable to the senses, how many more are there which only torment us? If the light of day is pleasant, the darkness of night is disagreeable: if the spring and the autumn are cheering, the cold of winter and the heat of summer are painful. In addition, we have to endure the pains of sickness, the persecution of men, and the inconveniences of poverty; we must submit to interior troubles, to fears, to temptations of the Devil, doubts of conscience, and to the uncertainty of eternal salvation.

2. But, after entering into Paradise, the blessed shall have no more sorrows. "God shall wipe away all tears from their eyes". The Lord shall dry up the tears which they have shed in this life. "And death shall be no more, nor mourning, nor crying, nor sorrow, shall be any more, for the former things are passed away. And he that sat on the throne, said: Behold, I make all things new"—*Apoc.*, xxi. 4, 5. In Paradise, death and the fear of death are no more: in that place of bliss, there are no sorrows, no infirmities, no poverty, no inconveniencies, no vicissitudes of day or night, of cold or of heat. In that kingdom, there is a continual day, always serene, a continual spring, always blooming. In Paradise there are no persecutions, no envy; for all love each other with tenderness, and each rejoices at the happiness of the others, as if it were his own. There is no more fear of eternal perdition; for the soul confirmed in grace, can neither sin nor lose God.

3. "Totum est quod velis". In Heaven, you have all you can desire. "Behold, I make all things new". There, every thing is new; new beauties, new delights, new joys. There, all our desires shall be satisfied. The sight shall be satiated with beholding the beauty of that city. How delightful to behold a city in which the streets should be of crystal, the houses of silver, the windows of gold, and all adorned with the most

beautiful flowers. But, oh! how much more beautiful shall be the city of Paradise: the beauty of the place shall be heightened by the beauty of the inhabitants, who are all clothed in royal robes; for, according to St. Augustine, they are all kings. "Quot cives, tot reges". How delightful to behold Mary, the queen of Heaven, who shall appear more beautiful than all the other citizens of Paradise! But, what it must be to behold the beauty of Jesus Christ! St. Teresa once saw one of the hands of Jesus Christ, and was struck with astonishment at the sight of such beauty. The smell shall be satiated with odours, but with the odours of Paradise. The hearing shall be satiated with the harmony of the celestial choirs. St. Francis once heard for a moment an angel playing on a violin, and he almost died through joy. How delightful must it be to hear the saints and angels singing the divine praises! "They shall praise thee for ever and ever"—*Ps.*, lxxxiii. 5. What must it be to hear Mary praising God! St. Francis de Sales says, that, as the singing of the nightingale in the wood surpasses that of all other birds, so the voice of Mary is far superior to that of all the other saints. In a word, there are in Paradise all the delights which man can desire.

4. But the delights of which we have spoken are the least of the blessings of Paradise. The glory of Heaven consists in seeing and loving God face to face. "Totum quod expectamus", says St. Augustine, "duæ syllabæ sunt, Deus". The reward which God promises to us, does not consist altogether in the beauty, the harmony, and other advantages of the city of Paradise. God himself, whom the saints are allowed to behold, is, according to the promise made to Abraham, the principal reward of the just in Heaven. "I am thy reward exceeding great"—*Gen.*, xv. 1. St. Augustine asserts, that, were God to show his face to the damned, "Hell would be instantly changed into a Paradise of delights"—*lib. de trip. habit.*, *tom.* IX. And he adds, that, were a departed soul allowed the choice of seeing God and suffering the pains of Hell, or of being freed from these pains and deprived of the sight of God, "she would prefer to see God and to endure these torments".

5. The delights of the soul infinitely surpass all the pleasures of the senses. Even in this life divine love infuses such

sweetness into the soul when God communicates himself to her, that the body is raised from the Earth. St. Peter of Alcantara once fell into such an ecstacy of love, that, taking hold of a tree, he drew it up from the roots, and raised it with him on high. So great is the sweetness of divine love, that the holy martyrs in the midst of their torments felt no pain, but were on the contrary filled with joy. Hence St. Augustine says, that, when St. Lawrence was laid on a red-hot gridiron, the fervour of divine love made him insensible to the burning heat of the fire. "Hoc igne incensus non sentit incendium". Even on sinners who weep for their sins, God bestows consolations which exceed all Earthly pleasures. Hence St. Bernard says: "If it be so sweet to weep for thee, what must it be to rejoice in thee!"

6. How great is the sweetness which a soul experiences when, in the time of prayer, God, by a ray of his own light, shows to her his goodness and his mercies towards her, and particularly the love which Jesus Christ has borne to her in his passion! She feels her heart melting and as it were dissolved through love. But in this life we do not see God as he really is: we see him as it were in the dark. "We see now through a glass in a dark manner, but then face to face"—I. *Cor.*, xiii. 12. Here below, God is hidden from our view; we can see him only with the eyes of faith: how great shall be our happiness when the veil shall be raised, and we shall be permitted to behold God face to face! We shall then see his beauty, his greatness, his perfection, his amiableness, and his immense love for our souls.

7. "Man knoweth not whether he be worthy of love or hatred"—*Eccl.*, ix. 1. The fear of not loving God, and of not being loved by him, is the greatest affliction which souls that love God endure on this Earth; but, in Heaven, the soul is certain that she loves God, and that he loves her; she sees that the Lord embraces her with infinite love, and that this love shall not be dissolved for all eternity. The knowledge of the love which Jesus Christ has shown her in offering himself in sacrifice for her on the cross, and in making himself her food in the sacrament of the altar, shall increase the ardour of her love. She shall also see clearly all the graces which God has bestowed upon her, all the helps which he has given her, to preserve her from falling into sin, and to draw her to his love. She

shall see that all the tribulations, the poverty, infirmities, and persecutions which she regards as misfortunes, have all proceeded from love, and have been the means employed by Divine Providence to bring her to glory. She shall see all the lights, loving calls, and mercies which God had granted to her after she had insulted him by her sins. From the blessed mountain of Paradise she shall see so many souls damned for fewer sins than she had committed, and shall see that she herself is saved and secured against the possibility of ever losing God.

8. The goods of this Earth do not satisfy our desires: at first, they gratify the senses; but, when we become accustomed to them, they cease to delight. But the joys of Paradise constantly satiate and content the heart. "I shall be satisfied when thy glory shall appear"—*Ps.*, xvi. 15. And though they satiate, they always appear to be as new as the first time they were experienced: they are always enjoyed and always desired, always desired and always possessed. "Satiety", says St. Gregory, "accompanies desire"—*lib.* XVIII. *Mor.*, *c.* xviii. Thus, the desires of the saints in Paradise do not beget pain, because they are always satisfied; and satiety does not produce disgust, because it is always accompanied with desire. Hence the soul shall be always satiated and always thirsty: she shall be for ever thirsty and always satiated with delights. The damned are, according to the Apostle, vessels full of wrath and of torments, "vessels of wrath, fitted for destruction"—*Rom.*, ix. 22. But the just are vessels full of mercy and of joy, so that they have nothing to desire. "They shall be inebriated with the plenty of thy house"—*Ps.*, xxxv. 9. In beholding the beauty of God, the soul shall be so inflamed and so inebriated with divine love, that she shall remain happily lost in God; for she shall entirely forget herself, and for all eternity shall think only of loving and praising the immense good which she shall possess for ever, without the fear of having it in her power ever to lose it. In this life, holy souls love God; but they cannot love him with all their strength, nor can they always actually love him. St. Thomas teaches, that this perfect love is only given to the citizens of Heaven, who love God with their whole heart, and never cease to love him actually. "Ut totum cor hominis semper actualiter in Deum feratur, ista est perfectio patriæ"—2, 2 *quæst.* 44, *art.* 4, *ad* 2.

9. Justly, then, has St. Augustine said, that, to gain the eternal glory of Paradise, we should cheerfully embrace eternal labour. "Pro æterna requie æternus labor subeundus esset". "For nothing", says David, "shalt thou save them"—*Ps.*, lv. 8. The saints have done but little to acquire Heaven. So many kings who have abdicated their thrones and shut themselves up in a cloister; so many holy anchorets who have confined themselves in a cave; so many martyrs, who have cheerfully submitted to torments—to the rack, and to red-hot plates—have done but little. "The sufferings of this life are not worthy to be compared to the glory to come"—*Rom.*, viii. 18. To gain Heaven, it would be but little to endure all the pains of this life.

10. Let us, then, brethren, courageously resolve to bear patiently with all the sufferings which shall come upon us during the remaining days of our lives: to secure Heaven they are all little and nothing. Rejoice then; for all these pains, sorrows, and persecutions shall, if we are saved, be to us a source of never-ending joys and delights. "Your sorrow shall be turned into joy"—*John*, xvi. 20. When, then, the crosses of this life afflict us, let us raise our eyes to Heaven, and console ourselves with the hope of Paradise. At the end of her life, St. Mary of Egypt was asked, by the abbot S. Zozimus, how she had been able to live for forty-seven years in the desert where he found her dying. She answered: *With the hope of Paradise.* If we be animated with the same hope, we shall not feel the tribulations of this life. Have courage! Let us love God and labour for Heaven. There the saints expect us, Mary expects us, Jesus Christ expects us, he holds in his hand a crown to make each of us a king in that eternal kingdom.

SERMON XVII.

FOR THE THIRD SUNDAY IN LENT.

On concealing sins in confession.

"And he was casting out a devil, and the same was dumb"—*Luke*, xi. 14.

THE Devil does not bring sinners to Hell with their eyes open: he first blinds them with the malice of their own sins. "For their own malice blinded them"—*Wis.*, ii. 21. He thus leads them to eternal perdition. Before we fall into sin, the enemy labours to blind us, that we may not see the evil we do, and the ruin we bring upon ourselves by offending God. After we commit sin, he seeks to make us dumb, that, through shame, we may conceal our guilt in confession. Thus he leads us to Hell by a double chain, inducing us, after our transgression, to consent to a still greater sin—the sin of sacrilege. I will speak on this subject to-day, and will endeavour to convince you of the great evil of concealing sins in confession.

1. In expounding the words of David, "Set a door, O Lord, round about my lips"—*Ps.*, cxl. 3, St. Augustine says: "Non dixit claustrum, sed ostium: ostium et aperitur et clauditur: aperiatur and confessionem peccati: claudatur ad excusationem peccati". We should keep a door to the mouth, that it may be closed against detraction, and blasphemies, and all improper words, and that it may be opened to confess the sins we have committed. "Thus", adds the holy doctor, "it will be a door of restraint, and not of destruction". To be silent when we are impelled to utter words injurious to God or to our neighbour, is an act of virtue; but, to be silent in confessing our sins, is the ruin of the soul. After we have offended God, the Devil labours to keep the mouth closed, and to prevent us from confessing our guilt. St. Antonine relates, that a holy solitary once saw the Devil standing beside a certain person who wished to go to confession. The solitary asked the fiend what he was doing there. The enemy said in reply: "*I now restore to these penitents what I before took away from them; I took*

away from them shame while they were committing sin; I now restore it, that they may have a horror of confession". "My sores are putrefied and corrupted, because of my foolishness"—*Ps.*, xxxvii. 6. Gangrenous sores are fatal; and sins concealed in confession, are spiritual ulcers, which mortify and become gangrenous.

2. "Pudorem", says St. Chrysostom, "dedit Deus peccato, confessioni fiduciam: invertit rem diabolis, peccato fiduciam præbet, confessioni pudorem"—*Proem in Isa.* God has made sin shameful, that we may abstain from it, and gives us confidence to confess it by promising pardon to all who accuse themselves of their sins. But the Devil does the contrary: he gives confidence to sin by holding out hopes of pardon; but when sin is committed, he inspires shame, to prevent the confession of it.

3. A disciple of Socrates, at the moment he was leaving a house of bad fame, saw his master pass: to avoid being seen by him, he went back into the house. Socrates came to the door, and said: My son, it is a shameful thing to enter, but not to depart from this house. "Non te pudeat, fili egredi ex hoc loco, intrasse pudeat". To you also, O brethren, who have sinned, I say, that you ought to be ashamed to offend so great and so good a God. But you have no reason to be ashamed of confessing the sins which you have committed. Was it shameful in St. Mary Magdalene to acknowledge publicly at the feet of Jesus Christ that she was a sinner? By her confession she became a saint. Was it shameful in St. Augustine not only to confess his sins, but also to publish them in a book, that, for his confusion, they might be known to the whole world? Was it shameful in St. Mary of Egypt to confess, that for so many years, she had led a scandalous life? By their confessions these have become saints, and are honoured on the altars of the Church.

4. We say that the man who acknowledges his guilt before a secular tribunal is condemned; but, in the tribunal of Jesus Christ, they who confess their sins, obtain pardon, and receive a crown of eternal glory. "After confession", says St. Chrysostom, "a crown is given to penitents". He who is afflicted with an ulcer must, if he wish to be cured, show it to a physician: otherwise it will fester and bring on death. "Quod ignorat", says

the Council of Trent, "medicina non curat". If then, brethren, your souls be ulcerated with sin, be not ashamed to confess it; otherwise you are lost. "For thy soul be not ashamed to say the truth"—*Eccl.*, iv. 24. But, you say, I feel greatly ashamed to confess such a sin. If you wish to be saved, you must conquer this shame. "For there is a shame that bringeth sin, and there is a shame that bringeth glory and grace"—*ib.*, iv. 25. There are, according to the inspired writer, two kinds of shame; one of which leads souls to sin, and that is the shame which makes them conceal their sins at confession: the other is the confusion which a Christian feels in confessing his sins; and this confusion obtains for him the grace of God in this life, and the glory of Heaven in the next.

5. St. Augustine says, that to prevent the sheep from seeking assistance by her cries, the wolf seizes her by the neck, and thus securely carries her away and devours her. The Devil acts in a similar manner with the sheep of Jesus Christ. After having induced them to yield to sin, he seizes them by the throat, that they may not confess their guilt; and thus he securely brings them to Hell. For those who have sinned grievously, there is no means of salvation but the confession of their sins. But, what hope of salvation can he have who goes to confession and conceals his sins, and makes use of the tribunal of penance to offend God, and to make himself doubly the slave of Satan? What hope would you entertain of the recovery of the man who, instead of taking the medicine prescribed by his physician, drank a cup of poison? O God! What can the sacrament of penance be to those who conceal their sins, but a deadly poison, which adds to their guilt the malice of sacrilege? In giving absolution, the confessor dispenses to his penitent the blood of Jesus Christ; for it is through the merits of that blood that he absolves from sin. What, then, does the sinner do, when he conceals his sins in confession? He tramples under foot the blood of Jesus Christ. And should he afterwards receive the holy communion in a state of sin, he is, according to St. Chrysostom, as guilty as if he threw the consecrated host into a sink. "Non minus detestabile est in os pollutum, quam in sterquilinium mittere Dei Filium"—*hom.*, lxxxiii. *in Mat.* Accursed shame! how many poor souls do you bring to Hell! "Magis memores pudoris", says Tertullian, "quam salutis".

Unhappy souls! they think only of the shame of confessing their sins, and do not reflect that, if they conceal them, they shall be certainly damned,

6. Some penitents ask: *What will my confessor say, when he hears that I have committed such a sin?* What will he say? He will say that you are, like all persons living on this Earth, miserable and prone to sin: he will say that, if you have done evil, you have also performed a glorious action, in overcoming shame and in candidly confessing your fault.

7. *But I am afraid to confess this sin.* To how many confessors, I ask, must you tell it? It is enough to mention it to one priest, who hears many sins of the same kind from others. It is enough to confess it once: the confessor will give you penance and absolution, and your conscience shall be tranquillized. *But*, you say, *I feel a great repugnance to tell this sin to my spiritual father.* Tell it, then, to another confessor, and, if you wish, to one to whom you are unknown. *But, if this come to the knowledge of my confessor, he will be displeased with me.* What then do you mean to do? Perhaps, to avoid giving displeasure to him, you intend to commit a heinous crime, and remain under sentence of damnation. This would be the very height of folly.

8. Are you afraid that the confessor will make known your sin to others? Would it not be madness to suspect that he is so wicked as to break the seal of confession by revealing your sin to others? Remember that the obligation of the seal of confession is so strict, that a confessor cannot speak, out of confession, even to the penitent, of the smallest venial fault; and if he did so,* he would be guilty of a most grievous sin.

9. But you say: *I am afraid that my confessor, when he hears my sin, will rebuke me with great severity.* O God! Do you not see that all these are deceitful artifices of the Devil to bring you to Hell? No; the confessor will not rebuke you; but he will give an advice suited to your state. A confessor cannot experience greater consolation than in absolving a penitent who confesses his sins with true sorrow and with sincerity. If a queen were mortally wounded by a slave, and you were in possession of a remedy by which she could be cured, how great would be your joy in saving her life! Such is the joy which a

* That is, without the permission of the penitent.

confessor feels in absolving a soul in the state of sin. By his act he delivers her from eternal death: and by restoring to her the grace of God, he makes her a queen of Paradise.

10. But you have so many fears, and are not afraid of damning your own soul by the enormous crime of concealing sins in confession. You are afraid of the rebuke of your confessor, and fear not the reproof which you shall receive from Jesus Christ, your Judge, at the hour of death. You are afraid that your sins shall become known (which is impossible), and you dread not the day of judgment, on which, if you conceal them, they shall be revealed to all men. If you knew that, by concealing sins in confession, they shall be made known to all your relatives and to all your neighbours, you would certainly confess them. But, do you not know, says St. Bernard, that, if you refuse to confess your sins to one man, who, like yourself, is a sinner, they shall be made known not only to all your relatives and neighbours, but to the entire human race? "Si pudor est tibi uni homini, et peccatori peccatum exponere, quid facturus es in die judicii, ubi omnibus exposita tua conscientia patebit?"—*S. Ber. super illud. Joan.*, *cap.* xi. "Lazare veni foras". If you do not confess your sin, God himself shall, for your confusion, publish not only the sin which you conceal, but also all your iniquities, in the presence of the angels and of the whole world. "I will discover thy shame to thy face, and will show thy wickedness to the nations"—*Nah.*, iii. 5.

11. Listen, then, to the advice of St. Ambrose: The Devil keeps an account of your sins, to charge you with them at the tribunal of Jesus Christ. Do you wish, says the saint, to prevent this accusation? Anticipate your accuser: accuse yourself now to a confessor, and then no accuser shall appear against you at the judgment seat of God. "Præveni accusatorem tuum; si te accusaveris, accusatorem nullum timebis"—*lib.* II. *de Pœnit.*, *cap.* ii. But according to St. Augustine, if you excuse yourself in confession, you shut up sin within your soul, and shut out pardon. "Excusas te, includis peccatum, excludis indulgentiam"—*hom.*, xii. 50.

12. If, then, brethren, there be a single soul among you who has ever concealed a sin, through shame, in the tribunal of penance, let him take courage, and make a full confession of all his faults. "Give glory to God with a good heart"—*Eccl.*,

xxxv. 10. Give glory to God and confusion to the Devil. A certain penitent was tempted by Satan to conceal a sin through shame; but she resolved to confess it; and while she was going to her confessor, the Devil came forward, and asked her where she was going. She courageously answered: *I am going to cover myself and you with confusion.* Act you in a similar manner; if you have ever concealed a mortal sin, confess it candidly to your director, and confound the Devil. Remember that the greater the violence you do to yourself in confessing your sins, the greater will be the love with which Jesus Christ will embrace you.

13. Courage, then! expel this viper which you harbour in your soul, and which continually corrodes your heart, and destroys your peace. Oh! what a Hell does a Christian suffer, who keeps in his heart a sin concealed through shame in confession! He suffers an anticipation of Hell. It is enough to say to the confessor: *Father, I have a certain scruple regarding my past life, but I am ashamed to tell it.* This will be enough: the confessor will help you to pluck out the serpent which gnaws your conscience. And, that you may not entertain groundless scruples, I think it right to tell you, that if the sin which you are ashamed to tell, be not mortal, or if you never considered it to be a mortal sin, you are not obliged to confess it; for we are bound only to confess mortal sins. Moreover, if you have doubts whether you ever confessed a certain sin of your former life, but know that, in preparing for confession, you always carefully examined your conscience, and that you never concealed a sin through shame; in this case, even though the sin, about the confession of which you are doubtful, had been a grievous fault, you are not obliged to confess it; because it is presumed to be morally certain that you have already confessed it. But, if you know that the sin was grievous, and that you never accused yourself of it in confession, then there is no remedy; you must confess it, or you must be damned for it. But, O lost sheep, go instantly to confession. Jesus Christ is waiting for you; he stands with arms open to pardon and embrace you, if you acknowledge your guilt. I assure you that, after having confessed all your sins, you shall feel such consolation at having unburdened your conscience and acquired the grace of God, that you shall for ever bless the day on which

you made this confession. Go as soon as possible in search of a confessor. Do not give the Devil time to continue to tempt you, and to make you put off your confession: go immediately; for Jesus Christ is waiting for you.

SERMON XVIII.

FOR THE FOURTH SUNDAY OF LENT.

On the tender compassion which Jesus Christ entertains towards sinners.

"Make the men sit down"—*John*, vi. 10.

WE read in this day's gospel, that, having gone up into a mountain with his disciples, and seeing a multitude of five thousand persons, who followed him because they saw the miracles which he wrought on them that were diseased, the Redeemer said to St. Philip: "Whence shall we buy bread, that these may eat?" "Lord", answered St. Philip, "two hundred pennyworth of bread is not sufficient that every one may take a little". St. Andrew then said: There is a boy here that has five barley loaves and two fishes; but what are these among so many? But Jesus Christ said: *Make the men sit down.* And he distributed the loaves and fishes among them. The multitude were satisfied: and the fragments of bread which remained filled twelve baskets. The Lord wrought this miracle through compassion for the bodily wants of these poor people; but far more tender is his compassion for the necessities of the souls of the poor,—that is, of sinners who are deprived of the divine grace. This tender compassion of Jesus Christ for sinners shall be the subject of this day's discourse.

1. Through the bowels of his mercy towards men, who groaned under the slavery of sin and Satan, our most loving Redeemer descended from Heaven to Earth, to redeem and save them from eternal torments, by his own death. Such was the language of St. Zachary, the father of the Baptist, when the

Blessed Virgin, who had already become the mother of the Eternal Word, entered his house: "Through the bowels of the mercy of our God, in which the Orient from on high hath visited us"—*Luke*, i. 78.

2. Jesus Christ, the good pastor, who came into the world to obtain salvation for us his sheep, has said: "I am come that they may have life and may have it more abundantly"—*John*, x. 10. Mark the expression, "*more abundantly*", which signifies that the Son of Man came on Earth not only to restore us to the life of grace which we lost, but to give us a better life than that which we forfeited by sin. Yes; for, as St. Leo says, the benefits which we have derived from the death of Jesus, are greater than the injury which the Devil has done us by sin. "Ampliora adepti sumus per Christi gratiam quam per diaboli amiseramus invidiam"—*ser.* i., *de Ascen.* The same doctrine is taught by the Apostle, who says that, "where sin abounded, grace did more abound"—*Rom.*, v. 20.

3. But, my Lord, since thou hast resolved to take human flesh, would not a single prayer offered by thee be sufficient for the redemption of all men? What need then was there of leading a life of poverty, humiliation, and contempt, for thirty-three years, of suffering a cruel and shameful death on an infamous gibbet, and of shedding all thy blood by dint of torments? I know well, answers Jesus Christ, that one drop of my blood, or a simple prayer, would be sufficient for the salvation of the world; but neither would be sufficient to show the love which I bear to men: and therefore, to be loved by men when they should see me dead on the cross for the love of them, I have resolved to submit to so many torments and to so painful a death. This, he says, is the duty of a good pastor. "I am the good shepherd. The good shepherd giveth his life for his sheep...I lay down my life for my sheep"—*John*, x. 11, 15.

4. O men, O men, what greater proof of love could the Son of God give us, than to lay down his life for us his sheep? "In this we have known the charity of God; because he hath laid down his life for us"—I. *John*, iii. 16. No one, says the Saviour, can show greater love to his friends, than to give his life for them. "Greater love than this no man hath, that a man lay down his life for his friends"—*John*, xv. 13. But thou, O Lord, hast died not only for friends, but for us who were

thy enemies by sin. "When we were enemies, we were reconciled to God by the death of his Son"—*Rom.*, v. 10. O infinite love of our God, exclaims St. Bernard; "to spare slaves, neither the Father has spared the Son, nor the Son himself". To pardon us, who were rebellious servants, the Father would not pardon the Son, and the Son would not pardon himself, but, by his death, has satisfied the divine justice for the sins which we have committed.

5. When Jesus Christ was near his passion, he went one day to Samaria: the Samaritans refused to receive him. Indignant at the insult offered by the Samaritans to their Master, St. James and St. John, turning to Jesus, said: "Lord, wilt thou that we command fire to come down from Heaven and consume them?"—*Luke*, ix. 54. But Jesus, who was all sweetness, even to those who insulted him, answered: "You know not of what spirit you are. The Son of Man came not to destroy souls, but to save"—*v.* 55 *and* 56. He severely rebuked the disciples. What spirit is this, he said, which possesses you? It is not my spirit: mine is the spirit of patience and compassion; for I am come, not to destroy, but to save the souls of men: and you speak of fire, of punishment, and of vengeance. Hence, in another place, he said to his disciples: "Learn of me, because I am meek and humble of heart"—*Mat.*, xi. 29. I do not wish you to learn of me to chastise, but to be meek, and to bear and pardon injuries.

6. How beautifully has he described the tenderness of his heart towards sinners in the following words!—"What man of you that hath an hundred sheep; and, if he lose one of them, doth he not leave the ninety-nine in the desert, and go after that which is lost until he find it: and when he hath found it, lay it upon his shoulder rejoicing; and coming home, call together his friends and neighbours, saying to them: Rejoice with me; because I have found my sheep that was lost?"—*Luke*, xv. 4, 5, *and* 6. But, O Lord, it is not thou that oughtest to rejoice, but the sheep that has found her pastor and her God. The sheep indeed, answers Jesus; rejoices at finding me, her shepherd; but far greater is the joy which I feel at having found one of my lost sheep. He concludes the parable in these words,—"I say to you, that even so there shall be joy in Heaven upon one sinner that doth penance, more than upon ninety-nine just, who

need not penance"—*Luke*, xv. 7. There is more joy in Heaven at the conversion of one sinner, than upon ninety-nine just men who preserve their innocence. What sinner, then, can be so hardened, as not to go instantly and cast himself at the feet of his Saviour, when he knows the tender love with which Jesus Christ is prepared to embrace him, and carry him on his shoulders, as soon as he repents of his sins?

7. The Lord has also declared his tenderness towards penitent sinners in the parable of the Prodigal Child (*Luke*, xv. 12, *&c.*). In that parable the Son of God says, that a certain young man, unwilling to be any longer under the control of his father, and desiring to live according to his caprice and corrupt inclinations, asked the portion of his father's substance which fell to him. The father gave it with sorrow, weeping over the ruin of his son. The son departed from his father's house. Having in a short time dissipated his substance, he was reduced to such a degree of misery, that, to procure the necessaries of life, he was obliged to feed swine. All this was a figure of a sinner, who, after departing from God, and losing the divine grace and all the merits he had acquired, leads a life of misery under the slavery of the Devil. In the gospel it is added, that the young man, seeing his wretched condition, resolved to return to his father: and the father, who is a figure of Jesus Christ, seeing his son return to him, was instantly moved to pity. "His father saw him, and was moved with compassion"—*v.* 20; and, instead of driving him away, as the ungrateful son had deserved, "running to him, he fell upon his neck and kissed him". He ran with open arms to meet him, and, through tenderness, fell upon his neck and consoled him by his embraces. He then said to his servants: "Bring forth quickly the first robe, and put it on him." According to St. Jerome and St. Augustine, *the first robe* signifies the divine grace, which, in addition to new celestial gifts, God, by granting pardon, gives to the penitent sinner. "And put a ring on his finger". Give him the ring of a spouse. By recovering the grace of God, the soul becomes again the spouse of Jesus Christ. "And bring hither the fatted calf, and kill it, and let us eat and make merry"—*v.* 23. Bring hither the fatted calf—which signifies the holy communion, or Jesus in the holy sacrament mystically killed and offered in sacrifice on the altar;—let us eat and rejoice.

But why, O divine Father, so much joy at the return of so ungrateful a child? Because, answers the Father, this my son was dead, and he is come to life again; he was lost, and I have found him.

8. This tenderness of Jesus Christ was experienced by the sinful woman (according to St. Gregory, Mary Magdalene) who cast herself at the feet of Jesus, and washed them with her tears (*Luke*, vii. 47 *and* 50). The Lord turning to her with sweetness, consoled her by saying: "Thy sins are forgiven;...thy faith hath made thee safe; go in peace"—*Luke*, vii. 48 *and* 50. Child, thy sins are pardoned; thy confidence in me has saved thee; go in peace. It was also felt by the man who was sick for thirty-eight years, and who was infirm both in body and soul. The Lord cured his malady, and pardoned his sins. "Behold", says Jesus to him, "thou art made whole; sin no more, lest some worse thing happen to thee"—*John*, v. 14. The tenderness of the Redeemer was also felt by the leper who said to Jesus Christ: "Lord, if thou wilt, thou canst make me clean"—*Matt.*, viii. 2. Jesus answered: "I will: be thou made clean"—*v.* 3. As if he said: Yes; I will that thou be made clean; for I have come down from Heaven for the purpose of consoling all: be healed, then, according to thy desire. "And forthwith his leprosy was cleansed".

9. We have also a proof of the tender compassion of the Son of God for sinners, in his conduct towards the woman caught in adultery. The scribes and pharisees brought her before him, and said: "This woman was even now taken in adultery. Now Moses, in the law, commands us to stone such a one. But what sayest thou?"—*John*, viii. 4 *and* 5. And this they did, as St. John says, tempting him. They intended to accuse him of transgressing the law of Moses, if he said that she ought to be liberated; and they expected to destroy his character for meekness, if he said that she should be stoned. "Si dicat lapidandam", says St. Augustine, "famam perdet mansuetudinis; sin dimittendam, transgressæ legis accusabitur"—*tract.* xxxiii., *in Joan.* But what was the answer of our Lord? He neither said that she should be stoned nor dismissed; but, "bowing himself down, he wrote with his finger on the ground". The interpreters say, that, probably, what he wrote on the ground was a text of Scripture admonishing the accusers of their own sins, which

were, perhaps, greater than that of the woman charged with adultery. "He then lifted himself up, and said to them: 'He that is without sin among you, let him first cast a stone at her'"—*v.* 7. The scribes and pharisees went away one by one, and the woman stood alone. Jesus Christ, turning to her, said: "Hath no one condemned thee? neither will I condemn thee. Go, and now sin no more"—*v.* 11. Since no one has condemned you, fear not that you shall be condemned by me, who have come on Earth, not to condemn, but to pardon and save sinners: go in peace, and sin no more.

10. Jesus Christ has come, not to condemn, but to deliver sinners from Hell, as soon as they resolve to amend their lives. And when he sees them obstinately bent on their own perdition, he addresses them with tears in the words of Ezechiel: "Why will you die, O house of Israel?"—xviii. 31. My children, why will you die? Why do you voluntarily rush into Hell, when I have come from Heaven to deliver you from it by my death? He adds: You are already dead to the grace of God. But I will not your death: return to me, and I will restore to you the life which you have lost. "For I desire not the death of him that dieth, saith the Lord God: return ye and live"—*v.* 32. But some sinners, who are immersed in the abyss of sin, may say: Perhaps, if we return to Jesus Christ, he will drive us away. No; for the Redeemer has said: "And him that cometh to me I will not cast out"—*John*, vi. 37. No one that comes to me with sorrow for his past sins, however manifold and enormous they may have been, shall be rejected.

11. Behold how, in another place, the Redeemer encourages us to throw ourselves at his feet with a secure hope of consolation and pardon. "Come to me, all you that labour and are burdened, and I will refresh you"—*Mat.*, xi. 28. Come to me, all ye poor sinners, who labour for your own damnation, and groan under the weight of your crimes; come, and I will deliver you from all your troubles. Again, he says: "Come and accuse me, saith the Lord; if your sins be as scarlet, they shall be made white as snow; and if they be red as crimson, they shall be made white as wool"—*Isa.*, i. 18. Come with sorrow for the offences you committed against me, and if I do not give you pardon, accuse me. As if he said: Upbraid me; rebuke me as a liar; for I promise that, though your

sins were of scarlet—that is, of the most horrid enormity—your soul, by my blood, in which I shall wash it, will become white and beautiful as snow.

12. Let us then, O sinners, return instantly to Jesus Christ. If we have left him, let us immediately return before death overtakes us in sin and sends us to Hell, where the mercies and graces of the Lord shall, if we do not amend, be so many swords which shall lacerate the heart for all eternity.

SERMON XIX.

FOR PASSION SUNDAY.

On the danger to which tepidity exposes the soul.

"But Jesus hid himself"—*John*, viii. 59.

JESUS CHRIST is "the true light which enlighteneth every man that cometh into this world"—*John*, i 9. He enlightens all; but he cannot enlighten those who voluntarily shut their eyes to the light; from them the Saviour hides himself. How then can they, walking in darkness, escape the many dangers of perdition to which we are exposed in this life, which God has given us as the road to eternal happiness? I will endeavour to-day to convince you of the great danger into which tepidity brings the soul, since it makes Jesus Christ hide his divine light from her, and makes him less liberal in bestowing upon her the graces and helps, without which she shall find it very difficult to complete the journey of this life without falling into an abyss—that is, into mortal sin.

1. A tepid soul is not one that lives in enmity with God, nor one that sometimes commits venial sins through mere frailty, and not with full deliberation. On account of the corruption of nature by original sin, no man can be exempt from such venial faults. This corruption of nature renders it impossible for us, without a most special grace, which has been given only to the mother of God, to avoid all venial sins during our whole lives.

Hence St. John has said: "If we say that we have no sin, we deceive ourselves, and the truth is not in us"—I. *John*, i. 8. God permits defects of this kind, even in the saints, to keep them humble, and to make them feel that, as they commit such faults in spite of all their good purposes and promises, so also, were they not supported by his divine hand, they would fall into mortal sins. Hence, when we find that we have committed these light faults, we must humble ourselves, and, acknowledging our own weakness, we must be careful to recommend ourselves to God, and implore of him to preserve us, by his almighty hand, from more grievous transgressions, and to deliver us from those we have committed.

2. What then are we to understand by a tepid soul? A tepid soul is one that frequently falls into fully deliberate venial sins,—such as deliberate lies, deliberate acts of impatience, deliberate imprecations, and the like. These faults may be easily avoided by those who are resolved to suffer death, rather than commit a deliberate venial offence against God. St. Teresa used to say, that one venial sin does us more harm than all the devils in Hell. Hence she would say to her nuns: "*My children, from deliberate sin, however venial it may be, may the Lord deliver you*". Some complain of being left in aridity and dryness, and without any spiritual sweetness. But how can we expect that God will be liberal of his favours to us, when we are ungenerous to him? We know that such a lie, such an imprecation, such an injury to our neighbour, and such detraction, though not mortal sins, are displeasing to God; and still we do not abstain from them. Why then should we expect that God will give us his divine consolations?

3. But some of you will say: Venial sins, however great they may be, do not deprive the soul of the grace of God: even though I commit them, I will be saved; and for me it is enough to obtain eternal life. You say, that, *for you, it is enough to be saved.* Remember that St. Augustine says, that, *where you have said, "It is enough", there you have perished.* To understand correctly the meaning of these words of St. Augustine, and to see the danger to which the state of tepidity exposes those who commit habitual and deliberate venial sins, without feeling remorse for them, and without endeavouring to avoid them, it is necessary to know that the habit of light faults leads

the soul insensibly to mortal sins. For example: the habit of venial acts of aversion leads to mortal hatred; the habit of small thefts leads to grievous rapine; the habit of venial attachments leads to affections which are mortally sinful. "*The soul*", says St. Gregory, "*never lies where it falls*"—*Moral., lib.* XXI. No; it continues to sink still deeper. Mortal diseases do not generally proceed from serious indisposition, but from many slight and continued infirmities: so, likewise, the fall of many souls into mortal sin follows from habitual venial sins; for, these render the soul so weak, that, when a strong temptation assails her, she has not strength to resist it, and she falls.

4. Many are unwilling to be separated from God by mortal sins; they wish to follow him, but at a distance, and regardless of venial sins. But to them shall probably happen what befell St. Peter. When Jesus Christ was seized in the garden, St. Peter was unwilling to abandon the Lord, but "followed him afar off" —*Matt.*, xxvi. 58. After entering the house of Caiphas, he was charged with being a disciple of Jesus Christ. He was instantly seized with fear, and three times denied his Master. The Holy Ghost says: "He that contemneth small things, shall fall by little and little"—*Eccl.*, xix. 1. They who despise small falls, will probably one day fall into an abyss; for, being in the habit of committing light offences against God, they will feel but little repugnance to offer to him some grievous insult.

5. The Lord says: "Catch us the little foxes that destroy the vines"—*Cant.*, ii. 15. He does not tell us to catch the lions or the bears, but the little foxes. Lions and bears strike terror, and therefore all are careful to keep at a distance through fear of being devoured by them; but the little foxes, though they do not excite dismay, destroy the vine by drying up its roots. Mortal sin terrifies the timorous soul; but, if she accustom herself to the commission of many venial sins with full deliberation, and without endeavouring to correct them, they, like the little foxes, shall destroy the roots—that is, the remorse of conscience, the fear of offending God, and the holy desires of advancing in divine love; and thus, being in a state of tepidity, and impelled to sin by some passion, the soul will easily abandon God and lose the divine grace.

6. Moreover, deliberate and habitual venial sins not only deprive us of strength to resist temptations, but also of the spe-

cial helps without which we fall into grievous sins. Be attentive, brethren; for this is a point of great importance. It is certain, that of ourselves we have not sufficient strength to resist the temptations of the Devil, of the flesh, and of the world. It is God that prevents our enemies from assailing us with temptations by which we would be conquered. Hence Jesus Christ has taught us the following prayer: *And lead us not into temptation.* He teaches us to pray that God may deliver us from the temptations to which we would yield, and thus lose his grace. Now, venial sins, when they are deliberate and habitual, deprive us of the special helps of God which are necessary for preservation in his grace. I say *necessary*, because the Council of Trent anathematizes those who assert that we can persevere in grace without a special help from God. "Si quis dixerit, justificatum vel sine speciali auxilio Dei in accepta justitia perseverare posse, vel cum eo non posse; anathema sit"—*sess.* 6, *can.* xxii. Thus with the ordinary assistance of God, we cannot avoid falling into some mortal sin: a special aid is necessary. But this special aid God will justly withhold from tepid souls who are regardless of committing, with full deliberation, many venial sins. Thus these unhappy souls shall not persevere in grace.

7. They who are ungenerous to God, well deserve that God should not be liberal to them. "He who soweth sparingly, shall also reap sparingly"—II. *Cor.*, ix. 6. To such souls the Lord will give the graces common to all, but will probably withhold his special assistance; and without this, as we have seen, they cannot persevere without falling into mortal sin. God himself revealed to B. Henry Suson, that, for tepid souls who are content with leading a life exempt from mortal sin, and continue to commit many deliberate venial sins, it is very difficult to preserve themselves in the state of grace. The venerable Lewis da Ponte used to say: *I commit many defects, but I never make peace with them.* Wo to him who is at peace with his faults! St. Bernard teaches, that, as long as a person who is guilty of defects detests his faults, there is reason to hope that he will one day correct them and amend his life; but when he commits faults without endeavouring to amend, he will continually go from bad to worse, till he loses the grace of God. St. Augustine says, that, like a certain disease of the

skin which makes the body an object of disgust, habitual faults, when committed without any effort of amendment, render the soul so disgusting to God, that he deprives her of his embraces. "Sunt velut scabies, et nostrum decus ita exterminant ut a sponsi amplexibus separent"—*hom.* l., *cap.* iii. Hence, the soul, finding no more nourishment and consolation in her devout exercises, in her prayers, communions, or visits to the blessed sacrament, will soon neglect them, and thus neglecting the means of eternal salvation, she shall be in great danger of being lost.

8. This danger will be still greater for those who commit many venial sins through attachment to any passion, such as pride, ambition, aversion to a neighbour, or an inordinate affection for any person. St. Francis of Assisium says, that, in endeavouring to draw to sin a soul that is afraid of being in enmity with God, the Devil does not seek in the beginning to bind her with the chain of a slave, by tempting her to commit mortal sin, because she would have a horror of yielding to mortal sin, and would guard herself against it. He first endeavours to bind her by a single hair; then by a slender thread; next by a cord; afterwards by a rope; and in the end by a chain of Hell,—that is, by mortal sin; and thus he makes her his slave. For example: A person cherishes an affection for a female through a motive of courtesy or of gratitude, or from an esteem for her good qualities. This affection is followed by mutual presents; to these succeed words of tenderness; and after the first violent assault of the Devil, the miserable man shall find that he has fallen into mortal sin. He meets with the fate of gamesters, who, after frequently losing large sums of money, yield to an impulse of passion, risk their all, and, in the end, lose their entire property.

9. Miserable the soul that allows herself to be the slave of any passion. "Behold how small a fire, what a great wood it kindleth"—*St. James*, iii. 5. A small spark, if it be not extinguished, will set fire to an entire wood; that is, an unmortified passion shall bring the soul to ruin. Passion blinds us; and the blind often fall into an abyss when they least expect it. According to St. Ambrose, the Devil is constantly endeavouring to find out the passion which rules in our heart, and the pleasures which have the greatest attraction for us. When he

discovers them, he presents occasions of indulging them: he then excites concupiscence, and prepares a chain to make us the slaves of Hell. "Tunc maxime insidiatur adversarius quando videt in nobis passiones aliquas generari: tunc fomites movet, laqueos parat".

10. St. Chrysostom asserts, that he himself knew many persons who were gifted with great virtues, and who, because they disregarded light faults, fell into an abyss of crime. When the Devil cannot gain much from us, he is in the beginning content with the little; by many trifling victories he will make a great conquest. No one, says St. Bernard, suddenly falls from the state of grace into the abyss of wickedness. They who rush into the most grievous irregularities, begin by committing light faults. "Nemo repente fit turpissimus: a minimis incipiunt qui in maxima proruunt"—*tract. de ord. vitæ.* It is necessary also to understand that, when a soul that has been favoured by God with special lights and graces, consents to mortal sin, her fall shall not be a simple fall, from which she will easily rise again, but it will be a precipitous one, from which she will find it very difficult to return to God.

11. Addressing a person in the state of tepidity, our Lord said: "I would that thou wert cold or hot; but, because thou art lukewarm, and neither cold nor hot, I will begin to vomit thee out of my mouth"—*Apoc.*, iii. 15, 16. "I would thou wert cold"—that is, it would be better for thee to be deprived of my grace, because there should then be greater hopes of thy amendment; but, because thou livest in tepidity, without any desire of improvement, "*I will begin to vomit thee out of my mouth*". By these words he means, that he will begin to abandon the soul; for, what is vomited, is taken back only with great horror.

12. A certain author says, that tepidity is a hectic fever which does not excite alarm, because it is not perceived; but it is, at the same time, so malignant that it is rarely cured. The comparison is very just; for tepidity makes the soul insensible to remorses of conscience; and, as she is accustomed to feel no remorse for venial faults, she will by degrees become insensible to the stings of remorse which arise from mortal sins.

13. Let us come to the remedy. The amendment of a tepid soul is difficult; but there are remedies for those who wish to adopt them. First, the tepid must sincerely desire to be de-

livered from a state which, as we have seen, is so miserable and dangerous; for, without this desire, they shall not take pains to employ the proper means. Secondly, they must resolve to remove the occasions of their faults; otherwise, they will always relapse into the same defects. Thirdly, they must earnestly beg of the Lord to raise them from so wretched a state. By their own strength they can do nothing; but they can do all things with the assistance of God, who has promised to hear the prayers of all. "Ask, and it shall be given; seek, and you shall find"—*Luke*, xi. 9. We must pray and continue to pray without interruption. If we cease to pray we shall be defeated; but if we persevere in prayer we shall conquer.

SERMON XX.

FOR PALM SUNDAY.

On the evil effects of bad habits.

"Go ye into the village that is over against you, and immediately you shall find an ass tied"—*Matt.*, xxi. 2.

WISHING to enter Jerusalem, to be there acknowledged as the promised Messiah sent by God for the salvation of the world, the Saviour said to his disciples: Go to a certain village, and you shall find an ass tied, and a colt with her: loose them, and bring them to me. "The ass which was tied", says St. Bonaventure, "denotes a sinner". This exposition is conformable to the doctrine of the Wise Man, who says, that the wicked are bound by the chains of their own sins. "His own iniquities catch the wicked, and he is fast bound with the rope of his own sins"—*Prov.*, v. 22. But, as Jesus Christ could not sit on the ass before she was loosed, so he cannot dwell in a soul bound with her own iniquities. If, then, brethren, there be among you a soul bound by any bad habit, let her attend to the admonition which the Lord addresses to her this morning. "Loose the bond from off thy neck, O captive daughter of Sion"—*Isa.*, lii. 2. Loose the bonds of your sins, which make you the slave of Satan. Loose the bonds before the habit of sin gains such power over you, as to render your conversion morally impossible, and thus to bring you to eternal perdition. This morning I will show, in three points, the evil effects of bad habits.

First point. A bad habit blinds the understanding.
Second point. It hardens the heart.
Third point. It diminishes our strength.

First point. A bad habit blinds the understanding.

1. Of those who live in the habit of sin, St. Augustine says: "Ipsa consuetudo non sinit videre malum, quod faciunt". The habit of sin blinds sinners, so that they no longer see the evil which they do, nor the ruin which they bring upon themselves; hence they live in blindness, as if there were neither God, nor Heaven, nor Hell, nor eternity. "Sins", adds the saint, "however enormous, when habitual, appear to be small, or not to be sins at all". How then can the soul guard against them, when she is no longer sensible of their deformity, or of the evil which they bring upon her?

2. St Jerome says, that habitual sinners "are not even ashamed of their crimes". Bad actions naturally produce a certain shame; but this feeling is destroyed by the habit of sin. St. Peter compares habitual sinners to swine wallowing in mire. "The sow that was washed *is returned* to her wallowing in the mire"—II. *Pet.*, ii. 22. The very mire of sin blinds them; and therefore, instead of feeling sorrow and shame at their uncleanness, they revel and exult in it. "A fool worketh mischief as it were for sport" —*Prov.*, x. 23. "Who are glad when they have done evil"—*Prov.*, ii. 14. Hence the saints continually seek light from God; for they know that, should he withdraw his light, they may become the greatest of sinners. How, then, do so many Christians, who know by faith that there is a Hell, and a just God, who cannot but chastise the wicked, how, I say, do they continue to live in sin till death, and thus bring themselves to perdition? "Their own malice blinded them"—*Wis.*, ii. 21. Sin blinds them, and thus they are lost.

3. Job says, that habitual sinners are full of iniquities. "His

bones shall be filled with the vices of his youth"—xx. 11. Every sin produces darkness in the understanding. Hence, the more sins are multiplied by a bad habit, the greater the blindness they cause. The light of the sun cannot enter a vessel filled with clay; and a heart full of vices cannot admit the light of God, which would make visible to the soul the abyss into which she is running. Bereft of light, the habitual sinner goes on from sin to sin, without ever thinking of repentance. "The wicked walk round about"—*Ps.*, xi. 9. Fallen into the dark pit of evil habits, he thinks only of sinning, he speaks only of sins, and no longer sees the evil of sin. In fine, he becomes like a brute devoid of reason, and seeks and desires only what pleases the senses. "And man, when he was in honour, did not understand: he is compared to senseless beasts, and is become like to them"—*Ps.*, xlviii. 13. Hence the words of the Wise Man are fulfilled with regard to habitual sinners. "The wicked man, when he comes into the depth of sins, contemneth"—*Prov.*, xviii. 3. This passage St. Chrysostom applies to habitual sinners, who, shut up in a pit of darkness, despise sermons, calls of God, admonitions, censures, Hell, and God, and become like the vulture that waits to be killed by the fowler, rather than abandon the corrupt carcass on which it feeds.

4. Brethren, let us tremble, as David did when he said: "Let not the tempests of water drown me, nor the deep swallow me up; and let not the pit shut her mouth upon me"—*Ps.*, lxviii. 16. Should a person fall into a pit, there is hope of deliverance as long as the mouth of the pit is not closed; but, as soon as it is shut, he is lost. When a sinner falls into a bad habit, the mouth of the pit is gradually closed as his sins are multiplied: the moment the mouth of the pit is shut, he is abandoned by God. Dearly beloved sinners, if you have contracted a habit of any sin, endeavour instantly to go out of that pit of Hell, before God shall deprive you entirely of his light, and abandon you; for, as soon as he abandons you by the total withdrawal of his light, all is over, and you are lost.

Second point. A bad habit hardens the heart.

5. The habit of sin not only blinds the understanding, but also hardens the heart of the sinner. "His heart shall be as

hard as a stone, and as firm as a smith's anvil"—*Job*, xli. 15. By the habit of sin the heart becomes like a stone; and, as the anvil is hardened by repeated strokes of the hammer, so, instead of being softened by divine inspirations, or by instructions, the soul of the habitual sinner is rendered more obdurate by sermons on the judgment of God, on the torments of the damned, and on the passion of Jesus Christ: *his heart shall be firm as a smith's anvil.* "Their heart", says St. Augustine, "is hardened against the dew of grace, so as to produce no fruit". Divine calls, remorses of conscience, terrors of divine justice, are showers of divine grace; but when, instead of drawing fruit from these divine blessings, the habitual sinner continues to commit sin, he hardens his heart, and thus, according to St. Thomas of Villanova, he gives a sign of his certain damnation—"*Induratio damnationis indicium*";—for, from the loss of God's light and the hardness of his heart, the sinner will, according to the terrible threat of the Holy Ghost, remain obstinate till death. "A hard heart shall fare evil at the end"—*Eccl.*, iii. 27.

6. Of what use are confessions, when, in a short time after them, the sinner returns to the same vices? "He who strikes his breast", says St. Augustine, "and does not amend, confirms, but does not take away sins". When you strike your breast in the tribunal of penance, but do not amend and remove the occasions of sin, you then, according to the saint, do not take away your sins, but you make them more firm and permanent; that is, you render yourself more obstinate in sin. "The wicked walk round about"—*Ps.*, xi. 9. Such is the unhappy life of habitual sinners. They go round about from sin to sin; and if they abstain for a little, they immediately, at the first occasion of temptation, return to their former iniquities. St. Bernard regards as certain the damnation of such sinners: "Væ homini, qui sequitur hunc circuitum"—*serm.* xii., *sup. Psalmos.*

7. But some young persons may say: I will hereafter amend, and sincerely give myself to God. But, if a habit of sin takes possession of you, when will you amend? The Holy Ghost declares, that a young man who contracts an evil habit, will not relinquish it even in his old age. "A young man, according to his way, even when he is old, he will not depart from it"—

Prov., xxii. 6. Habitual sinners have been known to yield, even at the hour of death, to the sins which they had been in the habit of committing. Father Recupito relates, that a person condemned to death, even while he was going to the place of execution, raised his eyes, saw a young female, and consented to a bad thought. We read in a work of Father Gisolfo, that a certain blasphemer, who had been likewise condemned to death, when thrown off the scaffold, broke out into a blasphemy, and died in that miserable state.

8. "He hath mercy on whom he will, and whom he will he hardeneth"—*Rom.*, ix. 18. God shows mercy for a certain time, and then he hardens the heart of the sinner. How does God harden the hearts of sinners? St. Augustine answers: "Obduratio Dei est non misereri". The Lord does not directly harden the heart of habitual sinners; but, in punishment of their ingratitude for his benefits, he withdraws from them his graces, and thus their hearts are hardened, and become like a stone. "*God does not harden the heart by imparting malice, but by withholding mercy*". God does not render sinners obdurate by infusing the malice of obstinacy, but by not giving them the efficacious graces by which they would be converted. By the withdrawal of the sun's heat from the earth, water is hardened into ice.

9. St. Bernard teaches, that hardness or obstinacy of heart does not take place suddenly; but, by degrees the soul becomes insensible to the divine threats, and more obstinate by divine chastisements. "Paulatim in cordis duritiam itur: cor durum non minis cedit, flagellis duratur". In habitual sinners are verified the words of David, "At thy rebuke, O God of Jacob, they have slumbered"—*Ps.*, lxxv. 7. Even earthquakes, thunders, and sudden deaths do not terrify an habitual sinner. Instead of awaking him to a sense of his miserable state, they rather bring on that deadly sleep in which he slumbers and is lost.

Third point. A bad habit diminishes our strength.

10. "He hath torn me with wound upon wound; he hath rushed in upon me like a giant"—*Job*, xvi. 15. On this text St. Gregory reasons thus: A person assailed by an enemy, is not rendered unable to defend himself by the first wound

which he receives; but, should he receive a second and a third, his strength will be so much exhausted, that death will be the consequence. It is so with sin: after the first and second wound which it inflicts on the soul, she shall still have some strength, but only through the divine grace. But, if she continue to indulge in vice, sin, becoming habitual, rushes upon her like a giant, and leaves her without any power to resist it. St. Bernard compares the habitual sinner to a person who has fallen under a large stone, which he is unable to remove. A person in such a case will rise only with difficulty. "The man on whom the weight of a bad habit presses, rises with difficulty". St. Gregory says: "Lapis superpositus, cum consuetudine mens in peccato demoratur ut etsi velit exsurgere, jam non possit quia moles desuper premit"—*Moral., lib.* XXVI. *c.* xxiv.

11. St. Thomas of Villanova teaches, that a soul which is deprived of the grace of God, cannot long abstain from new sins. "Anima a gratia destituta diu evadere ulteriora peccata non potest"—*Conc.* 4 *in Dom.* 4 *quadrages.* In expounding the words of David, "O my God, make them like a wheel, and as stubble before the wind"—*Ps.*, lxxxii. 14, St. Gregory says, that the man who struggled for a time before he fell into the habit of sin, as soon as he contracts the habit, yields, and yields again to every temptation, with as much facility as a straw is moved by the slightest blast of wind. Habitual sinners, according to St. Chrysostom, become so weak in resisting the attacks of the Devil, that, dragged to sin by their evil habit, they are sometimes driven to sin against their inclination. "Dura res est consuetudo, quæ nonnunquam nolentes committere cogit illicita". Yes; because, as St. Augustine says, a bad habit in the course of time brings on a certain necessity of falling into sin. "Dum consuetudini non resistitur, facta est necessitas".

12. St. Bernardine of Sienna says, that evil habits are changed into one's nature. "Usus veritur in natura". Hence, as it is necessary for men to breathe, so it appears that it becomes necessary for habitual sinners to commit sins. They are thus made the slaves of sin. I say, the *slaves.* In society there are servants, who serve for wages, and there are slaves, who serve by force and without remuneration. Having sold

themselves as slaves to the Devil, habitual sinners are reduced to such a degree of slavery, that they sometimes sin without pleasure, and sometimes even without being in the occasion of sin. St. Bernardine compares them to the wings of a wind-mill, which continue to turn the mill even when there is no corn to be ground; that is, they continue to commit sin, at least by indulging bad thoughts, even when there is no occasion of sin presented to them. The unhappy beings, as St. Chrysostom says, having lost the divine aid, no longer do what they wish themselves, but what the Devil wishes. "Homo perdito Dei auxilio, non quod vult agit, sed quod diabolus".

13. Listen to what happened in a city in Italy. A certain young man, who had contracted a vicious habit, though frequently called by God, and admonished by friends to amend his life, continued to live in sin. One day he saw his sister suddenly struck dead. He was terrified for a short time; but she was scarcely buried, when he forgot her death and returned to the vomit. In two months after he was confined to bed by a slow fever. He then sent for a confessor, and made his confession. But after all this, on a certain day, he exclaimed: Alas! how late have I known the rigour of divine justice! And turning to his physician, he said: Do not torment me any longer by medicines; for my disease is incurable. I know for certain that it will bring me to the grave. And to his friends, who stood around, he said: As for the life of this body of mine there is no remedy, so for the life of my poor soul there is no hope. I expect eternal death. God has abandoned me; this I see in the hardness of my heart. Friends and religious came to encourage him to hope in the mercy of God; but his answer to all their exhortations was, God has abandoned me. The writer who relates this fact says, that, being alone with the young man, he said to him: Have courage; unite yourself with God; receive the viaticum. Friend, replied the young man, you speak to a stone. The confession which I have made has been null for want of sorrow. I do not wish for a confessor, nor for the sacraments. Do not bring me the viaticum; for, should you bring it, I will do that which must excite horror. He then went away quite disconsolate; and returning to see the young man, learned from his relatives that he expired during

the night without the aid of a priest, and, that, near his room frightful howlings were heard.

14. Behold the end of habitual sinners! Brethren, if you have the misfortune of having contracted a habit of sin, make, as soon as possible, a general confession; for your past confessions can scarcely have been valid. Go forth instantly from the slavery of the Devil. Attend to the advice of the Holy Ghost. "Give not thy ears to the cruel"—*Prov.*, v. 9. Why will you serve the Devil, your enemy, who is so cruel a master—who makes you lead a life of misery here, to bring you to a life of still greater misery in Hell for all eternity? "*Lazarus, come forth*". Go out of the pit of sin; give yourself immediately to God, who calls you, and is ready to receive you if you return to him. Tremble! this may be for you the last call, to which, if you do not correspond, you shall be lost.

SERMON XXI.

FOR EASTER SUNDAY.

On the miserable state of relapsing sinners.

"Be not affrighted: you seek Jesus of Nazareth, who was crucified. He is risen: he is not here"—*Mark*, xvi. 6.

I HOPE, my dear Christians, that, as Christ is risen, you have, in this holy paschal time, gone to confession, and have risen from your sins. But, attend to what St. Jerome teaches—that many begin well, but few persevere. "Incipere multorum est, perseverare paucorum". Now the Holy Ghost declares, that he who perseveres in holiness to death, and not they who begin a good life, shall be saved. "But he that shall persevere to the end, he shall be saved"—*Matt.*, xxiv. 13. The crown of Paradise, says St. Bernard, is promised to those who commence, but is given only to those who persevere. "Inchoantibus præmium promittitur, perseverantibus datur"—*ser.* vi., *de modo bene viv.* Since, then, brethren, you have resolved to give yourselves to

God, listen to the admonition of the Holy Ghost: "Son, when thou comest to the service of God, stand in justice and in fear, and prepare thy soul for temptation"—*Eccl.*, ii. 1. Do not imagine that you shall have no more temptations, but prepare yourself for the combat, and guard against a relapse into the sins you have confessed; for, if you lose the grace of God again, you shall find it difficult to recover it. I intend this day to show you the miserable state of relapsing sinners; that is, of those who after confession, miserably fall back into the sins which they confessed.

1. Since, then, dearly beloved Christians, you have made a sincere confession of your sins, Jesus Christ says to you what he said to the paralytic: "Behold, thou art made whole. Sin no more, lest some worse thing happen to thee"—*John*, v. 14. By the confessions which you have made, your souls are healed, but not as yet saved; for, if you return to sin, you shall be again condemned to Hell, and the injury caused by the relapse shall be far greater than that which you sustained from your former sins. "Audis", says St. Bernard, "recidere quam incidere, esse deterius". If a man recover from a mortal disease, and afterwards fall back into it, he shall have lost so much of his natural strength, that his recovery from the relapse will be impossible. This is precisely what happens to relapsing sinners: returning to the vomit—that is, taking back into the soul the sins vomited forth in confession—they shall be so weak, that they will become objects of amusement to the Devil. St. Anselm says, that the Devil acquires a certain dominion over them, so that he makes them fall, and fall again as he wishes. Hence the miserable beings become like birds with which a child amuses himself. He allows them, from time to time, to fly to a certain height, and then draws them back again when he pleases, by means of a cord made fast to them. Such is the manner in which the Devil treats relapsing sinners. "Sed quia ab hoste tenentur, volantes in eadem vitia dejiciuntur".

2. St. Paul tells us, that we have to contend not with men like ourselves, made of flesh and blood, but with the princes of Hell. "Our wrestling is not against flesh and blood, but against principalities and powers"—*Ephes.*, vi. 12. By these words he wishes to admonish us that we have not strength to resist the powers of Hell, and that, to resist them, the divine aid is abso-

lutely necessary: without it, we shall be always defeated; but, with the assistance of God's grace, we shall, according to the same apostle, be able to do all things, and shall conquer all enemies. "I can do all things in him who strengtheneth me" —*Phil.*, iv. 13. But this assistance God gives only to those who pray for it. "Ask, and it shall be given you; seek, and you shall find"—*Matt.*, vii. 7. They who neglect to ask, do not receive. Let us, then, be careful not to trust in our resolutions: if we place our confidence in them, we shall be lost. When we are tempted to relapse into sin, we must put our whole trust in the assistance of God, who infallibly hears all who invoke his aid.

3. "He that thinketh himself to stand, let him take heed, lest he fall"—I. *Cor.*, x. 12. They who are in the state of grace should, according to St. Paul, be careful not to fall into sin, particularly if they have been ever guilty of mortal sins; for a relapse into sin brings greater evil on the soul. "And the last state of that man becomes worse than the first"—*Luke*, xi. 26.

4. We are told in the holy Scriptures, that the enemy "will offer victims to his drag, and will sacrifice to his net; because through them his meat is made dainty"—*Habac.*, i. 16. In explaining this passage, St. Jerome says, that the Devil seeks to catch in his nets all men, in order to sacrifice them to the divine justice by their damnation. Sinners, who are already in the net, he endeavours to bind with new chains; but the friends of God are his *dainty meats.* To make them his slaves, and to rob them of all they have acquired, he prepares stronger snares. "The more fervently", says Denis the Carthusian, "a soul endeavours to serve God, the more fiercely does the adversary rage against her". The closer the union of a Christian with God, and the greater his efforts to serve God, the more the enemy is armed with rage, and the more strenuously he labours to enter into the soul from which he has been expelled. "When", says the Redeemer, "the unclean spirit is gone out of a man, seeking rest, and not finding, he saith: I will return into my house, whence I came out"—*Luke*, xi. 24. Should he succeed in reëntering, he will not enter alone, but will bring with him associates to fortify himself in the soul of which he has again got possession. Thus, the second destruction of that miserable soul shall be greater

than the first. "And the last state of that man becomes worse than the first"—*Luke*, xi. 26.

5. To God, the relapse of ungrateful Christians is very displeasing. Because, after he had called and pardoned them with so much love, he sees that, forgetful of his mercies to them, they again turn their back upon him and renounce his grace. "If my enemy had reviled me, I would verily have borne with it. But thou, a man of one mind, my guide and familiar, who didst take sweet meats together with me"—*Ps.*, liv. 13, *etc.* Had my enemy, says the Lord, insulted me, I would have felt less pain; but to see you rebel against me, after I had restored my friendship to you, and after I had made you sit at my table, to eat my own flesh, grieves me to the heart, and impels me to take vengeance on you. Miserable the man who, after having received so many graces from God, becomes the enemy, from being the friend of God. He shall find the sword of divine vengeance prepared to chastise him. "And he that passes over from justice to sin, God hath prepared such an one for the sword"—*Eccl.*, xxvi. 27.

6. Some of you may say: If I relapse, I will soon rise again; for I will immediately prepare myself for confession. To those who speak in this manner shall happen what befell Samson. He allowed himself to be deluded by Dalila: while he was asleep she cut off his hair, and his strength departed from him. Awaking from sleep, he said: "I will go out as I did before, and shake myself, not knowing that the Lord was departed from him"—*Judges*, xvi. 20. He expected to deliver himself, as on former occasions, from the hands of the Philistines. But, because his strength had departed from him, he was made their slave. They pulled out his eyes, and binding him in chains, shut him up in prison. After relapsing into sin a Christian loses the strength necessary to resist temptations, because *the Lord departs from him.* He abandons him by withholding the efficacious aid necessary to overcome temptations; and the miserable man remains blind and abandoned in his sin.

7. "No man putting his hand to the plough, and looking back, is fit for the kingdom of God"—*Luke*, ix. 62. Behold a faithful picture of a relapsing sinner. Mark the words *no man:* no one, says Jesus Christ, who begins to serve me, and looks back, is fit to enter Heaven. According to Origen, the

addition of a new sin to one committed before is like the addition of a new wound to a wound just inflicted. "Cum peccatum peccato adjicitur, sicut vulnus vulneri"—*hom.* i. *in Ps.* If a wound be inflicted on any member of the body, that member certainly loses its original vigour. But, if it receives a second wound, it shall lose all strength and motion, without hope of recovery. The great evil of a relapse into sin is, that it renders the soul so weak, that she has but little strength to resist temptation. For, says St. Thomas, "after a fault has been remitted, the dispositions produced by the preceding acts remain"—1 *p.*, *qu.* 86, *art.* 5. Every sin, though pardoned, always leaves a wound on the soul. When to this wound a new one is added, the soul becomes so weak that, without a special and extraordinary grace from God, it is impossible for her to conquer temptations.

8. Let us, then, brethren, tremble at the thought of relapsing into sin, and let us beware of availing ourselves of the mercy of God to continue to offend him. "He", says St. Augustine, "who has promised pardon to penitents, has promised repentance to no one". God has indeed promised to pardon all who repent of their sins; but he has not promised to any one the grace to repent of the faults which he has committed. Sorrow for sin is a pure gift of God: if he withholds it, how will you repent? And without repentance, how can you obtain pardon? Ah! the Lord will not allow himself to be mocked. "Be not deceived", says St. Paul; "God is not mocked"—*Gal.*, vi. 7. St. Isidore tells us, that the man who repeats the sin which he before detested, is not a penitent, but a scoffer of God's majesty. "Irrisor, et non pœnitens est, pui adhuc agit, quod pœnitet"—*de Sum. Bono.* And Tertullian teaches, that, where there is no amendment, repentance is not sincere. "Ubi emendatio nulla, pœnitentia nulla"—*de Pœnit.*

9. "Be penitent", said St. Peter in a discourse to the Jews, "and be converted, that your sins may be blotted out"—*Acts*, iii. 19. Many repent, but are not converted. They feel a certain sorrow for the irregularities of their lives, but do not sincerely return to God. They go to confession, strike their breasts, and promise to amend; but they do not make a firm resolution to change their lives. They who resolve firmly on a change of life, persevere, or at least preserve themselves for a

considerable time in the grace of God. But they who relapse into sin soon after confession, show, as St. Peter says, that they repent, but are not converted; and such persons shall in the end die an unhappy death. "Plerumque", says St. Gregory, "mali sic compunguntur ad justitiam, sicut plerumque boni tentantur ad culpam" —*Pastor.*, *p.* 3, *admon.* 31. As the just have frequent temptations to sin, but yield not to them, because their will abhors them, so sinners feel certain impulses to virtue; but these are not sufficient to produce a true conversion. The Wise Man tells us that mercy shall be shown to him who confesses his sins and abandons them, but not to those who merely confess their transgressions. "He that shall confess *his sins*, and forsake them, shall obtain mercy"—*Prov.*, xxviii. 13. He, then, who does not give up, but returns to, sin after confession, shall not obtain mercy from God, but shall die a victim of divine justice. He may expect to die the death of a certain young Englishman, who, as is related in the history of England, was in the habit of relapsing into sins against purity. He always fell back into these sins after confession. At the hour of death he confessed his sins, and died in a manner which gave reason to hope for his salvation. But, while a holy priest was celebrating or preparing to celebrate Mass for his departed soul, the miserable young man appeared to him, and said that he was damned. He added that, at the point of death, being tempted to indulge a bad thought, he felt himself as it were forced to consent, and, as he was accustomed to do in the former part of his life, he yielded to the temptation, and thus was lost.

10. Is there then no means of salvation for relapsing sinners? I do not say this; but I adopt the maxim of physicians. "In magnis morbis a magnis initium medendi sumere oportet". In malignant diseases, powerful remedies are necessary. To return to the way of salvation, the relapsing sinner must do great violence to himself. "The kingdom of Heaven suffereth violence, and the violent bear it away"—*Mat.*, xi. 12. In the beginning of a new life, the relapsing sinner must do violence to himself in order to root out the bad habits which he has contracted, and to acquire habits of virtue; for when he has acquired habits of virtue, the observance of the divine commands shall become easy and even sweet. The Lord once said to St. Bridget, that, to those who bear with fortitude the first punctures of the

thorns which they experience in the attacks of the senses, in avoding occasions of sin, and in withdrawing from dangerous conversations, these thorns are by degrees changed into roses.

11. But, to use the necessary violence, and to lead a life of regularity, you must adopt the proper means; otherwise, you shall do nothing. After rising in the moning, you must make acts of thanksgiving, of the love of God, and of oblation of the actions of the day. You must also renew your resolution never to offend God, and beg of Jesus Christ and his holy mother to preserve you from sin during the day. Afterwards, make your meditation, and hear Mass. During the day, make a spiritual lecture and a visit to the most holy sacrament. In the evening, say the Rosary and make an examination of conscience. Receive the holy communion at least once a-week, or more frequently if your director advises you. Be careful to choose a confessor, to whom you will regularly go to confession. It is also very useful to make a spiritual retreat every year in some religious house. Honour the mother of God every day by some particular devotion, and by fasting on every Saturday. She is the mother of perseverance, and promises to obtain it for all who serve her "They that work by me shall not sin"—*Eccl.*, xxiv. 30. Above all, it is necessary to ask of God every morning the gift of perseverance, and to beg of the Blessed Virgin to obtain it for you, and particularly in the time of temptation, by invoking the name of Jesus and Mary as long as the temptation lasts. Happy the man who will continue to act in this manner, and shall be found so doing when Jesus Christ shall come to judge him. "Blessed is that servant, whom, when his Lord shall come, he shall find so doing"—*Matt.*, xxiv. 46.

SERMON XXII.

FOR THE FIRST SUNDAY AFTER EASTER.

On avoiding the occasions of sin.

" When the doors were shut, where the disciples were gathered together for fear of the Jews, Jesus came and stood in the midst"—*John*, xx. 19.

We find in this day's gospel, that, after his resurrection, Jesus Christ entered, though the doors were closed, into the house in which the apostles were assembled, and stood in the midst of them. St. Thomas says, that the mystic meaning of this miracle is, that the Lord does not enter into our souls unless we keep the door of the senses shut. " Mistice per hoc datur intelligi, quod Christus nobis apparet quando fores, id est sensus sunt clausi". If, then, we wish Jesus Christ to dwell within us, we must keep the doors of our senses closed against dangerous occasions, otherwise the Devil will make us his slaves. I will show to-day the great danger of perdition to which they who do not avoid the occasions of sin expose themselves.

1. We read in the Scriptures, that Christ and Lazarus arose from the dead. Christ rose to die no more—" Christ rising from the dead, dieth now no more"—*Rom.*, vi. 9; but Lazarus rose and died again. The Abbot Guerric remarks, that Christ rose free and unbound; " but Lazarus came forth bound feet and hands"—*John*, xi. 44. Miserable the man, adds this author, who rises from sin bound by any dangerous occasion: he will die again by losing the divine grace. He, then, who wishes to save his soul, must not only abandon sin, but also the occasions of sin: that is, he must renounce such an intimacy, such a house; he must renounce those wicked companions, and all similar occasions that incite him to sin.

2. In consequence of original sin, we all have an inclination to do what is forbidden. Hence St. Paul complained, that he experienced in himself a law opposed to reason. " But I see another law in my members, fighting against the law of my mind, and captivating me in the law of sin"—*Rom.*, vii. 23.

Now, when a dangerous occasion is present, it violently excites our corrupt desires, so that it is then very difficult to resist them; because God withholds efficacious helps from those who voluntarily expose themselves to the occasion of sin. "He that loveth danger shall perish in it"—*Eccl.*, iii. 27. "When", says St. Thomas, in his comment on this passage, "we expose ourselves to danger, God abandons us in it". St. Bernardine of Sienna teaches, that the counsel of avoiding the occasions of sin, is the best of all counsel, and as it were the foundation of religion. "Inter consilia Christi unum celeberrimum, et quasi religionis fundamentum est, fugere peccatorum occasiones".

3. St. Peter says, that "the Devil goeth about seeking whom he may devour"—I. *Pet.*, v. 8. He is constantly going about our souls, endeavouring to enter and take possession of them. Hence, he seeks to place before us the occasions of sin, by which he enters the soul. "Explorat", says St. Cyprian, "an sit pars cujus aditu penetret". When the soul yields to the suggestions of the Devil, and exposes herself to the occasions of sin, he easily enters and devours her. The ruin of our first parents arose from their not flying from the occasions of sin. God had prohibited them not only to eat, but even to touch the forbidden apple. In answer to the serpent tempting her, Eve said: "God hath commanded us that we should not eat, and that we should not touch it"—*Gen.*, iii. 3. But *she saw, took, and eat* the forbidden fruit: she first looked at it, she then took it into her hands, and afterwards eat it. This is what ordinarily happens to all who expose themselves to the occasions of sin. Hence, being once compelled by exorcisms to tell the sermon which displeased him most, the Devil confessed that it was the sermon on avoiding the occasions of sin. As long as we expose ourselves to the occasions of sin, the Devil laughs at all our good purposes and promises made to God. The greatest care of the enemy is, to induce us not to avoid evil occasions; for these occasions, like a veil placed before the eyes, prevent us from seeing either the lights received from God, or the eternal truths, or the resolutions we have made; in a word, they make us forget all, and as it were force us into sin.

4. "Know it to be a communication with death; for thou art going in the midst of snares"—*Eccl.*, ix. 20. Every one born in this world, enters into the midst of snares. Hence the Wise

Man advises those who wish to be secure, to guard themselves against the snares of the world, and to withdraw from them. "He that is aware of the snares shall be secure"—*Prov.*, xi. 15. But if, instead of withdrawing from them, a Christian approaches to them, how can he avoid being caught by them? Hence, after having, with so much loss, learned the danger of exposing himself to the danger of sin, David said, that, to continue faithful to God, he kept at a distance from every occasion which could lead him to relapse. "I have restrained my feet from every evil way, that I may keep thy words"—*Ps.*, cxviii. 101. He does not say, from every sin, but from every evil way which conducts to sin. The Devil is careful to find pretexts to make us believe that certain occasions to which we expose ourselves, are not voluntary, but necessary. When the occasion in which we are placed is really necessary, the Lord always helps us to avoid sin; but we sometimes imagine certain necessities which are not sufficient to excuse us. "A treasure is never safe", says St. Cyprian, "as long as a robber is harboured within; nor is a lamb secure while it dwells in the same den with a wolf"—*lib. de Sing. Cler.* The saint speaks against those who do not wish to remove the occasions of sin, and still say: *I am not afraid that I shall fall.* As no one can be secure of his treasure if he keeps a thief in his house, and as a lamb cannot be sure of its life if it remain in the den of a wolf, so likewise no one can be secure of the treasure of divine grace, if he is resolved to continue in the occasion of sin. St. James teaches, that every man has within himself a powerful enemy, that is, his own evil inclinations, which tempt him to sin. "Every man is tempted by his own concupiscence, drawn away, and allured"—*St. James*, i. 14. If, then, we do not fly from the external occasions, how can we resist temptation and avoid sin? Let us, therefore, place before our eyes the general remedy which Jesus Christ has prescribed for conquering temptations and saving our souls. "If thy right eye scandalize thee, pluck it out and cast it from thee"—*Matt.*, v. 29. If you find that your right eye is to you a cause of damnation, you must pull it out and cast it far from you; that is, when there is danger of losing your soul, you must fly from all evil occasions. St. Francis of Assisium used to say, as I have stated in another sermon, that the Devil does not seek, in the beginning, to bind timorous souls with the chain of mortal sin; because they would be alarmed at the thought of committing mortal sin, and would fly from it with horror: he endeavours to bind them by a single hair, which does not excite much fear; because by this means, he will succeed more easily in strengthening their bonds, till he makes them his slaves. Hence he who wishes to be free from the danger of being the slave of Hell, must break all the hairs by which the enemy attempts to bind him; that is, he must avoid all occasions of sin, such as certain salutations, billets, little presents, and words of affection. With regard to those who have had a habit of impurity, it will not be sufficient to avoid proximate occasions; if they do not fly from remote occasions, they will very easily relapse into their former sins.

5. Impurity, says St. Augustine, is a vice which makes war on all, and which few conquer. "*The fight is common; but the victory rare*". How many miserable souls have entered the contest with this vice, and have been defeated! But to induce you to expose yourselves to occasions of this sin, the Devil will tell you not to be afraid of being overcome by the temptation. "I do not wish", says St. Jerome, "to fight with the hope of victory, lest I should sometimes lose the victory". I will not expose myself to the combat with the hope of conquering; because, by voluntarily engaging in the fight, I shall lose my soul and my God. To escape defeat in this struggle, a great grace of God is necessary; and to render ourselves worthy of this grace, we must, on our part, avoid the occasions of sin. To practise the virtue of chastity, it is necessary to recommend ourselves continually to God: we have not strength to preserve it; that strength must be the gift of God. "And as I knew", says the Wise Man, "that I could not otherwise be continent, except God gave it,...I went to the Lord, and besought him"—*Wis.*, viii. 21. But if we expose ourselves to the occasions of sin, we ourselves shall provide our rebellious flesh with arms to make war against the soul. "Neither", says the Apostle, "yield ye your members as instruments of sin unto iniquity" —*Rom.*, vi. 13. In explaining this passage, St. Cyril of Alexandria says: "You stimulate the flesh; you arm it, and make it powerful against the spirit". St. Philip Neri used to say, that in the war against the vice of impurity, the victory is gained by cowards—that is, by those who fly from the occasions of this

sin. But the man who exposes himself to it, arms his flesh, and renders it so powerful, that it will be morally impossible for him to resist its attacks.

6. "Cry", says the Lord to Isaias; "all flesh is grass"—*Isa.*, xl. 6. Now, says St. John Chrysostom, if all flesh is grass, it is as foolish for a man who exposes himself to the occasion of sin to hope to preserve the virtue of purity, as to expect that hay, into which a torch has been thrown, will not take fire. "Put a torch into hay, and then dare to deny that the hay will burn". No, says St. Cyprian; it is impossible to stand in the midst of flames, and not to burn. "Impossibile est flammis circumdari et non ardere"—*de Sing. Cler.* "Can a man", says the Holy Ghost, "hide fire in his bosom, and his garments not burn? or can he walk upon hot coals, and his feet not be burnt?"—*Prov.*, vi 27, 28 Not to be burnt in such circumstances would be a miracle. St. Bernard teaches, that to preserve chastity, and, at the same time, to expose oneself to the proximate occasion of sin, "*is a greater miracle than to raise a dead man to life*".

7. In explaining the fifth Psalm, St. Augustine says, that "he who is unwilling to fly from danger, wishes to perish in it". Hence, in another place, he exhorts those who wish to conquer, and not to perish, to avoid dangerous occasions. "In the occasion of falling into sin, take flight, if you desire to gain the victory"—*serm.* ccl., *de temp.* Some foolishly trust in their own strength, and do not see that their strength is like that of tow placed in the fire. "And your strength shall be as the ashes of tow"—*Isa.*, i. 31. Others, trusting in the change which has taken place in their life, in their confessions, and in the promises they have made to God, say: Through the grace of the Lord, I have now no bad motive in seeking the company of such a person; her presence is not even an occasion of temptations. Listen, all you who speak in this manner. In Mauritania there are bears that go in quest of the apes, to feed upon them: as soon as a bear appears, the apes run up the trees, and thus save themselves. But what does the bear do? He stretches himself on the ground as if dead, and waits till the apes descend from the trees. The moment he sees that they have descended, he springs up, seizes on them, and devours them. It is thus the Devil acts: he makes the temptation appear to be

dead; but when a soul descends, and exposes herself to the occasion of sin, he stirs up temptation, and devours her. Oh! how many miserable souls, devoted to spiritual things, to mental prayer, to frequent communion, and to a life of holiness, have by exposing themselves to the occasion of sin, become the slaves of the Devil! We find in ecclesiastical history that a holy woman, who employed herself in the pious office of burying the martyrs, once found among them one who was not as yet dead. She brought him into her own house, and procured a physician and medicine for him, till he recovered. But, what happened? These two saints (as they might be called—one of them on the point of being a martyr, the other devoting her time to works of mercy with so much risk of being persecuted by the tyrants) first fell into sin and lost the grace of God, and, becoming weaker by sin, afterwards denied the faith. St. Macarius relates a similar fact regarding an old man who suffered to be half-burned in defence of the faith; but, being brought back into prison, he, unfortunately for himself, formed an intimacy with a devout woman who served the martyrs, and fell into sin.

8. The Holy Ghost tells us, that we must fly from sin as from a serpent. "Flee from sins as from the face of a serpent"—*Eccl.*, xxi. 2. Hence, as we not only avoid the bite of a serpent, but are careful neither to touch nor approach it, so we must fly not only from sin, but also from the occasion of sin—that is, from the house, the conversation, the person that would lead us to sin. St. Isidore says, that he who wishes to remain near a serpent will not remain long unhurt. "Juxta serpentem positus non erit diu illæsus"—*lib.* II. *Solit.* Hence, if any person is likely to prove an occasion of your ruin, the admonition of the Wise Man is, "Remove thy way far from her, and come not nigh the doors of her house"—*Prov.*, v. 8. He not only tells you not to enter the house which has been to you a road to Hell ("*Her house is the way to Hell*"—*Prov.*, vii. 27); but he also cautions you not to approach it, and even to keep at a distance from it. "Remove thy way far from her". But, you will say, if I abandon that house, my temporal affairs shall suffer. It is better that you should suffer a temporal loss, than that you should lose your soul and your God. You must be persuaded that, in whatever regards chastity, there cannot be too great caution.

If we wish to save our souls from sin and Hell, we must always fear and tremble. "With fear and trembling work out your salvation"—*Phil.*, ii. 12. He who is not fearful, but exposes himself to occasions of sin, shall scarcely be saved. Hence, in our prayers we ought to say every day, and several times in the day, that petition of the Our Father—"*and lead us not into temptation*". Lord, do not permit me to be attacked by those temptations which would deprive me of your grace. We cannot merit the grace of perseverance; but, according to St. Augustine, God grants it to every one that asks it, because he has promised to hear all who pray to him. Hence, the holy doctor says, that the Lord, "*by his promises, has made himself a debtor*".

SERMON XXIII.

FOR THE SECOND SUNDAY AFTER EASTER.

On scandal.

"The wolf catcheth and scattereth the sheep"—*John*, x. 12.

The wolves that catch and scatter the sheep of Jesus Christ, are the authors of scandal, who, not content with their own destruction, labour to destroy others. But the Lord says: "Wo to that man by whom the scandal cometh"—*Matt.*, xviii. 7. Wo to him who gives scandal, and causes others to lose the grace of God. Origen says, that "a person who impels another to sin, sins more grievously than the other". If, brethren, there be any among you who has given scandal, I will endeavour this day to convince him of the evil he has done, that he may bewail it, and guard against it for the future. I will show, in the first point, the great displeasure which the sin of scandal gives to God; and, in the second, the great punishment which God threatens to inflict on the authors of scandal.

First point. On the great displeasure which the sin of scandal gives to God.

1. It is, in the first place, necessary to explain what is meant by scandal. Behold how St. Thomas defines it: "Scandal is a word or act which gives occasion to the spiritual ruin of one's neighbour"—2, ii. *q.* 45, *art.* 1. Scandal, then, is a word or act by which you are to your neighbour the cause or occasion of losing his soul. It may be direct or indirect. It is direct, when you directly tempt and induce another to commit sin. It is indirect, when, although you foresee that sinful words or actions will be the cause of sin to another, you do not abstain from them. But, scandal, whether it be direct or indirect, if it be in a matter of great moment, is always a mortal sin.

2. Let us now see the great displeasure which the destruction of a neighbour's soul gives to God. To understand it, we must consider how dear every soul is to God. He has created the souls of all men to his own image. "Let us make man to our image and likeness"—*Gen.*, i. 26. Other creatures God has made by a *fiat*—by an act of his will; but the soul of man he has created by his own breath. And *the Lord* breathed into his face the breath of life"—*Gen.*, ii. 7. The soul of your neighbour God has loved for eternity. "I have loved thee with an everlasting love"—*Jer.*, xxxi. 3. He has, moreover, created every soul to be a queen in Paradise, and to be a partner in his glory. "That by these you may be made partakers of the divine nature"—II. *Peter*, i. 4. In Heaven he will make the souls of the saints partakers of his own joy. "Enter thou into the joy of thy Lord"—*Mat.*, xxv. 21. To them he shall give himself as their reward. "I am thy reward exceeding great"—*Gen.*, xv. 1.

3. But nothing can show the value which God sets on the souls of men, more clearly than what the Incarnate Word has done for their redemption from sin and Hell. "If", says St. Eucharius, "you do not believe your Creator, ask your Redeemer how precious you are". Speaking of the care which we ought to have of our brethren, St. Ambrose says: "The great value of the salvation of a brother is known from the death of Christ". We judge of the value of everything by the price paid for it by an intelligent purchaser. Now, Jesus Christ has, according to the Apostle, purchased the souls of men with his own blood. "You are bought with a great price"—I. *Cor.*, vi. 20. We can, then, say, that the soul is of as much value as the blood of a

God. Such, indeed, is the language of St. Hilary. "Tam copioso munere redemptio agitur, ut homo Deum valere videatur" Hence, the Saviour tells us, that whatsoever good or evil we do to the least of his brethren, we do to himself. "So long as you did it to one of these my least brethren, you did it to me"—*Mat.*, xxv. 40.

4. From all this we may infer how great is the displeasure given to God by scandalizing a brother and destroying his soul. It is enough to say, that they who give scandal rob God of a child, and murder a soul, for whose salvation he has spent his blood and his life. Hence, St. Leo calls the authors of scandal murderers. "Quisquis scandalizat, mortem infert animæ proximi". They are the most impious of murderers; because they kill not the body, but the soul, of a brother, and rob Jesus Christ of all his tears, of his sorrows, and of all that he has done and suffered to gain that soul. Hence the Apostle says: "Now, when you sin thus against the brethren, and wound their weak conscience, you sin against Christ"—I. *Cor.*, viii. 12. They who scandalize a brother, sin against Christ; because, as St. Ambrose says, they deprive him of a soul for which he has spent so many years, and submitted to so many toils and labours. It is related, that B. Albertus Magnus spent thirty years in making a head, which resembled the human head, and uttered words; and that St. Thomas, fearing that it was done by the agency of the Devil, took the head and broke it. B. Albertus complained of the act of St. Thomas, saying: "You have broken on me the work of thirty years". I do not assert that this is true; but it is certain that, when Jesus Christ sees a soul destroyed by scandal, he can reprove the author of it, and say to him: Wicked wretch, what have you done? You have deprived me of this soul, for which I have laboured thirty-three years.

5. We read in the Scriptures, that the sons of Jacob, after having sold their brother Joseph to certain merchants, told his father that wild beasts had devoured him. "Fera pessima devoravit eum"—*Gen.*, xxxvii. 20. To convince their father of the truth of what they said, they dipped the coat of Joseph in the blood of a goat, and presented it to him, saying: "See whether this be thy son's coat or not"—*v.* 32. In reply, the afflicted father said with tears: "It is my son's coat: an evil wild beast hath

eaten him"—*v.* 33. Thus, we may imagine that, when a soul is brought into sin by scandal, the devils present to God the garment of that soul dipped in the blood of the Immaculate Lamb, Jesus Christ—that is, the grace lost by that scandalized soul, which Jesus Christ had purchased with his blood—and that they say to the Lord: "See whether this be thy son's coat or not". If God were capable of shedding tears, he would weep more bitterly than Jacob did, at the sight of that lost soul—his murdered child—and would say: "It is my son's coat: an evil wild beast hath eaten him". The Lord will go in search of this wild beast, saying: *Where is the beast? where is the beast that has devoured my child?* When he finds the wild beast, what shall he do with him?

6. "I will", says the Lord by his Prophet Osee, "meet them as a bear that is robbed of her whelps"—*Osee*, xiii. 8. When the bear comes to her den, and finds not her whelps, she goes about the wood in search of the person that took them away. When she discovers the person, oh! with what fury does she rush upon him! It is thus the Lord shall rush upon the authors of scandal, who have robbed him of his children. Those who have given scandal, will say: My neighbour is already damned; how can I repair the evil that has been done? The Lord shall answer: Since you have been the cause of his perdition, you must pay me for the loss of his soul. "I will require his blood at thy hands"—*Ezec.*, iii. 20. It is written in Deuteronomy, "Thou shalt not pity him, but shall require life for life"—xix. 21. You have destroyed a soul; you must suffer the loss of your own. Let us pass to the second point.

Second point. The great punishment which God threatens to inflict on those who give scandal.

7. "Wo to that man by whom the scandal cometh"—*Mat.*, xviii. 7. If the displeasure given to God by scandal be great, the chastisement which awaits the authors of it must be frightful. Behold how Jesus Christ speaks of this chastisement: "But he that shall scandalize one of these little ones that believe in me, it were better for him that a millstone should be hanged about his neck, and that he should be drowned in the depth of the sea"—*Mat.*, xviii. 6. If a malefactor dies on the scaffold, he excites the compassion of the spectators, who, at least, pray for him, if

they cannot deliver him from death. But, were he cast into the depths of the sea, there should be no one present to pity his fate. A certain author says, that Jesus Christ threatens the person who scandalizes a brother with this sort of punishment, to signify that he is so hateful to the angels and saints, that they do not wish to recommend to God the man who has brought a soul to perdition. "He is declared unworthy not only to be assisted, but even to be seen"—*Mansi.*, *cap.* iii. *num.* 4.

8. St. John Chrysostom says, that scandal is so abominable in the eyes of God, that though he overlooks very grevious sins, he cannot allow the sin of scandal to pass without condign punishment. "Tam Deo horribile est scandalum, ut peccata graviora dissimulet non autem peccata ubi frater scandalizatur". God himself says the same by the Prophet Ezechiel: "Every man of the house of Israel, if he...set up the stumbling-block of his iniquity... I will make him an example and a proverb, and will cut him off from the midst of my people"—*Ezec.*, xiv. 7, 8. And, in reality, scandal is one of the sins which we find in the sacred Scriptures punished by God with the greatest rigour. Of Heli, because he did not correct his sons, who gave scandal by stealing the flesh offered in sacrifice (for parents give scandal, not only by giving bad example, but also by not correcting their children as they ought), the Lord said: "Behold I do a thing in Israel: and whosoever shall hear it, both his ears shall tingle"—I. *Kings*, iii. 11. And speaking of the scandal given by the sons of Heli, the inspired writer says: "Wherefore the sin of the young men was exceeding great before the Lord"—*ibid.*, ii. 17. What was this sin, exceeding great? It was, says St. Gregory in explaining this passage, drawing others to sin. "Quia ad peccandum alios pertrahebant". Why was Jeroboam chastised? Because he scandalized the people: he "hath sinned, and made Israel sin"—III. *Kings*, xiv. 16. In the family of Achab, all the members of which were the enemies of God, Jezabel was the most severely chastised. She was thrown down from a window, and devoured by dogs, so that nothing remained but her "skull, and the feet, and the extremities of her hands". And why was she so severely punished? Because *she set Achab on to every evil.*

9. For the sin of scandal Hell was created. "In the begin-

ning God created Heaven and Earth"—*Gen.*, i. 1. But, when did he create Hell? It was when Lucifer began to seduce the angels into rebellion against God. Lest he should continue to pervert those who remained faithful to God, he was banished from Heaven immediately after his sin. Hence Jesus Christ said to the Pharisees, who, by their bad example, scandalized the people, that they were children of the Devil, who was, from the beginning, a murderer of souls. "You are of *your* father, the Devil: he was a murderer from the beginning"—*John*, viii. 44. And when St. Peter gave scandal to Jesus Christ, by suggesting to him not to allow his life to be taken away by the Jews, and thus endeavouring to prevent the accomplishment of redemption, the Redeemer called him a devil. "Go behind me, Satan; thou art a scandal to me"—*Matt.*, xvi. 23. And, in reality, what other office do the authors of scandal perform, than that of a minister of the Devil? If he were not assisted by such impious ministers, he certainly would not succeed in gaining so many souls. A scandalous companion does more injury than a hundred devils.

10. On the words of Ezechias, "Behold, in peace is my bitterness most bitter"—*Isa.*, xxxviii. 17, St. Bernard, in the name of the Church, says: "*Peace from pagans, peace from heretics, but no peace from children*". At present the Church is not persecuted by idolaters, or by heretics, but she is persecuted by scandalous Christians, who are her own children. In catching birds, we employ decoys, that is, certain birds that are blinded, and tied in such a manner that they cannot fly away. It is thus the Devil acts. "When", says St. Ephrem, "a soul has been taken, she becomes a snare to decive others". After having made a young man fall into sin, the enemy first blinds him and binds him as his own slave, and then makes him his decoy to deceive others, and to draw them into the net of sin: he not only impels, but even forces him to deceive others. "The enemy", says St. Leo, "has many whom he compels to deceive others"—*serm. de Nativ.*

11. Miserable wretches! the authors of scandal must suffer in Hell the punishment of all the sins they have made others commit. Cesarius relates (*l.* 2, *c.* vi.) that, after the death of a certain person who had given scandal, a holy man witnessed his judgment and condemnation, and saw, that, at his arrival at

the gates of Hell, all the souls whom he had scandalized, came to meet him, and said to him: Come, accursed wretch, and atone for all the sins which you have made us commit. They then rushed in upon him, and like so many wild beasts, began to tear him in pieces. St. Bernard says, that, in speaking of other sinners, the Scriptures hold out hopes of amendment and pardon; but they speak of those who give scandal, as persons separated from God, of whose salvation there is very little hope. "Loquitur tanquam a Deo separati, unde hisce nulla spes vitæ esse poterit".

12. Behold, then, the miserable state of those who give scandal by their bad example, who utter immodest words before their companions, in the presence of young females, and even of innocent children, who, in consequence of hearing these words, commit a thousand sins. Consider how the angel-guardians of these little ones weep at seeing them in the state of sin, and how they call for vengeance from God against the sacrilegious tongues that have scandalized them. A great chastisement awaits all who ridicule those who practise virtue. For, many, through fear of the contempt and ridicule of others, abandon virtue, and give themselves up to a wicked life. What shall be the punishment of those who bring messages to induce others to sin? or of those who boast of their own wicked actions? O God! instead of weeping and repenting for having offended the Lord, they rejoice and glory in their iniquities! Some advise others to commit sin; others induce them to it; and some, worse than the devils, teach others how to sin. What shall we say of fathers and mothers, who, though it is in their power to prevent the sins of their children, allow them to associate with bad companions, or to frequent certain dangerous houses, and permit their daughters to hold conversations with young men? Oh! with what scourges shall we see such persons chastised on the day of judgment!

13. Perhaps some father of a family among you will say: Then, am I lost because I have given scandal? Is there no hope of salvation for me? No; I will not say that you are past hope—the mercy of God is great. He has promised pardon to all who repent. But, if you wish to save your soul, you must repair the scandal you have given. "Let him", says Eusebius Emissenus, "who has destroyed himself by the destruction of many, redeem

himself by the edification of many"—*hom.* x., *ad Mon.* You have lost your soul, and have destroyed the souls of many by your scandals. You are now bound to repair the evil. As you have hitherto drawn others to sin, so you are bound to draw them to virtue by words of edification, by good example, by avoiding sinful occasions, by frequenting the sacraments, by going often to the church to pray, and by attending sermons. And from this day forward avoid, as you would death, every act and word which could scandalize others. "Let their own ruin", says St. Cyprian, "suffice for those who have fallen"—*lib.* I., *epis.* iii. And St. Thomas of Villanova says: "Let your own sins be sufficient for you". What evil has Jesus Christ done to you, that it is not enough for you to have offended him yourselves, but you wish to make others offend him? This is an excess of cruelty.

14. Be careful, then, never again to give the smallest scandal. And if you wish to save your soul, avoid as much as possible those who give scandal. These incarnate devils shall be damned; but, if you do not avoid them, you will bring yourself to perdition. "Wo to the world because of scandals", says the Lord (*Mat.*, xviii. 7). That is, many are lost because they do not fly from occasions of scandal. But you may say: Such a person is my friend; I am under obligations to him; I expect many favours from him. But Jesus Christ says: "If thy right eye scandalize thee, pluck it out and cast it from thee. It is better for thee, having one eye, to enter into life, than, having two eyes, to be cast into Hell fire"—*Mat.*, xviii. 9. Although a certain person was your right eye, you must withdraw for ever from her; it is better for you to lose an eye and save your soul, than to preserve it and be cast into Hell.

SERMON XXIV.

FOR THE THIRD SUNDAY AFTER EASTER.

On the value of time.

"A little while, and now you shall not see me"—*John*, xvi. 16.

THERE is nothing shorter than time, but there is nothing more valuable. There is nothing shorter than time; because the past is no more, the future is uncertain, and the present is but a moment. This is what Jesus Christ meant when he said: "A little while, and now you shall not see me". We may say the same of our life, which, according to St. James, is but a vapour, which is soon scattered for ever. "For what is your life? It is a vapour which appeareth for a little while"—*James*, iv. 14. But the time of this life is as precious as it is short; for, in every moment, if we spend it well, we can acquire treasures of merits for Heaven; but, if we employ time badly, we may in each moment commit sin, and merit Hell. I mean this day to show you how precious is every moment of the time which God gives us, not to lose it, and much less to commit sin, but to perform good works and to save our souls.

1. "Thus saith the Lord: In an acceptable time I have heard thee, and in the day of salvation I have helped thee"—*Isa.*, xlix. 8. St. Paul explains this passage, and says, that *the acceptable time* is the time in which God has determined to confer his favours upon us. He then adds: "Behold, now is the acceptable time; behold, now is the day of salvation"—II. *Cor.*, vi. 2. The Apostle exhorts us not to spend unprofitably the present time, which he calls the day of salvation; because, perhaps, after this day of salvation, there shall be no salvation for us. "The time", says the same Apostle, "is short: it remaineth that......they that weep *be* as though they wept not; that they that rejoice, as if they rejoiced not; and they that buy, as though they possessed not; and they that use this world, as if they used it not"—I. *Cor.*, vii. 29, 30, 31. Since, then, the

time which we have to remain on this Earth is short, the Apostle tells those who weep, that they ought not to weep, because their sorrows shall soon pass away; and those who rejoice, not to fix their affections on their enjoyments, because they shall soon have an end. Hence he concludes, that we should use this world, not to enjoy its transitory goods, but to merit eternal life.

2. "Son", says the Holy Ghost, "observe the time"—*Eccl.*, iv. 23. Son, learn to preserve time, which is the most precious, and the greatest gift that God can bestow upon you. St. Bernardine of Sienna teaches, that time is of as much value as God; because in every moment of time well spent, the possession of God is merited. He adds, that in every instant of this life a man may obtain the pardon of his sins, the grace of God, and the glory of Paradise. "Modico tempore potest homo lucrari gratiam et gloriam". Hence St. Bonaventure says, that "no loss is of greater moment than the loss of time"—*ser.* xxxvii. *in Sept.*

3. But, in another place, St. Bernardine says, that, though there is nothing more precious than time, there is nothing less valuable in the estimation of men. "Nil pretiosius tempore, nil vilius reputatur"—*ser.* ii., *ad Schol.* You will see some persons spending four or five hours in play. If you ask them why they lose so much time, they answer: To amuse ourselves. Others remain half the day standing in the street, or looking out from a window. If you ask them what they are doing, they shall say in reply, that they are passing the time. And why, says the same saint, do you lose this time? Why should you lose even a single hour, which the mercy of God gives you to weep for your sins, and to acquire the divine grace? "Donec hora pertranseat, quam tibi ad agendam pœnitentiam, ad acquirendam gratiam, miseratio conditoris indulserit".

4. O time despised by men during life, how much shall you be desired at the hour of death, and particularly in the other world! Time is a blessing which we enjoy only in this life; it is not enjoyed in the next; it is not found in Heaven nor in Hell. In Hell, the damned exclaim with tears: "*Oh! that an hour were given to us*". They would pay any price for an hour or for a minute, in which they might repair their eternal ruin. But this hour or minute they never shall have. In Heaven, there is no weeping; but, were the saints capable of sorrow, all

their wailing should arise from the thought of having lost in this life the time in which they could have acquired greater glory, and from the conviction that this time shall never more be given to them. A deceased Benedictine nun appeared in glory to a certain person, and said, that she was in Heaven, and in the enjoyment of perfect happiness; but that, if she could desire anything, it would be to return to life, and to suffer affliction, in order to merit an increase of glory. And she added, that, to acquire the glory which corresponded to a single *Ave Maria*, she would be content to suffer till the day of judgment, the long and painful sickness which brought on her death. Hence St. Francis Borgia was careful to employ every moment of his time for God. When others spoke of useless things, he conversed with God by holy affections: and so recollected was he, that, when asked his opinion on the subject of conversation, he knew not what answer to make. Being corrected for this, he said: I am content to be considered stnpid, rather than lose my time in vanities.

5. Some of you will say: *What evil am I doing?* Is it not, I ask, an evil to spend your time in plays, in conversations, and useless occupations, which are unprofitable to the soul? Does God give you this time to lose it? "Let not", says the Holy Ghost, "the part of a good gift overpass thee"—*Eccl.*, xiv. 14. The workmen of whom St. Matthew speaks, did no evil; they only lost time by remaining idle in the streets. But they were rebuked by the father of the family, saying: "Why stand you here all the day idle?"—*Matt.*, xx. 6. On the day of judgment Jesus Christ shall demand an account, not only of every month and day that has been lost, but even of every idle word. "Every idle word that men shall speak, they shall render an account for it on the day of judgment"—*Matt.*, xii. 36. He shall likewise demand an account of every moment of the time which you shall lose. According to St. Bernard, all time which is not spent for God, is lost time. "Omne tempus quo de Deo non cogitasti, cogita te perdidisse"—*Coll.* I., *cap.* viii. Hence the Holy Ghost says: "Whatsoever thy hand is able to do, do it earnestly; for neither work nor reason......shall be in Hell, whither thou art hastening"—*Eccl.*, ix. 10. What you can do to-day, defer not till to-morrow; for, on to-morrow you may be dead, and may be gone into another world, where you

shall have no more time to do good, and where you shall only enjoy the reward of your virtues, or suffer the punishment due to your sins. "To-day, if you shall hear his voice, harden not your hearts"—*Ps.*, xciv. 8. God calls you to confess your sins, to restore ill-gotten goods, to be reconciled with your enemies. Obey his call to-day; for it may happen that, on to-morrow, time may be no more for you, or that God will call you no more. All our salvation depends on corresponding with the divine calls, and at the time that God calls us.

6. But some of you will perhaps say: I am young; after some time I will give myself to God. But, remember that the Gospel tells us, that Jesus Christ cursed the fig tree which he found without fruit, although the season for figs had not yet arrived. "*It was not the time for figs*"—*Mark*, xi. 13. By this the Saviour wished to signify, that man at all times, even in youth, should produce fruits of good works; and that otherwise, like the fig tree, he shall be cursed, and shall produce no fruit for the future. "May no man hereafter eat any more fruit of thee for ever"—*ibid.*, v. 14. "Delay not to be converted to the Lord, and defer it not from day to day; for his wrath shall come on a sudden"—*Eccl.*, v. 8, 9. If you find your soul in the state of sin, delay not your repentance nor your confession; do not put them off even till to-morrow; for, if you do not obey the voice of God calling you to-day to confess your sins, death may this day overtake you in sin, and to-morrow there may be no hope of salvation for you. The Devil regards the whole of our life as very short, and therefore he loses not a moment of time, but tempts us day and night. "The Devil is come down unto you having great wrath, knowing that he hath but a short time"—*Apoc.*, xii. 12. The enemy, then, never loses time in seeking to bring us to Hell: and shall we squander the time which God has given us to save our souls?

7. You say: *I will hereafter give myself to God.* But "why", answers St. Bernard, "do you, a miserable sinner, presume on the future, as if the Father placed time in your power?"—*serm.* xxxviii. *de Part., etc.* Why do you presume that you will hereafter give yourself to God, as if he had given to you the time and opportunity of returning to him whenever you wish? Job said with trembling, that he knew not whether

another moment of his life remained: "For I know not how long I shall continue, and whether after a while my Maker may take me away"—xxxii. 22. And you say: I will not go to confession to-day; I will think of it to-morrow. "Diem tenes", says St. Augustine, "qui horam non tenes". How can you promise yourself another day, when you know not whether you shall live for an hour? "*If*", says St. Teresa, "*you are not prepared to die to-day*, tremble, lest you die an unhappy death".

8. St. Bernardine weeps over the blindness of those negligent Christians, who squander the days of salvation, and never consider that a day once lost shall never return. "Transeunt dies, salutis et nemo recogitat sibi perire diem et nunquam rediturum"—*Serm. ad Scholar.* At the hour of death they shall wish for another year, or for another day; but they shall not have it: they shall then be told that *time shall be no more.* What price would they not then give for another week, for a day, or even for an hour, to prepare the account which they must then render to God? St. Lawrence Justinian says, that for a single hour they would give all their property, all their honours, and all their delights. "Erogaret opes, honores, delicias, pro una horula"—*Vit. Solit., cap.* x. But this hour shall not be granted to them. The priest who attends them shall say: Depart, depart immediately from this Earth; for you time is no more. "Go forth, Christian soul, from this world".

9. What will it profit the sinner who has led an irregular life, to exclaim at death: Oh! that I had led a life of sanctity! Oh! that I had spent my years in loving God! How great is the anguish of a traveller, who, when the night has fallen, perceives that he has missed the way, and that there is no more time to correct his mistake! Such shall be the anguish at death of those who have lived many years in the world, but have not spent them for God. "The night cometh, when no man can work"—*John*, ix. 4. Hence the Redeemer says to all: "Walk whilst you have light, that the darkness overtake you not"—*John*, xii. 35. Walk in the way of salvation, now that you have the light, before you are surprised by the darkness of death, in which you can do nothing. You can then only weep over the time which you have lost.

10. "He hath called against me the time"—*Thren.*, i. 15. At the hour of death, conscience will remind us of all the time which we have had to become saints, and which we have employed in multiplying our debts to God. It will remind us of all the calls and of all the graces which he has given us to make us love him, and which we have abused. At that awful moment, we shall also see that the way to salvation is closed for ever. In the midst of these remorses, and of the torturing darkness of death, the dying sinner shall say: Oh! fool that I have been! O life mispent! O lost years, in which I could have gained treasures of merits, and have become a saint! but, I have neglected both, and now the time of saving my soul is gone for ever. But, of what use shall these wailings and lamentations be, when the scene of this world is about to close, the lamp is on the point of being extinguished, and when the dying Christian has arrived at that great moment on which eternity depends?

11. "Be you then also ready; for, at what hour you think not, the Son of Man will come"—*Luke*, xii. 40. The Lord says: "*Be prepared*". He does not tell us to prepare ourselves when death approaches, but to be ready for his coming; because when we think least of death, the Son of Man shall come and demand an account of our whole life. In the confusion of death, it will be most difficult to adjust our accounts, so as to appear guiltless before the tribunal of Jesus Christ. Perhaps death may not come upon us for twenty or thirty years; but it may also come very soon, perhaps in a year or in a month. If any one had reason to fear that a trial should take place, on which his life depended, he certainly would not wait for the day of trial, but would as soon as possible employ an advocate to plead his cause. And what do we do? We know for certain that we must one day be judged, and that on the result of that judgment our eternal, not our temporal, life depends. We also know that that day may be very near at hand; and still we lose our time, and, instead of adjusting our accounts, we go on daily multiplying the crimes which will merit for us the sentence of eternal death.

12. If, then, we have hitherto employed our time in offending God, let us henceforth endeavour to bewail our misfortune for the remainder of our life, and say continually with the penitent King Ezechias: "I will recount to thee all my years in the

bitterness of my soul"—*Isa.*, xxxviii. 15. The Lord gives us the remaining days of life, that we may compensate the time that has been badly spent. "Whilst we have time, let us work good"—*Galat.*, vi. 10. Let us not provoke the Lord to punish us by an unhappy death; and if, during the years that are past, we have been foolish, and have offended him, let us now attend to the Apostle exhorting us to be wise for the future, and to redeem the time we have lost. "See, therefore, brethren, now you walk circumspectly, not as unwise, but as wise, redeeming the time, because the days are evil,...understanding what is the will of God" —*Eph.*, v. 15, 16, 17. "*The days are evil*". According to St. Anselm, the meaning of these words is, that the days of this life are evil, because in them we are exposed to a thousand temptations and dangers of eternal misery; and therefore, to escape perdition, all possible care is necessary. "What", says St. Augustine, "is meant by redeeming the time, unless, when necessary, to submit to temporal loss in order to gain eternal goods?"—*de hom.* 50, *hom.* 1. We should live only to fulfil with all diligence the divine will; and, should it be necessary, it is better to suffer in temporal things, than to neglect our eternal interests. Oh! how well did St. Paul redeem the time which he had lost! St. Jerome says, that though the last of the apostles, he was, on account of his great labours, the first in merits. "Paul, the last in order, but the first in merits, because he laboured more than all". Let us consider that, in each moment, we may lay up greater treasures of eternal goods. If the possession of all the land round which you could walk, or of all the money which you could count in a day, were promised you, would you lose time? or would you not instantly begin to walk over the ground, or to reckon the money? You now have it in your power to acquire, in each moment, eternal treasures; and will you, notwithstanding, mispend your time? Do not say, that what you can do to-day, you can also do to-morrow; because this day shall then be lost to you, and shall never return. You have this day; but perhaps to-morrow will not be given you.

SERMON XXV.

FOR THE FOURTH SUNDAY AFTER EASTER.

On obedience to your confessor.

"Whither goest thou?"—*John*, xiii. 36.

To gain Heaven we must walk in the path that leads to Paradise. Many Christians, who have faith, but not works, live in sin, intent only on the pleasures and goods of this world. If you say to one of them: You are a Christian; you believe that there is an eternity, a Heaven, and a Hell: tell me, do you wish to save your soul? If you do, I will ask you, in the words of this day's gospel, *whither goest thou?* He will answer: I do not know, but I hope to be saved. You know not whither you are going. How can you hope for salvation from God, if you live in a state of perdition? How can you expect Heaven, if you walk in the way that leads to Hell? It is necessary, then, to change the road; and for this purpose you must put yourself in the hands of a good confessor, who will point out to you the way to Heaven, and you must obey him punctually. "My sheep", said Jesus Christ, "hear my voice"—*John*, x. 27. We have not Jesus Christ on Earth, to make us sensibly hear his voice; but, in his stead, he has left us his priests, and has told us, that he who hears them, hears him, and he who despises them, despises him. "He that heareth you, heareth me, and he that despiseth you, despiseth me"—*Luke*, x. 16. Happy they who are obedient to their spiritual father: unhappy they who do not obey him; for, by their disobedience, they give a proof that they are not among the sheep of Jesus Christ. I intend this day to show, in the first point, how secure of salvation are all who obey their confessor; and, in the second point, how great the danger of perdition to which they who do not obey him are exposed.

First point. How secure of salvation are they who obey their confessor.

1. In leaving us spiritual fathers to guide us in the way of

salvation, Jesus Christ has bestowed upon us a great benefit. To obtain salvation, we must follow the will of God in all things. What, I ask, is necessary in order to save our souls and to become saints? Some imagine that sanctity consists in performing many works of penance; but, were a sick man to practise mortifications which would expose him to the proximate danger of death, he would, instead of becoming a saint, be guilty of a very grievous sin. Others think that perfection consists in long and frequent prayers; but, should the father of a family neglect the education of his children and go into the desert to pray, he too would commit sin; because, although prayer is good, a parent is bound to take care of his children, and he can fulfil the precept of prayer and of attention to their instruction, without going into the desert. Others believe that holiness consists in frequent communion; but if, in spite of a just command of her husband, and to the injury of her family, a married woman wished to communicate every morning, she would act improperly, and would have to render an account of her conduct to God. In what, then, does sanctity consist? It consists in the perfect fulfilment of the will of God. All the sins which bring souls to Hell proceed from self-will. Let us, then, says St. Bernard, cease to do our own will; let us follow the will of God, and for us there shall be no Hell. "Cesset propria voluntas, et infernus non erit"—*S. Bern.*, *serm.* iii. *de Resur.*

2. But some of you will ask: How shall we know what God wills us to do? This is a matter which, according to David, is involved in great doubts and obscurity. "Of the business that walketh about in the dark"—*Ps.*, xc. 6. Many deceive themselves; for, passion often makes them believe that they do the will of God, when, in reality, they do their own will. Let us thank without ceasing the goodness of Jesus Christ, who has taught us the secure means of ascertaining the will of God in our regard, by telling us, that, if we obey our confessor, we obey himself. "He that heareth you, heareth me". In the book of the foundations, chapter x., St. Teresa says: Let a soul take a confessor with a determination to think no more of directing herself, but to trust in the words of our Lord, *He that heareth you, heareth me.* She adds, that this is the secure way of finding the will of God. Hence the saint acknowledged that

it was by obedience to the voice of her director that she attained to the knowledge and love of God. Hence, speaking of obedience to one's confessor, St. Francis de Sales adopts the words of Father M. Avila: How much soever you seek, you shall never find the will of God so securely, as by this way of humble obedience so much recommended and practised by the ancient saints (*Introd.*, *etc.*, *cap.* iv.).

3. He that acts according to the advice of his confessor, always pleases God when, through obedience, he either practises or omits prayer, mortifications, or communions. He even merits a reward before God when, to obey his confessor, he takes recreation, when he eats or drinks, because he does the will of God. Hence the Scripture says, that "much better is obedience than the victories of fools"—*Eccl.*, iv. 17. Obedience is more pleasing to God than all the sacrifices of penitential works, or of alms-deeds, which we can offer to him. He that sacrifices to God his property by alms-deeds, his honour by bearing insults, or his body by mortifications, by fasts and penitential rigours, offers to him a part of himself and of what belongs to him; but he that sacrifices to God his will, by obedience, gives to him all that he has, and can say: Lord, having given you my will, I have nothing more to give you.

4. Thus, obedience to a confessor is the most acceptable offering which we can make to God, and the most secure way of doing the divine will. Blessed Henry Suson says, that God does not demand an account of what we do through obedience. Obey, says the Apostle, your spiritual fathers, and fear not any thing which you do through obedience; for they, and not you, shall have to render an account of your conduct. "Obey your prelates, and be subject to them; for they watch, as being to render and account of your souls: that they may do this with joy and not with grief"—*Hebr.*, xiii. 17. Mark the last words: they signify, that penitents should obey without reply, and without causing pain and sorrow to their confessor. Oh! what grief do confessors feel, when penitents endeavour, by certain pretexts and unjust complaints, to excuse themselves from obedience! Let us, then, obey our spiritual father without reply, and let us fear not that we shall have to account for any act which we do through obedience. "They", says St. Philip Neri, "who desire to advance in the way of God, should place

themselves under a learned confessor, whom they will obey in the place of God. They who do so, may be assured that they shall not have to render to God an account of their actions". Hence, if you practise obedience, and if Jesus Christ should ask you on the day of judgment, why you have chosen such a state of life? why you have communicated so frequently? why you have omitted certain works of penance? you will answer: O Lord, I have done all in obedience to my confessor, and Jesus Christ cannot but approve of what you have done.

5. Father Marchese relates, that St. Dominic once felt a scruple in obeying his confessor, and that our Lord said to him: "Why do you hesitate to obey your director? All that he directs will be useful to you". Hence St. Bernard says, that "whatever a man, holding the place of God, commands, provided it be not certainly sinful, should be received as if the command came from God himself"—*de Præcep. et Discip., cap.* xi. Gerson relates, that the same St. Bernard ordered one of his disciples, who, through scruples, was afraid to say Mass, to go, and, trusting in his advice, to offer the holy sacrifice. The disciple obeyed, and was cured of scruples. Some, adds Gerson, will say: Would to God that I had a St. Bernard for my director: my confessor is not a St. Bernard. "Whosoever you are, that speak in this manner, you err; for you have not put yourself under the care of a man because he is learned, but because he is placed over you. Obey him, then, not as a man, but as God"—*tract. de Præp. ad Miss.* You have entrusted the care of your soul to a confessor, not because he is a man of learning, but because God has given him to you as a guide; and therefore you ought to obey him, not as a man, but as God.

6. "An obedient man shall speak of victory"—*Prov.*, xxi. 28. Justly, says St. Gregory, has the Wise Man asserted, that they who are obedient shall overcome the temptations of Hell; because, as by their obedience they subject their own will to men, so they render themselves superior to the devils, who fell through disobedience. "The obedient are conquerors; because, whilst they subject their will to others, they rule over the angels that have fallen through disobedience"—*in lib. Reg., cap.* x. Cassian teaches, that he who mortifies self-will, beats down all vices; because all vices proceed from self-will. "By the mortification of the will all vices are dried up". He who

obeys his confessor, overcomes all the illusions of the Devil, who sometimes makes us expose ourselves to dangerous occasions under pretext of doing good, and makes us engage in certain undertakings which appear holy, but which may prove very injurious to us. Thus, for example, the enemy induces certain devout persons to practise immoderate austerities, which impair their health: they then give up all mortifications, and return to their former irregularities. This happens to those who direct themselves; but they who are guided by their confessor, are not in danger of falling into such an illusion.

7. The Devil labours to make scrupulous persons afraid that they will commit sin if they follow the advice of their confessor. We must be careful to overcome these vain fears. All theologians and spiritual writers commonly teach, that it is our duty to obey the directions of our confessors, and conquer our scruples. Natalis Alexander says, that we must act against scruples; and in support of this doctrine, he adduces the doctrine of St. Antonine, who, along with Gerson, censures scrupulous persons for refusing, through vain fears, to obey their confessor, and to overcome scruples. "Beware, lest, while you seek security, you rush into a pit". Be careful not, through an excess of fear, to fall into the illusions of the Devil, by disobeying your director. Hence all the spiritual masters exhort us to obey our confessors in every thing which is not manifestly sinful. B. Hubert, of the order of St. Dominic, says that, "unless what is commanded is evidently bad, it ought to be received as if it were commanded by God"—*lib. de Erud. Rel.*, *cap.* i. Blessed Denis the Carthusian teaches, that "in doubtful matters we must obey the precept of a superior; because, though it may be against God, a subject is excused from sin on account of obedience"—*in* 2, *dis.* xxxix. *qu.* 3. According to Gerson *(tr. de. consc. et scrup.)*, to act against a conscience formed with deliberation, and to act against a fear of sinning in some doubtful matter, are very different things. He adds, that we should banish this fear, and obey our confessor. "Iste timor, quam fieri potest abjiciendus". In a word, he who obeys his spiritual father, is always secure. St. Francis de Sales used to say, that *a truly obedient soul has never been lost;* and that we should be satisfied to know from our confessor, that we are

going on well in the way of God, without seeking further certainty of it.

Second point. How great is the danger of perdition to which they who do not obey their confessor are exposed.

8. Jesus Christ has said, that he who hears his priests, hears him; and that he who despises them, despises him. "Qui vos spernit, me spernit"—*Luc.*, x. 16. When the Prophet Eliseus complained of the contempt which he had received from the people, after God had charged him with the direction of them, the Lord said to him: "They have not rejected thee, but me, that I should not reign over them"—I. *Kings*, viii. 7. They, then, who despise the advice of their confessors, despise God himself, who has made confessors his own representatives.

9. "Obey your prelates", says St. Paul, "and be subject to them; for they watch, as being to render an account of your souls: that they may do this with joy, and not with grief; for, this is not expedient for you"—*Heb.*, xiii. 17. Some penitents contend with their confessors, and endeavour to make him adopt their own opinion. This is a cause of grief to spiritual directors. But the Apostle says, *this is not expedient for you;* because, when the confessor finds that you do not obey him, and that it is only with difficulty he can induce you to walk in the straight path, he will give up the direction of your soul. How deplorable the condition of a vessel which a pilot refuses to steer! How miserable the state of a sick man who is abandoned by his physician! When a patient refuses to obey, or to take the medicine which has been prescribed—when he eats and drinks what he pleases—the physician abandons him, and allows him to follow his own caprice. But, what hope can be entertained of the recovery of such a patient? "Wo to him that is alone,...he hath none to lift him up"—*Eccl.*, iv. 10. Wo to the penitent who wishes to direct himself: he shall have no one to enlighten or correct him, and will therefore rush into an abyss.

10. To every one that comes into this world, the Holy Ghost says: "Thou art going in the midst of snares"—*Eccl.*, ix. 20. We all, on this Earth, walk in the midst of a thousand snares; that is, in the midst of the temptations of the Devil, dangerous occasions, bad companions, and our own passions, which fre-

quently deceive us. Who shall be saved in the midst of so many dangers? The Wise Man says: "He that is aware of the snares shall be secure"—*Prov.*, xi. 15. They only who avoid these snares shall be saved. How shall we avoid them? If you had to pass by night through a wood full of precipices, without a guide to give you light, and to point out to you the dangerous passages, you would certainly run a great risk of losing your life. You wish to direct yourself: "Take heed, therefore, that the light which is in thee be not darkness"—*Luke*, xi. 35. The light which you think you possess will be your ruin; it will lead you into a pit.

11. God wills, that, in the way of salvation, we all submit to the guidance of our director. Such has been the practice of even the most learned among the saints. In spiritual things, the Lord wishes us to humble ourselves, and to put ourselves under a confessor, who will be our guide. Gerson teaches, that he who neglects the advice of his director, and directs himself, does not require a devil to tempt him; he becomes a devil to himself. "Qui spreto duce, sibi dux esse vult, non indiget dæmone tentante, quia factus est sibi ipsi dæmon"—*Cons. de Lib. Reg.* And when God sees that he will not obey his minister, he allows him to follow his own caprice. "So I let them go according to the desires of their own hearts"—*Ps.*, lxxx. 13.

12. "It is like the sin of witchcraft, to rebel: and like the crime of idolatry, to refuse to obey"—I. *Kings*, xv. 23. In explaining this text St. Gregory says, that the sin of idolatry consists in abandoning God and adoring an idol. This a penitent does when he disobeys his confessor to do his own will: he refuses to do the will of God, who has spoken to him by means of his minister; he adores the idol of self-will, and does what he pleases. Hence St. John of the Cross says, that, "not to follow the advice of our confessor, is pride and a want of faith"—*Tratt. delle spine, tom.* III., *col.* 4, § 2, *n.* 8; for it appears to proceed from a want of faith in the Gospel, in which Jesus Christ has said: "He that heareth you, heareth me".

13. If, then, you wish to save your souls, obey your confessor punctually. Be careful to have a fixed confessor, to whom you will ordinarily make your confession; and avoid going about from one confessor to another. Make choice of a learned priest; and, in the beginning, make to him a general confession, which,

as we know from experience, is a great help to a true change of life. After having made choice of a confessor, you should not leave him without a just and manifest cause. "Every time", says St. Teresa, "that I resolved to leave my confessor, I felt within me a reproof, more painful than that which I received from him".

SERMON XXVI.

FOR THE FIFTH SUNDAY AFTER EASTER.

On the conditions of prayer.

"Ask, and ye shall receive"—*John*, xvi. 24.

In the thirty-ninth Sermon, I shall show the strict necessity of prayer, and its infallible efficacy to obtain for us all the graces which can be conducive to our eternal salvation. "Prayer", says St. Cyprian, "is omnipotent; it is one; it can do all things". We read in Ecclesiasticus, that God has never refused to hear any one who invoked his aid. "Who hath called upon him, and he hath despised him?"—*Eccl.*, ii. 12. This he never can do; for he has promised to hear all who pray to him. "Ask, and ye shall receive". But this promise extends only to prayer which has the necessary conditions. Many pray; but, because they pray negligently, they do not obtain the graces they desire. "You ask, and receive not; because you ask amiss"—*St. James*, iv. 3. To pray as we ought, we must pray, first, with humility; secondly, with confidence; and thirdly, with perseverance.

First point. We must pray with humility.

1. St. James tells us, that God rejects the prayers of the proud: "God resisteth the proud, and giveth grace to the humble"—iv. 6. He cannot bear the proud; he rejects their petitions, and refuses to hear them. Let those proud Chris-

tians who trust in their own strength, and think themselves better than others, attend to this, and let them remember that their prayers shall be rejected by the Lord.

2. But he always hears the prayers of the humble: "The prayer of him that humbleth himself pierceth the clouds; and he will not depart till the Most High behold"—*Eccl.*, xxxv. 21. David says, that "the Lord hath had regard to the prayer of the humble"—*Ps.*, ci. 18. The cry of the humble man penetrates the Heavens, and he will not depart till God hears his prayer. "You humble yourself", says St. Augustine, "and God comes to you; you exalt yourself, and he flies from you". If you humble yourself, God himself comes, of his own accord, to embrace you; but, if you exalt yourself, and boast of your wisdom and of your actions, he withdraws from you, and abandons you to your own nothingness.

3. The Lord cannot despise even the most obdurate sinners, when they repent from their hearts, and humble themselves before him, acknowledging that they are unworthy to receive any favour from him. "A contrite and humble heart, O God, thou wilt not despise"—*Ps.*, l. 19. Let us pass to the other points, in which there is a great deal to be said.

Second point. We must pray with confidence.

4. "No one hath hoped in the Lord, and hath been confounded"—*Eccl.*, ii. 11. Oh! how encouraging to sinners are these words! Though they may have committed the most enormous crimes, they are told by the Holy Ghost, that "*no one hath hoped in the Lord, and hath been confounded*". No man has ever placed his trust in God, and has been abandoned. He that prays with confidence, obtains whatever he asks. "All things whatsoever you ask when you pray, believe that you shall receive, and they shall come unto you"—*Mark*, xi. 24. When we pray for spiritual favours, let us have a secure confidence of receiving them, and we shall infallibly obtain them. Hence the Saviour has taught us to call God, in our petitions for his graces, by no other name than that of Father *(Our Father)*, that we may have recourse to him with the confidence with which a child seeks assistance from an affectionate parent.

5. Who, says St. Augustine, can fear that Jesus Christ, who is truth itself, can violate his promise to hear all who pray to

him? "Who shall fear deception when truth promises?" Is God like men, who promise, and do not afterwards fulfil their promise; either because in making it they intend to deceive, or because, after having made it, they change their intention? "God is not a as man, that he should lie, nor as the Son of Man, that he should be changed. Hath he told, then, and will he not do?"—*Num.*, xxiii. 19. Our God cannot tell a lie; because he is truth itself: he is not liable to change; because all his arrangements are just and holy.

6. And because he ardently desires our welfare, he earnestly exhorts and commands us to ask the graces we stand in need of. "Ask, and it shall be given you; seek, and you shall find; knock, and it shall be opened to you?"—*Matt.*, vii. 7. Why, says St. Augustine, should the Lord exhort us so strongly to ask his graces, if he did not wish to give them to us? "Non nos hortaretur, ut peteremus, nisi dare vellet"—*de Verb. Dom.*, *ser.* v. He has even bound himself by his promise to hear our prayers, and to bestow upon us all the graces which we ask with a confidence of obtaining them. "By his promises he has made himself a debtor"—*S. Augus.*, *ibid.*, *ser.* ii.

7. But some will say: I have but little confidence in God, because I am a sinner. I have been too ungrateful to him, and therefore I see that I do not deserve to be heard. But St. Thomas tells us, that the efficacy of our prayers in obtaining graces from God, does not depend on our merits, but on the divine mercy. "Oratio in impetrando non innititur nostris meritis, sed soli divinæ misericordiæ"—2, 2, *qu.* 178, *a.* 2, *ad.* 1. As often as we ask with confidence favours which are conducive to our eternal salvation, God hears our prayer. I have said, *favours conducive to our salvation;* for, if what we seek be injurious to the soul, God does not, and cannot hear us. For example: if a person asked help from God to be revenged of an enemy, or to accomplish what would be offensive to God, the Lord will not hear his prayers; because, says St. Chrysostom, such a person offends God in the very act of prayer: he does not pray, but, in a certain manner mocks God. "Qui orat et peccat, non rogat Deum, sed eludit" —*hom.* xi., *in Matt.*, vi.

8. Moreover, if you wish to receive from God the aid which you ask, you must remove every obstacle which may render you

unworthy of being heard. For example: if you ask of God strength to preserve you from relapsing into a certain sin, but will not avoid the occasions of the sin, nor keep at a distance from the house, from the object, or the bad company, which led to your fall, God will not hear your prayer. And why? Because "thou hast set a cloud before thee, that prayer may not pass through"—*Thren.*, iii. 44. Should you relapse, do not complain of God, nor say: I have besought the Lord to preserve me from falling into sin, but he has not heard me. Do you not see that, by not taking away the occasions of sin, you have interposed a thick cloud, which has prevented your prayers from passing to the throne of divine mercy?

9. It is also necessary to remark, that the promise of Jesus Christ to hear those who pray to him does not extend to all the temporal favours which we ask—such as a plentiful harvest, a victory in a law-suit, or a deliverance from sickness or from certain persecutions. These favours God grants to those who pray for them; but only when they are conducive to their spiritual welfare. Otherwise, he refuses them; and he refuses them because he loves us, and because he knows that they would be injurious to our souls. "A physician", says St. Augustine, "knows better than his patient, what is useful for him"—*tom.* III., *cap.* ccxii. The saint adds, that God refuses to some, through mercy, what he grants to others as a chastisement. "Deus negat propitius, quæ concedit iratus". Hence St. John Damascene says, that sometimes, when we do not obtain the graces which we ask, we receive, by not receiving them; because it is better for us not to receive, than to receive them. "Etiam si non accipias, non accipendo accepisti, interdum enim non accipere quam accipere satius est"—*Paral.*, *lib.* 3, *cap.* xv. We often ask poison, which would cause our death. How many are there, who, had they died in the sickness or poverty with which they were afflicted, should be saved. But, because they recovered their health, or because they were raised to wealth and honours, they became proud and forgot God, and thus have been damned. Hence St Chrysostom exhorts us to ask in our prayers what God knows to be expedient for us. "Orantes in ejus potestate ponamus, ut nos illud petentes exaudiat, quod ipse nobis expedire cognoscit"—*hom.* xv. *in*

Matt. We should, then, always ask from God temporal favours on the condition that they will be useful to the soul.

10. But, spiritual favours—such as the pardon of our sins, perseverance in virtue, the gift of divine love, and resignation to the divine will—ought to be asked of God absolutely, and with a firm confidence of obtaining them. "If you, then, being evil, know how to give good gifts to your children, how much more will your Father from Heaven give the good spirit to them that ask him?"—*Luke*, xi. 13. If you, says Jesus Christ, who are so much attached to Earthly goods, cannot refuse your children the blessings which you have received from God, how much more will your Heavenly Father (who is in himself infinitely good, and who desires to give you his graces more ardently than you desire to receive them) give the good spirit—that is, a sincere contrition for their sins, the gift of divine love, and resignation to the will of God—to those who ask them? "Quando Deus negabit", says St. Bernard, "petentibus qui etiam non petentes hortatur ut petant?"—*ser.* ii. *de S. Andr.* How can God refuse graces conducive to salvation to those who seek them, when he exhorts even those who do not pray, to ask them?

11. Nor does God inquire whether the person who prays to him is a just man or a sinner; for he has declared, that "*every one that asketh, receiveth*"—*Luke*, xi. 10. "Every one", says the author of the *Imperfect Work*, "whether he be a just man or a sinner"—*hom.* xviii. And, to encourage us to pray and to ask with confidence for spiritual favours, he has said: "Amen, amen, I say to you: If you ask the Father anything in my name, he will give it you"—*John*, xvi. 23. As if he said: Sinners, though you do not deserve to receive the divine graces, I have merited them for you from my Father: ask, then, in my name—that is, through my merits—and I promise that you shall obtain whatsoever you demand.

Third point. We must pray with perseverance.

12. It is, above all, necessary to persevere in prayer till death, and never to cease to pray. This is what is inculcated by the following passages of Scripture. "We ought always to pray"—*Luke*, xviii. 1. "Watch ye, therefore, praying at all times"—xxi. 36. "Pray without ceasing"—I. *Thess.*, v. 17.

Hence the Holy Ghost says: "Let nothing hinder thee from praying always"—*Eccl.*, xviii. 22. These words imply, not only that we should pray always, but also that we should endeavour to remove every occasion which may prevent us from praying; for, if we cease to pray, we shall be deprived of the divine aid, and shall be overcome by temptations. Perseverance in grace is a gratuitous gift, which, as the Council of Trent has declared, we cannot merit (*ses.* 6, *cap.* xiii.). But St. Augustine says, that we may obtain it by prayer. "Hoc donum Dei suppliciter emereri potest, id est supplicando impetrari"—*de Dono. Per.*, *cap.* vi. Hence Cardinal Bellarmine teaches, that "*we must ask it daily, in order to obtain it every day*". If we neglect to ask it on any day, we may fall into sin on that day.

13. If, then, we wish to persevere and to be saved—for no one can be saved without perseverance—we must pray continually. Our perseverance depends, not on one grace, but on a thousand helps which we hope to obtain from God during our whole lives, that we may be preserved in his grace. Now, to this chain of graces a chain of prayers on our part must correspond: without these prayers, God ordinarily does not grant his graces. If we neglect to pray, and thus break the chain of prayers, the chain of graces shall also be broken, and we shall lose the grace of perseverance. If, says Jesus Christ to his disciples, one of you go during the night to a friend, and say to him: Lend me three loaves; an acquaintance has come to my house, and I have no refreshment for him. The friend will answer: I am in bed; the door is locked; I cannot get up. But, if the other continue to knock at the door, and will not depart, the friend will rise, and give him as many loaves as he wishes, not through friendship, but to be freed from his importunity. "Although he will not rise and give him because he is his friend; yet, because of his importunity, he will rise, and give him as many as he needeth"—*Luke*, xi. 8. Now, if a man will give his loaves to a friend because of his importunity, "how much more", says St. Augustine, "will God give, who exhorts us to ask, and is displeased if we do not ask?" How much more will the Lord bestow on us his graces, if we persevere in praying for them, when he exhorts us to ask them, and is offended if we do not ask them?

14. Men feel annoyed at being frequently and importunately asked for a favour. But God exhorts us to pray frequently; and, instead of being dissatisfied, he is pleased with those who repeatedly ask his graces. Cornelius a Lapide says, that "God wishes us to persevere in prayer, even to importunity"—*in Luc.*, *cap.* xi. St. Jerome says: "This importunity with the Lord is seasonable"—*in Luc.* xi. That God is pleased with frequent and persevering prayer, may be inferred from the words of Jesus Christ—"Ask, and it shall be given you; seek, and you shall find; knock, and it shall be opened to you"—*Luke*, xi. 9. It was not enough to have said *ask;* but he added, *seek*, *knock;* in order to show, that, during our whole lives, we should be as importunate in supplicating the divine graces, as beggars are in asking alms. Though they should be refused, they do not cease to cry out, or to knock at the door; they persist in asking relief till they obtain it.

15. If, then, we wish to obtain from God the gift of perseverance, we must ask him for it continually and with importunity. We must ask it when we rise in the morning, in our meditations, in hearing Mass, in our visits to the blessed sacrament, in going to bed at night, and particularly when we are tempted by the Devil to commit any sin. Thus, we must always have our mouths open praying to God, and saying: Lord, assist me; give me light; give me strength; keep thy hand upon me, and do not abandon me. We must do violence to the Lord. "Such violence", says Tertullian, "is agreeable to God". The violence which we offer to God by repeated prayers does not offend him: on the contrary, it is pleasing and acceptable in his sight. "Prayer", according to St. John Climacus, "piously offers violence to God" Our supplications compel him, but in a manner grateful to him. He takes great complacency in seeing his mother honoured, and therefore wishes, as St. Bernard says, that all the graces we receive should pass through her hands. Hence the holy doctor exhorts us, "to seek grace, and to seek it through Mary, because she is a mother, and her prayer cannot be fruitless"—*de Aquæd.* When we ask her to obtain any grace for us, she graciously hears our petitions and prays for us: and the prayers of Mary are never rejected.

SERMON XXVII.

FOR THE SIXTH SUNDAY AFTER PENTECOST, OR THE SUNDAY WITHIN THE OCTAVE OF THE ASCENSION.

On human respect.

"Whosoever killeth you, will think that he doth a service to God"—*John*, xvi. 2.

In exhorting his disciples to be faithful to him under the persecutions which they were to endure, the Saviour said: "Yea; the hour cometh, that whosoever killeth you, will think that he doth a service to God". Thus, the enemies of the faith believed that in putting Christians to death they did a service to God. It is thus that many Christians of the present day act. They kill their own souls by losing the grace of God through human respect and to please worldly friends. Oh! how many souls has human respect —that great enemy of our salvation—sent to Hell! I shall speak on this subject to-day, that, if you wish to serve God and save your souls, you may guard as much as possible against human respect. In the first point, I will show the importance of not being influenced by human respect; and in the second, I will point out the means by which this vice may be overcome.

First point. On the importance of not being influenced by human respect.

1. "Wo to the world because of scandals"—*Matt.*, xviii. 7. Jesus Christ has said, that through the scandals of the wicked many souls fall into Hell. But how is it possible to live in the midst of the world, and not to take scandal? This is impossible. To avoid taking scandal, St Paul says, we should leave this world. "Otherwise, you must needs go out of this world"—I. *Cor.*, v. 10. But it is in our power to avoid familiarity with scandalous sinners. Hence the Apostle adds: "But now I have written to you not to keep company......with such an one, not as much as to eat"—*ibid.*, v. 11. We should beware of contracting an intimacy with such sinners; for, should we be

united with them in the bonds of friendship, we shall feel an unwillingness to oppose their bad practices and bad counsels. Thus, through human respect and the fear of contradicting them, we will imitate their example, and lose the friendship of God.

2. Such lovers of the world not only glory in their own iniquities—("They rejoice in most wicked things"—*Prov.*, ii. 14)—but, what is worse, they wish to have companions, and ridicule all who endeavour to live like true Christians and to avoid the dangers of offending God. This is a sin which is very displeasing to God, and which he forbids in a particular manner. "Despise not a man that turneth away from sin, nor reproach him therewith"—*Eccl.*, viii. 6. Despise not those who keep at a distance from sin, and seek not to draw them to evil by your reproaches and irregularities. The Lord declares, that, for those who throw ridicule on the virtuous, chastisements are prepared in this and in the next life. "Judgments are prepared for scorners, and striking hammers for the bodies of fools"—*Prov.*, xix. 29. They mock the servants of God, and he shall mock them for all eternity. "But the Lord shall laugh them to scorn. And they shall fall after this without honour, and be a reproach among the dead for ever"—*Wis.*, iv. 18. They endeavour to make the saints contemptible in the eyes of the world, and God shall make them die without honour, and shall send them to Hell to suffer eternal ignominy among the damned.

3. Not only to offend God, but also to endeavour to make others offend him, is truly an enormous excess of wickedness. This execrable intention arises from a conviction that there are many weak and pusillanimous souls, who, to escape derision and contempt, abandon the practice of virtue, and give themselves up to a life of sin. After his conversion to God, St. Augustine wept for having associated with those ministers of Lucifer, and confessed, that he felt ashamed not to be as wicked and as shameless as they were. "Pudebat me", says the saint, "esse pudentem". How many, to avoid the scoffs of wicked friends, have been induced to imitate their wickedness! *Behold the saint*, these impious scoffers will say; *get me a piece of his garment; I will preserve it as a relic. He ought to go into the desert. Why does he not become a monk?* How many also,

when they receive an insult, resolve to take revenge, not so much through passion, as to escape the reputation of being cowards! How many are there who, after having inadvertently given expression to a scandalous maxim, neglect to retract it (as they are bound to do), through fear of losing the esteem of others! How many, because they are afraid of forfeiting the favour of a friend, sell their souls to the Devil! They imitate the conduct of Pilate, who, through the apprehension of losing the friendship of Cæsar, condemned Jesus Christ to death.

4. Be attentive. Brethren, if we wish to save our souls, we must overcome human respect, and bear the little confusion which may arise from the scoffs of the enemies of the cross of Jesus Christ. "For there is a shame that bringeth sin, and there is a shame that bringeth glory and grace"—*Eccl.*, iv. 25. If we do not suffer this confusion with patience, it will lead us into the pit of sin; but, if we submit to it for God's sake, it will obtain for us the divine grace here, and great glory hereafter. "As", says St. Gregory, "bashfulness is laudable in evil, so it is reprehensible in good"—*hom.* x., *in Ezech.*

5. But some of you will say: I attend to my own affairs; I wish to save my soul; why then should I be persecuted? But there is no remedy; it is impossible to serve God, and not be persecuted. "The wicked loathe them that are in the right way"—*Prov.*, xxix. 27. Sinners cannot bear the sight of the man who lives according to the Gospel, because his life is a continual censure on their disorderly conduct; and therefore they say: "Let us lie in wait for the just; because he is not for our turn, and he is contrary to our doings, and upbraideth us with transgressions of the law"—*Wis.*, ii. 12. The proud man, who seeks revenge for every insult which he receives, would wish that all should avenge the offences that may be offered to him. The avaricious, who grow rich by injustice, wish that all should imitate their fraudulent practices. The drunkard wishes to see others indulge like himself, in intoxication. The immoral, who boast of their impurities, and can scarcely utter a word which does not savour of obscenity, desire that all should act and speak as they do: and those who do not imitate their conduct, they regard as mean, clownish, and intractable—as men without honour and without education. "They are of the world; therefore of the world they speak"—I. *John*, iv. 5.

Worldlings can speak no other language than that of the world. Oh! how great is their poverty and blindness! Sin has blinded them, and therefore they speak so profanely. "These things they thought, and were deceived; for their own malice blinded them"—*Wis.*, ii. 21.

6. But I say again, that there is no remedy, All, as St. Paul says, who wish to live in union with Jesus Christ, must be persecuted by the world. "And all that will live godly in Christ, shall suffer persecution"—II. *Tim.*, iii. 12. All the saints have been persecuted. You say: I do not injure any one; why then am I not left in peace? What evil have the saints, and particularly the martyrs, done? They were full of charity; they loved all, and laboured to do good to all. And how have they been treated by the world? They have been flayed alive; they have been tortured with red-hot plates of iron; and have been put to death in the most cruel manner. And whom has Jesus Christ, the saint of saints, injured? He consoled all; he healed all. "Virtue went out from him, and healed all"—*Luke*, vi. 19. And how has the world treated him? It has persecuted him, so as to make him die through pain on the infamous gibbet of the cross.

7. This happens because the maxims of the world are diametrically opposed to the maxims of Jesus Christ. What the world esteems, Jesus Christ regards as folly. "For the wisdom of this world is foolishness with God"—I. *Cor.*, iii. 19. And what is foolish in the eyes of the world—that is crosses, sickness, contempt, and ignominies—Jesus Christ holds in great estimation. "For the word of the cross, to them indeed that perish, is foolishness"—I. *Cor.*, i. 18. How, says St. Cyprian, can a man think himself to be a Christian, when he is afraid to be a Christian? "Christianum se putat si Christianum esse veretur?"—*ser.* v., *de Lapsis.* If we are Christians, let us show that we are Christians in name and in truth; for, if we are ashamed of Jesus Christ, he will be ashamed of us, and cannot give us a place on his right hand on the last day. "For he that shall be ashamed of me and of my words, of him the Son of Man shall be ashamed when he shall come in his majesty"—*Luke*, ix. 26. On the day of Judgment he shall say: You have been ashamed of me on Earth: I am now ashamed to see you with me in Paradise. Begone, accursed souls; go into Hell to meet your compa-

nions, who have been ashamed of me. But mark the words, *he that shall be ashamed of me and of my words.* St. Augustine says, that some are ashamed to deny Jesus Christ, but do not blush to deny the maxims of Jesus Christ. "Erubescunt negare Christum, et non erubescunt negare verba Christi"—*serm.* xlviii. But you may tell me, that, if you say you cannot do such an act, because it is contrary to the Gospel, your friends will turn you into ridicule, and will call you a hypocrite. Then, says St. John Chrysostom, you will not suffer to be treated with derision by a companion, and you are content to be hated by God? "Non vis a conservo derideri, sed odio haberi a Deo tuo?"—*hom.* xci., *in Act.* xix.

8. The Apostle, who gloried in being a follower of Christ, said: "The world is crucified to me, and I to the world"—*Gal.*, vi. 14. As I am a person crucified to the world—an object of its scoffs and injustice, so the world is to me an object of contempt and abomination. It is necessary to be convinced, that if we do not trample on the world, the world will trample on our souls. But what is the world and all its goods? "All that is in the world, is the concupiscence of the flesh, and the concupiscence of the eyes, and the pride of life"—I. *John*, ii. 16. To what are all the goods of this Earth reduced? To riches, which are but dung; to honours, which are only smoke; and to carnal pleasures. But what shall all these profit us, if we lose our souls? "What doth it profit a man, if he gain the whole world, and suffer the loss of his own soul?"—*Matt.*, xvi. 26.

9. He that loves God and wishes to save his soul, must despise the world and all human respect; and to do this, every one must offer violence to himself. St. Mary Magdalene had to do great violence to herself, in order to overcome human respect and the murmurings and scoffs of the world, when in the presence of so many persons, she cast herself at the feet of Jesus Christ to wash them with her tears, and dry them with her hair. But she thus became a saint, and merited from Jesus Christ pardon of her sins and praise for her great love. "Many sins are forgiven her because she hath loved much"—*Luke*, vii. 47. One day, as St. Francis Borgia carried to certain prisoners a vessel of broth under his cloak, he met his son mounted on a fine horse and accompanied by several noblemen. The saint felt

ashamed to show what he carried under his cloak. But what did he do in order to conquer human respect? He took the vessel of broth, placed it on his head, and thus showed his contempt for the world. Jesus Christ, our Head and Master, when nailed to the cross, was mocked by the soldiers. "If thou be the Son of God, come down from the cross"—*Matt.*, xxvii. 40. He was mocked by the priests, saying: "He saved others; himself he cannot save"—*ibid.*, *v.* 42. But he remained firm on the cross; he cheerfully died upon it, and thus conquered the world.

10. "I give thanks to God", says St. Jerome, "that I am worthy to be hated by the world"—*Epis. ad Asellam.* The saint return thanks to God for having made him worthy of the hatred of the world. Jesus Christ pronounced his disciples blessed when they should be hated by men. "Blessed shall you be, when men shall hate you"—*Luke*, vi. 22. Christians, let us rejoice; for, if worldlings curse and upbraid us, God at the same time praises and blesses us. "They will curse, and thou wilt bless"—*Ps.*, cviii. 28. Is it not enough for us to be praised by God, to be praised by the queen of Heaven, by all the angels, by all the saints, and by all just men? Let worldlings say what they wish; but let us continue to please God, who will give us, in the next life, a reward proportioned to the violence we shall have done to ourselves in despising the contradictions of men. Each of you should figure to himself, that there is no one in the world but himself and God. When the wicked treat us with contempt, let us recommend to God these blind and miserable men, who run in the road to perdition; and let us thank the Lord for giving to us the light which he refuses to them. Let us continue in our own way: to obtain all, it is necessary to conquer all.

Second point. On the means of overcoming human respect.

11. To overcome human respect, it is necessary to fix in our hearts the holy resolution of preferring the grace of God to all the goods and favours of this world, and to say with St. Paul: "Neither death, nor life, nor angels, nor principalities, nor powers,......nor any other creature, shall be able to separate us from the love of God"—*Rom.*, viii. 38, 39. Jesus Christ exhorts us not to be afraid of those who can take away the life of the body; but to fear him only who can condemn the soul

and body to Hell. "And fear ye not them that kill the body;... but rather fear him that can destroy both soul and body into Hell"—*Matt.*, x. 28. We wish either to follow God or the world; if we wish to follow God, we must give up the world. "How long do you halt between two sides?" said Elias to the people. "If the Lord be God, follow him"—III. *Kings*, xviii. 21. You cannot serve God and the world. He that seeks to please men, cannot please God. "If", says the Apostle, "I yet pleased men, I should not be the servant of Christ"—*Gal.*, i. 10.

12. The true servants of God rejoice to see themselves despised and maltreated for the sake of Jesus Christ. The holy apostles "went from the presence of the council, rejoicing that they were accounted worthy to suffer reproach for the name of Jesus"—*Acts*, v. 41. Moses could have prevented the anger of Pharaoh by not contradicting the current report, that he was the son of Pharaoh's daughter. But he denied that he was her son, preferring, as St. Paul says, the opprobrium of Christ, to all the riches of the world. "Rather choosing to be afflicted with the people of God; ......esteeming the reproach of Christ greater riches than the treasure of the Egyptians"—*Heb.*, xi. 25, 26.

13. Wicked friends come to you and say: What extravagancies are those in which you indulge? Why do you not act like others? Say to them in answer: My conduct is not opposed to that of all men; there are others who lead a holy life. They are indeed few; but I will follow their example; for the Gospel says: "Many are called, but few are chosen"—*Matt.*, xx. 16. "If", says St. John Climacus, "you wish to be saved with the few, live like the few". But, they will add, do you not see that all murmur against you, and condemn your manner of living? Let your answer be: It is enough for me, that God does not censure my conduct. Is it not better to obey God than to obey men? Such was the answer of St. Peter and St. John to the Jewish priests: "If it be just in the sight of God to hear you rather than God, judge ye"—*Acts*, iv. 19. If they ask you how can you bear an insult? or how, after submitting to it, can you appear among your equals? answer them by saying, that you are a Christian, and that it is enough for you to appear well in the eyes of God. Such should be your answer to all these satellites of Satan: you must despise all their maxims and reproaches.

And when it is necessary to reprove those who make little of God's law, you must take courage and correct them publicly. "Them that sin, reprove before all"—I. *Tim.*, v. 20. And when there is question of the divine honour, we should not be frightened by the dignity of the man who offends God; let us say to him openly: This is sinful; it cannot be done. Let us imitate the Baptist, who reproved King Herod for living with his brother's wife, and said to him: "It is not lawful for thee to have her"—*Matt.*, xiv. 4. Men indeed shall regard us as fools, and turn us into derision; but, on the day of judgment they shall acknowledge that they have been foolish, and we shall have the glory of being numbered among the saints. They shall say: "These are they whom we had some time in derision......We fools esteemed their life madness, and their end without honour. Behold how they are numbered among the children of God, and their lot is among the saints"—*Wis.*, v. 3, 4, 5.

SERMON XXVIII.

FOR PENTECOST SUNDAY.

On conformity to the will of God.

"As the Father hath given me commandment, so do I"—*John*, xiv. 31.

Jesus Christ was given to us by God, as a saviour and as a master. Hence he came on Earth principally to teach us, not only by his words, but also by his own example, how we are to love God—our supreme good; hence, as we read in this day's Gospel, he said to his disciples: "That the world may know that I love the Father, and as the Father hath given me commandments, so do I". To show the world the love I bear to the Father, I will execute all his commands. In another place he said: "I came down from Heaven not to do my own will, but the will of him that sent me"—*John*, vi. 38. Devout souls, if you love God and desire to become saints, you must seek his will and wish what he wishes. St. Paul tells us, that the divine love is poured into our souls by means of the Holy Ghost. "The charity of God is poured into our hearts by the Holy Ghost, who is given to us"—*Rom.*, v. 5. If, then, we wish for the gift of divine love, we must constantly beseech the Holy Ghost to make us know and do the will of God. Let us continually implore his light to know, and his strength to fulfil the divine will. Many wish to love God, but they, at the same time, wish to follow their own, and not his will. Hence I shall show to-day, in the first point, that our sanctification consists entirely in conformity to the will of God; and in the second, I shall show how and in what we should, in practice, conform ourselves to the divine will.

First point. Our sanctification consists entirely in conformity to the will of God.

1. It is certain that our salvation consists in loving God. A soul that does not love God, is not living, but dead. "He that loveth not, abideth in death"—I. *John*, iii. 14. The perfection of love consists in conforming our will to the will of God. "And life in his *good* will"—*Ps.*, xxix. 6. "Have charity, which is the bond of perfection"—*Col.*, iii. 14. According to the Areopagite, the principal effect of love is to unite the wills of lovers, so that they may have but one heart and one will. Hence all our works, communions, prayers, penances, and alms, please God in proportion to their conformity to the divine will, and if they be contrary to the will of God, they are no longer acts of virtue, but defects deserving of chastisement.

2. Whilst preaching one day, Jesus Christ was told that his mother and brethren were waiting for him; in answer he said: "Whosoever shall do the will of my Father that is in Heaven, he is my brother, and sister and mother"—*Matt.*, xii. 50. By these words he gave us to understand that he acknowledged as friends and relatives those only who fulfil the will of his Father.

3. The saints in Heaven love God perfectly. In what, I ask, does the perfection of their love consist? It consists in an entire conformity to the divine will. Hence Jesus Christ has taught us to pray for grace to do the will of God on Earth, as the saints do it in Heaven. "Thy will be done on Earth, as it is in Heaven"—*Matt.*, vi. 10. Hence St. Teresa says, that "they

who practise prayer, should seek in all things to conform their will to the will of God". In this, she adds, consists the highest perfection. He that practises it in the most perfect manner, shall receive from God the greatest gifts, and shall make the greatest progress in an interior life. The accomplishment of the divine will has been the sole end of the saints in the practice of all virtues. Blessed Henry Suson used to say: "I would rather be the vilest man on Earth with the will of God, than be a seraph with my own will".

4. A perfect act of conformity is sufficient to make a person a saint. Behold, Jesus Christ appeared to St. Paul while he was persecuting the Church, and converted him. What did the saint do? He did nothing more than offer to God his will, that he might dispose of it as he pleased. "Lord", he exclaimed, "what wilt thou have me to do?"—*Acts*, ix. 6. And instantly the Lord declared to Ananias, that Saul was a vessel of election, and apostle of the Gentiles. "This man is a vessel of election to carry my name before the Gentiles"—*Acts*, ix. 15. He that gives his will to God, gives him all he has. He that mortifies himself by fasts and penitential austerities, or that gives alms to the poor for God's sake, gives to God a part of himself and of his goods; but he that gives his will to God, gives him all, and can say: Lord, having given thee my will, I have nothing more to give thee—I have given thee all. It is our heart—that is, our will—that God asks of us. "My son, give me thy heart"—*Prov.*, xxiii. 26. Since, then, says the holy Abbot Nilus, our will is so acceptable to God, we ought, in our prayers, to ask of him the grace, not that we may do what he will, but that we may do all that he wishes us to do. Every one knows this truth, that our sanctification consists in doing the will of God; but there is some difficulty in reducing it to practice. Let us, then, come to the second point, in which I have to say many things of great practical utility.

Second point. How, and in what we ought to practise conformity to the will of God.

5. That we may feel a facility of doing on all occasions the divine will, we must beforehand offer ourselves continually to embrace in peace, whatever God ordains or wills. Such was the practice of holy David. "My heart", he used to say, "is

ready; O God! my heart is ready"—*Ps.*, cvii. 2. And he continually besought the Lord to teach him to do his divine will. "Teach me to do thy will"—*Ps.*, cxlii. 10. He thus deserved to be called a man according to God's own heart. "I have found David, the son of Jesse, a man according to my own heart, who shall do all my wills"—*Acts*, xiii. 22. And why? Because the holy king was always ready to do whatever God wished him to do.

6. St. Teresa offered herself to God fifty times in the day, that he might dispose of her as he pleased; and declared her readiness to embrace either prosperity or adversity. The perfection of our oblation consists in offering ourselves to God without reserve. All are prepared to unite themselves to the divine will in prosperity; but perfection consists in conforming to it, even in adversity. To thank God in all things that are agreeable to us, is acceptable to him; but to accept with cheerfulness what is repugnant to our inclinations, is still more pleasing to him. Father M. Avila used to say, that "a single *blessed be God*, in adversity, is better than six thousand thanksgivings in prosperity".

7. We should conform to the divine will, not only in misfortunes which come directly from God—such as sickness, loss of property, privation of friends and relatives—but also in crosses which come to us from men, but indirectly from God—such as acts of injustice, defamations, calumnies, injuries, and all other sorts of persecutions. But you may ask, does God will that others commit sin, by injuring us in our property or in our reputation? No; God wills not their sin; but he wishes us to bear with such a loss, and with such a humiliation; and he wishes us to conform, on all such occasions, to his divine will.

8. "Good things and evil...are from God"—*Eccl.*, xi. 14. All blessings—such as riches and honours—and all misfortunes—such as sickness and persecutions—come from God. But mark that the Scripture calls them evils only because we, through a want of conformity to the will of God, regard them as evils and misfortunes. But, in reality, if we accepted them from the hands of God with Christian resignation, they should be blessings and not evils. The jewels which give the greatest splendour to the crown of the saints in Heaven, are the tribulations which they bore with patience, as coming from the hands of

the Lord. On hearing that the Sabeans had taken away all his oxen and asses, holy Job said: "The Lord gave, and the Lord hath taken away"—*Job*, i. 21. He did not say that the Lord gave, and that the Sabeans had taken away; but that the Lord gave, and that the Lord had taken away: and therefore he blessed the Lord, believing that all had happened through the divine will. "As it hath pleased the Lord, so it is done: blessed be the name of the Lord"—*ibid.* Being tormented with iron hooks and burning torches, the holy martyrs Epictetus and Atone said: "Lord, thy will be done in us". And their last words were: "Be blessed, O eternal God, for having given us the grace to accomplish thy will".

9. "Whatsoever shall befall the just man, it shall not make him sad"—*Prov.*, xii. 21. A soul that loves God is not disturbed by any misfortune that may happen to her. Cesarius relates (*lib.* X., *c.* vi.), that a certain monk, who did not perform greater austerities than his companions, wrought many miracles. Being astonished at this, the abbot asked him one day, what were the works of piety which he practised. He answered, that he was more imperfect than the other monks; but that his sole concern was, to conform himself to the divine will. Were you displeased, said the abbot, with the person who injured us so grievously a few days ago? No, father, replied the monk; I, on the contrary, thanked God for it; because I know that he does or permits all things for our good. From this answer, the abbot perceived the sanctity of the good religious. We should act in a similar manner under all the crosses that come upon us. Let us always say: "Yea, Father; for so hath it seemed good in thy sight"—*Matt.*, xi. 26. Lord, this is pleasing to thee; let it be done.

10. He that acts in this manner enjoys that peace which the angels announced at the birth of Jesus Christ to men of good will,—that is to those whose wills are united to the will of God. These, as the Apostle says, enjoy that peace which exceeds all sensual delights. "The peace of God, which surpasseth all understanding"—*Phil.*, iv. 7. A great and solid peace, which is not liable to change. "A holy man continueth in wisdom, like the sun; but a fool is changing, like the moon"—*Eccl.*, xxvii. 12. Fools—that is, sinners—are changed like the moon, which increases to-day, and grows less on to-morrow;—

to-day they are seen to laugh through folly, and to-morrow, to weep through despair; to-day they are humble and meek, to-morrow, proud and furious. In a word, sinners change with prosperity and adversity; but the just are like the sun, always the same, always serene in whatever happens to them. In the inferior part of the soul they cannot but feel some pain at the misfortunes which befall them; but, as long as the will remains united to the will of God, nothing can deprive them of that spiritual joy which is not subject to the vicissitudes of this life. "Your joy no man shall take from you"—*John*, xvi. 22.

11. He that reposes in the divine will, is like a man placed above the clouds: he sees the lightning, and hears the claps of thunder and the raging of the tempest below, but he is not injured or disturbed by them. And how can he be ever disturbed, when whatever he desires, always happens? He that desires only what pleases God, always obtains whatsoever he wishes, because all that happens to him, happens through the will of God. Salvian says, that Christians who are resigned, if they be in a low condition of life, wish to be in that state; if they be poor, they desire poverty; because they wish whatever God wills, and therefore they are always content. "Humiles sunt, hoc volunt, pauperes sunt, paupertate delectantur: itaque beati dicendi sunt". If cold, or heat, or rain, or wind come on, he that is united to the will of God says: I wish for this cold, this heat, this rain, and this wind, because God wills them. If loss of property, persecution, sickness, or even death come upon him, he says: I wish for this loss, this persecution, this sickness; I even wish for death, when it comes, because God wills it. And how can a person who seeks to please God, enjoy greater happiness than that which arises from cheerfully embracing the cross which God sends him, and from the conviction that, in embracing it, he pleases God in the highest degree? So great was the joy which St. Mary Magdalene de Pazzi used to feel at the bare mention of *the will of God*, that she would fall into an ecstasy.

12. But, how great is the folly of those who resist the divine will, and, instead of receiving tribulations with patience, get into a rage, and accuse God of treating them with injustice and cruelty! Perhaps they expect, that, in consequence of their opposition, what God wills shall not happen? "Who resisteth his will?"—*Rom.*, ix. 19. Miserable men! instead of lighten-

ing the cross which God sends them, they make it more heavy and painful. "Who hath resisted him, and hath peace?"—*Job*, ix. 4. Let us be resigned to the divine will, and we shall thus render our crosses light, and shall gain great treasures of merits for eternal life. In sending us tribulations, God intends to make us saints. "This is the will of God, your sanctification"—I. *Thess.*, iv. 3. He sends us crosses, not because he wishes evil to us, but because he desires our welfare, and because he knows that they are conducive to our salvation. "All things work together unto good"—*Rom.*, viii. 28. Even the chastisements which come from the Lord are not for our destruction, but for our good, and for the correction of our faults. "Let us believe that these scourges of the Lord...have happened for our amendment, and not for our destruction"—*Jud.*, viii. 27. God loves us so tenderly, that he not only desires, but is solicitous about our welfare. "The Lord", says David, "is careful for me"—*Ps.*, xxxix. 18.

13. Let us, then, always throw ourselves into the hands of God, who so ardently desires and so anxiously watches over our eternal salvation. "Casting all your care upon him; for he hath care of you"—I. *Peter*, v. 7. He who, during life, casts himself into the hands of God, shall lead a happy life and shall die a holy death. He who dies resigned to the divine will, dies a saint; but they who shall not have been united to the divine will during life, shall not conform to it at death, and shall not be saved. The accomplishment of the divine will should be the sole object of all our thoughts during the remainder of our days. To this end we should direct all our devotions, our meditations, communions, visits to the blessed sacrament, and all our prayers. We should constantly beg of God to teach and help us to do his will. "Teach me to do thy will"—*Ps.*, cxlii. 10. Let us, at the same time, offer ourselves to accept without reserve whatever he ordains, saying, with the Apostle: "Lord, what wilt thou have me to do?"—*Acts*, ix. 6. Lord, tell me what thou dost wish me to do; I desire to do thy will. And in all things, whether they be pleasing or painful, let us always have in our mouths that petition of the PATER NOSTER—"*thy will be done*". Let us frequently repeat it in the day, with all the affection of our hearts. Happy we, if we live and die saying: "*Thy will be done! thy will be done!*"

SERMON XXIX.

FOR TRINITY SUNDAY.

On the love of the Three Divine Persons for man.

"Going, therefore, teach ye all nations, baptizing them in the name of the Father, and of the Son, and of the Holy Ghost"—*Matt.*, xxviii. 19.

St. Leo has said, that the nature of God is, by its essence, goodness itself. "Deus cujus natura bonitas". Now, goodness naturally diffuses itself. "Bonum est sui diffusivum". And by experience we know that men of a good heart are full of love for all, and desire to share with all the goods which they enjoy. God being infinite goodness, is all love towards us his creatures. Hence St. John calls him pure love—pure charity. "God is charity"—I. *John*, iv. 8. And therefore he ardently desires to make us partakers of his own happiness. Faith teaches us how much the Three Divine Persons have done through love for man, and to enrich him with Heavenly gifts. In saying to his apostles, "Teach ye all nations, baptizing them in the name of the Father, and of the Son, and of the Holy Ghost", Jesus Christ wished that they should not only instruct the Gentiles in the mystery of the Most Holy Trinity, but that they should also teach them the love which the adorable Trinity bears to man. I intend to propose this day for your consideration the love shown to us by the Father in our creation; secondly, the love of the Son, in our redemption; and thirdly, the love of the Holy Ghost, in our sanctification.

First point. The love shown to us by the Father in our creation.

1. "I have loved thee with an everlasting love, therefore have I drawn thee, taking pity *on thee*"—*Jer.*, xxxi. 3. My son, says the Lord, I have loved you from eternity, and, through love for you, I have shown mercy to you by drawing you out of nothing. Hence, beloved Christians, of all those who love you, God has been your first lover. Your parents have been the first to love you on this Earth; but they have loved you only after they

had known you. But, before you had a being, God loved you. Before your father or mother was born, God loved you: yes; even before the creation of the world, he loved you. And how long before creation has God loved you? Perhaps for a thousand years, or for a thousand ages. It is needless to count years or ages; God loved you from eternity. "I have loved thee with an everlasting love". As long as he has been God, he has loved you: as long as he has loved himself, he has loved you. The thought of this love made St. Agnes the Virgin exclaim: "*I am prevented by another lover*". When creatures asked her heart, she answered: No; I cannot prefer you to my God. He has been the first to love me; it is then but just that he should hold the first place in my affections.

2. Thus, brethren, God has loved you from eternity, and through pure love, he has selected you from among so many men whom he could have created in place of you; but he has left them in their nothingness, and has brought you into existence, and placed you in the world. For the love of you, he has made so many other beautiful creatures, that they might serve you, and that they might remind you of the love which he has borne to you, and of the gratitude which you owe to him. "Heaven and Earth", says St. Augustine, "and all things tell me to love thee". When the saint beheld the sun, the stars, the mountains, the sea, the rains, they all appeared to him to speak, and to say: Augustine, love God; for he has created us that you might love him. When Abbé De Rancé, the founder of la Trappe, looked at the hills, the fountains, or flowers, he said, that all these creatures reminded him of the love which God had borne him. St. Teresa used to say, that these creatures reproached her with her ingratitude to God. Whilst she held a flower or fruit in her hand, St. Mary Magdalene de Pazzi used to feel her heart wounded with divine love, and would say within herself: Then, my God has thought from eternity of creating this flower and this fruit, that I might love him.

3. Moreover, seeing us condemned to Hell, in punishment of our sins, the Eternal Father, through love for us, has sent his Son on Earth to die on a cross, in order to redeem us from Hell, and to bring us with himself into Paradise. "God so loved the world, as to give his only begotten Son"—*John*, iii.

16:—love, which the Apostle calls an excess of love. "For his exceeding charity wherewith he loved us, even when we were dead in sins, has quickened us together in Christ"—*Eph.*, ii. 4, 5.

4. See also the special love which God has shown you in bringing you into life in a Christian country, and in the bosom of the Catholic or true Church. How many are born among the pagans, among the Jews, among the Mahometans and heretics, and all are lost. Consider that, compared with these, only a few—not even the tenth part of the human race—have the happiness of being born in a country where the true faith reigns: and, among that small number, he has chosen you. Oh! what an invaluable benefit is the gift of faith! How many millions of souls, among infidels and heretics, are deprived of the sacraments, of sermons, of good example, and of the other helps to salvation which we possess in the true Church. And the Lord resolved to bestow on us all these great graces, without any merit on our part, and even with the foreknowledge of our demerits. For, when he thought of creating us and of conferring these favours upon us, he foresaw our sins, and the injuries which we would commit against him.

Second point. The love which the Son of God has shown to us in our redemption.

5. Adam, our first father, sins by eating the forbidden apple, and is condemned to eternal death, along with all his posterity. Seeing the whole human race doomed to perdition, God resolved to send a redeemer to save mankind. Who shall come to accomplish their redemption? Perhaps an angel or a seraph. No; the Son of God, the supreme and true God, equal to the Father, offers himself to come on Earth, and there to take human flesh and to die for the salvation of men. O prodigy of divine love! Man, says St. Fulgentius, despises God, and separates himself from God, and through love for him, God comes on Earth to seek after rebellious man. "Homo Deum contemnens, a Deo discessit: Deus hominem diligens, ad homines venit"—*serm. in Nativ. Christ.* Since, says St. Augustine, we could not go to the Redeemer, he has deigned to come to us. "Quia ad mediatorem venire non poteramus, ipse ad nos venire dignatus est". And why has Jesus Christ resolved

to come to us? According to the same holy doctor, it is to convince us of his great love for us. "Christ came, that man might know how much God loves him".

6. Hence the Apostle writes: "The goodness and kindness of God our Saviour appeared"—*Tit.*, iii. 4. In the Greek text, the words are: "Singularis Dei erga homines apparuit amor": "The singular love of God towards men appeared". In explaining this passage, St. Bernard says, that before God appeared on Earth in human flesh, men could not arrive at a knowledge of the divine goodness; therefore, the Eternal Word took human nature, that, appearing in the form of man, men might know the goodness of God. "Priusquam apparet humanitas, latebat benignitas, sed unde tanta agnosci poterat? Venit in carne ut, apparente humanitate, cognosceretur benignitas"—*serm.* i., *in Epiph.* And what greater love and goodness could the Son of God show to us, than to become man and to become a worm like us, in order to save us from perdition? What astonishment would we not feel, if we saw a prince become a worm to save the worms of his kingdom! And what shall we say at the sight of a God made man like us, to deliver us from eternal death? "The word was made flesh" —*John*, i. 14. A God made flesh! if faith did not assure us of it, who could ever believe it? Behold then, as St. Paul says, a God, as it were, annihilated. "He emptied himself, taking the form of a servant......and in habit found as a man"—*Phil.*, ii. 7. By these words the Apostle gives us to understand, that the Son of God, who was filled with the divine majesty and power, humbled himself so as to assume the lowly and impotent condition of human nature, taking the form or nature of a servant, and becoming like men in his external appearance, although, as St. Chrysostom observes, he was not a mere man, but man and God. Hearing a deacon sing the words of St. John, *and the Word was made flesh*, St. Peter of Alcantara fell into an ecstasy, and flew through the air to the altar of the most holy sacrament.

7. But this God of love, the Incarnate Word, was not content with becoming flesh for the love of man; but, according to Isaias, he wished to live among us, as the last and lowest, and most afflicted of men. "There is no beauty in him, nor comeliness: and we have seen him......despised, and the most abject of men, a man of sorrows"—*Isa.*, liii. 2, 3. He was a man of

sorrows. Yes; for the life Jesus Christ was full of sorrows. *Virum dolorum.* He was a man made on purpose to be tormented with sorrows. From his birth till his death, the life of our Redeemer was all full of sorrows.

8. And because he came on Earth to gain our love, as he declared when he said: "I am come to cast fire on the Earth; and what will I but that it be kindled?"—*Luke*, xii. 49, he wished at the close of his life to give us the strongest marks and proofs of the love which he bears to us. "Having loved his own who were in the world, he loved them unto the end"—*John*, xiii. 1. Hence he not only humbled himself to death for us, but he also chose to die the most painful and opprobrious of all deaths. "He humbled himself, becoming obedient unto death, even unto the death of the cross"—*Phil.*, ii. 8. They who were crucified among the Jews, were objects of malediction and reproach to all. "He is accursed of God that hangeth on a tree"—*Deut.*, xxi. 23. Our Redeemer wished to die the shameful death of the cross, in the midst of a tempest of ignominies and sorrows. "I am come into the depths of the sea, and a tempest hath overwhelmed me"—*Ps.*, lxviii. 3.

9 "In this", says St. John, "we have known the charity of God, because he hath laid down his life for us"—I. *John*, iii. 16. And how could God give us a greater proof of his love than by laying down his life for us? Or, how is it possible for us to behold a God dead on the cross for our sake, and not love him? "For the charity of Christ presseth us"—II. *Cor.*, v. 14. By these words, St. Paul tells us, that it is not so much what Jesus Christ has done and suffered for our salvation, as the love which he has shown in suffering and dying for us, that obliges and compels us to love him. He has, as the same Apostle adds, died for all, that each of us may live no longer for himself, but only for that God who has given his life for the love of us. "Christ died for all, that they also who live, may not live to themselves, but unto him who died for them, and rose again"—II. *Cor.*, v. 15. And, to captivate our love, he has, after having given his life for us, left himself for the food of our souls. "Take ye and eat, this is my body"—*Matt.*, xxvi. 26. Had not faith taught that he left himself for our food, who could ever believe it? But of the prodigy of divine

love manifested in the holy sacrament, I shall speak on the second Sunday after Pentecost. Let us pass to a brief considera-tion of the third point.

Third point. On the love shown to us by the Holy Ghost in our sanctification.

10. The Eternal Father was not content with giving us his Son Jesus Christ, that he might save us by his death; he has also given us the Holy Ghost, that he may dwell in our souls, and that he may keep them always inflamed with holy love. In spite of all the injuries which he received on Earth from men, Jesus Christ, forgetful of their ingratitude, after having ascended into Heaven, sent us the Holy Ghost, that, by his holy flames, this divine spirit might kindle in our hearts the fire of divine charity, and sanctify our souls. Hence, when he descended on the apos-tles, he appeared in the form of tongues of fire. "And there appeared to them parted tongues, as it were of fire"—*Acts*, ii. 3. Hence the Church prescribes the following prayer: "We beseech thee, O Lord, that the Spirit may inflame us with that fire which the Lord Jesus Christ sent on the Earth, and vehemently wished to be enkindled". This is the holy fire which inflamed the saints with the desire of doing great things for God, which enabled them to love their most cruel enemies, to seek after contempt, to renounce all the riches and honours of the world, and even to em-brace with joy, torments and death.

11. The Holy Ghost is that divine bond which unites the Father with the Son; it is he that unites our souls, through love, with God. For, as St. Augustine says, an union with God is the effect of love. "*Charity is a virtue which unites us with God*". The chains of the world are chains of death, but the bonds of the Holy Ghost are bonds of eternal life, because they bind us to God, who is our true and only life.

12. Let us also remember, that all the lights, inspirations, divine calls, all the good acts which we have performed during our life, all our acts of contrition, of confidence in the divine mercy, of love, of resignation, have been the gifts of the Holy Ghost. "Likewise the Spirit also helpeth our infirmity; for we know not what we should pray for as we ought; but the Spirit himself asketh for us with unspeakable groanings"—

Rom., viii. 26. Thus, it is the Holy Ghost that prays for us; for we know not what we ought to ask, but the Holy Spirit teaches us what we should pray for.

13. In a word, the Three Persons of the Most Holy Trinity have endeavoured to show the love which God has borne us, that we may love him through gratitude. "When", says St. Bernard, "God loves, he wishes only to be loved". It is, then, but just that we love that God who has been the first to love us, and to put us under so many obligations by so many proofs of tender love. "Let us, therefore, love God, because God first hath loved us"—I. *John*, iv. 19. Oh! what a treasure is charity! it is an infinite treasure, because it makes us partakers of the friendship of God. "She is an infinite treasure to men, which they that use, become the friends of God"—*Wis.*, vii. 14. But, to acquire this treasure, it is necessary to detach the heart from Earthly things. "*Detach the heart from creatures*", says St. Teresa, "*and you shall find God*". In a heart filled with Earthly affections, there is no room for divine love. Let us therefore continually implore the Lord in our prayers, communions, and visits to the blessed sacrament, to give us his holy love; for this love will expel from our souls all affections for the things of this Earth. "*When*", says St. Francis de Sales, "*a house is on fire, all that is within is thrown out through the windows*". By these words the saint meant, that, when a soul is inflamed with divine love, she easily detaches herself from creatures: and Father Paul Segneri the younger used to say, that divine love is a thief that robs us of all Earthly affections, and makes us exclaim: *What, O my Lord, but thee alone, do I desire?*

14. "Love is strong as death"—*Cant.*, viii. 6. As no creature can resist death when the hour of dissolution arrives, so there is no difficulty which love, in a soul that loves God, does not overcome. When there is question of pleasing her beloved, love conquers all things: it conquers pains, losses, ignominies. "*Nihil tam durum, quod non amoris igne vincatur*". This love made the martyrs, in the midst of torments, racks, and burning gridirons, rejoice, and thank God for enabling them to suffer for him: it made the other saints, when there was no tyrant to torment them, become, as it were, their own executioners, by fasts, disciplines, and penitential austerities. St.

Augustine says, that in doing what one loves there is no labour, and if there be, the labour itself is loved. "In eo quod amatur aut non laboratur, aut ipse labor amatur".

SERMON XXX.

FOR THE FIRST SUNDAY AFTER PENTECOST.

On charity to our neighbour.

"For with the same measure that you shall mete withal, it shall be measured to you again"—*Luke*, vi. 38.

In this day's gospel we find, that Jesus Christ once said to his disciples: "Be ye merciful, as your Father also is merciful"—*Luke*, vi. 36. As your Heavenly Father is merciful towards you, so must you be merciful to others. He then proceeds to explain how, and in what, we should practise holy charity to our neighbour. "Judge not", he adds, "and you shall not be judged"—*v.* 37. Here he speaks against those who do not abstain from judging rashly of their neighbours. "Forgive, and you shall be forgiven"—*ibid.* He tells us that we cannot obtain pardon of the offences we have offered to God, unless we pardon those who have offended us. "Give, and it shall be given to you"—*v.* 38. By these words, he condemns those who wish that God should grant whatsoever they desire, and are, at the same time, niggardly and avaricious towards the poor. In conclusion he declares, that the measure of charity which we use to our neighbour, shall be the same that God will use towards us. Let us then see how we should practise charity to our neighbour: we ought to practise it, first, in our thoughts; secondly, in words; thirdly, by works.

First point. How we should practise charity to our neighbour in our thoughts.

1. "And this commandment we have from God, that he who loveth God, love also his brother"—I. *John*, iv. 21. The same precept, then, which obliges us to love God, commands us to love our neighbour. St. Catherine of Genoa said one day to

the Lord: "*My God, thou dost wish me to love my neighbour; but I can love no one but thee*". The Lord said to her in answer: *My child, he that loves me, loves whatsoever I love.* Hence St. John says: "If any man say: I love God; and hateth his brother, he is a liar"—I. *John*, iv. 20. And Jesus Christ has declared, that he will receive, as done to himself, the charity which we practise towards the least of his brethren.

2. Hence we must, in the first place, practise fraternal charity in our thoughts, by never judging evil of any one without certain foundation. "*Judge not, and you shall not be judged*". He who judges without certain grounds, that another has committed a mortal sin, is guilty of a grievous fault. If he only rashly suspects another of a mortal sin, he commits at least a venial offence. But, to judge or suspect evil of another is not sinful when we have certain grounds for the judgment or suspicion. However, he that has true charity thinks well of all, and banishes from his mind both judgments and suspicions. "Charity thinketh no evil"—I. *Cor.*, xiii. 5. The heads of families are obliged to suspect the evil which may be done by those who are under their care. Certain fathers and foolish mothers knowingly allow their sons to frequent bad company and houses in which there are young females, and permit their daughters to be alone with men. They endeavour to justify their neglect of their children by saying: *I do not wish to entertain bad thoughts of others.* O folly of parents! They are in such cases bound to suspect the evil which may happen; and, in order to prevent it, they should correct their children. But they that are not entrusted with the care of others, ought to abstain carefully from inquiring after the defects and conduct of others.

3. When sickness, loss of property, or any misfortune, happens to a neighbour, charity requires that we regret, at least with the superior part of the soul, the evil that has befallen him. I say, *with the superior part of the soul;* for, when we hear of the misfortunes of an enemy, our inferior appetite appears to feel delight; but, as long as we do not consent to that delight, we are not guilty of sin. However, it is sometimes lawful to desire, or to be pleased at, the temporal evil of another, when we expect that it will be productive of spiritual good to himself or to others. For example: it is lawful, according to St. Gregory, to rejoice at the sickness or

misfortune of an obstinate and scandalous sinner, and even to desire that he may fall into sickness or poverty, in order that he may cease to lead a wicked life, or at least to scandalize others. Behold the words of St. Gregory: "Evenire plerumque potest, ut non amissa charitate, et inimici nostri ruina lætificet, et ejus gloria sine invidiæ culpa contristet; cum et, ruente eo, quosdam bene erigi credimus, et proficiente illo, plerosque injuste opprimi formidamus"—*lib.* XXII. *Moral.*, *cap.* ii. But, except in such cases, it is unlawful to rejoice at the loss of a neighbour. It is also contrary to charity to feel regret at a neighbour's prosperity, merely because it is useful to him. This is precisely the sin of envy. The envious are, according to the Wise Man, on the side of the Devil, who, because he could not bear to see men in Heaven, from which he had been banished, tempted Adam to rebel against God. "But by the envy of the Devil death came into the world; and they follow him that are of his side"—*Wis.*, ii. 24. Let us pass to the next point.

Second point. On the charity which we ought to practise towards our neighbour in words.

4. With regard to the practice of fraternal charity in words, we ought, in the first place, and above all, to abstain from all detraction. "The tale-bearer shall defile his own soul, and shall be hated by all"—*Eccl.*, xxi. 31. As they who always speak well of others are loved by all, so he who detracts his neighbour is hateful to all—to God and to men, who, although they take delight in listening to detraction, hate the detracter, and are on their guard against him. St. Bernard says, that the tongue of a detracter is a three-edged sword. "Gladius equidem anceps, immo triplex est lingua detractoris"—*in Ps.*, lvi. With one of these edges it destroys the reputation of a neighbour; with the second it wounds the souls of those who listen to the detraction; and with the third it kills the soul of the detracter by depriving him of the divine grace. You will say: *I have spoken of my neighbour only in secret to my friends, and have made them promise not to mention to others what I told them.* This excuse will not stand: no; you are, as the Lord says, the serpent that bites in silence. "If a serpent bite in silence, he is nothing better that backbiteth secretly"—*Eccl.*, x. 11. Your secret defamation bites and destroys the cha-

racter of a neihgbour. They who indulge in the vice of detraction are chastised not only in the next, but also in this life; because their uncharitable tongues are the cause of a thousand sins, by creating discord in whole families and in entire villages. Thomas Cantaprensis (*Apum, etc., cap.* xxxvii.) relates, that he knew a certain detracter, who, at the end of life became raging mad, and died lacerating his tongue with his teeth. The tongue of another detracter, who was going to speak ill of St. Malachy, instantly swelled and was filled with worms. And, after seven days, the unhappy man died miserably.

5. Detraction is committed not only when we take away a neighbour's character by imputing to him a sin which he has not committed, or exaggerating his guilt, but also when we make known to others any of his secret sins. Some persons, when they know anything injurious to a neighbour, appear to suffer, as it were, the pains of childbirth, until they tell it to others. When the sin of a neighbour is secret and grievous, it is a mortal sin to mention it to others without a just cause. I say, *without a just cause;* for, to make known to a parent the fault of a child, that he may correct him and prevent a repetition of the fault, is not sinful, but is an act of virtue; for, according to St. Thomas (2, 2, *qu.* 2, *art.* 73), to let others know the sins of a neighbour is unlawful, when it is done to destroy his reputation, but not when it is done for his good, or for the good of others.

6. They who listen to detraction, and afterwards go and tell what was said to the person whose character had been injured, have to render a great account to God. These are called *talebearers.* Oh! how great is the evil produced by these talebearing tongues, that are thus employed in sowing discord. They are objects of God's hatred. "The Lord hateth......him that soweth discord among brethren"—*Prov.*, vi. 16, 19. Should the person who has been defamed speak of his defamer, the injury which he has received may, perhaps, give him some claim to compassion. But why should you relate what you have heard? Is it to create ill-will and hatred that shall be the cause of a thousand sins? If, from this day forward, you ever hear anything injurious to a neighbour, follow the advice of the Holy Ghost. "Hast thou heard a word against thy neighbour? let it die with thee"—*Eccl.*, xix. 10. You should not

only keep it shut up in your heart, but you must let it die within you. He that is only shut up, may escape and be seen; but he that is dead cannot leave the grave. When, then, you know anything injurious to your neighbour, you ought to be careful not to give any intimation of it to others by words, by motions of the head, or by any other sign. Sometimes greater injury is done to others by certain singular signs and broken words, than by a full statement of their guilt; because these hints make persons suspect that the evil is greater than it really is.

7. In your conversations, be careful not to give pain to any companion, either present or absent, by turning him into ridicule. You may say: *I do it through jest;* but, such jests are contrary to charity. "All things, therefore", says Jesus Christ, "that you would that men should do to you, do you also unto them"—*Mat.*, vii. 12. Would you like to be treated with derision before others? Give up, then, the practice of ridiculing your neighbours. Abstain also from contending about useless trifles. Sometimes, certain contests about mere trifles grow so warm, that they end in quarrels and injurious words. Some persons are so full of the spirit of contradiction, that they controvert what others say, without any necessity, and solely for the sake of contention, and thus violate charity. "Strive not", says the Holy Ghost, "in matters which do not concern thee"—*Eccl.*, xi. 9. But they will say: *I only defend reason; I cannot bear to hear assertions which are contrary to reason.* In answer to these defenders of reason, Cardinal Bellarmine says, that an ounce of charity is better than an hundred loads of reason. In conversation, particularly when the subject of it is unimportant, state your opinion, if you wish to take part in the discourse, and then keep yourself in peace, and be on your guard against obstinacy in defending your own opinion. In such contests it is always better to yield. B. Egidius used to say, that he who gives up, conquers; because he is superior in virtue, and preserves peace, which is far more valuable than a victory in such contests. St. Joseph Calasanctius was accustomed to say, that *he who loves peace never contradicts any one.*

8. Thus, dearly beloved brethren, if you wish to be loved by God and by men, endeavour always to speak well of all. And,

should you happen to hear a person speak ill of a neighbour, be careful not to encourage his uncharitableness, nor to show any curiosity to hear the faults of others. If you do, you will be guilty of the same sin which the detracter commits. "Hedge in thy ears with thorns", says Ecclesiasticus, "and hear not a wicked tongue"—*Eccl.*, xxviii. 28. When you hear any one taking away the character of another, place around your ears a hedge of thorns, that detraction may not enter. For this purpose it is necessary, at least, to show that the discourse is not pleasing to you. This may be done by remaining silent, by putting on a sorrowful countenance, by casting down the eyes, or turning your face in another direction. In a word, act, says St. Jerome, in such a way, that the detracter, seeing your unwillingness to listen to him, may learn to be more guarded for the future against the sin of detraction. "Discat detractor, dum te videt non libenter audire, non facile detrahere"—*S. Hier. ep. ad Nepot.* And when it is in your power to do it, it will be great act of charity to defend the character of the persons who have been defamed. The Divine Spouse wishes that the words of his beloved be a veil of scarlet. "Thy lips are as a scarlet lace"—*Cant.*, iv. 3. That is, as Theodoret explains this passage, her words should be dictated by charity—*(a scarlet lace)*—that they may cover, as much as possible, the defects of others, at least by excusing their intentions, when their acts cannot be excused. "If", says Bernard, "you cannot excuse the act, excuse the intention"—*serm.* xl., *in Cant.* It was a proverb among the nuns of the convent of St. Teresa, that, in the presence of their holy mother, their reputation was secure, because they knew she would take the part of those of whom any fault might be mentioned.

9. Charity also requires that we be meek to all, and particularly to those who are opposed to us. When a person is angry with you, and uses injurious language, remember that "a mild answer breaketh wrath"—*Prov.*, xv. 1. Reply to him with meekness, and you shall find that his anger will be instantly appeased. But, if you resent the injury, and use harsh language, you will increase the flame; the feeling of revenge will grow more violent, and you will expose yourself to the danger of losing your soul by yielding to an act of hatred, or by breaking out into expressions grievously injurious to your

neighbour. Whenever you feel the soul agitated by passion, it is better to force yourself to remain silent, and to make no reply; for, as St. Bernard says, an eye clouded with anger cannot distinguish between right and wrong. "Turbatus præ ira oculus rectum non videt"—*lib.* II. *de Consid.*, *cap.* xi. Should it happen that, in a fit of passion, you have insulted a neighbour, charity requires that you use every means to allay his wounded feelings, and to remove from his heart all sentiments of rancour towards you. The best means of making reparation for the violation of charity, is to humble yourself to the person whom you have offended. With regard to the meekness which we should practise towards others, I shall speak on that subject in the thirty-fourth Sermon, or the Sermon for the fifth Sunday after Pentecost.

10. It is also an act of charity to correct sinners. Do not say that you are not a superior. Were you a superior, you should be obliged by your office to correct all those who might be under your care; but, although you are not placed over others, you are, as a Christian, obliged to fulfil the duty of fraternal correction. "He gave to every one of them commandment concerning his neighbour"—*Eccl.*, xvii. 12. Would it not be great cruelty to see a blind man walking on the brink of a precipice, and not admonish him of his danger, in order to preserve him from temporal death? It would be far greater cruelty to neglect, for the sake of avoiding a little trouble, to deliver a brother from eternal death.

Third point. On the charity we ought to practise towards our neighbour by works.

11. Some say that they love all; but will not put themselves to any inconvenience in order to relieve the wants of a neighbour. "My little children", says St. John, "let us not love in word, nor in tongue, but in deed and in truth"—I. *John*, iii. 18. The Scripture tells us, that alms deliver men from death, cleanse them from sin, and obtain for them the divine mercy and eternal life. "Alms delivereth from death, and the same is that which purgeth away sins, and maketh to find mercy and life everlasting"—*Tob.*, xii. 9. God will relieve you in the same manner in which you give relief to your neighbour. "With what measure you shall mete, it shall be measured to

you again"—*Matt.*, vii. 2. Hence St. Chrysostom says, that the exercise of charity to others is the means of acquiring great gain with God. "Alms is, of all acts, the most lucrative". And St. Mary Magdalene de Pazzi used to say, that she felt more happy in relieving her neighbour, than when she was wrapt up in contemplation, "Because", she would add, "when I am in contemplation, God assists me; but in giving relief to a neighbour, I assist God"; for, every act of charity which we exercise towards our neighbour, God accepts as if it were done to himself. But, on the other hand, how, as St. John says, can he who does not assist a brother in want, be said to love God? "He that hath the substance of this world, and shall see his brother in need, and shall shut up his bowels from him, how doth the charity of God abide in him?"—I. *John*, iii. 17. By alms is understood, not only the distribution of money or other goods, but every succour that is given to a neighbour in order to relieve his wants.

12. If charity obliges us to assist all, it commands us still more strictly to relieve those who are in the greatest need; such as the souls in Purgatory. St. Thomas teaches, that charity extends not only to the living, but also to the dead. Hence, as we ought to assist our neighbours who are in this life, so we are bound to give relief to those holy prisoners, who are so severely tormented by fire, and who are incapable of relieving themselves. A deceased monk of the Cistercian order appeared to the sacristan of his monastery, and said to him: "*Brother, assist me by your prayers; for I can do nothing for myself*"—*Cron. Cist.* Let us, then, assist, to the utmost of our power, these beloved spouses of Jesus Christ, by recommending them every day to God, and by sometimes getting Mass offered for their repose. There is nothing which gives so much relief to those holy souls as the sacrifice of the altar. They certainly will not be ungrateful; they will in return pray for you, and will obtain for you still greater graces, when they shall have entered into the kingdom of God.

13. To exercise a special charity towards the sick, is also very pleasing to God. They are afflicted by pains, by melancholy, by the fear of death, and are sometimes abandoned by others. Be careful to relieve them by alms, or by little presents, and to serve them as well as you can, at least by endeavouring

to console them by your words, and by exhortations to practise resignation to the will of God, and to offer to him all their sufferings.

14. Above all be careful to practise charity to those who are opposed to you. Some say: I am grateful to all who treat me with kindness; but I cannot exercise charity towards those who persecute me. Jesus Christ says, that even pagans know how to be grateful to those who do them a service. "Do not also the heathens this?"—*Matt.*, v. 47. Christian charity consists in wishing well, and in doing good to those who hate and injure us. "But I say to you: Love your enemies; do good to them that hate you; and pray for them that persecute and calumniate you" —*Matt.*, v. 44. Some seek to injure you, but you must love them. Some have done evil to you, but you must return good for evil. Such the vengeance of the saints. This is the Heavenly revenge which St. Paulinus exhorts us to inflict on our enemies. "To repay good for evil is Heavenly revenge"—*epis.* xvi. St. Chrysostom teaches, that there is nothing which assimilates us so much to God, as the granting of pardon to enemies. "Nothing makes men so like to God as to spare enemies"—*hom.* xxvii., *in Gen.* Such has been the practice of the saints. St. Catherine of Genoa continued for a long time to relieve a woman who had endeavoured to destroy the saint's reputation. On an assassin, who had made an attempt on his life, St. Ambrose settled a sum for his support. Venustanus, governor of Tuscany, ordered the hands of St. Sabinus to be cut off, because the holy bishop confessed the true faith. The tyrant feeling a violent pain in his eyes, entreated the saint to assist him. The saint prayed for him, and raising his arm, from which the blood still continued to flow, blessed him, and obtained for him the cure of his eyes and of his soul; for the tyrant became a convert to the faith. Father Segneri relates, that the son of a certain lady in Bologna was murdered by an assassin, who by accident took refuge in her house (*Christ. Istr.*, *part.* 1, *disc.* 20, *n.* 20). What did she do? She first concealed him from the ministers of justice, and afterwards said to him: Since I have lost my son, you shall henceforth be my son and my heir. Take, for the present, this sum of money, and provide for your safety elsewhere; for here you are not secure. It is thus the saints resent injuries. With what

face, says St. Cyril of Jerusalem, can he that does not pardon the affronts which he receives from his enemies, say to God: Lord, pardon me the many insults which I have offered to thee? "Qua fronte dices Domino: remitte mihi multa peccata mea, si tu pauca conservo tuo non remiseris?"—*Catech.*, ii. But he that forgives his enemies, is sure of the pardon of the Lord, who says: "Forgive, and you shall be forgiven"—*Luke*, vi. 37. And when you cannot serve them in any other way, recommend to God those who persecute and calumniate you. "Pray for them that persecute and calumniate you". This is the admonition of Jesus Christ, who is able to reward those who treat their enemies in this manner.

SERMON XXXI.

FOR THE SECOND SUNDAY AFTER PENTECOST.

On holy communion.

"A certain man made a great supper"—*Luke*, xiv. 16.

In the gospel of this day we read that a rich man prepared a great supper. He then ordered one of his servants to invite to it all those whom he should find in the highways, even though they were poor, blind, and lame, and to compel those who should refuse, to come to the supper. "Go out into the highways and hedges, and compel them to come in, that my house may be filled"—*v.* 23. And he added, that of all those who had been invited and had not come, not one should ever partake of his supper. "But I say unto you, that none of those men that were invited, shall taste of my supper"—*v.* 24. This supper is the holy communion: it is a great supper, at which all the faithful are invited to eat the sacred flesh of Jesus Christ in the most holy sacrament of the altar. "Take ye, and eat: this is my body"—*Matt.*, xxvi. 26. Let us then consider to-day, in the first point, the great love which Jesus Christ has shown us in giving us himself in this sacrament; and, in the second point, how we ought to receive him in order to draw great fruit from the holy communion.

First point. On the great love which Jesus Christ has shown us in giving us himself in this sacrament.

1. "Jesus knowing that his hour was come, that he should pass out of this world to the Father, having loved his own that were in the world, he loved them unto the end"—*John*, xiii. 1. Knowing that the hour of his death had arrived, Jesus Christ wished, before his departure from this world, to leave us the greatest proof which he could give of his love, by leaving us himself in the holy eucharist. "He loved them to the end". That is, according to St. Chrysostom, *with an extreme love.* St. Bernardine of Sienna says, that the tokens of love which are given at death make a more lasting impression on the mind, and are more highly esteemed. "Quæ in fine in signum amicitiæ celebrantur, firmius memoriæ imprimuntur et cariora tenentur". But, whilst others leave a ring or a piece of money, as a mark of their affection, Jesus has left us himself entirely in this sacrament of love.

2. And when did Jesus Christ institute this sacrament? He instituted it, as the Apostle has remarked, on the night before his passion. "The Lord Jesus, the same night on which he was betrayed, took bread, and giving thanks, broke and said: 'Take ye and eat: this is my body'"—I. *Cor.*, xi. 23, 24. Thus, at the very time that men were preparing to put him to death, our loving Redeemer resolved to bestow upon us this gift. Jesus Christ, then, was not content with giving his life for us on a cross: he wished also, before his death, to pour out, as the Council of Trent says, all the riches of his love, by leaving himself for our food in the holy communion. "He, as it were, poured out the riches of his love towards man"—*sess.* 13, *cap.* ii. If faith had not taught it, who could ever imagine that a God would become man, and afterwards become the food of his own creatures? When Jesus Christ revealed to his followers this sacrament which he intended to leave us, St. John says, that they could not bring themselves to believe it, and departed from him saying: "How can this man give us his flesh to eat?...This saying is hard, and who can hear it?" —*St. John*, vi. 53, 61. But, what men could not imagine, the

great love of Jesus Christ has invented and effected. "*Take ye and eat: this is my body*". These words he addressed to his apostles on the night before he suffered, and he now, after his death, addresses them to us.

3. How highly honoured, says St. Francis de Sales, would that man feel, to whom the king sent from his table a portion of what he had on his own plate? But how should he feel if that portion were a part of the king's arm? In the holy communion Jesus gives us, not a part of his arm, but his entire body in the sacrament of the altar. "He gave you all", says St. Chrysostom, reproving our ingratitude; "he left nothing for himself". And St. Thomas teaches, that in the eucharist, God has given us all that he is, and all that he has. "Deus in eucharistia totum quod est et habet, dedit nobis"—*Opusc.* 63, *c.* ii. Justly then has the same saint called the eucharist, "*a sacrament of love; a pledge of love*". "*Sacramentum charitatis, pignus charitatis*". It is a sacrament of love, because it was pure love that induced Jesus Christ to give us this gift and pledge of love: for he wished that, should a doubt of his having loved us ever enter into our minds, we should have in this sacrament a pledge of his love. St. Bernard calls this sacrament, *love of loves.* "Amor amorum". By his incarnation, the Lord has given himself to all men in general; but, in this sacrament, he has given himself to each of us in particular, to make us understand the special love which he entertains for each of us.

4. Oh! how ardently does Jesus Christ desire to come to our souls in the holy communion! This vehement desire he expressed at the time of the institution of this sacrament, when he said to his apostles: "With desire I have desired to eat this Pasch with you"—*Luke*, xxii. 15. St. Lawrence Justinian says, that these words proceeded from the enamoured heart of Jesus Christ, who, by such tender expressions, wished to show us the ardent love with which he loved us. *This is the voice of the most burning charity.* "Flagrantissimæ charitatis est vox hæc". And, to induce us to receive him frequently in the holy communion, he promises eternal life—that is, the kingdom of Heaven—to those who eat his flesh. "He that eateth this bread shall live for ever"—*John*, vi. 59. On the other hand, he threatens to deprive us of his grace and of Paradise, if we

neglect communion. "Except you eat the flesh of the Son of Man, and drink his blood, you shall not have life in you"—*John*, vi. 54. These promises and these threats all sprung from a burning desire to come to us in this sacrament.

5. And why does Jesus Christ so vehemently desire that we receive him in the holy communion? It is because he takes delight in being united with each of us. By the communion, Jesus is really united to our soul and to our body, and we are united to Jesus. "He that eateth my flesh, and drinketh my blood, abideth in me, and I in him"—*John*, vi. 57. Thus, after communion, we are, says St. Chrysostom, one body and one flesh with Jesus Christ. "Huic nos unimur, et facti sumus unum corpus ut una caro"—*hom.* lxviii., *ad Pop. Ant.* Hence St. Lawrence Justinian exclaims: "Oh! how wonderful is thy love, O Lord Jesus, who hast wished to incorporate us in such a manner with thy body, that we should have one heart and one soul inseparably united with thee". Thus, to every soul that receives the eucharist, the Lord says what he once said to his beloved servant Margaret of Ipres—"Behold, my daughter, the close union made between me and thee; love me then, and let us remain for ever united in love; let us never more be separated". This union between us and Jesus Christ, is, according to St. Chrysostom, the effect of the love which Jesus Christ bears us. "Semetipsum nobis immiscuit, ut unum quid simus......ardenter enim amantium hoc est"—*hom.* lxi. But, O Lord, such intimate union with man is not suited to thy divine majesty. But love seeks not reason; it goes not where it ought to go, but where it is drawn. "Amor ratione caret, et vadit quo dicitur, non quo debeat"—*serm.* cxliii. St. Bernardine of Sienna says, that, in giving himself for our food, Jesus Christ loved us to the last degree; because he united himself entirely to us, as food is united to those who eat it. "Ultimus gradus amoris est, cum se dedit nobis in cibum, quia dedit se nobis ad omnimodam unionem, sicut cibus et cibans invicem uniuntur" —*tom.* II., *serm.* liv. The same doctrine has been beautifully expressed by St. Francis de Sales. "No action of the Saviour can be more loving or more tender than the institution of the holy eucharist, in which he, as it were, annihilates himself, and takes the form of food, to unite himself to the souls and bodies of his faithful servants".

6. Hence, there is nothing from which we can draw so much fruit as from the holy communion. St. Denis teaches, that the most holy sacrament has greater efficacy to sanctify souls, than all other spiritual means. "Eucharistia maximam vim habet perficiendæ sanctitatis". St. Vincent Ferrer says, that a soul derives more profit from one communion, than from fasting for a week on bread and water. The eucharist is, according to the holy Council of Trent, a medicine which delivers us from venial, and preserves us from mortal sins. "Antidotum quo a culpis quotidianis liberemur, et a mortalibus præservemur". Jesus himself has said, that they who eat him, who is the fountain of life, shall receive permanently the life of grace. "He that eateth me, the same shall also live by me"—*John*, vi. 58. Innocent the Third teaches, that by his passion, Jesus Christ delivers us from the sins we have committed, and by the eucharist from the sins we may commit. According to St. Chrysostom, the holy communion inflames us with the fire of divine love, and makes us objects of terror to the Devil. "The eucharist is a fire which inflames us, that, like lions breathing fire, we may retire from the altar being made terrible to the Devil"—*hom.* lxi. *ad Pop. Ant.* In explaining the words of the Spouse of the Canticles, "He brought me into the cellar of wine; he set in order charity in me" (ii. 4), St. Gregory says, that the communion is this cellar of wine, in which the soul is so inebriated with divine love, that she forgets and loses sight of all Earthly things.

7. Some will say: *I do not communicate often, because I am cold in divine love.* In answer to them, Gerson asks, will you then, because you feel cold, remove from the fire? When you are tepid, you should more frequently approach this sacrament. St. Bonaventure says: "Trusting in the mercy of God, though you feel tepid, approach: let him who thinks himself unworthy, reflect, that the more infirm he feels himself, the more he requires a physician"—*de Prof. Rel.*, *cap.* lxxviii. And, in *The Devout Life*, chapter xx., St. Francis de Sales writes: "Two sorts of persons ought to communicate often: the perfect, to preserve perfection; and the imperfect, to arrive at perfection". It cannot be doubted, that he who wishes to communicate, should prepare himself with great diligence, that he may communicate well. Let us pass to the second point.

Second point. On the preparation we ought to make in order to derive great fruit from the holy communion.

8. Two things are necessary in order to draw great fruit from communion—preparation for, and thanksgiving after communion. As to the preparation, it is certain that the saints derived great profit from their communions, only because they were careful to prepare themselves well for receiving the holy eucharist. It is easy then to understand why so many souls remain subject to the same imperfections, after all their communions. Cardinal Bona says, that the defect is not in the food, but in the want of preparation for it. "Defectus non in bibo est, sed in edentis dispositione". For frequent communion, two principal dispositions are necessary. The first is detachment from creatures, and disengagement of the heart from everything that is not God. The more the heart is occupied with Earthly concerns, the less room there is in it for divine love. Hence, to give full possession of the whole heart to God, it is necessary to purify it from worldly attachments. This is the preparation which Jesus himself recommended to St. Gertrude. "*I ask nothing more of thee*", said he to her, "*than that thou come to receive me with a heart divested of thyself*". Let us then, withdraw our affections from creatures, and our hearts shall belong entirely to the Creator.

9. The second disposition necessary to draw great fruit from communion, is a desire of receiving Jesus Christ in order to advance in his love. "He", says St. Francis de Sales, "who gives himself through pure love, ought to be received only through love". Thus, the principal end of our communions must be to advance in the love of Jesus Christ. He once said to St. Matilda: "When you communicate, desire all the love that any soul has ever had for me, and I will accept your love in proportion to the fervour with which you wished for it".

10. Thanksgiving after communion is also necessary. The prayer we make after communion is the most acceptable to God, and the most profitable to us. After communion the soul should be employed in affections and petitions. The affections ought to consist not only in acts of thanksgiving, but also in acts of humility, of love, and of oblation of ourselves to God. Let us then humble ourselves as much as possible at the sight of a God made our food after we had offended him. A learned

author says that, for a soul after communion, the most appropriate sentiment is one of astonishment at the thought of receiving a God. She should exclaim: *What! a God to me! a God to me!* Let us also make many acts of the love of Jesus Christ. He has come into our souls in order to be loved. Hence, he is greatly pleased with those who, after communion, say to him: "*My Jesus, I love thee; I desire nothing but thee.* Let us also offer ourselves, and all that we have, to Jesus Christ, that he may dispose of all as he pleases; and let us frequently say: *My Jesus, thou art all mine; thou hast given thyself entirely to me; I give myself entirely to thee.*

11. After communion, we should not only make these affections, but we ought also to present to God with great confidence many petitions for his graces. The time after communion is a time in which we can gain treasures of divine graces. St. Teresa says, that at that time Jesus Christ remains in the soul as on a throne, saying to her what he said to the blind man—"What wilt thou that I should do to thee?"—*Mark*, x. 51. As if he said: "But me you have not always"—*John*, xii. 8. Now that you possess me within you, ask me for graces; I have come down from Heaven on purpose to dispense them to you; ask whatever you wish, and you shall obtain it. Oh! what great graces are lost by those who spend but little time in prayer after communion. Let us also turn to the Eternal Father, and, bearing in mind the promise of Jesus Christ—"Amen, amen, I say to you, if you ask the Father anything in my name, he will give it you"—*John*, xvi. 23—let us say to him: My God, for the love of this thy Son, whom I have within my heart, give me thy love; make me all thine. And if we offer this prayer with confidence, the Lord will certainly hear us. He who acts thus may become a saint by a single communion.

SERMON XXXII.

FOR THE THIRD SUNDAY AFTER PENTECOST.

On the mercy of God towards sinners.

"There shall be joy in Heaven upon one sinner that doth penance, more than upon ninety-nine just, who need not penance"—*Luke*, xv. 7.

In this day's gospel it is related, that the Pharisees murmured against Jesus Christ, because he received sinners and eat with them. "This man receiveth sinners and eateth with them"—*v.* 2. In answer to their murmurings our Lord said: If any of you had a hundred sheep, and lost one of them, would he not leave the ninety-nine in the desert, and go in search of the lost sheep? would he not continue his search until he found it? and having found it, would he not carry it on his shoulders, and, rejoicing, say to his friends and neighbours: "Rejoice with me, because I have found my sheep that was lost"?—*v.* 6. In conclusion, the Son of God said: "I say to you, there shall be joy in Heaven upon one sinner that doth penance, more than upon ninety-nine just, that need not penance". There is more joy in Heaven upon one sinner who returns to God, than upon many just who preserve the grace of God. Let us then speak to-day on the mercy which God shows to sinners, first, in calling them to repentance; secondly, in receiving them when they return.

First point. Mercy of God in calling sinners to repentance.

1. After having sinned by eating the forbidden apple, Adam fled from the face of the Lord through shame of the sin he had committed. What must have been the astonishment of the angels when they saw God seeking after him, and calling him as it were with tears, saying: Adam, "where art thou?"—*Gen.*, iii. 9. My beloved Adam, where art thou? These words, says Father Pereyra, in his commentary on this passage, "are the words of a father in search of his lost son". Towards you, brethren, the Lord acts in a similar manner. You fled from him,

and he has so often invited you to repentance by means of confessors and preachers. Who was it that spoke to you when they exhorted you to penance? It was the Lord. Preachers are, as St. Paul says, his ambassadors. "For Christ, therefore, we are ambassadors; God, as it were, exhorting by us"—II. *Cor.*, v. 20. Hence he writes to the sinners of Corinth: "For Christ, we beseech you, be reconciled to God"—*ibid.* In explaining these words, St. Chrysostom says: "Ipse Christus vos obsecrat: quid autem obsecrat? Reconciliamini Deo". Then, says the holy doctor, Jesus Christ himself entreats you, O sinners: and what does he entreat you to do? To make peace with God. The saint adds: "Non enim ipse inimicus gerit, sed vos". It is not God that acts like an enemy, but you; that is, God does not refuse to make peace with sinners, but they are unwilling to be reconciled with him.

2. But, notwithstanding the refusal of sinners to return to God, he does not cease to continue to call them by so many interior inspirations, remorses of conscience, and terrors of chastisements. Thus, beloved Christians, God has spoken to you, and, seeing that you disregarded his words, he has had recourse to scourges: he has called you to repentance by such a persecution, by temporal losses, by the death of a relative, by sickness which has brought you to the brink of the grave. He has, according to holy David, placed before your eyes the bow of your damnation, not that you might be condemned to eternal misery, but that you might be delivered from Hell, which you deserved. "Thou hast given a warning to them that fear thee, that they may flee from before the bow; that thy beloved may be delivered"—*Ps.*, lix. 6. You regarded certain afflictions as misfortunes; but they were mercies from God; they were the voices of God calling on you to renounce sin, that you might escape perdition. "My jaws are become hoarse"—*Ps.*, lxviii. 4. My son, says the Lord, I have almost lost my voice in calling you to repentance. "I am weary of entreating thee"—*Jer.*, xv. 6. I have become weary in imploring you to offend me no more.

3. By your ingratitude you deserved that he should call you no more; but he has continued to invite you to return to him. And who is it that has called you? It is a God of infinite majesty, who is to be one day your judge, and on whom your

eternal happiness or misery depends. And what are you but miserable worms deserving Hell? Why has he called you? To restore to you the life of grace which you have lost. "Return ye and live"—*Ezec.*, xviii. 32. To acquire the grace of God, it would be but little to spend a hundred years in a desert in fasting and penitential austerities. But God offered it to you for a single act of sorrow; you refused that act, and, after your refusal, he has not abandoned you, but has sought after you, saying: "And why will you die, O house of Israel?"—*Ez.*, xviii. 31. Like a father weeping and following his son, who has voluntarily thrown himself into the sea, God has sought after you, saying through compassion to each of you: My son, why dost thou bring thyself to eternal misery? "Why will you die, O house of Israel?"

4. As a pigeon that seeks to take shelter in a tower, seeing the entrance closed on every side, continues to fly round it till she finds an opening through which she enters, so, says St. Augustine, did the divine mercy act towards me when I was in enmity with God. "Circuibat super me fidelis a longe misericordia tua". The Lord treated you, brethren, in a similar manner. As often as you sinned, you banished him from your souls. The wicked have said to God: "Depart from us"—*Job*, xxi. 14. And, instead of abandoning you, what has the Lord done? He has placed himself at the door of your ungrateful hearts, and, by his knocking, has made you feel that he was outside, and seeking for admission. "Behold, I stand at the gate and knock"—*Apoc.*, iii. 20. He, as it were, entreated you to have compassion on him, and to allow him to enter. "Open to me, my sister"—*Cant.*, v. 2. Open to me; I will deliver you from perdition; I will forget all the insults you have offered to me, if you give up sin. Perhaps you are unwilling to open to me through fear of becoming poor by restoring ill-gotten goods, or by separating from a person who provided for you? Am not I, says the Lord, able to provide for you? Perhaps you think that, if you renounce a certain friendship which separates you from me, you shall lead a life of misery? Am I not able to content your soul and to make your life happy? Ask those who love me with their whole hearts, and they will tell you that my grace makes them content, and that they would not ex-

change their condition, though poor and humble, for all the delights and riches of the monarchs of the Earth.

Second point. Mercy of God in waiting for sinners to return to him.

5. We have considered the divine mercy in calling sinners to repentance: let us now consider his patience in waiting for their return. That great servant of God, D. Sancia Carillo, a penitent of Father John Avila, used to say, that the consideration of God's patience with sinners, made her desire to build a church, and entitle it, *The patience of God.* Ah, sinners! who could ever bear with what God has borne from you? If the offences which you have committed against God had been offered to your best friends, or even to your parents, they surely would have sought revenge. When you insulted the Lord, he was able to chastise you; you repeated the insult, and he did not punish your guilt, but preserved your life and provided you with sustenance. He, as it were, pretended not to see the injuries you offered to him, that you might enter into yourselves, and cease to offend him. "Thou overlookest the sins of men for the sake of repentance"—*Wis.*, xi. 24. But how, O Lord, does it happen, that thou canst not behold a single sin, and that thou dost bear in silence with so many? "Thy eyes are too pure to behold evil, and thou canst not look on iniquity. Why lookest thou upon them that do unjust things, and holdest thy peace?"—*Hab.*, i. 13. Thou seest the vindictive prefer their own, before thy honour; thou beholdest the unjust, instead of restoring what they have stolen, continuing to commit theft; the unchaste, instead of being ashamed of their impurities, boasting of them before others; the scandalous, not content with the sins which they themselves commit, but seeking to draw others into rebellion against thee: thou seest all this, and holdest thy peace, and dost not inflict vengeance.

6. "Omnis creatura", says St. Thomas, "tibi factori deserviens excandescit adversus injustos". All creatures—the Earth, fire, air, water—because they all obey God, would, by a natural instinct, wish to punish the sinner, and to avenge the injuries which he does to the Creator; but God, through his mercy, restrains them. But, O Lord, thou waitest for the wicked that they may enter into themselves; and dost thou not see that

they abuse thy mercy to offer new insults to thy majesty? "Thou hast been favourable to the nation, O Lord, thou hast been favourable to the nation: art thou glorified?"—*Isa.*, xxvi. 15. Thou hast waited so long for sinners; thou hast abstained from inflicting punishment; but what glory have you reaped from thy forbearance? They have become more wicked. Why so much patience with such ungrateful souls? Why dost thou continue to wait for their repentance? Why dost thou not chastise their wickedness? The same Prophet answers: "The Lord waiteth that he may have mercy on you"—*Isa.*, xxx. 18. God waits for sinners that they may one day repent, and that after their repentance, he may pardon and save them. "As I live, saith the Lord, I desire not the death of the wicked, but that the wicked turn from his way and live"—*Ezech.*, xxxiii. 11. St. Augustine goes so far as to say, that the Lord, if he were not God, should be unjust on account of his excessive patience towards sinners. "Deus, Deus meus, pace tua dicam, nisi quia Deus esses, injustus esses". By waiting for those who abuse his patience to multiply their sins, God appears to do an injustice to the divine honour. "*We*", continues the saint, "*sin; we adhere to sin* (some of us become familiar and intimate with sin, and sleep for months and years in this miserable state); *we rejoice at sin* (some of us go so far as to boast of our wickedness); *and thou art appeased! We provoke thee to anger—thou dost invite us to mercy*". We and God appear to be, as it were, engaged in a contest, in which we labour to provoke him to chastise our guilt, and he invites us to pardon.

7. Lord, exclaimed holy Job, what is man, that thou dost entertain so great an esteem for him? Why dost thou love him so tenderly? "What is man that thou shouldst magnify him? or why dost thou set thy heart upon him?"—*Job*, vii. 17. St. Denis the Areopagite says, that God seeks after sinners like a despised lover, entreating them not to destroy themselves. "Deus etiam a se aversos amatorie sequitur, et deprecatur ne pereant". Why, O ungrateful souls, do you fly from me? I love you, and desire nothing but your welfare. Ah, sinners! says St. Teresa, remember that he who now calls and seeks after you, is that God who shall one day be your judge. If you are lost, the great mercies which he now shows you, shall be the greatest torments which you shall suffer in Hell.

Third point. Mercy of God in receiving penitent sinners.

8. Should a subject who has rebelled against an Earthly monarch go into the presence of his sovereign to ask pardon, the prince instantly banishes the rebel from his sight, and does not condescend even to look at him. But God does not treat us in this manner, when we go with humility before him to implore mercy and forgiveness. " The Lord your God is merciful, and will not turn away his face from you if you return to him"—II. *Par.*, xxx.
9. God cannot turn away his face from those who cast themselves at his feet with an humble and contrite heart. Jesus himself has protested, that he will not reject any one who returns to him. " And him that cometh to me, I will not cast out"—*John*, vi. 37. But how can he reject those whom he himself invites to return, and promises to embrace? " Return to me, saith the Lord, and I will receive thee"—*Jer.*, iii. 1. In another place he says: Sinners, I ought to turn my back on you, because you first turned your back on me; but be converted to me, and I will be converted to you. " Turn to me, saith the Lord of Hosts, and I will turn to you, saith the Lord of Hosts"—*Zach.*, i. 3.

9. Oh! with what tenderness does God embrace a sinner that returns to him! This tenderness Jesus Christ wished to declare to us when he said that he is the good pastor, who, as soon as he finds the lost sheep, embraces it, and places it on his own shoulders. " And when he hath found it, doth he not lay it upon his shoulders rejoicing?"—*Luke*, xv. 5. This tenderness also appears in the parable of the prodigal son, in which Jesus Christ tells us that he is the good father, who, when his lost son returns, goes to meet him, embraces and kisses him, and, as it were, swoons away through joy in receiving him. " And running to him, he fell upon his neck and kissed him"—*Luke*, xv. 20.

10. God protests that when sinners repent of their iniquities, he will forget all their sins, as if they had never offended him. " But, if the wicked do penance for all the sins which he hath committed...living, he shall live, and shall not die. I will not remember all his iniquities that he hath done"—*Ezech.*, xviii. 21, 22. By the Prophet Isaias, the Lord goes so far as to say: " Come and accuse me, saith the Lord. If your sins be as scarlet, they shall be made white as snow"—*Isa.*, i. 18. Mark the

words, *Come and accuse me.* As if the Lord said: Sinners, come to me, and if I do not pardon and embrace you, reprove me, upbraid me with violating my promise. But no! God cannot despise an humble and contrite heart. " A contrite and humbled heart, O God, thou wilt not despise"—*Ps.*, l. 19.

11. To show mercy and grant pardon to sinners, God regards as redounding to his own glory. " And therefore shall he be exalted sparing you"—*Isa.*, xxx. 18. The holy Church says, that God displays his omnipotence in granting pardon and mercy to sinners. " *O God, who manifestest thy omnipotence in sparing and showing mercy*". Do not imagine, dearly beloved sinners, that God requires of you to labour for a long time before he grants you pardon: as soon as you wish for forgiveness, he is ready to give it. Behold what the Scripture says: " Weeping, thou shalt not weep, he will surely have pity on thee"—*Isa.*, xxx. 19. You shall not have to weep for a long time: as soon as you shall have shed the first tear through sorrow for your sins, God will have mercy on you. " At the voice of thy cry, as soon as he shall hear, he will answer thee"—*ibid.* The moment he shall hear you say: Forgive me, O my God, forgive me: he will instantly answer and grant you pardon.

SERMON XXXIII.

FOR THE FOURTH SUNDAY AFTER PENTECOST.

Death is certain and uncertain.

" Let down your nets for a draught"—*Luke*, v. 4.

In this day's gospel we find that, having gone up into one of the ships, and having heard from St. Peter, that he and his companions had laboured all the night and had taken nothing, Jesus Christ said: " Launch out into the deep, and let down your nets for a draught". They obeyed; and having cast out their nets into the sea, they took such a multitude of fishes, that the nets were nearly broken. Brethren, God has placed us in the midst of the sea of this life, and has commanded us to cast out our nets, that we may catch fishes; that is, that we may perform good works, by which we can acquire merits for eternal life. Happy we, if we attain this end and save our souls! Unhappy we, if, instead of laying up treasures for Heaven, we by our sins merit Hell, and bring our souls to damnation! Our happiness or misery for eternity depends on the moment of our death, which is certain and uncertain. The Lord assures us that death is certain, that we may prepare for it; but, on the other hand, he leaves us uncertain as to the time of our death, that we may be always prepared for it —two points of the utmost importance.

First point. It is certain that we shall die.
Second point. It is uncertain when we shall die.

First point. It is certain that we shall die.

8. "It is appointed unto men once to die"—*Heb.*, ix. 27. The decree has been passed for each of us: we must all die. St. Cyprian says, that we are all born with the halter on the neck: hence, every step we make brings us nearer to the gibbet. For each of us the gibbet shall be the last sickness, which will end in death. As then, brethren, your name has been inserted in the registry of baptism, so it shall be one day written in the record of the dead. As, in speaking of your ancestors, you say: God be merciful to my father, to my uncle, or to my brother; so others shall say the same of you when you shall be in the other world: and as you have often heard the deathbell toll for many, so others shall hear it toll for you.

2. All things future, which regard men now living, are uncertain, but death is certain. "All other goods and evils", says St. Augustine, "are uncertain: death only is certain". It is uncertain whether such an infant shall be rich or poor, whether he shall enjoy good or ill health, whether he shall die at an early or at an advanced age. But it is certain that he shall die, though he be the son of a peer or of a monarch. And, when the hour arrives, no one can resist the stroke of death. The same St. Augustine says: "Fires, waters, and the sword are resisted; kings are resisted; death comes: who resists it?"—*in Ps.* xii. We may resist conflagrations, inundations,

the sword of enemies, and the power of princes; but who can resist death? A certain king of France, as Belluacensis relates, said in his last moments: "*Behold, with all my power, I cannot make death wait for a single hour*". No; when the term of life has arrived, death does not wait even a moment—"Thou hast appointed his bounds, which cannot be passed"—*Job*, xiv. 5.

3. We must all die. This truth we not only believe, but see with our eyes. In every age, houses, streets, and cities are filled with new inhabitants: their former possessors are shut up in the grave. And as for them the days of life are over, so a time shall come when not one of all who are now alive shall be among the living. "Days shall be formed, and no one in them"—*Ps.*, cxxxviii. 16. "Who is the man that shall live, and shall not see death?"—*Ps.*, lxxxviii. 49. Should any one flatter himself that he shall not die, he would not only be a disbeliever—for it is of faith that we shall all die—but he would be regarded as a madman. We know that all men, even potentates and princes and emperors, have, after a certain time, fallen victims to death. And where are they now? "Tell me", says St. Bernard, "where are the lovers of the world? Nothing has remained of them but ashes and worms". Of so many great men of the world, though buried in marble mausoleums, nothing has remained but a little dust and a few withered bones. We know that our ancestors are no longer among the living: of their death we are constantly reminded by their pictures, their memorandum books, their beds, and by the clothes which they have left us. And can we entertain a hope or a doubt that we shall not die? Of all who lived in this town a hundred years ago, how many are now alive? They are all in eternity—in an eternal day of delights, or in an eternal night of torments. Either the one or the other shall be our lot also.

4. But, O God! we all know that we shall die: the misfortune is, that we imagine death as distant as if it were never to come, and therefore we lose sight of it. But, sooner or later, whether we think or think not of death, it is certain and of faith that we shall die, and that we are drawing nearer to it every day. "For we have not here a lasting city, but we seek one that is to come"—*Heb.*, xiii. 14. This is not our country: here we are pilgrims on a journey. "While we are in the body we are

absent from the Lord"—II. *Cor.*, v. 6. Our country is Paradise, if we know how to acquire it by the grace of God and by our own good works. Our house is not that in which we live; we dwell in it only in passing; our dwelling is in eternity. "Man shall go into the house of his eternity"—*Eccl.*, xii. 5. How great would be the folly of the man, who, in passing through a strange country, should lay out all his property in the purchase of houses and possessions in a foreign land, and reduce himself to the necessity of living miserably for the remainder of his days in his own country! And is not he, too, a fool, who seeks after happiness in this world, from which he must soon depart, and, by his sins, exposes himself to the danger of misery in the next, where he must live for eternity?

5. Tell me, beloved brethren, if, instead of preparing for his approaching death, a person condemned to die were, on his way to the place of execution, to employ the few remaining moments of his life in admiring the beauty of the houses as he passed along, in thinking of balls and comedies, in uttering immodest words, and detracting his neighbours, would you not say that the unhappy man had either lost his reason, or that he was abandoned by God? And are not you on the way to death? Why then do you seek only the gratification of the senses? Why do you not think of preparing the accounts which you shall one day, and perhaps very soon, have to render at the tribunal of Jesus Christ? Souls that have faith, leave to the fools of this world the care of realizing a fortune on this Earth; seek you to make a fortune for the next life, which shall be eternal. The present life must end, and end very soon.

6. Go to the grave in which your relatives and friends are buried. Look at their dead bodies: each of them says to you: "Yesterday for me; to-day for thee"—*Eccl.*, xxxviii. 23. What has happened to me, must one day happen to thee. Thou shalt become dust and ashes, as I am. And where shall thy soul be found, if, before death, thou hast not settled thy accounts with God? Ah, brethren! if you wish to live well, and to have your accounts ready for that great day, on which your doom to eternal life or to eternal death must be decided, endeavour, during the remaining days of life, to live with death before your eyes. "O death, thy sentence is welcome"—*Eccl.*, xli. 3. Oh! how correct are the judgments, how well directed

the actions of those who form their judgments, and perform their actions, with death before their view! The remembrance of death destroys all attachment to the goods of this Earth "Let the end of life be considered", says St. Lawrence Justinian, "and there will be nothing in this world to be loved"—*de Ligno Vitæ., cap.* v. Yes; all the riches, honours, and pleasures of this world are easily despised by him who considers that he must soon leave them for ever, and that he shall be thrown into the grave to be the food of worms.

7. Some banish the thought of death, as if, by avoiding to think of death, they could escape it. But death cannot be avoided; and they who banish the thought of it, expose themselves to great danger of an unhappy death. By keeping death before their eyes, the saints have despised all the goods of this Earth. Hence St. Charles Borromeo kept on his table a death's head, that he might have it continually in view. Cardinal Baronius had the words, *Memento mori—Remember death*—inscribed on his ring. The venerable P. Juvenal Anzia, Bishop of Saluzzo, had before him a skull, on which was written: "*As I am, so thou shalt be*". In retiring to deserts and caves, the holy solitaries brought with them the head of a dead man; and for what purpose? To prepare themselves for death. Thus, a certain hermit being asked at death, why he was so cheerful, answered: I have kept death always before my eyes; and therefore, now that it has arrived, I feel no terror. But, oh! how full of terror is death, when it comes to those who have thought of it but seldom.

Second point. It is uncertain when we shall die.

8. "Nothing", says the Idiota, "is more certain than death, but nothing is more uncertain than the hour of death". It is certain that we shall die. God has already determined the year, the month, the day, the hour, the moment, in which each of us shall leave this Earth, and enter into eternity; but, this moment he has resolved not to make known to us. And justly, says St. Augustine, has the Lord concealed it; for, had he manifested to all the day fixed for their death, many should be induced to continue in the habit of sin by the certainty of not dying before the appointed day. "Si statuisset viam omnibus, faceret abundare peccata de securitate"—*in Ps.*, cxliv.

Hence the holy doctor teaches, that God has concealed from us the day of our death, that we may spend all our days well. "Latet ultimus dies, ut observentur omnes dies"—*hom.* xii. *inter.* 50. Hence Jesus Christ says: "Be you also ready; for at what hour you think not, the Son of Man will come"—*Luke*, xii. 40. That we may be always prepared to die, he wishes us to be persuaded that death will come when we least expect it. "Of death", says St. Gregory, "we are uncertain, that we may be found always prepared for death". St. Paul likewise admonishes us, that the day of the Lord—that is, the day on which the Lord shall judge us—shall come unexpectedly, like a thief in the night. "The day of the Lord shall so come as a thief in the night"—I. *Thess.*, v. 2. Since, then, says St. Bernard, death may assail you and take away your life in every place and at every time, you should, if you wish to die well and to save your soul, be at all times and places in expectation of death. "Mors ubique te expectat, tu, ubique eam expectabis". And St. Augustine says: "Latet ultimus dies, ut observentur omnes dies"—*hom.* xii. The Lord conceals from us the last day of our life, that we may always have ready the account which we must render to God after death.

9. Many Christians are lost, because many, even among the old, who feel the approach of death, flatter themselves that it is at a distance, and that it will not come without giving them time to prepare for it. "Dura mente", says St. Gregory, "abesse longe mors creditur, etiam cum sentitur"—*Moral.*, *lib.* 8. Death, even when it is felt, is believed to be far off. O brethren, are these your sentiments? How do you know that your death is near or distant? What reason have you to suppose that death will give you time to prepare for it? How many do we know to have died suddenly? Some have died walking; some sitting; and some during sleep. Did any one of these ever imagine that he should die in such a manner? But they have died in this way; and if they were in enmity with God, what has been the lot of their unhappy souls? Miserable the man who meets with an unprovided death! And I assert, that all who ordinarily neglect to unburthen their conscience, die without preparation, even though they should have seven or eight days to prepare for a good death; for, as I shall show in the forty-fourth sermon, it is very difficult, during these

days of confusion and terror, to settle accounts with God, and to return to him with sincerity. But I repeat, that death may come upon you in such a manner, that you shall not have time even to receive the sacraments. And who knows whether, in another hour, you shall be among the living or the dead? The uncertainty of the time of his death made Job tremble. "For I know not how long I shall continue, or whether, after a while, my Maker may take me away"—*Job*, xxxii. 22. Hence St. Basil exhorts us, in going to bed at night, not to trust that we shall see the next day. "Cum in lectulum ad quiescendum membra tua posueris, noli confidere de lucis adventu"—*Inst. ad fil. spirit.*

10. Whenever, then, the Devil tempts you to sin, by holding out the hope that you will go to confession and repair the evil you have done, say to him in answer: How do I know that this shall not be the last day of my life? And should death overtake me in sin, and not give me time to make my confession, what shall become of me for all eternity? Alas! how many poor sinners have been struck dead in the very act of indulging in some sinful pleasure, and have been sent to Hell! "As fishes are taken by the hook, and as birds are caught with the snare, so men are taken in the evil time"—*Eccl.*, ix. 12. Fishes are taken with the hook while they eat the bait that conceals the hook, which is the instrument of their death. *The evil time* is precisely that in which sinners are actually offending God. In the act of sin, they calm their conscience by a security of afterwards making a good confession and reversing the sentence of their damnation. But death comes suddenly upon them, and does not leave them time for repentance. "For, when they shall say peace and security, then shall sudden destruction come upon them"—I. *Thess.*, v. 3.

11. If a person lend a sum of money, he is careful instantly to get a written acknowledgment, and to take all the other means necessary to secure the repayment of it. Who, he says, can know what shall happen? Death may come, and I may lose my money. And how does it happen, that there are so many who neglect to use the same caution for the salvation of their souls, which is of far greater importance than all temporal interests? Why do they not also say: Who knows what may happen? death may come, and I may lose my soul? If you lose a sum

of money, all is not lost; if you lose it one way, you may recover the loss in another; but he that dies and loses his soul, loses all, and has no hope of ever recovering it. If we could die twice, we might, if we lost our soul the first time, save it the second. But we cannot die twice. "It is appointed unto men once to die"—*Heb.*, ix. 27. Mark the word *once:* death happens to each of us but once: he who has erred the first time, has erred for ever. Hence, to bring the soul to Hell is an irreparable error. *Periisse semel œternum est.*

12. The venerable Father John Avila was a man of great sanctity and apostle of Spain. What was the answer of this great servant of God, who had led a holy life from his childhood, when he was told that his death was at hand, and that he had but a short time to live? *Oh!* replied the holy man with trembling, *that I had a little more time to prepare for death!* St. Agatho, abbot, after spending so many years in penance, trembled at the hour of death, and said: *What shall become of me? who can know the judgments of God?* And, O brethren, what will you say when the approach of death shall be announced to you, and when, from the priest who attends you, you shall hear these words: "*Go forth, Christian soul, from this world*"? You will, perhaps, say: Wait a little; allow me to prepare better. No; depart immediately; death does not wait. You should therefore prepare yourselves now. "With fear and trembling work out your salvation"—*Phil.*, ii. 12. St. Paul admonishes us, that, if we wish to save our souls, we must live in fear and trembling, lest death may find us in sin. Be attentive, brethren: there is question of eternity. "If the tree fall to the south or to the north, in what place soever it shall fall, there shall it be"—*Eccl.*, xi. 3. If, when the tree of your life is cut down, you fall to the south—that is, if you obtain eternal life—how great shall be your joy at being able to say: I shall be saved; I have secured all; I can never lose God; I shall be happy for ever! But, if you fall to the north—that is, into eternal damnation—how great shall be your despair! Alas! you shall say, I have erred, and my error is irremediable! Arise, then, from your tepidity, and, after this sermon, make a resolution to give yourselves sincerely to God. This resolution will insure you a good death, and will make you happy for eternity.

SERMON XXXIV.

FOR THE FIFTH SUNDAY AFTER PENTECOST.

On the sin of anger.

"Whosoever is angry with his brother, shall be in danger of the judgment"—*Matt.*, v. 22.

ANGER resembles fire; hence, as fire is vehement in its action, and, by the smoke which it produces, obstructs the view, so anger makes men rush into a thousand excesses, and prevents them from seeing the sinfulness of their conduct; and thus exposes them to the danger of the judgment of eternal death. "Whosoever is angry with his brother, shall be in danger of the judgment". Anger is so pernicious to man, that it even disfigures his countenance. No matter how comely and gentle he may be, he shall, as often as he yields to the passion of anger, appear to be a monster and a wild beast full of terror. "Iracundus", says St. Basil, "humanam quasi figuram amittit, feræ speciem indutus"—*hom.* xxi. But, if anger disfigures us before men, how much more deformed will it render us in the eyes of God! In this discourse I will show, in the first point, the destruction which anger unrestrained brings on the soul; and, in the second, how we ought to restrain anger in all occasions of provocation which may occur to us.

First point. The ruin which anger unrestrained brings on the soul.

1. St. Jerome says that anger is the door by which all vices enter the soul. "Omnium vitiorum janua est iracundia"—*Inc.*, xxix. *Prov.* Anger precipitates men into resentments, blasphemies, acts of injustice, detractions, scandals, and other iniquities; for the passion of anger darkens the understanding, and makes a man act like a beast and a madman. "Caligavit ab indignatione oculus meus"—*Job*, xvii. 7. My eye has lost its sight, through indignation. David said: "My eye is

troubled with wrath"—*Ps.*, xxx. 10. Hence, according to St. Bonaventure, an angry man is incapable of distinguishing between what is just and unjust. "Iratus non potest videre quod justum est, vel injustum". In a word, St. Jerome says, that anger deprives a man of prudence, reason, and understanding. "Ab omni consilio deturpat, ut donec irascitur, insanire credatur". Hence St. James says: "The anger of man worketh not the justice of God"—*St. James*, i. 20. The acts of a man under the influence of anger cannot be conformable to the divine justice, and consequently cannot be faultless.

2. A man who does not restrain the impulse of anger, easily falls into hatred towards the person who has been the occasion of his passion. According to St. Augustine, hatred is nothing else than persevering anger. "Odium est ira diuturno tempore perseverans". Hence St. Thomas says, that "anger is sudden, but hatred is lasting"—*Opusc.*, v. It appears, then, that in him in whom anger perseveres, hatred also reigns. But some will say: I am the head of the house; I must correct my children and servants, and, when necessary, I must raise my voice against the disorders which I witness. I say in answer: It is one thing to be angry against a brother, and another to be displeased at the sin of a brother. To be angry against sin is not anger, but zeal; and therefore it is not only lawful, but it is sometimes a duty. But our anger must be accompanied with prudence, and must appear to be directed against sin, but not against the sinner; for, if the person whom we correct perceive that we speak through passion and hatred towards him, the correction will be unprofitable and even mischievous. To be angry, then, against a brother's sin, is certainly lawful. "He", says St. Augustine, "is not angry with a brother, who is angry against a brother's sin". It is thus, as David said, we may be angry without sin. "Be ye angry, and sin not" —*Ps.*, iv. 5. But, to be angry against a brother on account of the sin which he has committed, is not lawful; because according to St. Augustine, we are not allowed to hate others for their vices. "*Nec propter vitia* (licet) *homines odisse*"—*in Ps.*, cxviii.

3. Hatred brings with it a desire of revenge; for, according to St. Thomas, anger, when fully voluntary, is accompanied with a desire of revenge. *Ira est appetitus vindictæ.* But you will perhaps say: If I resent such an injury, God will have pity

on me, because I have just grounds for resentment. Who, I ask, has told you, that you have just grounds for seeking revenge? It is you, whose understanding is clouded by passions, that say so. I have already said, that anger obscures the mind, and takes away our reason and understanding. As long as the passion of anger lasts, you will consider your neighbour's conduct very unjust and intolerable; but, when your anger shall have passed away, you shall see that his act was not so bad as it appeared to you. But, though the injury be grievous, or even more grievous, God will not have compassion on you, if you seek revenge. No; he says: vengeance for sins belongs not to you, but to me; and when the time shall come, I will chastise them as they deserve. "Revenge is mine, and I will repay *them* in due time"—*Deut.*, xxxii. 35. If you resent an injury done to you by a neighbour, God will justly inflict vengeance on you for all the injuries you have offered to him, and particularly for taking revenge on a brother whom he commands you to pardon. "He that seeketh to revenge himself, shall find vengeance from the Lord......Man to man reserveth anger, and doth he seek remedy of God?......He that is but flesh nourisheth anger; and doth he ask forgiveness of God? Who shall obtain pardon for his sins?"—*Eccl.*, xxviii. 1, 3, 5. Man, a worm of flesh, reserves anger, and takes revenge on a brother: does he afterwards dare to ask mercy of God? And who, adds the sacred writer, can obtain pardon for the iniquities of so daring a sinner? "Qua fronte", says St. Augustine, "indulgentiam peccatorem obtinere poterit, qui præcipienti dare veniam non acquiescit". How can he who will not obey the command of God to pardon his neighbour, expect to obtain from God the forgiveness of his own sins?

4. Let us implore the Lord to preserve us from yielding to any strong passion, and particularly to anger. "Give me not over to a shameful and foolish mind"—*Eccl.*, xxiii. 6. For, he that submits to such a passion is exposed to great danger of falling into a grievous sin against God or his neighbour. How many, in consequence of not restraining anger, break out into horrible blasphemies against God or his saints! But, at the very time that we are in a flame of indignation, God is armed with scourges. The Lord said one day to the Prophet Jeremias: "What seest thou, Jeremias? And I said: I see a rod watch-

ing"—*Jer.*, i. 11. Lord, I behold a rod watching to inflict punishment. The Lord asked him again: "What seest thou? And I said: I see a boiling caldron"—*ibid.*, *v.* 13. The boiling caldron is the figure of a man inflamed with wrath, and threatened with the rod, that is, with the vengeance of God. Behold, then, the ruin which anger unrestrained brings on man. It deprives him, first, of the grace of God, and afterwards of corporal life. "Envy and anger shorten a man's days"—*Eccl.*, xxx. 26. Job says: "Anger indeed killeth the foolish"—*Job*, v. 2. All the days of their life, persons addicted to anger are unhappy, because they are always in a tempest. But let us pass to the second point, in which I have to say many things which will assist you to overcome this vice.

Second point. How we ought to restrain anger in the occasions of provocation which occur to us.

5. In the first place, it is necessary to know that it is not possible for human weakness, in the midst of so many occasions, to be altogether free from every motion of anger. No one, as Seneca says, can be entirely exempt from this passion. "Iracundia nullum genus hominum excipit"—*l.* III. *c.* xii. All our efforts must be directed to the moderation of the feelings of anger which spring up in the soul. How are they to be moderated? By meekness. This is called the virtue of the lamb—that is, the beloved virtue of Jesus Christ. Because, like a lamb, without anger or even complaint, he bore the sorrows of his passion and crucifixion. "He shall be led as a sheep to the slaughter, and dumb as a lamb before his shearer, and he shall not open his mouth"—*Isa.*, liii. 7. Hence he has taught us to learn of him meekness and humility of heart. "Learn of me, because I am meek and humble of heart"—*Mat.*, xi. 29.

6. Oh! how pleasing in the sight of God are the meek, who submit in peace to all crosses, misfortunes, persecutions, and injuries! To the meek is promised the kingdom of Heaven. "Blessed are the meek; for they shall possess the land"—*Mat.*, v. 4. They are called the children of God. "Blessed are the peacemakers; for they shall be called the children of God"—*ibid.*, *v.* 9. Some boast of their meekness, but without any grounds; for they are meek only towards those who praise and

confer favours upon them: but, to those who injure or censure them, they are all fury and vengeance. The virtue of meekness consists in being meek and peaceful towards those who hate and maltreat us. "With them that hated peace, I was peaceful"—*Ps.*, cxix. 7.

7. We must, as St. Paul says, put on the bowels of mercy towards all men, and bear one with another. "Put on ye the bowels of mercy, humility, modesty, patience, bearing with one another, and forgiving one another, if any have a complaint against another"—*Col.*, iii. 12, 13. You wish others to bear with your defects, and to pardon your faults; you should act in the same manner towards them. Whenever, then, you receive an insult from a person enraged against you, remember that "a mild answer breaketh wrath"—*Prov.*, xv. 1. A certain monk once passed through a corn field: the owner of the field ran out, and spoke to him in very offensive and injurious language. The monk humbly replied: Brother, you are right; I have done wrong; pardon me. By this answer the husbandman was so much appeased, that he instantly became calm, and even wished to follow the monk, and to enter into religion. The proud make use of the humiliations they receive to increase their pride; but the humble and the meek turn the contempt and insults offered them into an occasion of advancing in humility. "He", says St. Bernard, "is humble, who converts humiliation into humility"—*ser.* xxiv., *in Can.*

8. "A man of meekness", says St. Chrysostom, "is useful to himself and to others". The meek are useful to themselves: because, according to F. Alvarez, the time of humiliation and contempt is for them the time of merit. Hence, Jesus Christ calls his disciples happy when they shall be reviled and persecuted. "Blessed are ye when they shall revile you and persecute you"—*Mat.*, v. 11. Hence, the saints have always desired to be despised, as Jesus Christ has been despised. The meek are useful to others; because, as the same St. Chrysostom says, there is nothing better calculated to draw others to God, than to see a Christian meek and cheerful when he receives an injury or an insult. "Nihil ita conciliat Domino familiares ut quod illum vident mansuetudine jucundum". The reason is, because virtue is known by being tried; and, as gold is tried by fire, so the meekness of men is proved by humiliation. "Gold and

silver are tried in the fire, but acceptable men in the furnace of humiliation"—*Eccl.*, ii. 5. "My spikenard", says the spouse in the Canticles, "sent forth the odour thereof"—i. 11. The spikenard is an odoriferous plant, but diffuses its odours only when it is torn and bruised. In this passage the inspired writer gives us to understand, that a man cannot be said to be meek, unless he is known to send forth the odour of his meekness by bearing injuries and insults in peace and without anger. God wishes us to be meek even towards ourselves. When a person commits a fault, God certainly wishes him to humble himself, to be sorry for his sin, and to purpose never to fall into it again; but he does not wish him to be indignant with himself, and give way to trouble and agitation of mind; for, while the soul is agitated, a man is incapable of doing good. "My heart is troubled; my strength hath left me"—*Ps.*, xxxvii. 11.

9. Thus, when we receive an insult, we must do violence to ourselves in order to restrain anger. Let us either answer with meekness, as recommended above, or let us remain silent; and thus, as St. Isidore says, we shall conquer. "Quamvis quis irritet, tu dissimula, quia tacendo vinces". But, if you answer through passion, you shall do harm to yourself and others. It would be still worse to give an angry answer to a person who corrects you. "Medicanti irascitur", says St. Bernard, "qui non irascitur sagittanti"—*ser.* vi., *de Nativ.* Some are not angry, though they ought to be indignant with those who wound their souls by flattery; and are filled with indignation against the person who censures them in order to heal their irregularities. Against the man who abhors correction, the sentence of perdition has, according to the Wise Man, been pronounced. "Because they have despised all my reproofs,......the prosperity of fools shall destroy them"—*Prov.*, i. 30, *etc.* Fools regard as prosperity to be free from correction, or to despise the admonitions which they receive; but such prosperity is the cause of their ruin. When you meet with an occasion of anger, you must, in the first place, be on your guard not to allow anger to enter your heart. "Be not quickly angry"—*Eccles.*, vii. 10. Some persons change colour, and get into a passion, at every contradiction: and when anger has got admission, God knows to what it shall lead them. Hence, it is necessary to foresee

these occasions in our meditations and prayers; for, unless we are prepared for them, it will be as difficult to restrain anger as to put a bridle on a horse while he is running away.

10. Whenever we have the misfortune to permit anger to enter the soul, let us be careful not to allow it to remain. Jesus Christ tells all who remember that a brother is offended with them, not to offer the gift which they bring to the altar, without being first reconciled to their neighbour. "Go first to be reconciled to thy brother; and then coming thou shalt offer thy gift"—*Mat.*, v. 24. And he who has received any offence, should endeavour to root out of his heart not only all anger, but also every feeling of bitterness towards the persons who have offended him. "Let all bitterness", says St. Paul, "and anger, and indignation......be put away from you"—*Eph.*, iv. 31. As long as anger continues, follow the advice of Seneca—"When you shall be angry, do nothing, say nothing which may be dictated by anger". Like David, be silent, and do not speak, when you feel that you are disturbed. "I was troubled, and I spoke not"—*Ps.*, lxxvi. 5. How many, when inflamed with anger, say and do what they afterwards, in their cooler moments, regret, and excuse themselves by saying that they were in a passion? As long, then, as anger lasts, we must be silent, and abstain from doing or resolving to do anything; for, what is done in the heat of passion will, according to the maxim of St. James, be unjust. "The anger of man worketh not the justice of God"—i. 20. It is also necessary to abstain altogether from consulting those who might foment our indignation. "Blessed", says David, "is the man who hath not walked in the counsel of the ungodly"—*Ps.*, i. 1. To him who is asked for advice, Ecclesiasticus says: "If thou blow the spark, it shall burn as a fire; and if thou spit upon it, it shall be quenched"—*Eccl.*, xxviii. 14. When a person is indignant at some injury which he has received, you may, by exhorting him to patience, extinguish the fire; but, if you encourage revenge, you may kindle a great flame. Let him, then, who feels himself in any way inflamed with anger, be on his guard against false friends, who, by an imprudent word, may be the cause of his perdition.

11. Let us follow the advice of the apostle: "Be not overcome by evil, but overcome evil by good"—*Rom.*, xii. 21. *Be*

not overcome by evil: do not allow yourself to be conquered by sin. If, through anger, you seek revenge or utter blasphemies, you are overcome by sin. But you will say: *I am naturally of a warm temper.* By the grace of God, and by doing violence to yourself, you will be able to conquer your natural disposition. Do not consent to anger, and you shall subdue the warmth of your temper. But you say: *I cannot bear with unjust treatment.* In answer I tell you, first, to remember that anger obscures reason, and prevents us from seeing things as they are. "Fire hath fallen on them, and they shall not see the sun"—*Ps.*, lvii. 9. Secondly, if you return evil for evil, your enemy shall gain a victory over you. "If", said David, "I have rendered to them that repaid me evils, let me deservedly fall empty before my enemies"—*Ps.*, vii. 5. If I render evil for evil, I shall be defeated by my enemies. "*Overcome evil by good*". Render every foe good for evil. "Do good", says Jesus Christ, "to them that hate you"—*Matt.*, v. 44. This is the revenge of the saints, and is called by St. Paulinus, *Heavenly revenge.* It is by such revenge that you shall gain the victory. And should any of those, of whom the Prophet says, "The venom of asps is under their lips"—*Ps.*, cxxxix. 4, ask how you can submit to such an injury, let your answer be: "The chalice which my Father hath given me, shall I not drink it?"—*John*, xviii. 11. And then turning to God, you shall say: "I opened not my mouth, because thou hast done it"—*Ps.*, xxxviii. 10; for it is certain that every cross which befalls you, comes from the Lord. "Good things and evil are from God"—*Eccl.*, xi. 14. Should any one take away your property, recover it if you can; but, if you cannot, say with Job: "The Lord gave, and the Lord hath taken away"—i. 21. A certain philosopher, who lost some of his goods in a storm, said: "If I have lost my goods, I will not lose my peace". And do you say: If I have lost my property, I will not lose my soul.

12. In fine, when we meet with crosses, persecutions, and injuries, let us turn to God, who commands us to bear them with patience; and thus we shall always avoid anger. "Remember the fear of God, and be not angry with thy neighbour" —*Eccl.*, xxviii. 8. Let us give a look at the will of God, which disposes things in this manner for our merit, and anger,

shall cease. Let us give a look at Jesus crucified, and we shall not have courage to complain. St. Eleazar being asked by his spouse, how he bore so many injuries without yielding to anger, answered: I turn to Jesus Christ, and thus I preserve my peace. Finally, let us give a glance at our sins, for which we have deserved far greater contempt and chastisement, and we shall calmly submit to all evils. St. Augustine says, that though we are sometimes innocent of the crime for which we are persecuted, we are, nevertheless, guilty of other sins which merit greater punishment than that which we endure. "Esto non habemus peccatum, quod objicitur: habemus tamen, quod digne in nobis flagelletur"—*in Ps.*, lxviii.

SERMON XXXV.

FOR THE SIXTH SUNDAY AFTER PENTECOST.

On the vanity of the world.

"And they have nothing to eat"—*Mark*, viii. 2.

1. Such were the attractions of our Divine Saviour, and such the sweetness with which he received all, that he drew after him thousands of the people. He one day saw himself surrounded by a great multitude of men, who followed him and remained with him three days without eating anything. Touched with pity for them, Jesus Christ said to his disciples: "I have compassion on the multitude; for, behold! they have now been with me three days, and have nothing to eat"—*Mark*, viii. 2. He, on this occasion, wrought the miracle of the multiplication of the seven loaves and a few fishes, so as to satisfy the whole multitude. This is the literal sense; but the mystic sense is, that in this world there is no food which can fill the desire of our souls. All the goods of this Earth—riches, honours, and pleasures—delight the sense of the body, but cannot satiate the soul, which has been created for God, and which

God alone can content. I will, therefore, speak to-day on the vanity of the world, and will show how great is the illusion of the lovers of the world, who lead an unhappy life on this Earth, and expose themselves to the imminent danger of a still more unhappy life in eternity.

2. "O ye sons of men", exclaims the Royal Prophet against worldlings, "how long will you be dull at heart? Why do you love vanity, and seek after lying?"—*Ps.*, iv. 3. O men, O fools, how long will you fix the affections of your hearts on this Earth? Why do you love the goods of this world, which are all vanity and lies? Do you imagine that you shall find peace by the acquisition of these goods? But how can you expect to find peace, while you walk in the ways of affliction and misery? Behold how David describes the condition of worldlings. "Destruction and unhappiness in their ways: and the way of peace they have not known"—*Ps.*, xiii. 3. You hope to obtain peace from the world; but how can the world give you that peace which you seek, when St. John says, that "the whole world is seated in wickedness"?—I. *John*, v. 19. The world is full of iniquities; hence, worldlings live under the despotism of *the wicked one*—that is, of the Devil. The Lord has declared, that there is no peace for the wicked, who live without his grace. "There is no peace to the wicked"—*Isa.*, xlviii. 22.

3. The goods of the world are but apparent goods, which cannot satisfy the heart of man. "You have eaten", says the Prophet Aggeus, "and have not had enough"—*Ag.*, i. 6. Instead of satisfying our hunger, they increase it. "These", says St. Bernard, "provoke, rather than extinguish hunger". If the goods of this world made men content, the rich and powerful should enjoy complete happiness; but experience shows the contrary. We see every day that they are the most unhappy of men; they appear always oppressed by fears, by jealousies and sadness. Listen to King Solomon, who abounded in these goods: "And behold all is vanity and vexation of spirit"—*Eccl.*, i. 14. He tells us, that all things in this world are vanity, lies, and illusion. They are not only vanity, but also affliction of spirit. They torture the poor soul, which finds in them a continual source, not of happiness, but of affliction and bitterness. This is a just punishment on those who

instead of serving their God with joy, wish to serve their enemy—the world—which makes them endure the want of every good. "Because thou didst not serve the Lord thy God with joy and gladness of heart,.........thou shalt serve thy enemy in hunger, and thirst, and nakedness, and in want of all things" —*Deut.*, xxviii. 47, 48. Man expects to content his heart with the goods of this Earth; but, howsoever abundantly he may possess them, he is never satisfied. Hence, he always seeks after more of them, and is always unhappy. Oh! happy he who wishes for nothing but God; for God will satisfy all the desires of his heart. "Delight in the Lord, and he will give thee the requests of thy heart"—*Ps.*, xxxvi. 4. Hence St. Augustine ask: "What, O miserable man, dost thou seek in seeking after goods? Seek one good, in which are all goods". And, having dearly learned that the goods of this world do not content, but rather afflict the heart of man, the saint, turning to the Lord, said: "*All things are hard, and thou alone repose*". Hence in saying "*My God and my all*", the seraphic St. Francis, though divested of all worldly goods, enjoyed greater riches and happiness than all the worldlings on this Earth. Yes; for the peace which fills the soul that desires nothing but God, surpasses all the delights which creatures can give. They can only delight the senses; but cannot content the heart of man. "The peace of God which surpasseth all understanding"—*Phil.*, iv. 7. According to St. Thomas, the difference between God, the sovereign good, and the goods of the Earth, consists in this, that the more perfectly we possess God, the more ardently we love him, because the more perfectly we possess him, the better we comprehend his infinite greatness, and therefore the more we despise other things: but, when we possess temporal goods, we despise them, because we then see their emptiness, and desire other things which may make us content. "Summum bonum quanto perfectius possidetur, tanto magis amatur, et alia contemnuntur. Sed in appetitu temporalium bonorum, quando habentur, contemnentur, et alia appetuntur"—*S. Thom.*, i. 2, *qu.* 2, *art.* 1, *ad.* 3.

4. The Prophet Osee tells us, that the world holds in its hand a deceitful balance. "*He is like* Chanaan" *(that is the world)*; "there is a deceitful balance in his hand"—*Osee*, xii. 7. We must, then, weigh things in the balance of God, and not in that

of the world, which makes them appear different from what they are. What are the goods of this life? "My days", said Job, "have been swifter than a post: they have passed by as ships carrying fruits"—*Job*, ix. 25, 26. The ships signify the lives of men, which soon pass away and run speedily to death: and if men have laboured only to provide themselves with Earthly goods, these fruits decay at the hour of death; we can bring none of them with us to the other world. We, says St. Ambrose, falsely call these things our property, which we cannot bring with us to eternity, where we must live for ever, and where virtue alone will accompany us. "Non nostra sunt, quæ non possumus auferre nobiscum: sola virtus nos comitatur". You, says St. Augustine, attend only to what a rich man possessed; but tell me, which of his possessions shall he, now, that he is on the point of death, be able to take with him? "Quid hic habebat attendis, quid secum fert, attendo"—*serm.* xiii., *de Adv. Dom.* The rich bring with them a miserable garment, which shall rot with them in the grave. And should they, during life, have acquired a great name, they shall be soon forgotten. "Their memory hath perished with a noise"—*Ps.*, ix. 7.

5. Oh! that men would keep before their eyes that great maxim of Jesus Christ—"What doth it profit a man, if he gain the whole world, and suffer the loss of his own soul?"—*Matt.*, xvi. 26. If they did, they should certainly cease to love the world. What shall it profit them at the hour of death to have acquired all the goods of this world, if their souls must go into Hell to be in torments for all eternity? How many has this maxim sent into the cloister and into the deserts! How many martyrs has it encouraged to embrace torments and death! In the history of England, we read of thirty kings and queens, who left the world and became religious, in order to secure a happy death. The consideration of the vanity of Earthly goods made St. Francis Borgia retire from the world. At the sight of the Empress Isabella, who had died in the flower of youth, he came to the resolution of serving God alone. "Is such, then", he said, "the end of all the grandeur and crowns of this world! Henceforth I will serve a master who can never die". The day of death is called *the day of destruction* ("The day of destruction is at hand"—*Deut.*, xxxii.

35), because on that day we shall lose and give up all the goods of the world—all its riches, honours, and pleasures. The shade of death obscures all the treasures and grandeurs of this Earth; it obscures even the purple and the crown. Sister Margaret of St. Anne, a Discalced Carmelite, and daughter of the Emperor Rodolph the Second, used to say: *What do kingdoms profit us at the hour of death?* "The affliction of an hour maketh one forget great delights"—*Eccl.*, xi. 29. The melancholy hour of death puts an end to all the delights and pomps of this life. St. Gregory says, that all goods which cannot remain with us, or which are incapable of taking away our miseries, are deceitful. "Fallaces sunt quæ nobiscum permanere non possunt: fallaces sunt quæ mentis nostræ inopiam non expellunt"—*hom.* xv., *in Luc.* Behold a sinner whom the riches and honours which he had acquired made an object of envy to others. Death came upon him when he was at the summit of his glory, and he is no longer what he was. "I have seen the wicked highly exalted, and lifted up like the cedars of Libanus; and I passed by, and lo! he was not; and I sought him, and his place was not found"—*Ps.*, xxxvi. 35, 36.

6. These truths the unhappy damned fruitlessly confess in Hell, where they exclaim with tears: "What hath pride profited us? or what advantage hath the boasting of riches brought us? All those things are passed away like a shadow"—*Wis.*, v. 8, 9. What, they say, have our pomps and riches profited us, now they are all passed away like a shadow, and for us nothing remains but eternal torments and despair? Dearly beloved Christians, let us open our eyes, and now that we have it in our power, let us attend to the salvation of our souls; for, if we lose them, we shall not be able to save them in the next life. Aristippus the philosopher was once shipwrecked, and lost all his goods; but such was the esteem which the people entertained for him on account of his learning, that, as soon as he reached the shore, they presented him with an equivalent for all that he had lost. He then wrote to his friends, and exhorted them to attend to the acquisition of goods which cannot be lost by shipwreck. Our relatives and friends who have passed into eternity, exhort us, from the other world, to labour in this life for the attainment of goods which are not lost at death. If at that awful moment we shall be found to have attended only to the

accumulation of Earthly goods, we shall be called fools, and shall receive the reproach addressed to the rich man in the gospel, who, after having reaped an abundant crop from his fields, said to himself: "Soul, thou hast much goods laid up for many years; take thy rest, eat, drink, make good cheer. But God said to him: Thou fool, this night do they require thy soul of thee: and whose shall those things be which thou hast provided?"—*Luke*, xii. 19, 20. He said, *they require thy soul of thee*, because to every man his soul is given, not with full power to dispose of it as he pleases; but it is given to him in trust, that he may preserve and return it to God in a state of innocence, when it shall be presented at the tribunal of the Sovereign Judge. The Redeemer concludes this parable by saying: "So is he that layeth up treasure for himself, and is not rich towards God"—*v.* 21. This is what happens to those who seek to enrich themselves with the goods of this life, and not with the love of God. Hence St. Augustine asks: "What has the rich man if he has not charity? If the poor man has charity, what is there that he has not?" He that possesses all the treasures of this world, and has not charity, is the poorest of men; but the poor who have God, possess all things, though they should be bereft of all Earthly goods.

7. "The children of this world", said Jesus Christ, "are wiser in their generation, than the children of light"—*Luke*, xvi. 8. O how wise in Earthly affairs are worldlings, who live in the midst of the darkness of the world! "Behold", says St. Augustine, "how much men suffer for things for which they entertain a vicious love". What fatigue do they endure for the acquisition of property, or of a situation of emolument! With what care do they endeavour to preserve their bodily health! They consult the best physician, and procure the best medicine. And Christians, who are the children of light, will take no pains, will suffer nothing, to secure the salvation of their souls! O God! at the light of the candle which lights them to death, at that hour, at that time, which is called the time of truth, worldlings shall see and confess their folly. Then each of them shall exclaim: O that I had led the life of a saint! At the hour of death, Philip the Second, king of Spain, called in his son, and having shown him his breast devoured with worms, said to him: Son, behold how we die; behold the end of all

worldly greatness. He then ordered a wooden cross to be fastened to his neck; and, having made his arrangements for death, he turned again to his son, and said: My son, I wished you to be present at this scene, that you might understand how the world in the end treats even monarchs. He died saying: Oh! that I had been a lay brother in some religious order, and that I had not been a king! Such is the language, at the hour of death, even of the princes of the Earth, whom worldlings regard as the most fortunate of men. But these desires and sighs of regret serve only to increase the anguish and remorse of the lovers of the world at the hour of death, when the scene is about to close.

8. And what is the present life but a scene, which soon passes away for ever? It may end when we least expect it. Cassimir, king of Poland, while he sat at table with his grandees, died in the act of raising a cup to take a draught; thus the scene ended for him. The Emperor Celsus was put to death in seven days days after his election; and the scene closed for him. Ladislaus, king of Bohemia, in his eighteenth year, while he was preparing for the reception of his spouse, the daughter of the king of France, was suddenly seized with a violent pain, which took away his life. Couriers were instantly despatched to announce to her that the scene was over for Ladislaus, that she might return to France. "The fashion of this world passeth away"—I. *Cor.*, vii. 31. By these words St. Paul meant, that this world is but a scene—a comedy. "The world", says Cornelius a Lapide, in his comment upon this passage, "is like a stage. One generation passes away, and a new generation comes. The king does not take with him the purple. Tell me, O villa, O house, how many masters had you?" In every age the inhabitants of this Earth are changed. Cities and kingdoms are filled with new people. The first generation passes to the other world, a second comes on, and this is followed by another. He who, in the scene of this world, has acted the part of a king, is no longer a king. The master of such a villa or palace, is no longer its master. Hence the Apostle gives us the following advice. "The time is short; it remaineth that... they that use this world, be as if they used it not; for the fashion of this world passeth away"—I. *Cor.*, vii. 29, 30. Since the time of our dwelling on this Earth is short, and since all

must end with our death, let us make use of this world to despise it, as if it did not exist for us; and let us labour to acquire the eternal treasures of Paradise, where, as the gospel says, there are no moths to consume, nor thieves to steal them. "But lay up to yourselves treasures in Heaven, where neither the rust nor the moth doth consume, and where thieves do not break through nor steal"—*Matt.*, vi. 20. St. Teresa used to say: "We should not set value on what ends with life; the true life consists in living in such a manner as not to be afraid of death". Death shall have no terror for him who, during life, is detached from the vanities of this world, and is careful to provide himself only with goods which shall accompany him to eternity, and make him happy for ever.

SERMON XXXVI.

FOR THE SEVENTH SUNDAY AFTER PENTECOST.

On the education of children.

"A good tree cannot bring forth evil fruit, neither can an evil tree bring forth good fruit"—*Matt.*, vii. 18.

THEN the gospel of this day tells us, that a good plant cannot produce bad fruit, and that a bad one cannot produce good fruit. Learn from this, brethren, that a good father brings up good children. But, if parents be wicked, how can the children be virtuous? Have you ever, says the Redeemer, in the same gospel, seen grapes gathered from thorns, or figs from thistles? "Do men gather grapes from thorns, or figs from thistles?"—*v.* 16. And, in like manner, it is impossible, or rather very difficult, to find children virtuous, who are brought up by immoral parents. Fathers and mothers, be attentive to this sermon, which is of great importance to the eternal salvation of yourselves and of your children. Be attentive, young men and young women, who have not as yet chosen a state of life. If you wish to marry, learn this day the obligations which you contract with regard to the education of your children; and learn also, that, if you do not fulfil them, you shall bring yourselves and all your children to damnation. I shall divide this sermon into two points. In the first, I shall show how important it is to bring up children in habits of virtue; and, in the second, I shall show with what care and diligence a parent ought to labour to bring them up well.

First point. How very important it is to bring up children in habits of virtue.

1. A father owes two obligations to his children; he is bound to provide for their corporal wants, and to educate them in habits of virtue. It is not necessary at present to say more on the first obligation, than that there are some fathers more cruel than the most ferocious of wild beasts; for these do not neglect to nourish their offspring; but certain parents squander away in eating and drinking and gaming, all their property, or all the fruits of their industry, and allow their children to die of hunger. But let us come to the education, which is the subject of my discourse.

2. It is certain that a child's future good or ill conduct depends on his being brought up well or ill. Nature itself teaches every parent to attend to the education of his offspring. He who has given them being ought to endeavour to make life useful to them. God gives children to parents, not that they may assist the family, but that they may be brought up in the fear of God, and be directed in the way of eternal salvation. "We have", says St. Chrysostom, "a great deposit in children; let us attend to them with great care"—*hom.* ix., *in* I. *ad Tit.* Children have not been given to parents as a present, which they may dispose of as they please, but as a trust, for which, if lost through their negligence, they must render an account to God. The Scripture tells us, that when a father observes the divine law, both he and his children shall prosper. "That it may be well with thee and thy children after thee, when thou shalt do that which is pleasing in the sight of God" —*Deut.*, xii. 25. The good or ill conduct of a parent may be known, by those who have not witnessed it, from the life which his children lead. "For by the fruit the tree is known"—*Matt.*, xii. 33. A father, says Ecclesiasticus, who leaves a

family, when he departs this life, is as if he had not died; because his sons remain, and exhibit his habits and character. "His father is dead, and he is as if he were not dead; for he hath left one behind him that is like himself"—*Eccl.*, xxx. 4. When we find a son addicted to blasphemies, to obscenities, and to theft, we have reason to suspect that such too was the character of the father. "For a man is known by his children" —*Eccl.*, xi. 30.

3. Hence Origen says, that on the day of judgment, parents shall have to render an account for all the sins of their children. "Omnia quæcumque deliquerint filii, a parentibus requiruntur" —*Orig.*, *lib.* II., *in Job.* Hence, he who teaches his son to live well, shall die a happy and tranquil death. "He that teacheth his son...when he died was not sorrowful, neither was he confounded"—*Eccl.*, xxx. 3, 5. And he shall save his soul by means of his children; that is, by the virtuous education which he has given them. "She shall be saved through child-bearing" —I. *Tim.*, ii. 15. But, on the other hand, a very uneasy and unhappy death shall be the lot of those who have laboured only to increase the possessions, or to multiply the honours of their family; or who have sought only to lead a life of ease and pleasure, but have not watched over the morals of their children. St. Paul says, that such parents are worse than infidels. "But if any man have not care of his own, and especially of those of his house, he hath denied the faith, and is worse than an infidel"—I. *Tim.*, v. 8. Were fathers or mothers to lead a life of piety and continual prayer, and to communicate every day, they should be damned if they neglected the care of their children. Would to God that certain parents paid as much attention to their children as they do to their horses! How careful are they to see that their horses are fed and well trained! And they take no pains to make their children attend at catechism, hear mass, or go to confession. "We take more care", says St. Chrysostom, "of our asses and horses, than of our children"—*hom.* x., *in Matt.*

4. If all fathers fulfilled their duty of watching over the education of their children, we should have but few crimes and few executions. By the bad education which parents give to their offspring, they cause their children, says St. Chrysostom, to rush into many grievous vices; and thus they deliver them

up to the hands of the executioner. "Majoribus illos malis involvimus, et carnificum manibus damus"—*serm.* xx., *de divers.* Hence, in Lacedemon, a parent, as being the cause of all the irregularities of his children, was justly punished for their crimes with greater severity than the children themselves. Great indeed is the misfortune of the child that has vicious parents, who are incapable of bringing up their children in the fear of God, and who, when they see their children engaged in dangerous friendships and in quarrels, instead of correcting and chastising them, rather take compassion on them, and say: "*What can be done? They are young; they must take their course*". Oh! what wicked maxims! what a cruel education! Do you hope that when your children grow up, they shall become saints? Listen to what Solomon says: "A young man, according to his way, even when he is old, he will not depart from it"—*Prov.*, xxii. 6. A young man who has contracted a habit of sin, will not abandon it even in his old age. "His bones", says Job, "shall be filled with the vices of his youth, and they shall sleep with him in the dust"—*Job*, xx. 11. When a young person has lived in evil habits, his bones shall be filled with the vices of his youth, so that he will carry them with him to death; and the impurities, blasphemies, and hatred to which he was accustomed in his youth, shall accompany him to the grave, and shall sleep with him after his bones shall be reduced to dust and ashes. It is very easy, when they are small, to train up children to habits of virtue; but, when they have come to manhood, it is equally difficult to correct them, if they have learned habits of vice. But, let us come to the second point—that is, to the means of bringing up children in the practice of virtue. I entreat you, fathers and mothers, to remember what I now say to you; for on it depends the eternal salvation of your own souls, and of the souls of your children.

Second point. On the care and diligence with which parents ought to endeavour to bring up their children in habits of virtue.

5. St. Paul teaches sufficiently, in a few words, in what the proper education of children consists. He says, that it consists in discipline and correction. "And you, fathers, provoke not

your children to anger; but bring them up in the discipline and correction of the Lord"—*Ephes.*, vi. 4. *Discipline*, which is the same as the religious regulation of the morals of children, implies an obligation of educating them in habits of virtue by word and example. First, by words: a good father should often assemble his children, and instil into them the holy fear of God. It was in this manner that Tobias brought up his little son. The father taught him from his childhood to fear the Lord and to fly from sin. "And from his infancy he taught him to fear God and to abstain from sin"—*Tob.*, i. 10. The Wise Man says, that a well educated son is the support and consolation of his father. "Instruct thy son, and he shall refresh thee, and shall give delight to thy soul"—*Prov.*, xxix. 17. But, as a well instructed son is the delight of his father's soul, so an ignorant child is a source of sorrow to a father's heart; for the ignorance of his obligations as a Christian is always accompanied with a bad life. Cantipratensis relates (*lib.* I. *cap.* xx.), that, in the year 1248, an ignorant priest was commanded, in a certain synod, to make a discourse. But while he was greatly agitated by the command, the Devil appeared to him, and instructed him to say: "The rectors of infernal darkness salute the rectors of parishes, and thank them for their negligence in instructing the people; because from ignorance proceed the misconduct and the damnation of many". The same is true of negligent parents. In the first place, a parent ought to instruct his children in the truths of faith, and particularly in the four principal mysteries. First, that there is but one God, the Creator and Lord of all things; secondly, that this God is a remunerator, who, in the next life, shall reward the good with the eternal glory of Paradise, and shall punish the wicked with the everlasting torments of Hell; thirdly, the mystery of the most holy Trinity,—that is, that in God there are Three Persons, who are only one God, because they have but one essence; fourthly, the mystery of the incarnation of the Divine Word—the Son of God, and true God, who became man in the womb of Mary, and suffered and died for our salvation. Should a father or a mother say: I myself do not know these mysteries, can such an excuse be admitted?—that is, can one sin excuse another? If you are ignorant of these mysteries, you are obliged to learn them, and afterwards to teach them to your children. At least, send your children to the catechism. Oh! what a misery to see so many fathers and mothers, who are unable to instruct their children in the most necessary truths of faith, and who, instead of sending their sons and daughters to the Christian doctrine on festivals, employ them in messages, or other occupations of little moment: and when grown up, they know not what is meant by mortal sin, by Hell, or eternity. They do not even know the *Creed*, the *Pater Noster*, or the *Hail Mary*, which every Christian is bound to learn under pain of mortal sin.

6. Religious parents not only instruct their children in these things, which are the most important, but they also teach them the acts which ought to be made every morning after rising. They teach them, first, to thank God for having preserved their life during the night; secondly, to offer to God all the good actions which they will perform, and all the pains which they shall suffer during the day; thirdly, to implore of Jesus Christ and most holy Mary to preserve them from all sin during the day. They teach them to make, every evening, an examen of conscience and an act of contrition. They also teach them to make, every day, the acts of Faith, Hope, and Charity, to recite the Rosary, and to visit the blessed sacrament. Some good fathers of families are careful to get a book of meditations read, and to have mental prayer in common for half an hour every day. This is what the Holy Ghost exhorts you to practise. "Hast thou children? Instruct them and bow down their neck from their childhood"—*Eccl.*, vii. 25. Endeavour to train them from their infancy to these religious habits; and when they grow up, they shall persevere in them. Accustom them also to go to confession and communion every week. Be careful to make them go to confession when they arrive at the age of seven, and to communion at the age of ten. This is the advice of St. Charles Borromeo. As soon as they attain the use of reason, make them receive the sacrament of confirmation.

7. It is also very useful to infuse good maxims into the infant minds of children. Oh! what ruin is brought upon his children by the father who teaches them worldly maxims! *You must*, some parents say to their children, *seek the esteem and applause of the world. God is merciful; he takes compassion*

on certain sins. Miserable the young man who sins in obedience to such maxims. Good parents teach very different maxims to their children. Queen Blanche, the mother of St. Louis, king of France, used to say to him: "My son, I would rather see you dead in my arms, than in the state of sin". Oh! brethren, let it be your practice also to infuse into your children certain maxims of salvation, such as, *What will it profit us to gain the whole world, if we lose our own souls? Every thing on this Earth has an end; but eternity never ends. Let all be lost, provided God is not lost.* One of these maxims well impressed on the mind of a young person, will preserve him always in the grace of God.

8. But parents are obliged to instruct their children in the practice of virtue, not only by words, but still more by example. If you give your children bad example, how can you expect that they will lead a good life? When a dissolute young man is corrected for a fault, he answers: Why do you censure me, when my father does worse? "The children will complain of an ungodly father, because for his sake they are in reproach" —*Eccl.*, xli. 10. How is it possible for a son to be moral and religious, when he has had the example of a father who was accustomed to utter blasphemies and obscenities; who spent the entire day in the tavern, in gaming and drunkenness; who was in the habit of frequenting houses of bad fame, and of defrauding his neighbour? Do you expect that your son will go frequently to confession, when you yourself approach the tribunal of penance scarcely once a year? Children are like apes; they do what they see their parents do. It is related in the fables, that a crab-fish one day rebuked its young for walking crookedly. They replied: Father, let us see you walk. The father walked before them more crookedly than they did. This is what happens to the parent who gives bad example. Hence, he has not even courage to correct his children for the sins which he himself commits.

9. But though he should correct them by words, of what use is his correction, when he sets them a bad example by his acts? It has been said in the council of Bishops, that "men believe the eyes rather than the ears". And St. Ambrose says: "The eyes convince me of what they see, more quickly than the ear can insinuate what is past"—*serm.* xxiii. *de S. S.* According

to St. Thomas, scandalous parents compel, in a certain manner, their children to lead a bad life. "Eos ad peccatum, quantum in eis fuit obligaverunt"—*in Ps.*, xvi. They are not, says St. Bernard, fathers, but murderers; they kill, not the bodies, but the souls of their children. "Non parentes, sed peremptores". It is useless for them to say: *My children have been born with bad dispositions.* This is not true; for, as Seneca says, "you err, if you think that vices are born with us; they have been engrafted"—*Ep.*, xciv. Vices are not born with your children, but have been communicated to them by the bad example of the parents. If you had given good example to your sons, they should not be so vicious as they are. O brethren, frequent the sacraments, assist at sermons, recite the Rosary every day, abstain from all obscene language, from detraction, and from quarrels; and you shall see that your sons will go often to confession, will assist at sermons, will say the Rosary, will speak modestly, and will fly from detraction and disputes. It is particularly necessary to train up children to virtue in their infancy: "Bow down their neck from their childhood"; for when they have grown up, and contracted bad habits, it will be very difficult for you to produce, by words, any amendment in their lives.

10. To bring up children in the discipline of the Lord, it is also necessary to take away from them the occasion of doing evil. Hence a father must, in the first place, forbid his children to go out at night, or to go to a house in which their virtue might be exposed to danger, or to keep bad company. "Cast out", said Sarah to Abraham, "this bondwoman and her son"—*Gen.*, xxi. 10. She wished to have Ishmael, the son of Agar the bondwoman, banished from her house, that her son Isaac might not learn his vicious habits. Bad companions are the ruin of young persons. A father should not only remove the evil which he witnesses, but he is also bound to inquire after the conduct of his children, and to seek information from domestics and from externs regarding the places which his sons frequent when they leave home, regarding their occupations and companions. Secondly, he should take from them every musical instrument, which is to them an occasion of going out at night, and all forbidden weapons, which may lead them into quarrels or disputes. Thirdly, he should dismiss all immoral servants; and, if his sons be grown up, he should not keep in his house any young female servant. Some parents

pay little attention to this; and when the evil happens, they complain of their children, as if they expected that tow thrown into the fire should not burn. Fourthly, a father ought to forbid his children ever to bring into his house stolen goods—such as fowl, fruit, and the like. When Tobias heard the bleating of a goat in his house, he said: "Take heed, lest perhaps it be stolen; restore ye it to its owners"—*Tob.*, ii. 21. How often does it happen, that, when a child steals something, the mother says to him: *Bring it to me, my son.* Parents should prohibit to their children all games, which bring destruction on their families and on their own souls, and also masks, scandalous comedies, and certain dangerous conversations and parties of pleasures. Fifthly, a father should remove from his house romances, which pervert young persons, and all bad books which contain pernicious maxims, tales of obscenity, or of profane love. Sixthly, he ought not to allow his children to sleep in his own bed, nor the males and females to sleep together. Seventhly, he should not permit his daughters to be alone with men, whether young or old. But some will say: *Such a man teaches my daughters to read and write, etc.; he is a saint.* The saints are in Heaven; but the saints that are on Earth are flesh, and by proximate occasions, they may become devils. Eighthly, if he has daughters, he should not permit young men to frequent his house. To get their daughters married, some mothers invite young men to their houses. They are anxious to see their daughters married; but they do not care to see them in sin. These are the mothers who, as David says, immolate their daughters to the Devil. "They sacrifice their sons and their daughters to devils"—*Ps.*, cv. 37. And, to excuse themselves, they will say: *Father, there is no harm in what I do.* There is no harm! Oh! how many mothers shall we see condemned on the day of judgment, on account of their daughters! The conduct of such mothers is at least a subject of conversation among their neighbours and equals; and, for all, the parents must render an account to God. O fathers and mothers! confess all the sins you have committed in this respect, before the day on which you shall be judged, arrives.

11. Another obligation of parents is, to correct the faults of the family. "Bring them up in the discipline and correction of the Lord". There are fathers and mothers who witness faults in the family, and remain silent. A certain mother was in the habit

of acting in this manner. Her husband one day took a stick and began to beat her severely. She cried out, and said: *I am doing nothing. Why do you beat me?* *I beat you*, replied the husband, *because you see and do not correct, the faults of the children—because you do nothing.* Through fear of displeasing their children, some fathers neglect to correct them: but, if you saw your son falling into a pool of water, and in danger of being drowned, would it not be savage cruelty not to catch him by the hair, and save his life? "He that spareth the rod hateth his son"—*Prov.*, xiii. 24. If you love your sons, correct them, and, while they are growing up, chastise them, even with the rod, as often as it may be necessary. I say, *with the rod*, but not with a stick; for you must correct them like a father, and not like a galley sergeant. You must be careful not to beat them when you are in a passion: for, you shall then be in danger of beating them with too much severity, and the correction will be without fruit; for they then believe that the chastisement is the effect of anger, and not of a desire on your part to see them amend their lives. I have also said, that you should correct them *while they are growing up;* for when they arrive at manhood, your correction will be of little use. You must then abstain from correcting them with the hand; otherwise, they shall become more perverse, and shall lose their respect for you. But of what use is it to correct children by so many injurious words and by so many imprecations? Deprive them of some part of their meals, of certain articles of dress, or shut them up in a room. But I have said enough. Dearly beloved brethren, draw from the discourse which you have heard, the conclusion, that he who has brought up his children badly, shall be severely punished; and that he who has trained them to habits of virtue, shall receive a great reward.

SERMON XXXVII.

FOR THE EIGHTH SUNDAY AFTER PENTECOST.

On the particular judgment.

"Give an account of thy stewardship"—*Luke*, xvi. 2.

Beloved Christians, of all the goods of nature, of fortune, and of grace, which we have received from God, we are not the masters, neither can we dispose of them as we please; we are but the administrators of them; and therefore we should employ them according to the will of God, who is our Lord. Hence, at the hour of death, we must render a strict account of them to Jesus Christ, our Judge. "For we must all be manifested before the judgment seat of Christ, that every one may receive the proper things of the body as he hath done, whether it be good or evil"—II. *Cor.*, v. 10. This is the precise meaning of that "*give an account of thy stewardship*", in the gospel of this day. "You are not", says St. Bonaventure, in his comment on these words, "a master, but a steward over the things committed to you; and therefore you are to render an account of them". I will place before your eyes to-day, the rigour of this judgment, which shall be passed on each of us on the last day of our life. Let us consider the terror of the soul, *first*, when she shall be presented to the Judge; *secondly*, when she shall be examined; and *thirdly*, when she shall be condemned.

First point. Terror of the soul when she shall be presented to the Judge.

1. "It is appointed unto men once to die, and, after this, the judgment"—*Heb.*, ix. 27. It is of faith that we shall die, and that, after death, a judgment shall be passed on all the actions of our life. Now, what shall be the terror of each of us, when we shall be at the point of death, and shall have before our eyes the judgment which must take place the very moment the soul departs from the body? Then shall be decided our doom to

eternal life, or to eternal death. At the time of the passage of their souls from this life to eternity, the sight of their past sins, the rigour of God's judgment, and the uncertainty of their eternal salvation, have made the saints tremble. St. Mary Magdalene de Pazzi trembled in her sickness, through the fear of judgment; and to her confessor, when he endeavoured to give her courage, she said: *Ah father, it is a terrible thing to appear before Christ in judgment.* After spending so many years in penance in the desert, St. Agatho trembled at the hour of death, and said: *What shall become of me when I shall be judged?* The venerable Father Louis da Ponte was seized with such a fit of trembling at the thought of the account which he should render to God, that he shook the room in which he lay. The thought of judgment inspired the venerable Juvenal Ancina, Priest of the Oratory, and afterwards Bishop of Saluzzo, with the determination to leave the world. Hearing the *Dies Iræ* sung, and considering the terror of the soul when presented before Jesus Christ, her Judge, he took, and afterwards executed, the resolution of giving himself entirely to God.

2. It is the common opinion of theologians, that, at the very moment and in the very place in which the soul departs from the body, the divine tribunal is erected, the accusation is read, and the sentence is passed by Jesus Christ, the Judge. At this terrible tribunal each of us shall be presented, to give an account of all our thoughts, of all our words, and of all our actions. "For we must all be manifested before the judgment seat of Christ, that every one may receive the proper things of the body, according as he hath done, whether it be good or evil"—II. *Cor.*, v. 10. When presented before an Earthly judge, criminals have been seen to fall into a cold sweat through fear. It is related of Piso, that, so great and insufferable was the confusion which he felt at the thought of appearing as a criminal before the senate, that he killed himself. How great is the pain of a vassal, or of a son, in appearing before an angry prince or an enraged father, to account for some crime which he has committed! Oh! how much greater shall be the pain and confusion of the soul in standing before Jesus Christ enraged against her for having despised him during her life! Speaking of judgment, St. Luke says: "Then they shall see the Son of Man"—*Luke*, xxi. 27. They shall see Jesus Christ

as man, with the same wounds with which he ascended into Heaven. "Great joy of the beholders!" says Robert the Abbot, "great terror of those who are in expectation!" These wounds shall console the just, and shall terrify the wicked. In them sinners shall see the Redeemer's love for themselves, and their ingratitude to him.

3. "Who", says the Prophet Nahum, "can stand before the face of his indignation?"—i. 6. How great, then, shall be the terror of a soul that finds herself in sin before this Judge, the first time she shall see him, and shall see him full of wrath! St. Basil says that she shall be tortured more by her shame and confusion than by the very fire of Hell. "Horridior quam ignis, erit pudor". Philip the Second rebuked one of his domestics for having told him a lie. "*Is it thus*", said the king to him, "*you deceive me?*" The domestic, after having returned home, died of grief. The Scripture tells us, that when Joseph reproved his brethren, saying: "*I am Joseph, whom you sold*", they were unable to answer through fear, and remained silent. "His brethren could not answer him, being struck with exceeding great fear"—*Gen.*, xlv. 3. Now, what answer shall sinners make to Jesus Christ when he shall say to them: I am your Redeemer and your Judge, whom you have so much despised? Where shall the miserable beings fly, says St. Augustine, when they shall see an angry Judge above, Hell open below, on one side their own sins accusing them, and on the other the devils dragging them to punishment, and their conscience burning them within? "Above shall be an enraged Judge; below a horrid chaos; on the right, sins accusing him; on the left, demons dragging him to punishment; within, a burning conscience. Whither shall a sinner, beset in this manner, fly?" Perhaps he will cry for mercy? But how, asks Eusebius Emissenus, can he dare to implore mercy, when he must first render an account of his contempt for the mercy which Jesus Christ had shown to him? "With what face will you, who are to be first judged for contempt of mercy, ask for mercy?" But let us come to the rendering of the accounts.

Second point. Terror of the soul when she shall be examined.

4. As soon as the soul shall be presented before the tribunal

of Jesus Christ, he will say to her: "Give an account of thy stewardship": render instantly an account of thy entire life. The Apostle tells us, that to be worthy of eternal glory, our lives must be found conformable to the life of Jesus Christ. "For whom he foreknew, he also predestinated to be made conformable to the image of his Son;...them he also glorified"—*Rom.*, viii. 29, 30. Hence St. Peter has said, that in the judgment of Jesus Christ, the just man, who has observed the divine law, has pardoned enemies, has respected the saints, has practised chastity, meekness, and other virtues, shall scarcely be saved. "The just man shall scarcely be saved". The Apostle adds: "Where shall the ungodly and the sinner appear?"—I. *Pet.*, iv. 18. What shall become of the vindictive and the unchaste, of blasphemers, and slanderers? What shall become of those whose entire life is opposed to the life of Jesus Christ?

5. In the first place, the Judge shall demand of sinners an account of all the blessings and graces which he bestowed upon them in order to bring them to salvation, and which they have rendered fruitless. He will demand an account of the years granted to them that they might serve God, and which they have spent in offending him. "He hath called against me the time"—*Lam.*, i. 15. He will then demand an account of their sins. Sinners commit sins, and afterwards forget them; but Jesus Christ does not forget them: he keeps, as Job says, all our iniquities numbered, as it were in a bag. "Thou hast sealed up my iniquities, as it were in a bag"- *Job*, xiv. 17. And he tells us that, on the day of accounts, he will take a lamp to scrutinize all the actions of our life. "And it shall come to pass at that time, that I will search Jerusalem with lamps"—*Soph.*, i. 12. The lamp, says Mendoza on this passage, penetrates all the corners of the house—that is, God will discover all the defects of our conscience, great and small. According to St. Anselm, an account shall be demanded of every glance of the eyes. "Exigitur usque ad ictum oculi". And, according to St. Matthew, of every idle word. "Every idle word that men shall speak, they shall render an account for it on the day of judgment"—*Matt.*, xii. 36.

6. The Prophet Malachy says, that as gold is refined by taking away the dross, so on the day of judgment, all our

actions shall be examined; and every defect which may be discovered shall be punished. "He shall purify the sons of Levi, and shall refine them as gold"—*Mal.*, iii. 3. Even our justices—that is, our good works, confessions, communions, and prayers—shall be examined. "When I shall take a time, I will judge justices"—*Ps.*, lxxiv. 3. But, if every glance, every idle word, and even good works, shall be judged, with what rigour shall immodest expressions, blasphemies, grievous detractions, thefts, and sacrileges, be judged? Alas! on that day every soul shall, as St. Jerome says, see to her own confusion, all the evils which she has done. "Videbit unusquisque quod fecit".

7. "Weight and balance are judgments of the Lord"—*Prov.*, xvi. 11. In the balance of the Lord, a holy life and good works make the scale descend; but nobility, wealth, and science, have no weight. Hence, if found innocent, the peasant, the poor, and the ignorant, shall be rewarded. But the man of rank, of wealth, or of learning, if found guilty, shall be condemned. "Thou art weighed in the balance", said Daniel to Balthassar, "and art found wanting"—*Dan.*, v. 27. "Neither his gold, nor his wealth", says father Alvares, "but the king alone was weighed".

8. At the divine tribunal, the poor sinner shall see himself accused by the Devil, who, according to St. Augustine, "will recite the words of our profession, and will charge us before our face with all that we have done, will state the day and hour in which we sinned"—*Con. jud., tom.* VI. *He will recite the words of our profession;* that is, he will enumerate the promises which we have made to God, and which we afterwards violated. *He will charge us before our face;* he will upbraid us with all our wicked deeds, pointing to the day and hour in which they were committed. And he will, as the same saint says, conclude his accusation by saying: "I have suffered neither stripes nor scourges for this man". Lord, I have suffered nothing for this ungrateful sinner, and, to make himself my slave, he has turned his back on thee, who hast endured so much for his salvation. He, therefore, justly belongs to me. Even his angel-guardian will, according to Origen, come forward to accuse him, and will say: I have laboured so many years for his salvation; but he has despised all my admonitions. "Unus-

quisque angelorum perhibet testimonium, quot annis circa eum laboraverit, sed ille monita sprevit"—*hom.*, lxvi. Thus, even friends shall treat with contempt the guilty soul. "All her friends have despised her"—*Lamen.*, i. 2. Her very sins shall, says St. Bernard, accuse her. "And they shall say: You have made us; we are your work; we shall not desert you"—*Lib.*, *Medit.*, *cap.* ii. We are your offspring; we shall not leave you; we shall be your companions in Hell for all eternity.

9. Let us now examine the excuses which the sinner will be able to advance. He will say, that the evil inclinations of nature had drawn him to sin. But he shall be told, that, if concupiscence impelled him to sins, it did not oblige him to commit them; and that, if he had recourse to God, he should have received from him grace to resist every temptation. For this purpose Jesus Christ has left us the sacraments; but, when we do not make use of them, we can complain only of our ourselves. "But", says the Redeemer, "now they have no excuse for their sin"—*John*, xv. 22. To excuse himself, the sinner shall also say, that the Devil tempted him to sin. But, as St. Augustine says, "the enemy is bound like a dog in chains, and can bite only him who has united himself to him with a deadly security". The Devil can bark, but cannot bite, unless you adhere and listen to him. Hence the saint adds: "See how foolish is the man whom a dog loaded with chains bites". Perhaps he will advance his bad habits as an excuse; but this shall not stand; for the same St. Augustine says, that though it is difficult to resist the force of an evil habit, "if any one does not desert himself, he will conquer it with the divine assistance". If a man does not abandon himself to sin, and invokes God's aid, he will overcome evil habits. The Apostle tells us, that the Lord does not permit us to be tempted above our strength. "God is faithful, who will not suffer you to be tempted above that which you are able"—I. *Cor.*, x. 13.

10. "For what shall I do", said Job, "when God shall rise to judge me? and when he shall examine, what shall I answer him?"—*Job.*, xxxi. 14. What answer shall the sinner give to Jesus Christ? How can he, who sees himself so clearly convicted, give an answer? He shall be covered with confusion, and shall remain silent, like the man found without the nuptial garment. "But he was silent"—*Matt.*, xxii. 12. His very sins

shall shut the sinner's mouth. "And all iniquity shall stop her mouth"—*Ps.*, cvi. 42. There, says St. Thomas of Villanova, there shall be no intercessors, to whom the sinner can have recourse. "There, there is no opportunity of sinning; there, no intercessor, no friend, no father shall assist". Who shall then save you? Is it God? But how, asks St. Basil, can you expect salvation from him whom you have despised? "Who shall deliver you? Is it God, whom you have insulted?"—*S. Bas.*, *Or.* 4, *de Pen.* Alas! the guilty soul that leaves this world in sin, is condemned by herself before the Judge pronounces sentence. Let us come to the sentence of the Judge.

Third point. Terror of the soul when she shall be condemned.

11. How great shall be the joy of a soul when, at death, she hears from Jesus Christ these sweet words: "Well done, good and faithful servant; because thou hast been faithful over a few things, I will place thee over many things. Enter thou into the joy of thy Lord"—*Matt.*, xxv. 21. Equally great shall be the anguish and despair of a guilty soul, that shall see herself driven away by the Judge with the following words: "Depart from me, you cursed, into everlasting fire"—*verse* 41. Oh! what a terrible thunderclap shall that sentence be to her! "O how frightfully", says the Carthusian, "shall that thunder resound!" Eusebius writes, that the terror of sinners at hearing their condemnation shall be so great, that, if they could, they would die again. "The wicked shall be seized with such terror at the sight of the Judge pronouncing sentence, that, if they were not immortal, they should die a second time." But, brethren, let us, before the termination of this sermon, make some reflections which will be profitable to us. St. Thomas of Villanova says, that some listen to discourses on the judgment and condemnation of the wicked, with as little concern as if they themselves were secure against these things, or as if the day of judgment were never to arrive for them. "Heu quam securi hæc dicimus et audimus, quasi nos non tangeret hæc sententia, aut quasi dies hæc nunquam esset venturus!"—*Conc.* i., *de Jud.* The saint then asks: Is it not great folly to entertain security in so perilous an affair? "Quæ est ista stulta securitas in discrimine tanto?" There are some, says St. Augustine, who,

though they live in sin, cannot imagine that God will send them to Hell. "Will God", they say, "really condemn us?" Brethren, adds the saint, do not speak thus. So many of the damned did not believe that they should be sent to Hell; but the end came, and, according to the threat of Ezechiel, they have been cast into that place of darkness. "The end is come, the end is come... and I will send my wrath upon thee, and I will judge thee"—*Ezec.*, vii. 2, 3. Sinners, perhaps vengeance is at hand for you, and still you laugh and sleep in sin. Who will not tremble at the words of the Baptist, "For now the axe is laid to the root of the trees. Every tree, therefore, that doth not yield good fruit, shall be cut down and cast into the fire"?—*Matt.*, iii. 10. He says, that every tree that does not bring forth good fruit, shall be cut down and cast into the fire: and he promises that, with regard to the trees, which represent sinners, the axe is already laid to the roots—that is, chastisement is at hand. Dearly beloved brethren, let us follow the counsel of the Holy Ghost—"Before judgment, prepare thee justice"—*Eccl.*, xviii. 19. Let us adjust our accounts before the day of accounts. Let us seek God, now that we can find him; for the time shall come when we will wish, but shall not be able to find him. "You shall seek me, and shall not find me"—*John*, vii. 36. "Before judgment", says St. Augustine, "the Judge can be appeased, but not in judgment". By a change of life, we can now appease the anger of Jesus Christ, and recover his grace; but when he shall judge, and find us in sin, he must execute justice, and we shall be lost.

SERMON XXXVIII.

FOR THE NINTH SUNDAY AFTER PENTECOST.

On the death of the sinner.

"Thy enemies shall cast a trench about thee"—*Luke*, xix. 43.

Seeing from a distance the city of Jerusalem, in which the Jews were soon to put him to death, Jesus Christ wept over it. "Videns civitatem flevit super illam". Our merciful Redeemer wept at the consideration of the chastisement which was soon to be inflicted on the city, and which he foretold to her inhabitants. "Thy enemies shall cast a trench about thee". Unhappy city! thou shalt one day see thyself encompassed by enemies, who shall beat thee flat to the ground, and thy children in thee, and shall not leave in thee a stone upon a stone. Most beloved brethren, this unhappy city is a figure of the soul of a sinner, who, at the hour of death, shall find himself surrounded by his enemies, *first*, by remorses of conscience; *secondly*, by the assaults of the devils; and *thirdly*, by the fears of eternal death.

First point. The sinner at death shall be tortured by remorses of conscience.

1. "Their soul shall die in a storm"—*Job*, xxxvi. 14. The unhappy sinners who remain in sin, die in a tempest, with which God has beforehand threatened them. "A tempest shall break out and come upon the head of the wicked"—*Jer.*, xxiii. 19. At the commencement of his illness the sinner is not troubled by remorse or fear; because his relatives, friends, physicians, and all tell him that his sickness is not dangerous; thus he is deceived and hopes to recover. But when his illness increases, and malignant symptoms, the harbingers of approaching death, begin to appear, then the storm with which the Lord has threatened the wicked, shall commence. "When sudden calamity shall fall on you, and destruction as a tempest shall be at

hand"—*Prov.*, i. 27. This tempest shall be formed as well by the pains of sickness as by the fear of being obliged to depart from this Earth, and to leave all things; but still more by the remorses of conscience, which shall place before his eyes all the irregularities of his past life. "They shall come with fear at the thought of their sins, and their iniquities shall stand against them to convict them"—*Wis.*, iv. 20. Then shall his sins rush upon his mind, and fill him with terror. His iniquities shall stand against him to convict him, and, without the aid of other testimony, shall assail him, and prove that he deserves Hell.

2. The dying sinner will confess his sins; but, according to St. Augustine, "The repentance which is sought from a sick man is infirm"—*serm.* xxxvii., *de Temp.* And St. Jerome says, that of a hundred thousand sinners who continue till death in the state of sin, scarcely one shall be saved. "Vix de centum millibus, quorum mala vita fuit, meretur in morte a Deo indulgentiam, unus"—*in Epis. de Mort. Eus.* St. Vincent Ferrer writes, that it is a greater miracle to save such sinners, than to raise the dead to life. "Majus miraculum est, quod male viventes faciant bonum finem, quam suscitare mortuos"—*serm.* i., *de Nat. Virg.* They shall feel convinced of the evil they have done; they will wish, but shall not be able, to detest it. Antiochus understood the malice of his sins when he said: "Now I remember the evils that I have done in Jerusalem"—I. *Mach.*, vi. 12. He remembered his sins, but did not detest them. He died in despair and oppressed with great sadness, saying: "Behold, I perish with great grief in a strange land"—*v.* 13. According to St. Fulgentius, the same happened to Saul at the hour of death: he remembered his sins; he dreaded the punishment which they deserved; but he did not detest them. "Non odit quod fecerat, sed timuit quod nolebat".

3. Oh! how difficult is it for a sinner, who has slept many years in sin, to repent sincerely at the hour of death, when his mind is darkened, and his heart hardened! "His heart shall be as hard as a stone, and as firm as a smith's anvil"—*Job*, xli. 15. During life, instead of yielding to the graces and calls of God, he became more obdurate, as the anvil is hardened by repeated strokes of the hammer. "A hard heart shall fare evil at the last"—*Eccl.*, iii. 27. By loving sin till, death, he

has loved the danger of his damnation, and therefore God will justly permit him to perish in the danger in which he wished to live till death.

4. St. Augustine says, that he who is abandoned by sin before he abandons it, will scarcely detest it as he ought at the hour of death; for he will then detest it, not through a hatred of sin, but through necessity. "Qui prius a peccato relinquitur, quam ipse relinquat, non libere, sed quasi ex necessitate condemnat". But how shall he be able to hate from his heart the sins which he has loved till death? He must love the enemy, whom till then he has hated, and he must hate the person whom he has till that moment loved. Oh! what mountains must he pass! He shall probably meet with a fate similar to that of a certain person, who kept in confinement a great number of wild beasts in order to let them loose on the enemies who might assail him. But the wild beasts, as soon as he unchained them, instead of attacking his enemies, devoured himself. When the sinner will wish to drive away his iniquities, they shall cause his destruction, either by complacency in objects till then loved, or by despair of pardon at the sight of their numbers and enormity. "Evils shall catch the unjust man unto destruction"—*Ps.*, cxxxix. 12. St. Bernard says, that at death the sinner shall see himself chained and bound by his sins. "We are your works; we will not desert you". We will not leave you; we will accompany you to judgment, and will be your companions for all eternity in Hell.

Second point. The dying sinner shall be tortured by the assaults of the devils.

5. "The Devil is come down unto you, having great wrath, knowing that he hath but a short time"—*Apoc.*, xii. 12. At death, the Devil exerts all his powers to secure the soul that is about to leave this world; for he knows, from the symptoms of the disease, that he has but little time to gain her for eternity. The Council of Trent teaches, that Jesus Christ has left us the sacrament of Extreme Unction as a most powerful defence against the temptations of the Devil at the hour of death. "Extremæ Unctionis sacramento finem vitæ tanquam firmissimo quodam præsidio munivit". And the holy council adds, that there is no time in which the enemy combats against us with so

much violence in order to effect our damnation, and to make us despair of the divine mercy, as at the end of life. "Nullum tempus est, quo vehementius ille omnes suæ versutiæ nervos intendat ad perdendos nos penitus, et a fiducia, etiam, si possit, divinæ misericordiæ deturbandos, quam cum impendere nobis exitum vitæ perspicet"—*sess.* 14, *cap.* ix., *in Doctr. de Sacr. Extr. Unct.*

6. Oh! how terrible are the assaults and snares of the Devil against the souls of dying persons, even though they have led a holy life! After his recovery from a most severe illness, the holy king Eleazar said, that the temptations by which the Devil assails men at death, can be conceived only by him who has felt them. We read in the life of St. Andrew Avellino, that in his agony he had so fierce a combat with Hell, that all the religious present were seized with trembling. They perceived that, in consequence of the agitation, his face swelled and became black, all his members trembled, and a flood of tears gushed from his eyes. All began to weep through compassion, and were filled with terror at the sight of a saint dying in such a manner. But they were afterwards consoled, when they saw that as soon as an image of most holy Mary was held before him, he became perfectly calm, and breathed forth his blessed soul with great joy.

7. Now, if this happens to the saints, what shall become of poor sinners, who have lived in sin till death? At that awful moment the Devil does not come alone to tempt them in a thousand ways in order to bring them to eternal perdition, but he calls companions to his assistance. "Their house shall be filled with serpents"—*Isa.*, xiii. 21. When a Christian is about to leave this world, his house is filled with devils, who unite together in order to effect his ruin. "All her pesecutors have taken her in the midst of straits"—*Lamen.*, i. 3. All his enemies will encompass him in the straits of death. One shall say: Be not afraid; you shall not die of this sickness! Another will say: You have been for so many years deaf to the calls of God, and can you now expect that he will save you? Another will ask: How can you repair the frauds of your past life, and the injuries you have done to your neighbour in his property and character? Another shall ask: What hope can there be for you? do you not see that all your confessions have been null—that they have been made with-

out true sorrow, and without a firm purpose of amendment? How can you now repair them with this heart, which you feel so hard? Do you not see that you are lost? And in the midst of these straits and attacks of despair, the dying sinner, full of agitation and confusion, must pass into eternity. "The people shall be troubled,...and they shall pass"—*Job*, xxxiv. 20.

Third point. The dying sinner shall be tortured by the fears of eternal death.

8. Miserable the sick man who takes to his bed in the state of mortal sin! He that lives in sin till death, shall die in sin. "You shall die in your sin"—*John*, viii. 21. It is true that, in whatsoever hour the sinner is converted, God promises to pardon him; but to no sinner has God promised the grace of conversion at the hour of death. "Seek the Lord while he may be found" —*Isa.*, lv. 6. Then, there is for some sinners a time when they shall seek God and shall not find him. "You shall seek me, and shall not find me"—*John*, vii. 34. The unhappy beings will go to confession at the hour of death; they will promise and weep, and ask mercy of God, but without knowing what they do. A man who sees himself under the feet of a foe pointing a dagger to his throat, will shed tears, ask pardon, and promise to serve his enemy as a slave during the remainder of his life. But, will the enemy believe him? No; he will feel convinced that his words are not sincere—that his object is to escape from his hands, and that, should he be pardoned, he will become more hostile than ever. In like manner, how can God pardon the dying sinner, when he sees that all his acts of sorrow, and all his promises, proceed not from the heart, but from a dread of death and of approaching damnation?

9. In the recommendation of the departing soul, the assisting priest prays to the Lord, saying: *Recognise, O Lord, thy creature.* But God answers: I know that he is my creature; but, instead of regarding me as his Creator, he has treated me as an enemy. The priest continues his prayer, and says: *Remember not his past iniquities.* I would, replies the Lord, pardon all the past sins of his youth; but he has continued to despise me till this moment—the very hour of his death. "They have turned their back upon me, and not their face: and, in the time of affliction, they will say:

Arise and deliver us. Where are the gods which thou hast made thee? let them rise and deliver thee"—*Jer.*, ii. 27, 28. You, says the Lord, have turned your back upon me till death; and do you now want me to deliver you from vengeance? Invoke your own gods—the creatures, the riches, the friends you loved more than you loved me. Call them now to come to your assistance, and to save you from Hell, which is open to receive you. It now justly belongs to me to take vengeance on the insults you have offered me. You have despised my threats against obstinate sinners, and have paid no regard to them. "Revenge is mine, and I will repay them in *due* tme, that their foot may slide"—*Deut.*, xxxii. 35. The time of my vengeance is now arrived; it is but just to execute it. This is precisely what happened to a certain person in Madrid, who led a wicked life, but, at the sight of the unhappy death of a companion, went to confession, and resolved to enter a strict religious order. But, in consequence of having neglected to put his resolution into immediate execution, he relapsed into his former irregularities. Being reduced to great want, he wandered about the world, and fell sick at Lima. From the hospital in which he took refuge, he sent for a confessor, and promised again to change his life, and to enter religion. But, having recovered from his illness, he returned to his wickedness; and, behold! the vengeance of God fell upon him. One day, his confessor, who was a missionary, in passing over a mountain, heard a noise, which appeared to be the howling of a wild beast. He drew near the place from which the noise proceeded, and saw a dying man, half rotten, and howling through despair. He addressed to him some words of consolation. The sick man opening his eyes, recognised the missionary, and said: Have you, too, come to be a witness of the justice of God? I am the man who made my confession in the hospital of Lima. I then promised to change my life, but have not done so; and now I die in despair. And thus the miserable man, amid these acts of despair, breathed forth his unhappy soul. These facts are related by Father Charles Bovio, *part* iii. *example* 9.

10. Let us conclude the discourse. Tell me, brethren, were a person in sin seized with apoplexy, and instantly deprived of his senses, what sentiments of pity would you feel at seeing him die in this state, without the sacraments, and without signs of repen-

tance. Is not he a fool, who, when he has time to be reconciled with God, continues in sin, or returns to his sins, and thus exposes himself to the danger of dying suddenly, and of dying in sin? "At what hour you think not", says Jesus Christ, "the Son of Man will come"—*Luke*, xii. 40. An unprovided death, which has happened to so many, may also happen to each of us. And it is necessary to understand, that all who lead a bad life meet with an unprovided death, though their last illness may allow them some time to prepare for eternity; for the days of that mortal illness are days of darkness—days of confusion, in which it is difficult and even morally impossible, to adjust a conscience burdened with many sins. Tell me, brethren, if you were now at the point of death, given over by physicians, and in the last agony, how ardently would you desire another month, or another week, to settle the accounts you must render to God? And God gives you this time. He calls you, and warns you of the danger of damnation to which you are exposed. Give yourself, then, instantly to God. What do you wait for? Will you wait till he sends you to Hell? "Walk whilst you have light"—*John*, xii. 35. Avail yourselves of this time and this light, which God gives you at this moment, and now, while it is in your power, repent of all your past sins: for, a time shall come when you will be no longer able to avert the punishment which they deserve.

[*I entreat my reader to read Sermon* xliv., *or the sermon for the fifteenth Sunday after Pentecost, on the practical death, or that which practically happens at the death of men of the world. I know by experience, that, though it does not contain Latin texts, whenever I preached that sermon, it produced a great impression, and left the audience full of terror. A greater impression is made by practical than by speculative truths.*]

SERMON XXXIX.

FOR THE TENTH SUNDAY AFTER PENTECOST.

On the efficacy and necessity of prayer.

"O God, be merciful to me, a sinner"—*Luke*, xviii. 13.

In this day's gospel we read, that two men, one a Pharisee and the other a Publican, went to the temple. Instead of bowing down to beg of God to assist him by his graces, the Pharisee said: I thank thee, O Lord, that I am not as the rest of men, who are sinners. "Deus gratias ago tibi, quia non sum sicut cæteri homines". But the Publican, filled with sentiments of humility, cried out: "O God, be merciful to me a sinner". St. Luke tells us, that this Publican returned to his house justified; and that the Pharisee went home as guilty and as proud as when he entered the temple. From this, most beloved brethren, you may infer how pleasing to God, and how necessary for us, are our humble petitions to obtain from the Lord all the graces which are indispensable for salvation. In this sermon I will show, in the first point, the efficacy of prayer; and in the second, the necessity of prayer.

First point. On the efficacy of prayer.

1. To understand the efficacy and value of our prayers, we need only consider the great promises which God has made to every one who prays. "Call upon me, and I will deliver thee" —*Ps.*, xlix. 15. Call upon me, and I will save you from every danger. "He shall cry to me, I will hear him"—*Ps.*, xc. 15. "Cry to me, and I will hear thee"—*Jer.*, xxxiii. 3. "You shall ask whatever you will, and it shall be done unto you"—*John*, xv. 7. Ask whatsoever you wish, and it shall be given to you. There are a thousand similar passages in the Old and New Testament. By his nature, God is, as St. Leo says, goodness itself. "Deus cujus natura bonitas". Hence he desires, with a great desire, to make us partakers of his own goods. St.

Mary Magdalene de Pazzi used to say, that when a soul prays to God for any grace, he feels in a certain manner under an obligation to her, and thanks her; because by prayer the soul opens to him a way of satisfying his desire to dispense his graces to us. Hence in the holy Scriptures, the Lord appears to recommend and inculcate to us nothing more forcibly than to ask and pray. To show this, the words which we read in the seventh chapter of St. Matthew are sufficient. "Ask, and it shall be given you; seek, and you shall find; knock, and it shall be opened to you"—vii. 7. St. Augustine teaches, that by these promises God has bound himself to grant all that we ask in prayer. "By his promises he has made himself a debtor"—*de Verb. Dom.*, *serm.* ii. And, in the fifth sermon, the saint says, that if the Lord did not wish to bestow his graces upon us, he would not exhort us so strenuously to ask them. "He would not exhort us to ask, unless he wished to give". Hence we see that the Psalms of David, and the Books of Solomon and of the Prophets, are full of prayers.

2. Theodoret has writen, that prayer is so efficacious before God, that, "*though it be one, it can do all things*". "Oratio cum sit una, omnia potest". St. Bernard teaches, that when we pray, the Lord, if he does not give the grace we ask, will grant a more useful gift. "He will give either what we ask, or what he knows to be more profitable to us"—*serm.* v., *in Fer.* 4 *cin.* And whom has God, when asked for aid, ever despised by not listening to his petition? "Who hath called upon him, and he despised him?"—*Eccl.*, ii. 12. The Scripture says, that among the nations there is none that has gods so willing to hear our prayers, as our true God. "Neither is there any other nation so great, that hath gods so nigh to them, as our God is present to all our petitions"—*Deut.*, iv. 7. The princes of the Earth, says St. Chrysostom, give audience only to a few; but God grants it to every one that wishes for it. "Aures principis paucis patent, Dei vero omnibus volentibus"—*lib.* II. *de Orat.* David tells us that this goodness of God in hearing us at whatever time we pray to him, shows us that he is our true God, whose love for us surpasses the love of all others. "In what day soever I shall call upon thee, behold I know thou art my God"—*Ps.*, lv. 10. He wishes and ardently desires to confer favours upon us; but he requires us to

pray for them. Jesus Christ said one day to his disciples: "Hitherto you have not asked anything in my name: ask, and you shall receive, that your joy may be full"—*John*, xvi. 24. As if he said: You complain of me for not making you perfectly content; but you ought to complain of yourselves for not having asked of me all the gifts you stood in need of: ask, henceforth, whatsoever you want, and your prayer shall be heard. Many, says St. Bernard, complain that the Lord is wanting to them. But he complains with more justice, that they are wanting to him, by neglecting to ask him for his graces. "Omnes nobis causamur deesse gratiam, sed justius forsitan ista sibi queritur deesse nonnullos"—*S. Bern. de Tripl. Cust.*

3. The ancient fathers, after having consulted together about the exercise most conducive to salvation, came to the conclusion, that the best means of securing eternal life is, to pray continually, saying: Lord, assist me; Lord, hasten to my assistance. "Incline unto my aid, O God; O Lord, make haste to help me". Hence the holy Church commands these two petitions to be often repeated in the canonical hours by all the clergy and by all religious, who pray not only for themselves, but also for the whole Christian world. St. John Climacus says, that our prayers as it were compel God by a holy violence to hear us. "Prayer piously does violence to God". Hence, when we pray to the Lord, he instantly answers by bestowing upon us the grace we ask. "At the voice of thy cry, as soon as he shall hear, he will answer thee"—*Isa.*, xxx. 19. Hence St. Ambrose says, that "he who asks of God, receives while he asks"—*Ep.*, lxxxiv., *ad Demetr.* And he not only grants his graces instantly, but also abundantly, giving us more than we pray for. St. Paul tells us that God is rich—that is, liberal of his graces to every one that prays to him. "Rich unto all that call upon him"—*Rom.*, x. 12. And St. James says: "If any of you want wisdom, let him ask of God, who giveth to all men abundantly, and upbraideth not"—*St. James*, i. 5. *He upbraideth not;* when we pray to him, he does not reproach us with the insults we have offered to him, but he appears then to forget all the injuries we have done him, and to delight in enriching us with his graces.

Second point. On the necessity of prayer.

4. "God", as St. Paul has written, "will have all men to be saved, and to come to the knowledge of the truth"—I. *Tim.*, ii. 4. According to St. Peter, he does not wish any one to be lost. "The Lord dealeth patiently for your sake, not willing that any soul should perish, but that all should return to penance"—II. *Pet.*, iii. 9. Hence St. Leo teaches, that as God wishes us to observe his commands, so he prevents us by his assistance, that we may fulfil them. "Juste instat præcepto qui præcurrit auxilio"—*Serm.* xvi., *de Pass.* And Saint Thomas, in explaining the words of the Apostle,—"God, who will have all men to be saved", says: "Therefore grace is wanting to no one; but he, on his part, communicates it to all"—*in Epist. ad Hebr.*, *cap.* xii., *lect.* 3. And in another place the holy doctor writes: "To provide every man with the means necessary for his salvation, provided on his part he puts no obstacle to it, belongs to Divine Providence". But, according to Gennadius, this assistance of his grace the Lord grants only to those who prays for it. "We believe...that no one works out his salvation, but by God's assistance; and that he only who prays, merits aid from God"—*de Eccles. Dogm.* And St Augustine teaches, that, except the first graces of vocation to the faith and to repentance, all other graces, and particularly the grace of perseverance, are granted to those only who ask them. "It is evident that God gives some graces, such as the beginning of faith—without prayer, and that he has prepared other graces such as perseverance to the end, only for those who pray"—*de Dono Persev.*, c. xvi. And in another place he writes, that "God wishes to bestow his favours; but he gives them only to those who ask"—*in Ps.*, c.

5. Hence theologians commonly teach, after St. Basil, St. John Chrysostom, St. Augustine, Clement of Alexandria, and others, that, for adults prayer is necessary *as a means* of salvation; that is, that without prayer it is impossible for them to be saved. This doctrine may be inferred from the following passages of Scripture. "We ought always to pray"—*Luke*, xviii. 1. "Ask, and you shall receive"—*John*, xvi. 24. "Pray without ceasing"—I. *Thess.*, v. 17. The words *we ought*, *ask*, *pray*, according to St. Thomas (3 *part*, *qu.* xxxix., *art.* 5) and the generality of theologians, imply a precept,

which obliges, under grievous sin, particularly in three cases. First, when a man is in the state of sin; secondly, when he is in great danger of falling into sin; and, thirdly, when he is in danger of death. Theologians teach, that he who, at other times, neglects prayer for a month, or at most for two months, cannot be excused from mortal sin; because, without prayer we cannot procure the helps necessary for the observance of the law of God. St. Chrysostom teaches, that as water is necessary to prevent trees from withering, so prayer is necessary to save us from perdition. "Non minus quam arbores aquis, precibus indigemus" —*tom.* I., *hom.* lxxvii.

6. Most groundless was the assertion of Jansenius, that there are some commands the fulfilment of which is impossible to us; and that we have not even the grace to render their observance possible. For, the Council of Trent teaches, in the words of St. Augustine, that, though man is not able, with the aid of the grace ordinarily given, to fulfil all the commandments, still he can, by prayer, obtain the additional helps necessary for their observance. "God does not command impossibilities; but, by his precepts, he admonishes you to do what you can, and to ask what you cannot do; and he assists you, that you may be able to do it"—*sess.* 6, *cap.* xi. To this may be added another celebrated passage of St. Augustine:—"By our faith, which teaches that God does not command impossibilities, we are admonished what to do in things that are easy, and what to ask in things that are difficult"—*lib. de Nat. et Grat.*, *cap.* lxix. *n.* 83.

7. But why does God, who knows our weakness, permit us to be assailed by enemies which we are not able to resist? The Lord, answers the holy doctor, seeing the great advantages which we derive from the necessity of prayer, permits us to be attacked by enemies more powerful than we are, that we may ask his assistance. Hence they who are conquered, cannot excuse themselves by saying that they had not strength to resist the assault of the enemy; for had they asked aid from God, he should have given it; and had they prayed, they should have been victorious. Therefore, if they are defeated, God will punish them. St. Bonaventure says, that if a general lose a fortress in consequence of not having sought timely succour from his sovereign, he shall be branded as a traitor. "Reputaretur infidelis, nisi expectaret a rege

auxilium"—*S. Bon. Diœt. tit.*, *c.* v. Thus God regards as a traitor the Christian who, when he finds himself assailed by temptations, neglects to seek the divine aid. "Ask", says Jesus Christ, "and you shall receive". Then, concludes St. Teresa, he that does not ask, does not receive. This is conformable to the doctrine of St. James—"You have not, because you do not ask"—*St. James*, iv. 2. St. Chrysostom says, that prayer is a powerful weapon of defence against all enemies. "Truly prayer is a great armour"—*hom.* xli., *ad Pop.* St. Ephrem writes, that he who fortifies himself beforehand by prayer, prevents the entrance of sin into the soul. "If you pray before you work, the passage into the soul will not be open to sin"—*serm. de Orat.* David said the same—"Praising I will call upon the Lord, and I shall be saved from my enemies"—*Ps.*, xvii. 4.

8. If we wish to lead a good life, and to save our souls, we must learn to pray. "He", says St. Augustine, "knows how to live well, who knows how to pray well"—*hom.* xliii. In order to obtain God's graces by prayer, it is necessary, first, to take away sin; for God does not hear obstinate sinners. For example: if a person entertains hatred towards another, and wishes to take revenge, God does not hear his prayer. "When you multiply prayer, I will not hear; for your hands are full of blood"—*Isa.*, i. 15. St. Chrysostom says, that he who prays while he cherishes a sinful affection, does not pray, but mocks God. "Qui orat et peccat, non rogat Deum sed illudit"—*hom.* xi., *in Matt.* vi. But if he ask the Lord to take away hatred from his heart, the Lord will hear him. Secondly, it is necessary to pray with attention. Some imagine that they pray by repeating many *Our Fathers* with such distractions that they do not know what they say. These speak, but do not pray. Of them the Lord says, by the Prophet Isaias: "With their lips they glorify me, but their hearts are far from me"—*Is.*, xxix. 13. Thirdly, it is necessary, as the Holy Ghost exhorts us, to take away the occasions which hinder us to pray. "Let nothing hinder thee from praying always"—*Eccl.*, xviii. 22. He who is occupied in a thousand affairs unprofitable to the soul, places a cloud before his prayers, which prevents their passing to the throne of grace. "Thou hast set a cloud before thee, that *our* prayer may not pass through"—*Lamen.*, iii. 44. I will not omit here the exhortation of St. Bernard, to ask

graces of God through the intercession of his divine mother. "Let us ask grace, and ask it through Mary; for she is a mother, and her prayer cannot be fruitless"—*serm. de Aquæd.* St. Anselm says: "Many things are asked of God, and are not obtained: what is asked of Mary is obtained, not because she is more powerful, but because God decreed thus to honour her, that men may know that she can obtain all things from God".

SERMON XL.

FOR THE ELEVENTH SUNDAY AFTER PENTECOST.

On the vice of speaking immodestly.

"He touched his tongue,....and the string of his tongue was loosed"—*Mark*, vii. 33, 35.

In this day's gospel St. Mark relates the miracle which our Saviour wrought in healing the man that was dumb by barely touching his tongue. "He touched his tongue,...and the string of his tongue was loosed". From the last words we may infer that the man was not entirely dumb, but that his tongue was not free, or that his articulation was not distinct. Hence St. Mark tells us, that, after the miracle, *he spoke right.* Let us make the application to ourselves. The dumb man stood in need of a miracle to loose his tongue, and to take away the impediment under which he laboured. But how many are there on whom God would confer a great grace, if he bound their tongues, that they might cease to speak immodestly? This vice does great injury to others. Secondly, it does great injury to themselves. These shall be the two points of this Sermon.

First point. The man who speaks immodestly does great injury to others who listen to him.

1. In explaining the 140th Psalm, St. Augustine calls those who speak obscenely, "*the mediators of Satan*", the ministers of Lucifer; because, by their obscene language, the demon of

impurity gets access to souls, which by his own suggestions, he could not enter. Of their accursed tongues St. James says: "And the tongue is a fire,...being set on fire by Hell"—*James*, iii. 6. He says that the tongue is a fire kindled by Hell, with which they who speak obscenely burn themselves and others. The obscene tongue may be said to be the tongue of the third person, of which Ecclesiasticus says: "The tongue of a third person hath disquieted many and scattered them from nation to nation" —*Eccl.*, xxviii. 16. The spiritual tongue speaks of God, the worldly tongue talks of worldly affairs, but the tongue of a third person is a tongue of Hell, which speaks of the impurities of the flesh; and this is the tongue that perverts many, and brings them to perdition.

2. Speaking of the life of men on this Earth, the Royal Prophet says: "Let their way become dark and slippery"—*Ps.*, xxxiv. 6. In this life men walk in the midst of darkness, and in a slippery way. Hence, they are in danger of falling at every step, unless they cautiously examine the road on which they walk, and carefully avoid dangerous steps—that is, the occasions of sin Now, if, in treading this slippery way, frequent efforts were made to throw them down, would it not be a miracle if they did not fall? *The mediators of Satan*, who speak obscenely, impel others to sin, who, as long as they live on this Earth, walk in the midst of darkness, and, as long as they remain in the flesh, are in danger of falling into the vice of impurity. Now, of those who indulge in obscene language, it has been well said: "Their throat is an open sepulchre"—*Ps.*, v. 11. The mouths of those who can utter nothing but filthy obscenities are, according to St. Chrysostom, so many open sepulchres of putrefied carcasses. "Talia sunt ora hominum qui turpia proferunt"—*hom.* ii., *de Proph. Obs.* The exhalation which arises from the rottenness of a multitude of dead bodies thrown together into a pit, communicates infection and disease to all who feel the stench.

3. "The stroke of a whip", says Ecclesiasticus, "maketh a blue mark; but the stroke of a tongue will break the bones"—*Eccl.*, xxviii. 21. The wounds of the lash are wounds of the flesh, but the wounds of the obscene tongue are wounds which infect the bones of those who listen to its language. St. Bernardine of Sienna relates, that a virgin who led a holy life, at

hearing an obscene word from a young man, fell into a bad thought, and afterwards abandoned herself to the vice of impurity to such a degree, that, the saint says, if the Devil had taken human flesh, he could not have committed so many sins of that kind, as she committed.

4. The misfortune is, that these mouths of Hell that frequently utter immodest words, regard them as trifles, and are careless about confessing them: and when rebuked for them, they answer: *I say these words in jest, and without malice.* In jest! Unhappy man, these jests make the Devil laugh, and shall make you weep for eternity in Hell. In the first place, it is useless to say that you utter such words without malice; for, when you use such expressions, it is very difficult for you to abstain from acts against purity. According to St. Jerome, "he that delights in words is not far from the act". Besides, immodest words spoken before persons of a different sex, are always accompanied with sinful complacency. And is not the scandal you give to others criminal? Utter a single obscene word, and you shall bring into sin all who listen to you. Such is the doctrine of St. Bernard. "One speaks, and he utters only one word; but he kills the souls of a multitude of hearers" —*serm.* xxiv. *in Cant.* A greater sin than if, by one discharge of a blunderbuss, you murdered many persons; because you would then only kill their bodies; but, by speaking obscenely, you have killed their souls.

5. In a word, obscene tongues are the ruin of the world. One of them does more mischief than a hundred devils; because it is the cause of the perdition of many souls. This is not my language; it is the language of the Holy Ghost. "A slippery mouth worketh ruin"—*Prov.*, xxvi. 28. And when is it that this havock of souls is effected, and that such grievous insults are offered to God? It is in the summer, at the time when God bestows upon you the greatest temporal blessings. It is then that he supplies you for the entire year with corn, wine, oil, and other fruits of the Earth. It is then that there are as many sins committed by obscene words, as there are grains of corn or bunches of grapes. O ingratitude! How does God bear with us? And who is the cause of these sins? They who speak immodestly are the cause of them. Hence they must render an account to God, and shall be punished for all the

sins committed by those who hear them. "But I will require his blood at thy hand"—*Ezec.*, iii. 18. But let us pass to the second point.

Second point. He who speaks immodestly does great injury to himself.

6. Some young men say: *I speak without malice.* In answer to this excuse, I have already said, in the first point, that it is very difficult to use immodest language without taking delight in it; and that speaking obscenely before young females, married or unmarried, is always accompanied with a secret complacency in what is said. Besides, by using immodest language, you expose yourself to the proximate danger of falling into unchaste actions; for, according to St. Jerome, as we have already said, "he who delights in words, is not far from the act". All men are inclined to evil. "The imagination and thought of man's heart are prone to evil"—*Gen.*, viii. 21. But, above all, men are prone to the sin of impurity, to which nature itself inclines them. Hence St. Augustine has said, that in struggling against that vice, "*the victory is rare*", at least for those who do not use great caution. "Communis pugna, et rara victoria". Now, the impure objects of which they speak are always presented to the mind of those who freely utter obscene words. These objects excite pleasure, and bring them into sinful desires and morose delectations, and afterwards into criminal acts. Behold the consequence of the immodest words which young men say they speak without malice.

7. "Be not taken in thy tongue", says the Holy Ghost (*Eccl.*, v. 16). Beware lest by your tongue you forge a chain which will drag you to Hell. "The tongue", says St. James, "defileth the whole body, and inflameth the wheel of our nativity" —*St. James*, iii. 6. The tongue is one of the members of the body, but, when it utters bad words, it infects the whole body, and "*inflames the wheels of our nativity*"; it inflames and corrupts our entire life from our birth to old age. Hence we see that men who indulge in obscenity, cannot, even in old age, abstain from immodest language. In the life of St. Valerius, Surius relates, that the saint, in travelling, went one day into a house to warm himself. He heard the master of the house and a judge of the district, though both were advanced in years,

speaking on obscene subjects. The saint reproved them severely; but they paid no attention to his rebuke. However, God punished both of them: one became blind, and a sore broke out on the other, which produced deadly spasms. Henry Gragerman relates (*in Magn. Spec., dist.* 9, *ex.* 58), that one of these obscene talkers died suddenly and without repentance, and that he was afterwards seen in Hell tearing his tongue in pieces; and when it was restored, he began again to lacerate it.

8. But how can God have mercy on him who has no pity on the souls of his neighbours? "Judgment without mercy to him that hath not done mercy"—*St. James*, ii. 13. Oh! what a pity to see one of those obscene wretches pouring out his filthy expressions before girls and young married females! The greater the number of such persons present, the more abominable is his language. It often happens that little boys and girls are present, and he has no horror of scandalizing these innocent souls! Cantipratano relates, that the son of a certain nobleman in Burgundy was sent to be educated by the monks of Cluni. He was an angel of purity; but the unhappy boy having one day entered into a carpenter's shop, heard some obscene words spoken by the carpenter's wife, fell into sin, and lost the divine grace. Father Sabatino, in his work entitled *Evangelical Light*, relates, that another boy, fifteen years old, having heard an immodest word, began to think of it the following night, consented to a bad thought, and died suddenly the same night. His confessor having heard of his death, intended to say Mass for him. But the soul of the unfortunate boy appeared to him, and told the confessor not to celebrate Mass for him—that, by means of the word which he had heard, he was damned—and that the celebration of Mass would add to his pains. O God! how great, were it in their power to weep, would be the wailing of the angel-guardians of these poor children that are scandalized and brought to Hell by the language of obscene tongues! With what earnestness shall the angels demand vengeance from God against the authors of such scandals! That the angels shall cry for vengeance against them, appears from the words of Jesus Christ—"See that you despise not one of these little ones; for I say to you, that their angels in Heaven always see the face of my Father"—*Matt.*, xviii. 10.

9. Be attentive, then, my brethren, and guard yourselves

against speaking immodestly, more than you would against death. Listen to the advice of the Holy Ghost: "Make a balance for thy words, and a just bridle for thy mouth; and take heed lest thou slip with thy tongue...and thy fall be incurable unto death" —*Eccl.*, xxviii. 29, 30. *Make a balance*—you must weigh your words before you utter them—and *a bridle for thy mouth*—when immodest words come to the tongue, you must surpress them; otherwise, by uttering them, you shall inflict on your own soul, and on the souls of others, a mortal and incurable wound. God has given you the tongue, not to offend him, but to praise and bless him. "But", says St. Paul, "fornication and all uncleanness, let it not so much as be named among you, as becometh saints"—*Ephes.*, v. 3. Mark the words *all uncleanness.* We must not only abstain from obscene language and from every word of double meaning spoken in jest, but also from every improper word unbecoming a saint—that is, a Christian. It is necessary to remark, that words of a double meaning sometimes do greater evil than open obscenity, because the art with which they are spoken makes a deeper impression on the mind.

10. Reflect, says St. Augustine, that your mouths are the mouths of Christians, which Jesus Christ has so often entered in the holy communion. Hence, you ought to have a horror of uttering all unchaste words, which are a diabolical poison. "See, brethren, if it be just that, from the mouths of Christians, which the body of Christ enters, an immodest song, like diabolical poison, should proceed"—*serm.* xv., *de Temp.* St. Paul says, that the language of a Christian should be always seasoned with salt. "Let your speech be always in grace, seasoned with salt"—*Col.*, iv. 6. Our conversation should be seasoned with words calculated to excite others not to offend, but to love God. "Happy the tongue", says St. Bernard, "that knows only how to speak of holy things!" Happy the tongue that knows only how to speak of God! O brethren, be careful not only to abstain from all obscene language, but to avoid, as you would a plague, those who speak immodestly. When you hear any one begin to utter obscene words, follow the advice of the Holy Ghost. "Hedge in thy ears with thorns; hear not a wicked tongue"—*Eccl.*, xxviii. 28. *Hedge in thy ears with thorns*—that is, reprove with zeal the man who speaks obscenely; at

least turn away your face, and show that you hate such language. Let us not be ashamed to appear to be followers of Jesus Christ, unless we wish Jesus Christ to be ashamed to bring us with him into Paradise.

SERMON XLI.

FOR THE TWELFTH SUNDAY AFTER PENTECOST.

On the abuse of divine mercy.

"Take care of him"—*Luke*, x. 35.

In this day's gospel we read, that a certain man fell into the hands of robbers, who, after having taken his money, wounded him, and left him half dead. A Samaritan who passed by, saw him, and taking pity on him, bound up his wounds, brought him to an inn, and left him in the care of the host, saying: *Take care of him.* These words I this day address to those, if there be any such among you, who, though their souls are wounded by sin, instead of attending to the care of them, continually aggravate the wounds by new sins, and thus abuse the mercy of God, who preserves their lives, that they may repent, and not be lost for ever. I say to you: Brethren, take care of your souls, which are in a very bad state; have compassion on them. "Have pity on thy own soul" —*Eccl.*, xxx. 24. Your souls are sick, and—what is worse—they are near the eternal death of Hell; for, he who abuses to excess the divine mercy, is on the point of being abandoned by the mercy of God. This shall be the subject of the present discourse.

1. St. Augustine says, that the Devil deludes Christians in two ways—"by despair and hope". After a person has committed sin, the enemy, by placing before his eyes the rigour of divine justice, tempts him to despair of the mercy of God. But, before he sins, the Devil, by representing to him the divine mercy, labours to make him fearless of the chastisement due to

sin. Hence the saint gives the following advice: "After sin, hope for mercy; before sin, fear justice". If, after sin, you despair of God's pardon, you offend him by a new and more grievous sin. Have recourse to his mercy, and he will pardon you. But, before sin, fear God's justice, and trust not to his mercy; for, they who abuse the mercy of God to offend him, do not deserve to be treated with mercy. Abulensis says, that the man who offends justice, may have recourse to mercy; but to whom can they have recourse, who offend and provoke mercy against themselves?

2. When you intend to commit sin, who, I ask, promises you mercy from God? Certainly God does not promise it. It is the Devil that promises it, that you may lose God and be damned. "Beware", says St. John Chrysostom, "never to attend to that dog who promises the mercy from God"—*hom*. 50. *ad Pop*. If, beloved sinners, you have hitherto offended God, hope and tremble: if you desire to give up sin, and if you detest it, hope; because God promises pardon to all who repent of the evil they have done. But if you intend to continue in your sinful course, tremble lest God should wait no longer for you, but cast you into Hell. Why does God wait for sinners? Is it that they may continue to insult him? No; he waits for them that they may renounce sin, and that thus he may have pity on them, and forgive them. "Therefore the Lord waiteth, that he may have mercy on you"—*Isa*., xxx. 1. 8 But when he sees that the time which he gave them to weep over their past iniquities, is spent in multiplying their sins, he begins to inflict chastisement, and he cuts them off in the state of sin, that, by dying, they may cease to offend him. Then he calls against them the very time he had given them for repentance. "He hath called against me the time"—*Lam*., i. 15. "The very time", says St. Gregory, "comes to judge".

3. O common illusion of so many damned Christians! We seldom find a sinner so abandoned to despair, as to say: *I will damn myself*. Christians sin, and endeavour to save their souls. They say: *God is merciful; I will commit this sin, and will afterwards confess it*. Behold the illusion, or rather the snare, by which Satan draws so many souls to Hell. *Commit sin*, he says, *and confess it afterwards*. But listen to what the Lord says—"And say not: The mercy of the Lord is great;

he will have mercy on the multitude of my sins"—*Eccl.*, v. 6. Why does he tell you not to say, that the mercy of God is great? Attend to the words contained in the following verse: "For mercy and wrath quickly come from him, and his wrath looketh upon sinners"—*ibid.*, *verse* 7. The mercy of God is different from the acts of his mercy: the former is infinite, the latter are finite. God is merciful, but he is also just. St. Basil says, that sinners only consider God as merciful and ready to pardon, but not as just and prepared to inflict punishment. Of this the Lord complained one day to St. Bridget: "I am just and merciful: sinners regard me only as merciful". St. Basil's words are: "Bonus est Dominus sed etiam justus; nolimus Deum ex dimidia parte cogitare". God is just, and, being just, he must punish the ungrateful. Father John Avila used to say, that to bear with those who avail themselves of the mercy of God to offend him, would not be mercy, but a want of justice. Mercy, as the divine mother, said, is promised to those who fear, and not to those who insult the Lord. "And his mercy to them that fear him"—*Luke*, i. 50.

4. Some rash sinners will say: God has hitherto shown me so many mercies; why should he not hereafter treat me with the same mercy? I answer: he will show you mercy, if you wish to change your life; but if you intend to continue to offend him, he tells you that he will take vengeance on your sins by casting you into Hell. "Revenge is mine, and I will repay them in *due* time, that their foot may slide"—*Deut.*, xxxii. 35. David says, that "except you be converted, he will brandish his sword"—*Ps.*, vii. 13. The Lord has bent his bow, and waits for your conversion; but if you resolve not to return to him, he will in the end cast the arrow against you, and you shall be damned. O God! there are some who will not believe that there is a Hell until they fall into it. Can you, beloved Christians, complain of the mercies of God, after he has shown you so many mercies by waiting for you so long? You ought to remain always prostrate on the earth to thank him for his mercies, saying: "The mercies of the Lord that we are not consumed"—*Lamen.*, iii. 32. Were the injuries which you offered to God, committed against a brother, he would not have borne with you. God has had so much patience with you; and he now calls you again. If, after all this, he shall send you to

Hell, will he do you any wrong? "What is there", he will say, "that I ought to do more for my vineyard, that I have not done to it?"—*Isa.*, v. 4. Impious wretch, what more ought I to do for you that I have not done?

5. St. Bernard says, that the confidence which sinners have in God's goodness, when they commit sin, procures for them, not a blessing, but a malediction from the Lord. "Est infidelis fiducia solius ubique maledictionis capax, cum videlicet in spe peccamus" —*serm.* iii. *de Annunc.* O deceitful hope, which sends so many Christians to Hell! St. Augustine says: "Sperant, ut peccent! Væ a perversa spe"—*in Ps.*, cxliv. They do not hope for the pardon of the sins of which they repent; but they hope that though they continue to commit sin, God will have mercy upon them; and thus they make the mercy of God serve as a motive for continuing to offend him. O accursed hope! hope which is an abomination to the Lord! "And their hope the abomination"—*Job*, xi. 20. This hope will make God hasten the execution of his vengeance; for surely a master will not defer the punishment of servants who offend him because he is good. Sinners, as St. Augustine observes, trusting in God's goodness, insult him, and say: "God is good; I will do what I please"—*Tract.* xxxiii., *in Joan.* But, alas! how many, exclaims the same St. Augustine, has this vain hope deluded! "They who have been deceived by this shadow of vain hope, cannot be numbered". St. Bernard writes, that Lucifer's chastisement was accelerated, because, in rebellion against God, he hoped that he should not be punished for his rebellion. Ammon, the son of king Manasses, seeing that God had pardoned the sins of his father, gave himself up to a wicked life with the hope of pardon; but, for Ammon there was no mercy. St. John Chrysostom says, that Judas was lost because, trusting in the goodness of Jesus Christ, he betrayed him. "Fidit in lenitate Magistri".

6. He that sins with the hope of pardon, saying: *I will afterwards repent, and God will pardon me*, is, according to St. Augustine, "not a penitent, but a scoffer". The Apostle tells us, that "God is not mocked"—*Gal.*, vi. 7. It would be a mockery of God to offend him as often and as long as you please, and always to receive the pardon of your offences. "For what things a man shall sow", says St. Paul, "those also shall he

reap"—*ibid.*, *verse* 8. They who sow sins, can hope for nothing but the hatred of God and Hell. "Despisest thou the riches of his goodness, and patience, and long suffering?"—*Rom.*, ii. 4. Do you, O sinner, despise the riches of the goodness, of the patience, and long suffering of God towards you? He uses the word *riches*, because the mercies which God shows us, in not punishing our sins, are riches more valuable to us than all treasures. "Knowest thou not", continues the Apostle, "that the benignity of God leadeth thee to penance?"—*ibid.* Do you not know that the Lord waits for you, and treats you with so much benignity, not that you may continue to sin, but that you may weep over the offences you have offered to him? For, says St. Paul, if you persevere in sin and do not repent, your obstinacy and impenitence shall accumulate a treasure of wrath against the day of wrath, that is, the day on which God shall judge you. "According to thy hardness and impenitent heart, thou treasurest up wrath against the day of wrath, and revelation of the just judgment of God"—*ibid.*, *verse* 5.

7. To the hardness of the sinner shall succeed his abandonment by God, who will say of the soul that is obstinate in sin, what he said of Babylon: "We would have cured Babylon; but she is not healed: let us forsake her"—*Jer.*, li. 9. And how does God abandon the sinner? He either sends him a sudden death, and cuts him off in sin, or he deprives him of the graces which would be necessary to bring him to true repentance: he leaves him with the sufficient graces with which he can, but will not, save his soul. The darkness of his understanding, the hardness of his heart, and the bad habits which he has contracted, will render his conversion morally impossible. Thus, he shall not be absolutely, but morally abandoned. "I will take away the hedge thereof, and it shall be wasted"—*Is.*, v. 5. When the master of a vineyard destroys its hedges, does he not show that he abandons it? It is thus that God acts when he abandons a soul. He takes away the hedge of holy fear and remorse of conscience, and leaves the soul in darkness, and then vices crowd into the heart. "Thou hast appointed darkness, and it is night: in it shall all the beasts of the wood go about"—*Ps.*, ciii. 20. And the sinner, abandoned in an abyss of sins, will despise admonitions, excommunications, divine grace, chastisement, and Hell: he will make a jest of his

own damnation. "The wicked man, when he is come into the depth of sin, contemneth"—*Prov.*, xviii. 3.

8. "Why", asks the Prophet Jeremias, "doth the way of the wicked prosper?"—*Jer.*, xii. 1. He answers: "Gather them together as sheep for a sacrifice"—*verse* 3. Miserable the sinner who is prosperous in this life! The prosperity of sinners is a sign that God wishes to give them a temporal reward for some works which are morally good, but that he reserves them as victims of his justice for Hell, where, like the accursed cockle, they shall be cast to burn for all eternity. "In the time of the harvest I will say to the reapers: Gather up first the cockle, and bind it in bundles to burn"—*Mat.*, xiii. 30.

9. Thus, not to be punished in this life is the greatest of God's chastisements on the wicked, and has been threatened against the obstinate sinner by the Prophet Isaias. "Let us have pity on the wicked, but he will not learn justice"—*Isa.*, xxvi. 10. On this passage, St. Bernard says: This mercy I do not wish for: it is above all wrath. "Misericordiam hanc nolo; super omnem iram misericordia ista"—*serm.* xlii. *in Cant.* And what greater chastisement than to be abandoned into the hands of sin, so that, being permitted by God to fall from sin to sin, the sinner must in the end go to suffer as many hells as he has committed sins? "Add thou iniquity upon their iniquity......let them be blotted out of the book of the living"—*Ps.*, lxviii. 28, 29. On these words Bellarmine writes: "There is no punishment greater than when sin is the punishment of sin". It would be better for such a sinner to die after the first sin; because by dying under the load of so many additional iniquities, he shall suffer as many hells as he has committed sins. This is what happened to a certain comedian in Palermo, whose name was Cæsar. He one day told a friend that Father La Nusa, a missionary, foretold him that God should give him twelve years to live, and that if within that time he did not change his life, he should die a bad death. Now, said he to his friend, I have travelled through so many parts of the world: I have had many attacks of sickness, one of which nearly brought me to the grave; but in this month the twelve years shall be completed, and I feel myself in better health than in any of the past years. He then invited the friend to listen to a new comedy which he had composed. But, what happened? On the 24th November, 1688, the day fixed

for the comedy, as he was going on the stage, he was seized with apoplexy, and died suddenly. He expired in the arms of a female comedian. Thus the scene of this world ended miserably for him.

10. Let us make the application to ourselves, and conclude the discourse. Brethren, I entreat you to give a glance at all the bygone years of your life: look at the grievous offences you have commited against God, and at the great mercies which he has shown to you, the many lights he has bestowed upon you, and the many times he has called you to a change of life. By this sermon he has to-day given you a new call. He appears to me to say to you: "What is there that I ought to do to my vineyard, that I have not done to it?"—*Isa.*, v. 4. What more ought I to do for you, that I have not done? What do you say? What answer have you to make? Will you give yourselves to God, or will you continue to offend him? Consider, says St. Augustine, that the punishment of your sins has been deferred, not remitted. "O unfruitful tree! the axe has been deferred. Be not secure: you shall be cut off". If you abuse the divine mercy, *you shall be cut off;* vengeance shall soon fall upon you. What do you wait for? Do you wait till God sends you to Hell? The Lord has been hitherto silent; but he is not silent for ever. When the time of vengeance shall arrive, he will say: "These things hast thou done, and I was silent. Thou thoughtest unjustly that I should be like to thee: but I will reprove thee, and set before thy face"—*Ps.*, xlix. 21. He will set before your eyes the graces which he bestowed upon you, and which you have despised: these very graces shall judge and condemn you. O brethren, resist no longer the calls of God; tremble lest the call which he gives you to-day may be the last call for you. Go to confession as soon as possible, and make a firm resolution to change your lives. It is useless to confess your sins, if you afterwards return to your former vices. But you will perhaps say, that you have not strength to resist the temptations by which you are assailed. Listen to the words of the Apostle: "God is faithful, who will not permit you to be tempted above that which you are able"—I. *Cor.*, x. 13. God is faithful: he will not permit you to be tempted above your strength. And if of yourself you have not strength to overcome the Devil, ask it from God, and he will give it to you. "Ask,

and you shall receive"—*John*, xvi. 24. "Praising", said David, "I will call on the Lord, and I shall be saved from my enemies" —*Ps.*, xvii. 4. And St. Paul said: "I can do all things in him who strengtheneth me"—*Phil.*, iv. 13. Of myself I can do nothing; but with the divine assistance I can do all things. Recommend yourself to God in all temptations, and God will enable you to resist them, and you shall not fall.

SERMON XLII.

FOR THE THIRTEENTH SUNDAY AFTER PENTECOST.

On avoiding bad company.

"There met him ten men that were lepers....As they went, they were made clean"—*Luke*, xvii. 12, 14.

In this day's gospel it is related, that ten lepers of a certain town met Jesus Christ, and entreated him to heal the leprosy under which they laboured. The Lord bid them go and present themselves to the priests of the temple; but, before they reached the temple, they were cured. Now, it may be asked, why our Saviour, who could heal them in an instant, wished them to go to the priests, and healed them on the way. A certain author (Anthony of Lisbon) says, that Jesus Christ foresaw that, had he cured them on the spot, they, by remaining in the place and conversing with the other lepers, from whom they took the leprosy, should easily relapse into the same disease. Therefore, he first wished them to depart from the place, and then healed them. Whatever may be thought of this reason, let us come to the moral sense which may be deduced from it. The leprosy resembles sin. As the leprosy is a contagious disease, so the bad habits of the wicked infect others who associate with them. Hence, the leper who wishes to be cured, shall never be healed unless he separates from bad companions. He that keeps company with robbers, soon becomes a thief. In this discourse I shall show that, to lead a good life, it is necessary to avoid bad companions.

1. "A friend of fools", says the Holy Ghost, "shall become like them"—*Prov.*, xiii. 20. Christians who live in enmity with God, are, Father M. Avila used to say, all fools, who deserve to be shut up in a madhouse. For, what greater madness can be conceived than to believe in Hell, and to live in sin? But the man who contracts an intimacy with these fools, shall soon become like them. Although he should hear all the sermons of the sacred orators, he will continue in vice, according to the celebrated maxim: "*Examples make greater impressions than words*". Hence the Royal Prophet has said: "With the elect thou wilt be elect, and with the perverse thou wilt be perverted"—*Ps.*, xvii. 27. St. Augustine says, that familiarity with sinners is as it were a hook, which draws us to communicate in their vices. Let us, said the saint, avoid wicked friends, "lest by their company we may be drawn to a communion of vice". St. Thomas teaches, that to know whom we should avoid, is a great means of saving our souls. "Firma tutela salutis est, scire quem fugiamus".

2. "Let their way become dark and slippery, and let the angel of the Lord pursue them"—*Ps.*, xxxiv. 6. All men in this life walk in the midst of darkness, and in a slippery way. If, then, a bad angel—that is, a wicked companion, who is worse than any devil—pursue them, and endeavour to drive them into an abyss, who shall be able to escape death? "Talis eris", says Plato, "qualis conversatio quam sequeris?" And St. John Chrysostom said, that if we wish to know a man's moral habits, we have only to observe the character of the friends with whom he associates; because friendship finds or makes him like his friends. "Vis nosse hominem, attende quorum familiaritate assuescat: amicitia aut pares invenit, aut pares facit". First, because, to please his friends, a man will endeavour to imitate them; secondly, because, as Seneca says, nature inclines men to do what they see others do. And the Scripture says: "They were mingled among the heathens, and learned their works"—*Ps.*, cv. 35. According to St. Basil, as air which comes from pestilential places causes infection, so, by conversation with bad companions, we almost inperceptibly

contract their vices. "Quemadmodum in pestilentibus locis sensim attractus aër latentem corporibus morbum injicit, sic itidem in prava conversatione maxima a nobis mala hauriuntur, etiamsi statim incommodum non sentiatur"—*S. Bas., hom.* ix. *ex var. Quod Deus, etc.* And St. Bernard says, that St. Peter, in consequence of associating with the enemies of Jesus Christ, denied his Master. "Existens cum passionis dominicæ ministris, Dominum negavit".

3. But how, asks St. Ambrose, can bad companions give you the odour of chastity, when they exhale the stench of impurity? How can they infuse into you sentiments of devotion, when they themselves fly from it? How can they impart to you a shame of offending God, when they cast it away? "Quid tibi demonstrant castitatem, quem non habent? Devotionem quam non sequuntur? Verecundiam quam projiciunt?" St. Augustine writes of himself, that when he associated with bad companions, who boasted of their wickedness, he felt himself impelled to sin without shame; and to appear like them, he gloried in his evil actions. "Pudebat", he says, "me esse pudentem"—*lib.* 2, *de Conf.*, *c.* ix. Hence Isaias admonishes you to "touch no unclean thing"—*Isa.*, lii. 11. Touch not what is unclean: if you do, you too shall be polluted. He that handles pitch, says Ecclesiasticus, shall certainly be defiled with it; and they who keep company with the proud, shall be clothed with pride. The same holds for other vices: "He that toucheth pitch, shall be defiled with it; and he that hath fellowship with the proud, shall put on pride"—*Eccl.*, xiii. 1.

4. What then must we do? The Wise Man tells us, that we ought not only to avoid the vices of the wicked, but also to beware of treading in the ways in which they walk. "Restrain thy foot from their paths"—*Prov.*, i. 15. That is, we should avoid their conversations, their discourses, their feasts, and all the allurements and presents with which they will seek to entice us into their net. "My son", says Solomon, "if sinners shall entice thee, consent not to them"—*Prov.*, i. 10. Without the decoy, birds are not enticed into the fowler's net. "Will the bird fall into the snare upon the earth, if there be no fowler?"—*Amos*, iii. 5. The Devil employs vicious friends as decoys, to draw so many souls into the snare of sin. "My enemies", says Jeremias, "have chased me, and have caught me

like a bird without cause"—*Lamen.*, iii. 52. He says, *without cause.* Ask the wicked why they have made a certain innocent young man fall into sin; and they will answer: We have done it *without cause;* we only wish to see him do what we ourselves do. This, says St. Ephrem, is one of the artifices of the Devil: when he has caught a soul in his net, he makes him a snare, or a decoy, to deceive others. "Cum primum capta fuerit anima, ad alias decipiendas fit quasi laqueus".

5. Hence it is necessary to avoid, as you would a plague, all familiarity with those scorpions of Hell. I have said that you must avoid *familiarity* with them—that is, all fellowship in their banquets or conversation; for, never to meet them is, as the Apostle says, impossible. "Otherwise you must needs go out of this world"—I. *Cor.*, v. 10. But, it is in our power to abstain from familiar intercourse with them. "But now I have written to you, not to keep company, etc.......with such an one, not so much as to eat"—*ibid.*, v. 11. I have called them *scorpions:* so they have been called by the Prophet Ezechiel. "Thou art among unbelievers and destroyers, and thou dwellest among scorpions"—*Ezech.*, ii. 6. Would you live in the midst of scorpions? You must then fly from scandalous friends, who, by their bad examples and words, poison your soul. "A man's enemies shall be they of his own household"—*Matt.*, x. 36. Wicked friends that are very familiar and intimate with us, become the most pernicious enemies of our souls. "Who", says Ecclesiasticus, "will pity an enchanter struck by a serpent, or any that come near wild beasts? So it is with him that keepeth company with a wicked man"—*Eccl.*, xii. 13. If the man that makes free with serpents, or with ferocious wild beasts, be bitten or devoured by them, who will take pity on him? And so it is with him who associates with scandalous companions; if, by their bad example, he be contaminated and lost, neither God nor man will have compassion on him; because he was cautioned to fly from their society.

6. One scandalous companion is enough to corrupt all who treat him as a friend. "Know you not", says St. Paul, "that a little leaven corrupts the whole lump?"—I. *Cor.*, v. 6. One of these scandalous sinners is able, by a perverse maxim, to infect all his companions. They are the false prophets whom Jesus Christ warns us to avoid. "Beware of false prophets",

—*Matt.*, vii. 15. False prophets deceive, not only by false predictions, but also by false maxims or doctrines, which are productive of the greatest mischief. For, as Seneca says, they leave in the soul certain seeds of iniquity which lead to evil. "Semina in animo relinquunt, quæ inducunt ad malum". It is too true that scandalous language, as experience proves, corrupts the morals of those who hear it. "Evil communications", says the Apostle, "corrupt good manners"—I. *Cor.*, xv. 33. A young man refuses, through the fear of God, to commit a certain sin: an incarnate Devil, a bad companion, comes, and says to him what the serpent said to Eve—"No; you shall not die the death"—*Gen.*, iii. 4. What are you afraid of? How many others commit this sin? You are young; God will have pity on your youth. They will, as is written in the book of Wisdom, say: "Come, therefore, let us enjoy the good things that are present,...let us everywhere leave tokens of joy"—ii. 6, 9. Come with us; let us spend our time in amusements and in joy. "O nimis iniqua amicitia", says St. Augustine, "cum dicitur, eamus, faciamus: pudet non esse impudentem". O cruel friendship of those who say: Let us go and do, etc.; it is a shame not to be shameless. He who hears such language is ashamed not to yield to it, and not to be as shameless as they who utter it.

7. When any passion is kindled within us, we must be particularly careful in selecting the persons whom we will consult. For, then the passion itself will incline us to seek counsel from those who will probably give the advice which is most agreeable to the passion. But from such evil counsellors, who do not speak according to God, we should fly with greater horror than from an enemy; for their evil counsel, along with the passion which is excited, may precipitate us into horrible excesses. As soon as the passion shall subside, we shall see the error committed, and the delusion into which we have been led by false friends. But the good advice of a friend, who speaks according to Christian truth and meekness, preserves us from every disorder, and restores calm to the soul.

8. "Depart from the unjust", says the Lord, "and evils shall depart from thee"—*Eccl.*, vii. 2. Fly, separate from wicked companions, and you shall cease to commit sin. "Neither let the way of evil men please thee. Flee from it: pass not by it: go aside and

forsake it"—*Prov.*, iv. 14, 15. Avoid the ways in which these vicious friends walk, that you may not even meet them. "Forsake not an old friend; for the new will not be like to him"—*Eccl.*, ix. 14. Do not leave your first friend, who loved you before you came into the world. "I have loved thee with an everlasting love"—*Jer.*, xxxi. 3. Your new friends do not love you; they hate you more than your greatest enemy; they seek not your welfare, as God does, but their own pleasures, and the satisfaction of having companions of their wickedness and perdition. You will, perhaps, say: I feel a repugnance to separate from such a friend, who has been solicitous for my welfare; to break off from him would appear to be an act of ingratitude. What welfare? what ingratitude? God alone wishes your welfare, because he desires your eternal salvation. Your friend wishes your eternal ruin; he wishes you to follow him, but cares not if you be damned. It is not ingratitude to abandon a friend who leads you to Hell; but it is ingratitude to forsake God, who has created you, who has died for you on the cross, and who desires your salvation.

9. Fly then from the conversation of these wicked friends. "Hedge in thy ears with thorns, hear not a wicked tongue"—*Eccl.*, xxviii. 28. Beware of listening to the language of such friends; their words may bring you to perdition. And when you hear them speak improperly, arm yourself with thorns, and reprove them, not only for the purpose of rebuking, but also of converting them. "Ut non solum", says St. Augustine, "repellantur sed etiam compungantur". Listen to a frightful example, and learn the evil which a wicked friend does. Father Sabatino relates, in his *Evangelical Light*, that two friends of that kind were one day together. One of them, to please the other, committed a sin; but, after they separated, he died suddenly. The other, who knew nothing of his death, saw, in his sleep, his friend, and according to his custom, ran to embrace him. But the deceased appeared to be surrounded with fire, and began to blaspheme the other, and to upbraid him for being the cause of his damnation. The other awoke, and changed his life. But his unhappy friend was damned; and for his damnation there is not, and shall not be, any remedy for all eternity.

SERMON XLIII.

FOR THE FOURTEENTH SUNDAY AFTER PENTECOST.

All ends, and soon ends..

"The grass of the field, which is to-day, and to-morrow is cast into the oven"—*Matthew*, vii. 30.

BEHOLD! all the goods of this Earth are like the grass of the field, which to-day is blooming and beautiful; but, in the evening, it withers and loses its flowers, and the next day is cast into the fire. This is what God commanded the Prophet Isaias to preach, when he said to him: "Cry. And I said: What shall I cry? All flesh is grass, and all the glory thereof as the flower of the field"—*Isa.*, xl. 6. Hence St. James compares the rich of this world to the flower of grass: at the end of their journey through life, they rot along with all their riches and pomps. "The rich...... because as the flower of the grass shall he pass away. For the sun rose with a burning heat, and parched the grass, and the flower thereof fell off, and the beauty of the shape thereof perished: so also shall the rich man fade away in his ways"—*St. James*, i. 10, 11. They fade away and are cast into the fire, like the rich glutton, who made a splendid appearance in this life, but afterwards "*was buried in Hell*"—*Luke*, xvi. 22. Let us, then, dearly beloved Christians, attend to the salvation of our souls, and to the acquisition of riches for eternity, which never ends; for every thing in this world ends, and ends very soon.

First point. Every thing ends.

1. When one of the great of this world is in the full enjoyment of the riches and honours which he has acquired, death shall come, and he shall be told: "Take order with thy house; for thou shalt die, and not live"—*Isa.*, xxxviii. 1. Oh! what doleful tidings! The unhappy man must then say: Farewell, O world! farewell, O villa! farewell, O grotto! farewell, rela-

tives! farewell, friends! farewell, sports! farewell, balls! farewell, comedies! farewell, banquets! farewell, honours! all is over for me. There is no remedy; whether he will or not, he must leave all. "For when he shall die, he shall take nothing away; nor shall his glory descend with him"—*Ps.*, xlviii. 18. St. Bernard says, that death produces a horrible separation of the soul from the body and from all the things of this Earth. "Opus mortis horrendum divortium"—*serm.* xxvi., *in Cant.* To the great of this world, whom worldlings regard as the most fortunate of mortals, the bare name of death is so full of bitterness, that they are unwilling even to hear it mentioned; for their entire concern is to find peace in their Earthly goods. "O death!" says Ecclesiasticus, "how bitter is the remembrance of thee to a man that hath peace in his possessions"—*Eccl.*, xli. 1. But, how much greater bitterness shall death itself cause, when it actually comes! Miserable the man who is attached to the goods of this world! Every separation produces pain. Hence, when the soul shall be separated by the stroke of death from the goods on which she had fixed all her affections, the pain must be excruciating. It was this that made king Agag exclaim, when the news of approaching death was announced to him: "Doth bitter death separate me in this manner?"—I. *Kings*, xv. 32. The great misfortune of worldlings is, that when they are on the point of being summoned to judgment, instead of endeavouring to adjust the accounts of their soul, they direct all their attention to Earthly things. But, says St. John Chrysostom, the punishment which awaits sinners, on account of having forgotten God during life, is that they forget themselves at the hour of death. "Hac animadversione percutitur impius, ut moriens obliviscatur sui, qui vivens oblitus est Dei".

2. But how great soever a man's attachment to the things of this world may be, he must take leave of them at death. Naked he has entered into this world, and naked he shall depart from it. "Naked", says Job, "I came out of my mother's womb, and naked shall I return thither"—*Job*, i. 21. In a word, they who have spent their whole life, have lost their sleep, their health, and their soul, in accumulating riches and possessions, shall take nothing with them at the hour of death: their eyes shall then be opened; and of all they had so dearly acquired,

they shall find nothing in their hands. Hence, on that night of confusion, they shall be overwhelmed in a tempest of pains and sadness. "The rich man, when he shall sleep, shall take away nothing with him. He shall open his eyes, and find nothing...a tempest shall oppress him in the night"—*Job*, xxvii. 19, 20. St. Antonine relates, that Saladin, king of the Saracens, gave orders at the hour of death, that the winding sheet in which he was to be buried should be carried before him to the grave, and that a person should cry out: "Of all his possessions, this only shall Saladin bring with him". The saint also relates, that a certain philosopher, speaking of Alexander the Great, after his death, said: Behold the man that made the Earth tremble. "The Earth", as the Scripture says, "was quiet before him"—I. *Mach.*, i. 3. He is now under the earth. Behold the man whom the dominion of the whole world would not satisfy: now four palms of ground are sufficient for him. "Qui terram heri conculcabat, hodie ab ea conculcatur; et cui heri non sufficiebat mundus hodie sufficiunt quatuor ulnæ terræ". St. Augustine, or some other ancient writer, says, that, having gone to see the tomb of Cesar, he exclaimed: "Princes feared thee, cities worshipped thee; all trembled before thee;—where is thy magnificence gone?"—*serm.* xxxviii., *ad Fratr.* Listen to what David says:—"I have seen the wicked highly exalted and lifted up, like the cedars of Libanus. And I passed by, and lo! he was not"—*Ps.*, xxxvi. 35, 36. Oh! how many such spectacles are seen every day in the world! A sinner who had been born in lowliness and poverty, afterwards acquires wealth and honours, so as to excite the envy of all. When he dies, every one says: He made a fortune in the world; but now he is dead, and with death all is over for him.

3. "Why is earth and ashes proud?"—*Eccl.*, x. 9. Such the language which the Lord addresses to the man who is puffed up by Earthly honours and Earthly riches. Miserable creature, he says, whence comes such pride? If you enjoy honours and riches, remember that you are dust. "For dust thou art, and into dust thou shalt return"—*Gen.*, iii. 19. You must die; and after death, what advantage shall you derive from the honours and possessions which now inflate you with pride? Go, says St. Ambrose, go to a cemetery, in which are buried the rich and poor, and see if you can discern among them who has

been rich and who has been poor;—all are naked, and nothing remains of the richest among them, but a few withered bones. "Respice sepulchra, dic mihi, quis ibi dives, quis pauper sit"—*lib.* VI., *exam. cap.* viii. How profitable would the remembrance of death be to the man who lives in the world! "He shall be brought to the grave, and shall watch in the heap of the dead"—*Job*, xxi. 32. At the sight of these dead bodies, he would remember death, and that he shall be one day like them. Thus, he should be awakened from the deadly sleep in which perhaps he lives in a state of perdition. But the misfortune is, that worldlings are unwilling to think of death until the hour comes when they must depart from this Earth to go into eternity; and therefore they live as attached to the world, as if they were never to be separated from it. But, our life is short, and shall soon end: thus, all things must end, and must soon end.

Second point. All soon ends.

4. Men know well, and believe firmly, that they shall die; but they imagine death as far off as if it were never to arrive. But Job tells us that the life of man is short. "Man born of a woman, living for a short time, is filled with many miseries. Who cometh forth like a flower and is destroyed"—*Job*, xiv. 2. At present the health of men is so much impaired, that, as we see by experience, the greater number of them die before they attain the age of seventy. And what, says St. James, is our life, but a vapour, which a blast of wind, a fever, a stroke of apoplexy, a puncture, an attack of the chest, causes to disappear, and which is seen no more? "For what is your life? It is a vapour which appeareth for a little while"—*St. James*, iv. 15. "We all die", said the woman of Thecua to David, "and like waters that return no more, we fall down into the earth"—II. *Kings*, xiv. 14. She spoke the truth;—as all rivers and streams run to the sea, and as the gliding waters return no more, so our days pass away, and we approach to death.

5. They pass; they pass quickly. "My days", says Job, "have been swifter than a post"—*Job*, ix. 25. Death comes to meet us, and runs more swiftly than a post; so that every step we make, every breath we draw, we approach to death. St. Jerome felt, that even while he was writing, he was drawing

nearer to death. Hence he said: "What I write is taken away from my life". "Quod scribo de mea vita tollitur". Let us, then, say with Job: Years pass by, and with them pleasures, honours, pomps, and all things in this world pass away, "and only the grave remaineth for me"—*Job*, xvii. 1. In a word, all the glory of the labours we have undergone in this world, in order to acquire a large income, a high character for valour, for learning and genius, shall end in our being thrown into a pit to become the food of worms. The miserable worldling then shall say at death: My house, my garden, my fashionable furniture, my pictures and rich apparel, shall, in a short time, belong no more to me; "and only the grave remaineth for me".

6. But, how much soever the worldling may be distracted by his worldly affairs and by his pleasures—how much soever he may be entangled in them, St. Chrysostom says, that, when the fear of death, which sets fire to all things of the present life, begins to enter the soul, it will compel him to think and to be solicitous about his lot after death. "Cum pulsare animam incipit metus mortis (ignis instar præsentis vitæ omnia succendens) philosophari eam cogit, et futura solicita mente versari"—*serm. in* II. *Tim.* Alas! at the hour of death, "the eyes of the blind shall be opened" —*Isa.*, xxxv. 5. Then indeed shall be opened the eyes of those blind worldlings who have employed their whole life in acquiring Earthly goods, and have paid but little attention to the interests of the soul. In all these shall be verified what Jesus Christ has told them—that death shall come when they least expect it. "At what hour you think not, the Son of Man will come"—*Luke*, xii. 40. Thus, on these unhappy men death always comes unexpectedly. Hence, because the lovers of the world are not usually warned of their approaching dissolution till it is very near, they must, in the last few days of life, adjust the accounts of their soul for the fifty or sixty years which they lived on this Earth. They will then desire another month, or another week, to settle their accounts, and to tranquillize their conscience. But, "they will seek for peace, and there shall be none"—*Ezec.*, vii. 25. The time which they desire is refused. The assisting priest reads the divine command to depart instantly from this world: "Proficiscere anima Christiana de hoc mundo". *Depart, Christian soul, from this world.* Oh! how dangerous the entrance of

worldlings into eternity, dying, as they do, amid so much darkness and confusion, in consequence of the disorderly state of the accounts of their souls.

7. "Weight and balance are the judgments of the Lord"—*Prov.*, xvi. 11. At the tribunal of God, nobility, dignities, and riches have no weight: two things only—our sins, and the graces bestowed on us by God—make the scales ascend or descend. They who shall be found faithful in corresponding with the lights and calls which they have received, shall be rewarded; and they who shall be found unfaithful, shall be condemned. We do not keep an account of God's graces; but the Lord keeps an account of them; he measures them; and when he sees them despised to a certain degree, he leaves the soul in her sins, and takes her out of life in that miserable state. "For what things a man shall sow, those also shall he reap"—*Gal.*, vi. 8. From labours undertaken for the attainment of posts of honour and emolument, for the acquisition of property and of worldly applause, we reap nothing at the hour of death: all are then lost. We gather fruits of eternal life only from works performed, and tribulations suffered, for God.

8. Hence St. Paul exhorts us to attend to our own business. "But we must entreat you, brethren,......that you do your own business"—I. *Thess.*, iv. 10, 11. Of what business, I ask, does the Apostle speak? Is it of acquiring riches, or a great name in the world? No; he speaks of the business of the soul, of which Jesus Christ spoke, when he said: "Trade till I come"—*Luke*, xix. 13. The business for which the Lord has placed, and for which he keeps us on this Earth, is, to save our souls, and by good works to gain eternal life. This is the end for which we have been created. "And the end eternal life"—*Rom.*, vi. 22. The business of the soul is for us not only the most important, but also the principal and only affair; for, if the soul be saved, all is safe; but, if the soul be lost, all is lost. Hence we ought, as the Scripture says, to strive for the salvation of our souls, and to combat to death for justice—that is, for the observance of the divine law. "Strive for justice for thy soul, and, even unto death, fight for justice"—*Eccl.*, iv. 33. The business which our Saviour recommends to us, saying: *Trade till I come*, is, to have always before our eyes the day

on which he shall come to demand an account of our whole life.

9. All things in this world—acquisitions, applause, grandeur—must, as we have said, all end, and end very soon. "The fashion of this world passeth away"—I. *Cor.*, vii. 31. The scene of this life passes away: happy they who, in this scene, act their part well, and save their souls, preferring the eternal interests of the soul to all the temporal interests of the body. "He that hateth his life in this world, keepeth it unto life eternal"—*John*, xii. 26. Worldlings say: Happy the man who hoards up money! happy they who acquire the esteem of the world, and enjoy the pleasures of this life! O folly! Happy he who loves God and saves his soul! The salvation of his soul was the only favour which king David asked of God. "One thing have I asked of the Lord, this will I seek after"—*Ps.*, xxvi. 4. And St. Paul said, that to acquire the grace of Jesus Christ, which contains eternal life, he despised as dung all worldly goods. "I count all things as loss......and I count them as dung, that I may gain Christ"—*Phil.*, iii. 8.

10. But certain fathers of families will say: I do not labour so much for myself as for my children, whom I wish to leave in comfortable circumstances. But I answer: If you dissipate the goods which you possess, and leave your children in poverty, you do wrong, and are guilty of sin. But will you lose your soul in order to leave your children comfortable? If you fall into Hell, perhaps they will come and release you from it? O folly! Listen to what David said: "I have not seen the just man forsaken, nor his seed seeking bread"—*Ps.*, xxxvi. 25. Attend to the service of God; act according to justice; the Lord will provide for the wants of your children; and you shall save your souls, and shall lay up that eternal treasure of happiness which can never be taken from you—a treasure not like Earthly possessions, of which you may be deprived by robbers, and which you shall certainly lose at death. This is the advice which the Lord gives you—"But lay up to yourselves treasures in Heaven, where neither the rust nor the moth doth consume, and where thieves do not break through nor steal"—*Matt.*, vi. 20. In conclusion, attend to the beautiful admonition which St. Gregory gives to all who wish to live well and to gain eternal life. "Sit nobis in intentione æternitas, in usu

temporalitas". Let the end of all our actions in this life be, the acquisition of eternal goods; and let us use temporal things only to preserve life for the little time we have to remain on this Earth. The saint continues: "Sicut nulla est proportio inter æternitatem et nostræ vitæ tempus, ita nulla debet esse proportio inter æternitatis, et hujus, vitæ curas". As there is an infinite distance between eternity and the time of our life, so there ought to be, according to our mode of understanding, an infinite distance between the attention which we should pay to the goods of eternity, which shall be enjoyed for ever, and the care we take of the goods of this life, which death shall soon take away from us.

SERMON XLIV.

FOR THE FIFTEENTH SUNDAY AFTER PENTECOST.

On the practical death, or on what ordinarily happens at the death of men of the world.

"Behold, a dead man was carried out, the only son of his mother"—*Luke*, vii. 12.

It is related in this day's gospel, that, going to the city of Naim, Jesus Christ met a dead man, the only son of his mother, who was carried out to be buried. "*Behold, a dead man was carried out*". Before we proceed farther, let us stop at these words, and remember death. The holy Church directs her ministers to say to Christians every year, on Ash Wednesday: *Memento homo quia pulvis es, et in pulverem reverteris.* Remember, man, thou art but dust, and into dust thou shalt return. Oh! would to God that men had death always before their eyes: if they had, they certainly should not lead such bad lives. Now, beloved brethren, that the remembrance of death may be impressed upon you, I will this day place before your eyes the practical death, or a description of what ordinarily happens at the death of men of the world, and of all the circumstances attending it. Hence we shall consider, in the first point, what happens at the time of his last illness; in the second point, what happens when the last sacraments are received; and, in the third, what happens at the time of death.

First point. What happens at the time of the last illness.

1. I do not intend in this discourse to speak of a sinner who has always lived in habitual sin; but of a worldling, who is careless about his salvation, and always entangled in the affairs of the world, in contracts, enmities, courtships, and gaming. He has frequently fallen into mortal sins, and after a considerable time has confessed them. In a word, he has been a relapsing sinner, and has generally lived in enmity with God, or, at least, has been generally perplexed with grievous doubts of conscience. Let us consider the death of such persons, and what ordinarily happens at their death.

2. Let us commence with the time at which his last illness appears He rises in the morning, he goes out to look after his temporal affairs; but while he is engaged in business, he is assailed by a violent pain in the head, his legs totter, he feels a cold shivering, which runs through every member, a sickness of the stomach, and great debility over the whole body. He immediately returns home and throws himself on the bed. His relatives, his wife and sisters, run to him, and say: *Why have you retired so early? Are you unwell?* He answers: *I feel sick. I am scarcely able to stand; I have a great head-ache. Perhaps,* they say, *you have got a fever. It must be so,* he replies; *send for a physician.* The physician is immediately sent for. In the mean time, the sick man is put to bed, and there he is seized with a cold fit, which makes him shiver from head to foot. He is loaded with covering, but the cold continues for an hour or two, and is succeeded by a burning heat. The physician arrives, asks the sick man how he feels; he examines the pulse, and finds he has a severe attack of fever. But, not to alarm him, the physician says: You have fever: but it is trifling. Have you given any occasion to it? The sick man replies: I went out by night, a few days ago, and caught cold: or, I dined with a friend, and indulged my appetite to excess. It is worth nothing, the physician says: it is a fulness of stomach, or more probably one of those attacks which occur at the change of season. Eat nothing to-day; take a cup of tea; be not un-

easy: be cheerful: there is no danger. I will see you to-morrow. Oh! that there was an angel, who, on the part of God, would say to the physician: What do you say? Do you tell me that there is no danger in this disease? Ah! the trumpet of the divine justice has, by the first symptoms of his illness, given the signal of the death of this man: for him the time of God's vengeance has already arrived.

3. The night comes, and the poor invalid gets no rest. The difficulty of breathing and head-ache increase. The night appears to him a thousand years. The light scarcely dawns when he calls for some of the family. His relatives come, and say to him: Have you rested well? Ah! I have not been able to close my eyes during the entire night. O God! how much do I feel oppressed! Oh! how violent are the spasms in my head! I feel my temples pierced by two nails. Send immediately for the physician; tell him to come as soon as possible. The physician comes, and finds the fever increased; but still he continues to say: *Have courage; there is no danger. The disease must take its course. The fever which accompanies it will make it disappear.* He comes the third day, and finds the sick man worse. He comes on the fourth day, and the symptoms of malignant fever appear. The taste on the mouth is disagreeable; the tongue is black; every part of the body is restless; and delirium has commenced. The physician, finding that the fever is acute, prescribes purging, blood-letting, and iced water. He says to the relatives: Ah! the sickness is most severe; I do not wish to be alone. Let other physicians be called in, that we may have a consultation. This he says in secret to the relatives, but not to the sick man—on the contrary, not to frighten him, he continues to say: *Be cheerful; there is no danger.*

4. Thus, they speak of remedies, of more physicians, and of a consultation; but not a word about confession or the last sacraments. I know not how such physicians can be saved. Where the bull of Pope Pius the Fifth is in force, they expressly swear, when they receive the diploma, that, after the third day of his illness, they will pay no more visits to any sick man until he has made his confession. But some physicians do not observe this oath, and thus so many poor souls are damned. For, when a sick man has lost his reason, of what use is confession to

him? He is lost. Brethren, when you fall sick, do not wait till the physician tells you to send for a confessor; send for him of your own accord; for, physicians, through fear of displeasing a patient, do not warn him of his danger until they despair, or nearly despair of his recovery. Thus, brethren, send first for your confessor—call first for the physician of the soul, and afterwards for the physician of the body. Your soul is at stake, eternity is at stake; if you err then, you have erred for ever; your mistake shall be for ever irreparable.

5. The physician then conceals from the sick man his danger; his relatives do what is still worse—they deceive him by lies. They tell him that he is better, and that the physicians give strong hopes of his recovery. O treacherous relatives! O barbarous relatives, who are the worst of enemies! Instead of warning the sick man of his danger (as is their duty, particularly if they are parents, children, or brothers), that he may settle the accounts of his soul, they flatter him, they deceive him, and cause him to die in the state of damnation. But, from the pains, oppression, and restlessness, which he feels, from the studied silence of friends who visit him, and from the tears which he sees in the eyes of his relatives, the poor invalid perceives that his disease is mortal. Alas! he says, the hour of death is come; but, through fear of giving me annoyance, they do not warn me of it.

6. No; his relatives do not let him know that he is in danger of death; but, because they attend to their own interest, about which they are more solicitous than they are about anything else, they bring in a scrivener, in the hope that the dying man will leave them a large portion of his property. The scrivener arrives. Who is this? asks the sick man. The relatives answer: He is a scrivener. Perhaps, for your own satisfaction, you would like to make your will. Then, is my sickness mortal? Am I near my end? No, father, or brother, they say; we know that there is no necessity for making a will; but you must one day make it, and it would be better to do it now, while you have the full use of all your faculties. Very well, he replies; since the scrivener is come, and since you wish me to do it, I will make my last will. The scrivener first asks the sick man in what church he wishes to be buried, in case he should die. Oh! what a painful question! After choosing the place of his in-

terment, he begins to dispose of all his goods. I bequeath such an estate or farm to my children; such a house to my brother; such a sum of money to a friend; and such an article of furniture to an acquaintance. O miserable man, what have you done? You have submitted to so much fatigue, you have burdened your conscience with so many sins, in order to acquire these goods; and now you leave them for ever, and bequeath them to such and such persons. But there is no remedy; when death comes we must leave all things. This separation from all worldly possessions is very painful to the sick man, whose heart was attached to his property, his house, his garden, his money, and his amusements. Death comes, gives the stroke, and separates the heart from all the objects of its love. This stroke tortures the sick man with excruciating pain. Ah brethren! let us detach our hearts from the things of this world before death separates us from them with so much pain, and with such great danger to our salvation.

Second point. What happens at the time in which the sacraments are received.

7. Behold! the dying man has made his will. After the eighth or tenth day of his illness, seeing that he is daily growing worse, and that he is near his end, one of his relatives asks: *When shall we send for his confessor? He has been a man of the world. We know that he has not been a saint.* They all agree that the confessor should be sent for; but all refuse to speak to the sick man on the subject. Hence they send for the parish priest, or for some other confessor, to make known to the dying man his danger, and the necessity of receiving the last sacraments. But this is done only when he has nearly lost the use of his faculties. The confessor comes; he inquires from the family about the state of the sick man, and the sort of life which he led. He finds that he has been careless about the duties of religion, and, from the circumstances which he hears, he trembles for the salvation of the poor soul. Understanding that the dying man has but a short time to live, the confessor, first of all, orders the relatives to leave the room, and to return to it no more. He then approaches and salutes the sick man. The latter asks: Who are you? I am, replies the confessor, the parish priest, Father Such-a-one. Do you wish me to do

anything for you? Having heard that you had a severe attack of illness, I have come to reconcile you with your Creator. Father, I am obliged to you; but I beg of you for the present to let me take a little rest; for I have got no sleep for several nights, and I am scarcely able to speak. Recommend me to God.

8. Knowing the dangerous state of the soul and body of the sick man, the confessor says: We hope that the Lord and the most holy Virgin will deliver you from this illness; but, sooner or later, you must die. Your illness is very severe. You would do well to make your confession, and to adjust the affairs of your soul. Perhaps you have scruples of conscience: I have come on purpose to calm the troubles of your mind. Father, I should have to make a long confession; for my conscience is perplexed and burdened with sin. At present I am not able to do it. I feel a lightness in my head, and I can scarcely breathe. Father, we will see about it to-morrow; at present I am not able. But who knows what may happen? Some attack may come on, which will not leave you time to make your confession. Father, do not torment me any longer. I have said that I am not able; it is impossible for me do it. But the confessor, who knows that there is no hope of recovery, feels himself obliged to speak more plainly, and says: I think it my duty to inform you that your life is about to close. I entreat you to make your confession; for, perhaps, to-morrow you shall be dead. Why, father, do you say so? Because, replies the confessor, so the physicians have said. The poor dying man then begins to rage against the physicians and against his friends. Ah! the traitors have deceived me. They knew my danger, and have not informed me of it. Ah! unhappy me! The confessor rejoins, and says: Be not alarmed at the difficulties of making your confession; it is enough to mention the most grievous sins which you remember. I will assist you. Be not afraid. Begin at once to tell your sins. The dying man forces himself to commence his confession; but his mind is all confusion; he knows not where to begin; he tries to tell his sins, but is not able to explain himself. He feels but little, and understands still less, what the confessor says to him. O God! At such a time, and in such a state, worldlings are obliged to attend to the most important of all affairs—the affair of eternal

salvation! The confessor hears, perhaps, many sins, bad habits, injuries done to the property and character of others, confessions made with little sorrow, and with little purpose of amendment. He assists the dying man as well as he can, and, after a short exhortation, tells him to make an act of contrition. But, God grant that he may not be as insensible to sorrow as the sick man who was attended by Cardinal Bellarmine. When the cardinal exhorted him to make an act of contrition, he said: Father, do not trouble yourself; these things are too high for me; I do not understand them. In the end, the confessor absolves the dying man; but who knows if God absolves him?

9. After giving him absolution, the confessor says: Prepare yourself, now, to receive Jesus Christ for your *viaticum*. It is now, replies the sick man, four or five hours after night; I will communicate in the morning. No: perhaps in the morning, time shall be no more for you; you must at present receive the viaticum and extreme unction. Ah, unhappy me! the dying man says; am I then at the point of death? He has reason to say so; for the practice of some physicians is, to put off the viaticum till the patient is near his last, and till he has lost, or nearly lost his senses. This is a common delusion. According to the common opinion of theologians, the viaticum ought always to be administered when there is danger of death. It will be useful here to observe, that Benedict the Fourteenth, in his fifty-third bull, *in Euchol. Græc.*, § 46, *ap Bullar, tom.* 4, says, that extreme unction may be given whenever the sick man *labours under a grievous illness.* Hence, whenever the sick can receive the viaticum, they can also receive the sacrament of extreme unction. It is not necessary to wait, as some physicians recommend, till they are near the agony, or till they lose their senses.

10. Behold! the viaticum arrives, the sick man hears the bell. Oh! how he trembles! The trembling and terror increase when he sees the priest coming into the room with the holy sacrament, and when he beholds around his bed the torches of those who assisted at the procession. The priest recites the words of the ritual: "Accipe frater viaticum corporis Domini nostri Jesu Christi qui te custodiat ab hoste maligno, et perducat in vitam eternam. Amen". Brother, receive the viaticum of the body of our Lord Jesus Christ, that he may preserve you from the wicked enemy, and that he may bring

you to eternal life. He receives the consecrated host upon his tongue: the priest then gives him a little water, to enable him to swallow it; for his throat is dry and parched.

11. The priest afterwards gives the extreme unction; and begins by anointing the eyes while he says the following words: "Per istam sanctam unctionem, et suam piissimam misericordiam, indulgeat tibi Deus, quidquid per visum deliquisti". He then anoints the other senses—the ears, the nostrils, the mouth, the hands, the feet, and the loins, saying: "Quidquid per auditum deliquisti per odoratum, per gustum et locutionem, per tactum, per gressum, et lumborum delectationem". And, during the administration of the extreme unction, the Devil is employed in reminding the sick man of all the sins he committed by the senses—by the eyes, the ears, the tongue, the hands; and says to him: After so many sins, can you expect to be saved? Oh! what terror is then caused by every one of those mortal sins, which are now called human frailties, and which, worldlings say, God will not punish! Now they are disregarded; but then every mortal sin shall be a sword that will pierce the soul with terror. But let us come to what happens at death!

Third point. What happens at the time of death.

12. After having administered the sacraments, the priest departs, and leaves the dying man alone. He feels more terror and alarm after the sacraments, than before he received them; for he knows that his entire preparation for them was made in the midst of great confusion of mind and great uneasiness of conscience. But the signs of approaching death appear: the sick man falls into a cold sweat; the sight grows dim, and he no longer knows the persons that attend him: he has lost his speech, and can scarcely breathe. In the midst of this darkness of death, he continues to say: *Oh! that I had time; that I had another day, with the use of my faculties, to make a good confession!* For, the unhappy man has great doubts about the confession which he has made: he feels that he was not able to excite himself to make a true act of sorrow. But, what time? what day? "Time shall be no longer"—*Apoc.*, x. 6. The confessor has the book open to announce to him his departure from this world. Proficiscere anima Christiana de hoc mundo. Depart, Christian soul, from this world. The

dying man continues to say within himself: *O lost years of my life! O fool that I have been!* But when does he say this? When the scene is about to close for him; when the oil in the lamp is just consumed; and when the great moment has arrived, on which his eternal happiness or misery depends.

13. But behold! his eyes are petrified; his body takes the posture of a corpse; the extremities, the hands and feet, have become cold. The agony commences; the priest begins to recite the prayers for the recommendation of a departing soul. After having read the *recommendation*, he feels the pulse of the dying man, and feels that it has ceased to beat. *Light*, he says, *immediately the blessed candle.* O candle, O candle, show us light, now that we have health; for, at the hour of death, thy light shall serve only to terrify us the more. But already the breathing of the sick man is not so frequent; it has begun to fail. This is a sign that death is very near. The assisting priest raises his voice, and says to the poor man in his agony: Say after me: O God, come to my aid; have mercy on me. My crucified Jesus, save me through thy passion. Mother of God, intercede for me. St. Joseph, St. Michael the Archangel, my holy angel-guardian, and all ye saints in Paradise, pray to God for me. Jesus, Jesus, Jesus and Mary, I give you my heart and my soul. But, behold the last signs of death; the phlegm is confined in the throat; the dying man sends forth feeble moans; the tears rush from his eyes; finally he twists the mouth, he distorts the eyes, he makes a few pauses, and at the last opening of the mouth, he expires and dies.

14. The priest then brings a candle to the mouth of the dead man, to try if he be still alive: he sees that the flame is not moved, and thence infers that life is extinct. He says: Requiescat in pace. May he rest in peace. And turning to the bystanders, announces that he is dead. *I hope*, he adds, *he is gone to Heaven.* He is dead; and how has he died? No one knows whether he is saved or damned; but he has died in a great tempest. Such is the death of those unfortunate men who, during life, have cared little about God. "Their souls shall die in a storm" —*Job*, xxxvi. 14. Of every one that dies, it is usual to say, that *he is gone to Heaven.* He is gone to Heaven, if he deserved Heaven; but, if he merited Hell, he has gone to Hell. Do all go to Heaven? Oh! how few enter into that abode of bliss!

15. Before the body is cold, he is covered with a worn-out garment; because it must soon rot with him in the grave. Two lighted candles are placed in the chamber; the curtain of the bed on which the dead man lies, is let down; and he is left alone. The parish priest is sent for, and requested to come in the morning and take away the corpse. The priest comes; the deceased is carried to the church; and this is his last journey on this Earth. The priests begin to sing the "*De profundis clamavi ad te Domine*", *etc.* The spectators, who look at the funeral as it passes, speak of the deceased. One says: *He was a proud man.* Another: *O that he had died ten years ago.* A third: *He was fortunate in the world; he made a great deal of money; he had a fine house; but now he takes nothing with him.* And while they speak of him in this manner, he is burning in Hell. He arrives at the church, and is placed in the middle, surrounded by six candles. The bystanders look at him, but suddenly turn away their eyes, because his appearance excites horror. The Mass is sung for his repose, and, after Mass, the "*Libera*"; and the function is concluded with these words: *Requiescat in pace*—May he rest in peace. May he rest in peace, if he died in peace with God; but, if he has died in enmity with God, what peace! what peace can he enjoy? He shall have no peace as long as God shall be God. The sepulchre is then opened; the corpse is thrown into it; the grave is covered with a tombstone; and he is left there to rot, and to be the food of worms. It is thus that the scene of this world ends for each of us. His relatives put on mourning; but they first divide among themselves the property which he has left. They shed an occasional tear for two or three days, and afterwards forget him. And what shall become of him? If he be saved, he shall be happy for ever; if damned, he must be miserable for eternity.

SERMON XLV.

FOR THE SIXTEENTH SUNDAY AFTER PENTECOST.

On impurity.

"And behold, there was a certain man before him, who had the dropsy"—*Luke*, xiv. 2.

The man who indulges in impurity is like a person labouring under the dropsy. The latter is so much tormented by thirst, that the more he drinks, the more thirsty he becomes. Such, too, is the nature of the accursed vice of impurity; it is never satiated. "As", says St. Thomas of Villanova, "the more the dropsical man abounds in moisture, the more he thirsts; so too is it with the waves of carnal pleasures". I will speak to-day of the vice of impurity, and will show, in the first point, the delusion of those who say, that this vice is but a small evil; and, in the second, the delusion of those who say, that God takes pity on this sin, and that he does not punish it.

First point. Delusion of those who say, that sins against purity are not a great evil.

1. The unchaste, then, say, that sins contrary to purity are but a small evil. Like "*the sow wallowing in the mire*" ("Sus lota in volutabro luti"—II. *Pet.*, ii. 22), they are immersed in their own filth, so that they do not see the malice of their actions; and therefore they neither feel nor abhor the stench of their impurities, which excite disgust and horror in all others. Can you, who say that the vice of impurity is but a small evil—can you, I ask, deny that it is a mortal sin? If you deny it, you are a heretic; for as St. Paul says: "Do not err. Neither fornicators, nor adulterers, nor the effeminate, etc., shall possess the kingdom of God"—I. *Cor.*, vi. 9. It is a mortal sin; it cannot be a small evil. It is more sinful than theft, or detraction, or the violation of the fast. How then

can you say that it is not a great evil? Perhaps mortal sin appears to you to be a small evil? Is it a small evil to despise the grace of God, to turn your back upon him, and to lose his friendship, for a transitory, beastly pleasure?

2. St. Thomas teaches, that mortal sin, because it is an insult offered to an infinite God, contains a certain infinitude of malice. "A sin committed against God, has a certain infinitude, on account of the infinitude of the Divine Majesty"—*S. Thom.*, 3*p.*, *qu.* 1, *art.* 2, *ad* 2. Is mortal sin a small evil? It is so great an evil, that if all the angels and all the saints, the apostles, martyrs, and even the Mother of God, offered all their merits to atone for a single mortal sin, the oblation would not be sufficient. No; for, that atonement or satisfaction would be finite; but the debt contracted by mortal sin is infinite, on account of the infinite majesty of God, which has been offended. The hatred which God bears to sins against purity is great beyond measure. If a lady find her plate soiled, she is disgusted, and cannot eat. Now with what disgust and indignation must God, who is purity itself, behold the filthy impurities by which his law is violated? He loves purity with an infinite love; and consequently he has an infinite hatred for the sensuality which the lewd, voluptuous man calls a small evil. Even the devils who held a high rank in Heaven before their fall, disdain to tempt men to sins of the flesh.

3. St. Thomas says (*lib.* 5, *de Erud. Princ.*, *c.* li.), that Lucifer, who is supposed to have been the Devil that tempted Jesus Christ in the desert, tempted him to commit other sins, but scorned to tempt him to offend against chastity. Is this sin a small evil? Is it then a small evil to see a man endowed with a rational soul, and enriched with so many divine graces, bring himself, by the sin of impurity, to the level of a brute? "Fornication and pleasure", says St. Jerome, "pervert the understanding, and change men into beasts"—*in Oseam.*, *c.* iv. In the voluptuous and unchaste, are literally verified the words of David—"And man, when he was in honour, did not understand: he is compared to senseless beasts, and is become like to them"—*Ps.*, xlviii. 13. St. Jerome says, that there is nothing more vile or degrading, than to allow oneself to be conquered by the flesh. "Nihil vilius quam vinci a carne". Is it a small evil to forget God, and to banish him from the soul, for the sake

of giving the body a vile satisfaction, of which, when it is over, you feel ashamed? Of this the Lord complains by the Prophet Ezechiel. "Thus saith the Lord God: Because thou hast forgotten me, and hast cast me off behind thy back"—xxiii. 35. St. Thomas says, that by every vice, but particularly by the vice of impurity, men are removed far from God. "Per luxuriam maxime recedit a Deo"—*in Job*, *cap.* xxxi.

4. Moreover, sins of impurity, on account of their great number, are an immense evil. A blasphemer does not always blaspheme, but only when he is drunk, or provoked to anger. The assassin, whose trade is to murder others, does not, at the most commit more than eight or ten homicides. But the unchaste are guilty of an unceasing torrent of sins, by thoughts, by words, by looks, by complacencies, and by touches; so that, when they go to confession, they find it impossible to tell the number of the sins they have committed against purity. Even in their sleep, the Devil represents to them obscene objects, that, on awaking, they may take delight in them; and because they are made the slaves of the enemy, they obey and consent to his suggestions; for it is easy to contract a habit of this sin. To other sins, such as blasphemy, detraction, and murder, men are not prone; but to this vice nature inclines them. Hence St. Thomas says, that there is no sinner so ready to offend God, as the votary of lust is, on every occasion that occurs to him. "Nullus ad Dei contemptum promptior". The sin of impurity brings in its train the sins of defamation, of theft, hatred, and of boasting of its own filthy abominations. Besides, it ordinarily involves the malice of scandal. Other sins, such as blasphemy, perjury, and murder, excite horror in those who witness them; but this sin excites and draws others, who are flesh, to commit it, or at least, to commit it with less horror.

5. "Totum hominem", says St. Cyprian, "agit in triumphum libidinis"—*lib. de bono pudic.* By lust the Devil triumphs over the entire man, over his body and over his soul; over his memory, filling it with the remembrance of unchaste delights, in order to make him take complacency in them; over his intellect, to make him desire occasions of committing sin; over the will, by making it love its impurities as his last end, and as if there were no God. "I made", said Job, "a covenant with my eyes, that I would not so much as think upon a virgin. For

what part should God from above have in me?"—xxxi. 1, 2. Job was afraid to look at a virgin; because he knew that if he consented to a bad thought, God should have no part in him. According to St. Gregory, from impurity arises blindness of understanding, destruction, hatred of God, and despair of eternal life. "De luxuria cœcitas mentis, præcipitatio, odium Dei, desperatio futuri sæculi generantur"—*S. Greg.*, *Mor.*, *lib.* 13. St. Augustine says, that though the unchaste may grow old, the vice of impurity does not grow old in them. Hence St. Thomas says, that there is no sin in which the Devil delights so much as in this sin; because there is no other sin to which nature clings with so much tenacity. To the vice of impurity it adheres so firmly, that the appetite for carnal pleasures becomes insatiable. "Diabolus dicitur gaudere maxime de peccato luxuriæ, quia est maximæ adhœrentiæ: et difficile ab eo homo eripi potest; inasatiabilis est enim delectabilis appetitus"—1, 2, *qu.* 73, *a.* 5, *ad.* 2. Go now, and say that the sin of impurity is but a small evil. At the hour of death you shall not say so: every sin of that kind shall then appear to you a monster of Hell. Much less, shall you say so before the judgment-seat of Jesus Christ, who will tell you what the Apostle has already told you—"No fornicator, or unclean......hath inheritance in the kingdom of Christ and God"—*Eph.*, v. 5. The man who has lived like a brute, does not deserve to sit with the angels.

6. Most beloved brethren, let us continue to pray to God to deliver us from this vice: if we do not, we shall lose our souls. The sin of impurity brings with it blindness and obstinacy. Every vice produces darkness of understanding; but impurity produces it in a greater degree than all other sins. "Fornication, and wine, and drunkenness take away the understanding"—*Osee*, iv. 11. Wine deprives us of understanding and reason; so does impurity. Hence St. Thomas says, that the man who indulges in unchaste pleasures, does not live according to reason. "In nullo procedit secundum judicium rationis". Now, if the unchaste are deprived of light, and no longer see the evil which they do, how can they abhor it, and amend their lives? The Prophet Osee says, that being blinded by their own mire, they do not even think of returning to God; because their impurities take away from them all knowledge of God. "They will not set their thought to return to their God; for the spirit of fornication is in the midst of

them, and they have not known the Lord"—*Osee*, v. 4. Hence St. Lawrence Justinian writes, that this sin makes men forget God. "Delights of the flesh induce forgetfulness of God". And St. John Damascene teaches, that "the carnal man cannot look at the light of truth". Thus, the lewd and voluptuous no longer understand what is meant by the grace of God, by judgment, Hell, and eternity. "Fire hath fallen upon them, and they shall not see the sun"—*Ps.*, lvii. 9. Some of these blind miscreants go so far as to say, that fornication is not in itself sinful. They say, that it was not forbidden in the Old Law; and in support of this execrable doctrine, they adduce the words of the Lord to Osee: "Go, take thee a wife of fornication, and have of her children of fornication" —*Osee*, i. 2. In answer I say, that God did not permit Osee to commit fornication; but wished him to take for his wife a woman who had been guilty of fornication: and the children of this marriage were called children of fornication, because the mother had been guilty of that crime. This is, according to St. Jerome, the meaning of the words of the Lord to Osee. "Idcirco", says the holy doctor, "fornicationis appellandi sunt filii, quod sunt de meretrice generati". But fornication was always forbidden, under pain of mortal sin, in the Old, as well as in the New Law. St. Paul says: "No fornication or unclean...hath inheritance in the kingdom of Christ and of God"—*Eph.*, v. 5. Behold the impiety to which the blindness of such sinners carries them! From this blindness it arises, that, though they go to the sacraments, their confessions are null for want of true contrition; for how is it possible for them to have true sorrow, when they neither know nor abhor their sins?

7. The vice of impurity also brings with it obstinacy. To conquer temptations, particularly against chastity, continual prayer is necessary. "Watch ye, and pray, that ye enter not into temptation"—*Mark*, xiv. 38. But how will the unchaste, who are always seeking to be tempted, pray to God to deliver them from temptation? They sometimes, as St. Augustine confessed of himself, even abstain from prayer, through fear of being heard and cured of the disease, which they wish to continue. "I feared", said the saint, "that you would soon hear and heal the disease of concupiscence, which I wished to be satiated, rather than extinguished"—*Conf.*, *lib.* 8, *cap.* vii. St. Peter calls this

vice an unceasing sin. "Having eyes full of adultery and sin that ceaseth not"—II. *Pet.*, ii. 14. Impurity is called an unceasing sin on account of the obstinacy which it induces. Some persons addicted to this vice say: *I always confess the sin.* So much the worse; for, since you always relapse into the sin, these confessions serve to make you persevere in the sin. The fear of punishment is diminished by saying: *I always confess the sin.* If you felt that this sin certainly merits Hell, you would scarcely say: I will not give it up; I do not care if I am damned. But the Devil deceives you. Commit this sin, he says; for you afterwards confess it. But, to make a good confession of your sins, you must have true sorrow of the heart, and a firm purpose to sin no more. Where are this sorrow and this firm purpose of amendment, when you always return to the vomit? If you had had these dispositions, and had received sanctifying grace at your confessions, you should not have relapsed, or at least you should have abstained for a considerable time from relapsing. You have always fallen back into sin in eight or ten days, and perhaps in a shorter time, after confession. What sign is this? It is a sign that you were always in enmity with God. If a sick man instantly vomits the medicine which he takes, it is a sign that his disease is incurable.

8. St. Jerome says, that the vice of impurity, when habitual, will cease when the unhappy man who indulges in it, is cast into the fire of Hell. "O infernal fire, lust, whose fuel is gluttony, whose sparks are brief conversations, whose end is Hell". The unchaste become like the vulture that waits to be killed by the fowler, rather than abandon the rottenness of the dead bodies on which it feeds. This is what happened to a young female, who, after having lived in the habit of sin with a young man, fell sick, and appeared to be converted. At the hour of death, she asked leave of her confessor to send for the young man, in order to exhort him to change his life at the sight of her death. The confessor very imprudently gave the permission, and taught her what she should say to her accomplice in sin. But listen to what happened. As soon as she saw him, she forgot her promise to the confessor and the exhortation she was to give to the young man. And what did she do? She raised herself up, sat in the bed, stretched her arms to him, and said: Friend, I have

always loved you, and even now, at the end of my life, I love you: I see that, on your account, I shall go to Hell; but I do not care; I am willing, for the love of you, to be damned. After these words, she fell back on the bed and expired. These facts are related by Father Segneri (*Crist. Istr. Rag.* xxiv. *n.* 10). Oh! how difficult is it for a person who has contracted a habit of this vice, to amend his life and return sincerely to God! how difficult is it for him not to terminate this habit in Hell, like the unfortunate young woman of whom I have just spoken!

Second point. Illusion of those who say, that God takes pity on this sin.

9. The votaries of lust say that God takes pity on this sin; but, such is not the language of St. Thomas of Villanova. He says, that in the sacred Scriptures we do not read of any sin so severely chastised as the sin of impurity. "Luxuriæ facinus præ aliis punitum legimus"—*serm.* iv. *Dom.* 1, *Quadrag.* We find in the Scriptures, that in punishment of this sin, a deluge of fire descended from Heaven on four cities, and, in an instant, consumed not only the inhabitants, but even the very stones. "And the Lord rained upon Sodom and Gomorrha brimstone and fire from the Lord out of Heaven. And he destroyed these cities, and all things that spring from the Earth"—*Gen.*, xix. 24. St. Peter Damian relates, that a man and woman who had sinned against purity, were found burnt and black as a cinder.

10. Salvian writes, that it was in punishment of the sin of impurity that God sent on the Earth the universal deluge, which was caused by continued rain for forty days and forty nights. In this deluge, the waters rose fifteen cubits above the tops of the highest mountains; and only eight persons along with Noah were saved in the ark. The rest of the inhabitants of the Earth, who were more numerous then than at present, were punished with death in chastisement of the vice of impurity. Mark the words of the Lord in speaking of this chatisement which he inflicted on that sin. "My spirit shall not remain in man for ever; because he is flesh"—*Gen.*, vi. 3. "That is", says Liranus, "too deeply involved in carnal sins". The Lord added: "For it repenteth me that I made man"—*Gen.*, vi. 7. The indignation of God is not like ours, which clouds

the mind, and drives us into excesses: his wrath is a judgment perfectly just and tranquil, by which God punishes and repairs the disorders of sin. But to make us understand the intensity of his hatred for the sin of impurity, he represents himself as if sorry for having created man, who offended him so grievously by this vice. We, at the present day, see more severe temporal punishment inflicted on this, than on any other sin. Go into the hospitals, and listen to the shrieks of so many young men, who, in punishment of their impurities, are obliged to submit to the severest treatment and to the most painful operations, and who, if they escape death, are, according to the divine threat, feeble, and subject to the most excruciating pain for the remainder of their lives. "Thou...hast cast me off behind thy back, bear thou also thy wickedness and thy fornications"—*Ezech,*, xxiii. 35.

11. St. Remigius writes, that, if children be excepted, the number of adults that are saved, is few, on account of the sins of the flesh. "Exceptis parvulis ex adultis propter vitiam carnis pauci salvantur"—*Apud S. Cypr. de bono pudic.* In conformity with this doctrine, it was revealed to a holy soul, that as pride has filled Hell with devils, so impurity fills it with men (*Col. disp.* ix., *ex.* 192). St. Isidore assigns the reason. He says, that there is no vice which so much enslaves men to the Devil, as impurity. "Magis per luxuriam, humanum genus subditur diabolo, quam per aliquod aliud"—*S. Isid., lib.* 2, *c.* xxxix. Hence St. Augustine says, that with regard to this sin, *the combat is common, and the victory rare.* Hence it is, that on account of this sin, Hell is filled with souls.

12. All that I have said on this subject, has been said, not that any one present, who has been addicted to the vice of impurity, may be driven to despair, but that such persons may be cured. Let us then come to the remedies. There are two great remedies—prayer, and the flight of dangerous occasions. Prayer, says St. Gregory of Nyssa, is the safeguard of chastity. "Oratio pudicitiæ præsidium et tutamen est"—*de Orat.* And before him, Solomon, speaking of himself, said the same. "And as I knew that I could not otherwise be continent, except God gave it,...I went to the Lord, and besought him"—*Wis.*, viii. 21. Thus, it is impossible for us to conquer this vice without God's assistance.

Hence, as soon as a temptation against chastity presents itself, the remedy is, to turn instantly to God for help, and to repeat several times the most holy names of Jesus and Mary, which have a special virtue to banish bad thoughts of that kind. I have said immediately, without listening to, or beginning to argue with the temptation. When a bad thought occurs to the mind, it is necessary to shake it off instantly, as you would a spark that flies from the fire, and instantly to invoke aid from Jesus and Mary.

13. As to the flight of dangerous occasions, St. Philip Neri used to say, that cowards—that is, they who fly from the occasions—gain the victory. Hence, you must, in the first place, keep a restraint on the eyes, and must abstain from looking at young females. Otherwise, says St. Thomas, you can scarcely avoid this sin. "Luxuria vitari vix potest nisi vitatur aspectus mulieris pulchræ"—*S. Thom.*, 1, 2, *qu.* 167, *a.* 2. Hence Job said: "I made a covenant with my eyes, that I would not so much as think upon a virgin"—xxxi. 1. He was afraid to look at a virgin; because from looks it is easy to pass to desires, and from desires to acts. St. Francis de Sales used to say, that to look at a woman does not do so much evil, as to look at her a second time. If the Devil has not gained a victory the first, he will gain it the second time. And if it be necessary to abstain from looking at females, it is much more necessary to avoid conversation with them. "Tarry not among women"—*Eccl.*, xlii. 12. We should be persuaded that, in avoiding occasions of this sin, no caution can be too great. Hence we must be always fearful, and fly from them. "A wise man feareth and declineth from evil; a fool is confident"—*Prov.*, xiv. 16. A wise man is timid, and flies away; a fool is confident, and falls.

SERMON XLVI.

FOR THE SEVENTEENTH SUNDAY AFTER PENTECOST.

On the love of God.

"Thou shalt love the Lord thy God with thy whole heart"—*Matt.*, xxii. 37.

"But one thing is necessary"—*Luke*, x. 42. What is this one thing necessary? It is not necessary to acquire riches, nor to obtain dignities, nor to gain a great name. The only thing necessary is to love God. Whatever is not done for the love of God is lost. This is the greatest and the first commandment of the divine law. To the Pharisee who asked what was the greatest commandment of the law, Jesus Christ answered: "Thou shalt love the Lord thy God with thy whole heart......This is the greatest and first commandment"—*Matt.*, xxii. 37, 38. But this, which is the greatest of the commandments, is the most despised by men: there are few who fulfil it. The greater part of men love their relatives, their friends, and even brute animals, but do not love God. Of these St. John says, that they have not life,—that they are dead. "He that loveth not, abideth in death"—I. *John*, iii. 14. St. Bernard writes, that the reward of a soul is estimated by the measure of her love for God. "Quantitas animæ æstimatur de mensura charitatis quam habet"— *serm.* xxvii., *in Cant.* Let us consider to-day, in the first point, how dear this command of loving God with our whole heart, ought to be to us; and, in the second, what we ought to do in order to love God with our whole heart.

First point. How dear this command of loving God with our whole heart, ought to be to us.

1. What object more noble, more magnificent, more powerful, more rich, more beautiful, more bountiful, more merciful, more grateful, more amiable, or more loving, than himself, could God give us to love? Who more noble than God? Some boast

of the nobility of their family for five hundred or a thousand years; but the nobility of God is eternal. He is the Lord of all. Before God, all the angels in Heaven or all the nobles on Earth are but as a drop of water or a grain of dust. "Behold the Gentiles are as a drop of a bucket,...behold the islands are as a little dust"—*Isa.*, xl. 15. Who more powerful than God? He can do whatsoever he wills. By an act of his will he has created this world, and by another act he can destroy it when he pleases. Who more wealthy? He possesses all the riches of Heaven and Earth. Who more beautiful? Before the beauty of God, all the beauties of creatures disappear. Who more bountiful? St. Augustine says, that God has a greater desire to do good to us, than we have to receive it. Who more merciful? If the most impious sinner on Earth humble himself before God, and repent of his sins, God instantly pardons and embraces him. Who more grateful? He does not leave unrewarded the smallest act we perform for his sake. Who more amiable? God is so amiable, that, by barely seeing and loving him in Heaven, the saints feel a joy which makes them perfectly happy and content for all eternity. The greatest of the torments of the damned arises from knowing that this God is so amiable, and that they cannot love him.

2. Finally, who more loving than God? In the Old Law, men might doubt whether God loved them with a tender love; but, after seeing him die on a cross for us, how can we doubt of the tenderness and the ardent affection with which he loves us? Let us raise our eyes, and look at Jesus, the true Son of God, fastened with nails to a gibbet, and let us consider the intensity of the love which he bears us. The cross, the wounds, says St. Bernard, cry out, and proclaim to us, that he truly loves us. "Clamat crux, clamat vulnus, quod ipse vere dilexit". And what more could he do to convince us of his great love, than to lead a life of sorrow for thirty-three years, and afterwards die in torments on the infamous tree of the cross, in order, to wash away our sins with his own blood? "Christ also hath loved us, and hath delivered himself up for us"—*Eph.*, v. 2. "Who hath loved us, and washed us from our sins in his own blood" —*Apoc.*, i. 5. "How", says St. Philip Neri, "is it possible for him who believes in God to love anything but God?" Contemplating God's love towards men, St. Mary Magdalene de

Pazzi began one day to ring the bell, saying that she wished to invite all the nations of the Earth to love so loving a God. St. Francis de Sales used to say with tears: "To love our God, it would be necessary to have an infinite love; and we throw away our love on vain, contemptible things".

3. O inestimable value of divine love, which makes us rich before God! It is the treasure by which we gain his friendship. "She is an infinite treasure to men, which they that use, become the friends of God"—*Wis.*, vii. 14. The only thing we ought to fear, says St. Gregory of Nyssa *(de Vita Moysis)*, is the loss of God's friendship; and the only object of our desires should be its attainment. "Unum terribile arbitror, ab amicitia Dei repelli; unum solum expetibile, amicitia Dei". It is love that obtains the friendship of God. Hence, according to St. Lawrence Justinian, by love the poor become rich, and without love the rich are poor. "No greater riches than to have charity. In charity the poor man is rich, and without charity the rich man is poor"—*S. Laur. Just. in Matt.*, xiii. 44. How great is the joy which a person feels in thinking that he is loved by a man of exalted rank! But how much greater must be the consolation which a soul derives from the conviction that God loves her! "I love them that love me"—*Prov.*, viii. 17. In a soul that loves God, the Three Persons of the Adorable Trinity dwell. "If any one love me, he will keep my word; and my Father will love him; and we will come to him, and will make our abode with him"—*John*, xiv. 23. St. Bernard writes, that among all the virtues, charity is the one that unites us to God. "Charitas est virtus conjungens nos Deo". St. Catherine of Bologna used to say, that love is the golden chain that binds the soul to God. St. Augustine says that "love is a joint connecting the lover with the beloved". Hence, were God not immense, where should he be found? Find a soul that loves God; and there God is certainly found. Of this St. John assures us. "He that abideth in charity, abideth in God, and God in him"—I. *John*, iv. 16. A poor man loves riches; but he does not therefore enjoy them: he may love a throne; but he does not therefore possess a kingdom. But the man that loves God, possesses God. "He abideth in God, and God in him".

4. Besides, St. Thomas says *(Tr. de Virt., art.* 3), that love

draws in its train all other virtues, and directs them all to unite us more closely to God. Hence, because from charity all virtues are born, St. Lawrence Justinian called it *the mother of virtues.* Hence, St. Augustine used to say: "Love, and do what you wish". He that loves God, can only do what is good; if he does evil, he shows that he has ceased to love God. And when he ceases to love him, all things can profit him nothing. If, said the Apostle, I give all my possessions to the poor, and my body to the flames, and have not charity, I am nothing. "And if I should distribute all my goods to feed the poor, and if I should deliver my body to be burned, and have not charity, it profiteth me nothing"—I. *Cor.*, xiii. 3.

5. Love also prevents us from feeling the pains of this life. St. Bonaventure says, that the love of God is like honey; it sweetens things the most bitter. And what more sweet to a soul that loves God, than to suffer for him? She knows that, by cheerfully embracing sufferings she pleases God, and that her pains shall be the brightest jewels in her crown in Paradise. And who is there that will not willingly suffer and die in imitation of Jesus Christ, who has gone before us carrying his cross, to offer himself in sacrifice for the love of us, and inviting us to follow his example? "If any man will come after me, let him take up his cross and follow me"—*Matt.*, xvi. 24. For this purpose, he has condescended to humble himself to death, and to the opprobrious death of the cross, for the love of us. "He humbled himself, becoming obedient unto death, even to the death of the cross"—*Phil.*, ii. 8.

Second point. What we ought to do in order to love God with our whole heart.

6. St. Teresa used to say, that in calling a soul to his love, God bestows upon her an exceedingly great favour. Since, then, most beloved brethren, God calls us all to his love, let us thank and love him with our whole heart. Because he loves us intensely, he wishes to be tenderly loved by us. "When", says St. Bernard, "God loves, he desires nothing else than to be loved; for he loves only that he may be loved"—*serm.* lxiii. *in Cant.* It was to inflame us with his divine love, that the Eternal Word descended from Heaven. So he himself has declared; adding, that he only desires to see this fire lighted up in our

hearts. "I am come to cast fire on the Earth, and what will I but that it be kindled?"—*Luke*, xii. 49. Let us now see what means we ought to adopt in order to love God.

7. In the first place, we ought to guard against every sin, whether mortal or venial. "If", says Jesus Christ, "any one love me, he will keep my word"—*John*, xiv. 23. The first mark of love, is to endeavour not to give the smallest displeasure to the beloved. How can he be said to love God with his whole heart, who is not afraid to commit deliberate venial offences against God? St. Teresa used to say to her spiritual children: "From deliberate sin, however small, may God deliver you". But some will say: Venial sin is a small evil. Is it a small evil to displease a God, who is so good, and who loves us so tenderly?

8. In the second place, to love God with the whole heart, it is necessary to have a great desire to love him. Holy desires are the wings with which we fly to God; for, as St. Lawrence Justinian says, a good desire gives us strength to go forward, and lightens the labour of walking in the way of God. "Vires subministrat, pœnam exhibet leviorem". According to the spiritual masters, he that does not advance in the way of the Lord, goes back; but, on the other hand, God cheerfully gives himself to those who seek after him. "The Lord is good to the soul that seeketh him"—*Lamen.*, iii. 25. He fills with his own good things all who desire him through love. "He hath filled the hungry with good things"—*Luke*, i. 53.

9. In the third place, it is necessary to resolve courageously to arrive at the perfect love of God. Some persons desire to belong entirely to God, but do not resolve to adopt the means. It is of them the Wise Man says, "desires kill the soul"—*Prov.*, xxi. 25. I would wish, they say, to become a saint; but still, with all their desires, they never advance a single step. St. Teresa used to say, that "of these irresolute souls the Devil is never afraid". Because, if they do not resolve sincerely to give themselves to God without reserve, they shall always continue in the same imperfections. But, on the other hand, the saint says, that God wishes only from us a true resolution to become saints; he himself will do the rest. If, then, we wish to love God with our whole heart, we must resolve to do without reserve what is most pleasing to him, and to

begin at once to put our hands to the work. "Whatsoever thy hand is able to do, do it earnestly"—*Eccl.*, ix. 10. What you can do to-day, do not put off till to-morrow; do it as soon as possible. A certain nun in the convent of *Torri degli Specchi*, in Rome, led a tepid life; but, being called by God, in a retreat, to his perfect love, she resolved to correspond immediately to the divine call, and said to her director, with a sincere resolution: *Father, I wish to become a saint, and to become one immediately.* And from that moment, with the aid of God's grace, she lived and died a saint. We must, then, resolve to acquire the perfect love of God, and must immediately adopt the means of becoming saints.

10. The first means is, to detach the heart from all creatures, and to banish from the soul every affection which is not for God. The first question which the ancient fathers of the desert put to every one who sought admission into their society, was, *Do you bring an empty heart, that the Holy Ghost may be able to fill it?* If the world be not expelled from the heart, God cannot enter it. St. Teresa used to say: "Detach the heart from creatures; seek God, and you shall find him". St. Augustine writes, that the Romans worshiped thirty thousand gods; but, among these gods the Roman Senate refused to admit Jesus Christ. Because, said they, he is a proud God, who requires that he alone should be adored. This they had reason to say; for our God wishes to possess our whole souls. He is, as St. Jerome says, a jealous God. "*Zelotypus est Jesus*". And therefore he will have no rival in the affections of our heart. Hence, the Spouse in the Canticles is called "an enclosed garden". "My sister, my spouse is an enclosed garden"—*Cant.*, iv. 12. The soul, then, that wishes to belong entirely to God, must be shut against all love which is not for God.

11. Hence the Divine Spouse is said to be wounded by one of the eyes of his spouse. "Thou hast wounded my heart, my sister, my spouse; thou hast wounded my heart with one of thy eyes"—*Cant.*, iv. 9. One of her eyes signifies, that in all her thoughts and actions, the only end of the spouse is to please God: while, in their devout exercises, worldlings propose to themselves different objects,—sometimes their own interest, sometimes to please their friends, and sometimes to please them-

selves. But the saints seek only to please God, to whom they turn, and say: "What have I in Heaven? and, besides thee, what do I desire upon Earth?.....Thou art the God of my heart, and the God that is my portion for ever"—*Ps.*, lxxii. 25, 26. We should do the same, if we wish to be saints. If, says St. Chrysostom, we do some things pleasing to God, what else but his pleasure do we seek? "Si dignus fueris agere aliquid, quod Deo placet, aliam præter id mercedem requiris?"—*lib.* II., *de Compunct. Cord.* What greater reward can a creature obtain than to please its Creator? Hence, in all we desire or do, we should seek nothing but God. A certain solitary, called Zeno, walking through the desert, absorbed in thought, met the Emperor Macedonius going to hunt. The emperor asked him what he was doing. In answer the solitary said: You go in quest of animals, and I seek God alone. St. Francis de Sales used to say, that the pure love of God consumes all that is not God.

12. Moreover, to love God with our whole heart, it is necessary to love him without reserve. Hence we must love him with a love of *preference.* We must prefer him before every other good, and must be resolved to lose a thousand lives, rather than forfeit his friendship. We must say with St. Paul: "Neither death, nor life, nor angels, nor principalities, nor powers, nor things present, nor things to come,.....nor any other creature, shall be able to separate us from the love of God"—*Rom.*, viii. 38, 39. We must also love him with a love of *benevolence*, desiring to see him loved by all; and therefore, if we love God, we should seek as much as possible to kindle in others the fire of his love, or, at least, should pray for the conversion of all who do not love him. We must love him with a love of *sorrow*, regretting every offence offered to him more than every evil which we could suffer. We must love him with a love of *conformity to the divine will.* The principal office of love is to unite the wills of lovers, and to make the soul say: "Lord, what wilt thou have me to do?"—*Acts*, ix. 6. Lord, tell me what thou dost wish from me; I desire to do it. I wish for nothing; I wish only what thou willest. Hence, we ought frequently to offer ourselves to God without reserve, that he may do with us, and with all we have, whatever he pleases. We must love God with a love of *patience.* This is that strong

love by which true lovers are known. "Love is strong as death" —*Cant.*, viii. 6. "There is nothing too difficult", says St. Augustine, "to be conquered by the fire of love"—*lib. de Mor. Eccl.*, *c.* xxii. For, adds the saint, in doing what we love, labour is not felt, or, if it be felt, the very labour is loved. "In eo quod amatur, aut non laboratur, aut labor amatur". St. Vincent of Paul used to say, that love is measured by the desire of the soul to suffer and to be humbled in order to please God. Let God be pleased, though it should cost us the loss of our life and of all things. To gain all, it is necessary to leave all. *All for all*, said Thomas a Kempis. The reason we do not become saints is, as St. Teresa says, because, as we do not give God all our affections, so he does not give us his perfect love. We must then say with the spouse in the Canticles: "My beloved to me, and I to him"—*Cant.*, ii. 16. My beloved has given himself entirely to me: it is but just that I give myself without reserve to him. St. John Chrysostom says, that when a soul has given herself entirely to God, she no longer cares for ignominies and sufferings; she loses the desire of all things; and not finding repose in any creature, she is always in search of her beloved; her sole concern is to find her beloved.

13. To obtain and to preserve divine love, three things are necessary: meditation, communion, and prayer. First, meditation is necessary. He who thinks but little on God, loves him but little. "In my meditation", said David, "a fire shall flame out"—*Ps.*, xxxviii. 4. Meditation, and particularly meditation on the passion of Jesus Christ, is the blessed furnace in which the love of God is kindled and fanned. "He brought me into the wine cellar; he set in order charity in me"—*Cant.*, ii. 4. The souls that are introduced into this Heavenly cellar, by a single glance of Jesus Christ crucified and dying for the love of us, are wounded and inebriated with holy love. For St. Paul says, that Jesus Christ died for us all, that each of us may live only to love him. "And Christ died for all, that they also may not now live to themselves, but unto him who died for them"—II. *Cor.*, v. 15. The communion is another holy furnace, in which we are inflamed with divine love. "The holy eucharist", says St. Chrysostom, "is a fire which inflames us, that, like lions breathing fire, we may retire from the holy

table, being made terrible to the Devil"—*hom.* xli., *ad Pop.* Above all, prayer *(the prayer of petition)* is necessary. It is by means of prayer that God dispenses all his favours, but particularly the great gift of divine love. To make us ask this love, meditation is a great help. Without meditation we shall ask little or nothing from God. We must, then, always, every day, and several times in the day, ask God to give us the grace to love him with our whole heart. St. Gregory says, that God wishes to be compelled and importuned by our petitions, to bestow upon us his graces. "God wishes to be entreated—to be compelled: he wishes in a certain manner to be overcome by importunity". Let us, then, continually ask of Jesus Christ his holy love; and let us ask his divine mother Mary, who is the treasurer of all his graces, to obtain it for us. *Thesauraria gratiarum (Idiota).* She is called by St. Bernardine, the dispensatrix of God's graces. "*All graces are dispensed through her hands*". It is through her intercession that we must obtain the great gift of divine love.

SERMON XLVII.

FOR THE EIGHTEENTH SUNDAY AFTER PENTECOST

On bad thoughts.

"And Jesus, seeing their thoughts, said: Why do you think evil in your hearts?"—*Matt.*, ix. 4.

In the gospel of this day it is related, that a paralytic was presented to Jesus Christ, that he might heal him. The Lord healed not only his body, but also his soul, and said to him: "Be of good heart, son; thy sins are forgiven thee"—*verse* 2. Some of the Scribes, as soon as they heard these words, said in their hearts: *He blasphemeth.* But our Saviour soon let them know that he saw their evil thoughts, saying: "Why do you think evil in your hearts?" Let us come to the subject of this discourse. God sees the most secret evil thoughts of our hearts;

he sees and punishes them. Human judges forbid and chastise only external crimes; for men only see what appears externally. "Men seeth those things that appear; but the Lord beholdeth the heart"—I. *Kings*, xvi. 7. God prohibits and punishes bad thoughts. We shall examine, in the first point, when bad thoughts are sinful; in the second, the great danger of bad thoughts, when indulged; and in the third, the remedies against bad thoughts.

First point. When bad thoughts are sinful.

1. In two ways men err regarding bad thoughts. Some who have the fear of God are scrupulous, and are afraid that every bad thought which presents itself to the mind, is a sin. This is an error. It is not the bad thought, but the consent to it, that is sinful. All the malice of mortal sin consists in a bad will, in giving to sin a perfect consent, with full advertence to the malice of the sin. Hence St. Augustine teaches, that where there is no consent, there can be no sin. "Nullo modo sit peccatum, si non sit voluntarium"—*de Vera Rel.*, *cap.* xiv. Though the temptation, the rebellion of the senses, or the evil motion of the inferior parts, should be very violent, there is no sin, as long as there is no consent. "Non nocet sensus", says St. Bernard, "ubi non est consensus"—*de Inter. domo.*, *cap.* xix.

2. Even the saints have been tormented by temptations. The Devil labours harder to make the saints fall, than to make the wicked sin: he regards the saints as more valuable prey. The Prophet Habacuc says, that the saints are the dainty food of the enemy. "Through them his portion is made fat, and his meat dainty"—*Hab.*, i. 16. And therefore the prophet adds, that the evil one stretches out his net for all, to deprive them of the life of grace: and that he spares no one. "For this cause, therefore, he spreadeth out his net, and will not spare, continually to slay the nations"—*ib.*, *v.* 17. Even St. Paul, after he had been made a vessel of election, groaned under temptations against chastity. "There was", said he, "given me a sting of the flesh, an angel of Satan to afflict me"—II. *Cor.*, xii. 7. He three times prayed to the Lord to deliver him from these temptations; but in answer the Lord told him, that his grace was sufficient for him. "For which thing thrice I besought the Lord, that it

might depart from me. And he said: My grace is sufficient for thee"—*ver.* 8, 9. God permits even his servants to be tempted, as well to try their fidelity, as to purify them from their imperfections. And, for the consolation of timid and scrupulous souls, I will here state, that according to the common opinion of theologians, when a soul that fears God and hates sin, is in doubt whether she gave consent to a bad thought, she is not bound, as long as she is not certain of having given consent, to confess it; for it is then morally certain that she has not consented to it. Had she really fallen into grievous sin, she would have no doubt about it; for mortal sin is so horrible a monster, that it is impossible for him who fears God to admit it into the soul without his knowledge.

3. Others, who are not scrupulous, but are ignorant, and have lax consciences, think that evil thoughts, though wilfully indulged, are not mortal sins, unless the act is consummated. This is an error worse than the former. What we cannot lawfully do, we cannot lawfully desire. Hence it is, that a bad thought to which a person consents, has the same malice as the bad act. As sinful works separate us from God, so also do sinful thoughts. "Perverse thoughts separate us from God"—*Wis.*, i. 3. And as all bad actions are known to God, so also he sees all evil thoughts, and will condemn and punish them. "The Lord is a God of all knowledge, and to him are thoughts prepared"—I. *Kings*, ii. 3.

4. However, all bad thoughts are not equally sinful: nor have all those that are sinful, equal malice. In a bad thought we may consider three things: the suggestion, the delectation, and the consent. The suggestion is the first bad thought that is presented to the mind; this is no sin, but, when rejected, is an occasion of merit. "As often", says St. Antonine, "as you resist, you are crowned". The delectation takes place when the person stops as it were, to look at the bad thought, which, by its pleasing appearance, causes delight. Unless the will consent to it, this delectation is not a mortal sin; but it is a venial sin, and, if not resisted, the soul is in danger of consenting to it: but, when this danger is not proximate, the sin is only venial. But it is necessary to remark, that when the thought which excites the delight is against chastity, we are, according to the common opinion of theologians, bound under pain of mortal sin to give a

positive resistance to the delectation caused by the thought; because, if not resisted, the delight easily obtains the consent of the will. "Unless a person repel delectations", says St. Anselm, "the delight passes to consent, and kills the soul"—*St. Ans. Simil.*, *c.* xl. Hence, though a person, should not consent to the sin, if he delight in the obscene object, and do not endeavour to resist the delectation, he is guilty of a mortal sin, by exposing himself to the proximate danger of consent. "How long shall hurtful thoughts abide in thee?"—*Jer.*, iv. 14. Why, says the Prophet, do you allow hurtful thoughts to remain in the mind? Why do you not make an effort to banish them from the heart? God wishes us to watch over the heart with great care; because on the heart—that is, the will—our life depends. "With all watchfulness keep thy heart; because life issueth out from it"—*Prov.*, iv. 23. Finally, the consent, which is the cause of mortal sin, takes place when the person clearly knows that the object is mortally sinful, and embraces it perfectly with the will.

5. A person may sin grievously by thought in two ways: by desire, and by complacency. A person sins by desire, when he wishes to do the bad act which he desires, or would wish to do it if he had the opportunity: the desire is a mortal or a venial sin, according as the act which he desires to do, is mortally or venially sinful. However, in practice, the commission of the external act always increases the malice of the will; either because it ordinarily increases the complacency which the will indulges, or causes it to continue for a longer time. Hence, if the act followed, it is necessary to mention it in confession. A person sins by complacency, when he does not desire to commit the sinful act, but delights in it as if he had committed it. This complacency is called *morose delectation.* It is called *morose*, not because the complacency in the thought of the unchaste act lasts for a considerable time, but, because the will dwells with delight on the thought. Hence the sin of complacency may, as St. Thomas teaches, be committed in a moment. "Dicitur morosa", says the holy doctor, "non ex mora temporis, sed ex eo quod ratio deliberans circa eam immoratur revolvens libenter quæ statim respui debuerunt"—1, 2, *qu.* 74, *a.* 1, *ad.* 3. He says *libenter* (wilfully), to remove scruples from persons of timorous conscience, who suffer against their will certain carnal motions and delights, although they do all in their power to banish

them. Though the inferior part should feel a certain delight, as long as the will does not consent, there is no sin, at least no mortal sin. I repeat with St. Augustine, that what is not voluntary is by no means sinful. "Malum nullo modo sit peccatum, si non sit voluntarium"—*de Vera Rel.*, *c.* xiv. In temptations against chastity, the spiritual masters advise us, not so much to contend with the bad thought, as to turn the mind to some spiritual, or, at least, indifferent object. It is useful to combat other bad thoughts face to face, but not thoughts of impurity.

Second point. The great danger of bad thoughts.

6. It is necessary to guard with all possible caution against bad thoughts, which are an abomination to God. "Evil thoughts are an abomination to the Lord"—*Prov.*, xv. 26. They are called *an abomination to the Lord*, because, as the holy Council of Trent says, bad thoughts, particularly thoughts against the ninth and tenth commandments, sometimes inflict on the soul a deeper wound, and are more dangerous than external acts. "Nonnumquam animam gravius sauciant, et periculosiora sunt iis quæ in manifesto admittuntur"—*sess.* 14, *de Pœna.*, *cap.* v. They are more dangerous on many accounts; first, because sins of thought are more easily committed than sins of action. The occasions of sinful acts are frequently wanting; but sins of thought are committed without the occasion. When a soul has turned her back on God, the heart is continually intent on evil, which causes delight, and thus multiplies sins without number. "All the thought of their heart was bent upon evil at all times"—*Gen.*, vi. 5.

7. Secondly, at the hour of death sinful actions cannot be committed; but we may then be guilty of sins of thought; and he who has had a habit of consenting to bad thoughts during life, will be in danger of indulging them at death: for then the temptations of the Devil are most violent. Knowing that he has but little time to gain the soul, he makes great efforts to bring her into sin. "The Devil is come down unto you, having great wrath, knowing that he hath but a short time"—*Apoc.*, xii. 12. Being in danger of death, St. Eleazar, as Surius relates, was so severely tempted with bad thoughts, that, after his recovery, he said: *Oh! how great is the power of the devils at the hour of death!* The saint conquered the temptations, because he was accustomed

to reject bad thoughts. But miserable the man that has contracted the habit of committing them. Father Segneri relates, that a certain sinner indulged evil thoughts during life. At death he made a sincere confession of all his sins, and was truly sorry for them; but, after death, he appeared to a person and said he was damned. He stated, that his confession was valid, and that God had pardoned all his sins: that, before death, the Devil represented to him, that should he recover from his illness, it would be an act of ingratitude to forsake a certain woman who had a great affection for him. He banished the first temptation: a second came, which he also rejected; but having continued to think on it for a little, he was tempted a third time, yielded to the temptation, and thus he was lost.

Third point. On the remedies against bad thoughts.

8. The Prophet Isaias says that to be freed from bad thoughts, we must take away the evil of our thoughts. "Take away the evil of your devices"—*Isa.*, i. 16. What does he mean by taking away the evil of our devices? He means that we should take away the occasions of evil thoughts, avoid dangerous occasions, and keep at a distance from bad company. I knew a young man who was an angel; but, in consequence of a word which he heard from a bad companion, he had an evil thought and consented to it. He was of opinion that this was the only grievous sin which he committed in his whole life; for he afterwards became a religious, and, after some years, died a holy death. Thus, it is also necessary to abstain from reading books that are obscene, or otherwise bad. You must, moreover, avoid dances with females, and profane comedies: at least when the dances or comedies are immodest.

9. Some young men will ask: Father, is it sinful to make love? I say: I cannot assert, that of itself it is a mortal sin; but persons who do so, are often in the proximate occasion of mortal sin; and experience shows that few of them are found free from grievous faults. It is useless for them to say, that they neither had a bad motive, nor bad thoughts. This is an illusion of the Devil: in the beginning he does not suggest bad thoughts; but when by frequent conversations together, and by frequently speaking of love, the affection of these lovers has

become strong, the Devil will make them blind to the danger and sinfulness of their conduct, and they shall find that, without knowing how, they have lost their souls and God by many sins of impurity and scandal. Oh! how many young persons of both sexes does the Devil gain in this way! And of all those sins of scandal God will demand an account of fathers and mothers, who are bound, but neglect, to prevent these dangerous conversations. Hence they are the cause of all these evils, and shall be severely chastised by God for them.

10. Above all, in order to avoid bad thoughts, men must abstain from looking at women, and females must be careful not to look at men. I repeat the words of Job which I have frequently quoted. "I made a covenant with my eyes, that I would not so much as think upon a virgin"—*Job*, xxxi. 1. He says, that he made a covenant with his eyes that he would not think. What have the eyes to do with thinking? The eyes do not think; the mind alone thinks. But he had just reason to say, that he made a covenant with his eyes that he would not think on women; for St. Bernard says, that through the eyes the darts of impure love, which kills the soul, enter into the mind. "Per oculos intrat in mentem sagitta impuri amoris". Hence the Holy Ghost says: "Turn away thy face from a woman dressed up"—*Eccl.*, ix. 8. It is always dangerous to look at young persons elegantly dressed; and to look at them purposely and without a just cause, is, at least, a venial sin.

12. When thoughts against chastity, which often occur without any immediate occasion, present themselves, it is, as I have said, necessary to banish them at once, without beginning to argue with the temptation. The instant you perceive the thought, reject it, without giving ear to it, or examining what it says or represents to you. It is related in the book of the sentences of the fathers, § 4, that St. Pachomius one day saw a devil boasting that he often made a certain monk fall into sin; because, when tempted, the monk, instead of turning to God, listened to his suggestions, and began to reason with the temptations. But the saint heard another devil complaining, that he could gain nothing from the monk whom he tempted; because the monk immediately had recourse to God for help, and thus he was always victorious. This is the advice of St. Jerome: As soon as lust shall suggest evil, let us exclaim: The

Lord is my helper. "Statim ut libido titillaverat sensum, erumpamus in vocem: Domine auxiliator meus"—*Epist.* 22, *ad Eustoch.*

12. Should the temptation continue, it will be very useful to make it known to your confessor. St. Philip Neri used to say, that "*a temptation disclosed is half conquered*". In assaults of impurity, some saints have had recourse to very severe mortifications. St. Benedict rolled his naked body among thorns. St. Peter of Alcantara threw himself into a frozen pool. But I consider the best means of overcoming these temptations to be, to have recourse to God, who will certainly give us the victory. "Praising, I will call on the Lord", said David, "and I shall be saved from my enemies"—*Ps.*, xvii. 4. And when, after asking aid from God, the temptation continues, we must not cease to pray, but must multiply prayers: we must sigh and groan before the most holy sacrament in the chapel, or before a crucifix in our own room, or before some image of most holy Mary, who is the mother of purity. It is true, all our efforts are useless unless God sustains us by his own hand; but he sometimes requires these efforts on our part, that he may supply our deficiency, and secure to us the victory. In such combats with Hell, it is useful in the beginning to renew our purpose never to offend God, and to forfeit life rather than lose his grace; and then, we must make repeated petitions to him, saying: Lord, give me strength to resist this temptation: do not permit me to be separated from thee: deprive me of life, rather than allow me to lose thee.

SERMON XLVIII.

FOR THE NINETEENTH SUNDAY AFTER PENTECOST.

On the pain of loss which the damned suffer in Hell.

"Cast him into the exterior darkness: there shall be weeping and gnashing of teeth"—*Mat.*, xxii. 13.

According to all laws, divine and human, the punishment of crime should be proportioned to its grievousness. "According to the measure of the sin shall the measure also of the stripes be"—*Deut.*, xxv. 2. Now, the principal injury which sinners do to God by mortal sin, consists in turning their back upon their Creator and their Sovereign Good. St. Thomas defines mortal sin to be "*a turning away from the immutable good*"—*p.* 1, *qu.* 24, *art.* 4. Of this injury the Lord complains in the following words: "Thou hast forsaken me, saith the Lord; thou hast gone backward"—*Jer.*, xv. 6. Since, then, the greatest guilt of the sinner consists in deliberately consenting to lose God, the loss of God shall constitute his greatest punishment in Hell. *There shall be weeping.* In Hell there is continual weeping; but what is the object of the bitterest tears of the unhappy damned? It is the thought of having lost God through their own fault. This shall be the subject of the present discourse. Be attentive, brethren.

1. No, dearly beloved Christians; the goods of the Earth are not the end for which God has placed you in the world; the end for which he has created you is the attainment of eternal life. "And the end life eternal"—*Rom.*, vi. 22. Eternal life consists in loving God, and possessing him for eternity. Whosoever attains this end shall be for ever happy; but he who, through his own fault, does not attain it, loses God; he shall be miserable for eternity, and shall weep for ever, saying: "My end is perished"—*Lamen.*, iii. 18.

2. The pain produced by loss is proportioned to the value of what has been lost. If a person lose a jewel—a diamond worth a hundred crowns, he feels great pain; if the diamond were worth two hundred crowns, the pain is double: if worth four hundred, the pain is still greater. Now, I ask, what is the good which a damned soul has lost? She has lost God; she has lost an infinite good. The pain, then, arising from the loss of God is an infinite pain. "The pain of the damned", says St. Thomas, "is infinite, because it is the loss of an infinite good"—1, 2, *qu.* 87, *a.* 4. Such, too, is the doctrine of St. Bernard, who says, that the value of the loss of the damned is measured from the infinitude of God, the supreme good. Hence, Hell does not consist in its devouring fire, nor in its intolerable stench, nor in the unceasing shrieks and howlings of the damned, nor in the terrific sight of the devils, nor in the narrowness of that pit of torments, in which the damned are thrown one over the other: the pain which constitutes Hell, is the loss of God. In comparison of this pain, all the other torments of Hell are trifling. The reward of God's faithful servants in Heaven is, as he said to Abraham, God himself. "I am thy reward, exceeding great"—*Gen.*, xv. 1. Hence, as God is the reward of the blessed in Heaven, so the loss of God is the punishment of the damned in Hell.

3. Hence, St. Bruno has truly said, that how great soever the torments which may be inflicted on the damned, they never can equal the great pain of being deprived of God. Add torments to torments, but do not deprive them of God. "Addantur tormenta tormentis, et Deo non priventur"—*serm. de Jud. Fin.* According to St. Chrysostom, a thousand Hells are not equal to this pain. Speaking of the loss of God, he said: "Si mille dixeris gehennas, nihil par dices illius doloris"—*hom.* xlix., *ad Pop.* God is so lovely, that he deserves infinite love. He is so amiable, that the saints in Heaven are so replenished with joy, and so absorbed in divine love, that they desire nothing but to love God, and think only of loving him with all their strength. At present, sinners, for the sake of their vile pleasures, shut their eyes, and neither know God, nor the love which he deserves; but in Hell, they shall, in punishment of their sins, be made to know that God is an infinite good, and infinitely amiable. "The Lord shall be known when he executeth judgment"—*Ps.*, ix. 17.

The sinner, drowned in sensual pleasures, scarcely knows God: he sees him only in the dark, and therefore he disregards the loss of God. But in Hell he shall know God, and shall be tormented for ever by the thought of having voluntarily lost this infinite good. A certain Parisian doctor appeared after death to his bishop, and said that he was damned. His bishop asked him if he remembered the sciences in which he was so well versed in this life. He answered, that in Hell the damned think only of the pain of having lost God.

4. "Depart from me, ye cursed, into everlasting fire"—*Mat.*, xxv. 41. *Depart from me*. This command constitutes the Hell of the damned. Begone from me; you shall be no longer mine, and I shall be no longer yours. "You are not my people, and I will not be yours"—*Osee*, i. 9. At present, this punishment is, as St. Augustine says, dreaded only by the saints. "Hæc amantibus non contemnentibus pœna est". It is a punishment which affrights the soul that loves God, more than all the torments of Hell; but it does not terrify sinners, who are immersed in the darkness of sin. But at death they shall, for their greater chastisement, understand the infinite good which they have lost through their own fault.

5. It is necessary to know that men have been created for God, and that nature draws them to love him. In this life, the darkness of sin, and the Earthly affections which reign in their hearts, stifle their natural tendency and inclination to a union with God, their sovereign good; and therefore the thought of being separated from him does not produce much pain. But when the soul leaves the body, and is freed from the senses, which keep her in darkness, she then clearly sees that she has been created for God, and that he is the only good which can make her happy. "But", says St. Antonine, "the soul separated from the body, understands that God is her sovereign good, and that she has been created for him". Hence, as soon as she is loosed from the bondage of the body, she rushes forward to embrace her supreme good; but because she is in sin, and his enemy, God will cast her off. Though driven back and chased away, she retains her invincible tendency and inclination to a union with God; and her Hell shall consist in seeing herself always drawn to God, and always banished from him.

6. If a dog see a hare, what efforts does he not make to break

his chain, and seize his prey. Thus, at her separation from the body, the natural inclinations of the soul draw her to God, while at the same time, sin separates her from him, and drags her with it to Hell. Sin, says the prophet, like a wall of immense thickness, is placed between the soul and God, and separates her from him. "But your iniquities have divided between you and your God"—*Isa.*, lix. 2. Hence, the unhappy soul, confined in the prison of Hell, at a distance from God, shall weep for ever, saying: Then, O my God, I shall be no longer thine, and thou wilt be no longer mine. I shall love thee no more, and thou wilt never again love me. This separation from God terrified David, when he said: "Will God then cast off for ever? or will he never be more favourable again?"—*Ps.*, lxxvi. 8. How great, he says, would be my misery if God should cast me from him, and never again be merciful to me! But this misery every damned soul in Hell suffers, and shall suffer for eternity. As long as he remained in sin, David felt his conscience reproaching him, and asking, *Where is thy God?* O David, where is thy God, who once loved thee? Thou hast lost him; he is no longer thine. David was so afflicted at the loss of his God, that he wept night and day. "My tears have been my bread day and night, whilst it has been said to me daily: Where is thy God?"—*Ps.*, xli. 4. Thus, even the devils will say to the damned: Where is your God? By his tears, David appeased and recovered his God; but the damned shall shed an immense sea of tears, and shall never appease nor recover their God.

7. St. Augustine says, that if the damned saw the beauty of God, "they should feel no pain, and Hell itself would be converted into a Paradise"—*lib. de Trip. hab.* But the damned shall never see God. When David forbade his son Absalom to appear in his presence, the sorrow of Absalom was so great, that he entreated Joab to tell his father, that he would rather be put to death, than never more be permitted to see his face. "I beseech thee, therefore, that I may see the face of the king; and if he be mindful of my iniquity, let him kill me"—II. *Kings*, xiv. 32. To a certain grandee, who acted irreverently in the church, Philip the Second said: *Do not dare ever to appear again in my presence.* So intense was the pain which the nobleman felt, that after having returned home, he died of grief.

What then must be the feelings of the reprobate at the hour of death, when God shall say to them: Begone; let me never see you again: you shall never more see my face? "I will hide my face from them; all evils and afflictions shall find them"—*Deut.*, xxxi. 17. What sentiments of pity should we feel at seeing a son who was always united with his father, who always eat and slept with him, weeping over a parent whom he loved so tenderly, and saying: My father, I have lost you; I shall never see you more. Ah! if we saw a damned soul weeping bitterly, and asked her the cause of her wailing, she would answer: I weep because I have lost God, and shall never see him again.

8. The pain of the reprobate shall be increased by the knowledge of the glory which the saints enjoy in Paradise, and from which they see, and shall for ever see, themselves excluded. How great would be the pain which a person should feel, if, after being invited by his sovereign to his own theatre, to be present at the singing, dancing, and other amusements, he should be excluded in punishment of some fault! How bitter should be his anguish and disappointment, when, from without, he would hear the shouts of joy and applause within! At present, sinners despise Heaven, and lose it for trifles, after Jesus Christ shed the last drop of his blood to make them worthy of entering into that happy kingdom. But when they shall be confined in Hell, the knowledge of the glory of Heaven shall be the greatest of all their torments. St. John Chrysostom says, that to see themselves banished from that land of joy, shall be to the damned a torment ten thousand times as great as the Hell which they suffer. "Decem mille quis ponat gehennas, nihil tale dicet quale est a beata gloria excidere"—*S. Joan. Chry., ap S. Thom. Suppl., qu.* 98, *art.* 9. Oh! that I had at least the hope, the damned will say, that after a thousand, or even a million of ages, I could recover the divine grace, and become worthy of entering into Heaven, there to see God! But no; he shall be told, "When the wicked man is dead, there shall be no hope any more"—*Prov.*, xi. 7. When he was in this life, he could have saved his soul; but, because he has died in sin, his loss is irreparable. Hence, with tears of despair, he shall say: "I shall not see the Lord God in the land of the living"—*Isa.*, xxxviii. 11.

9. The thought of having lost God and Paradise solely through their own fault, shall increase the torture of the damned.

Every damned soul shall say: It was in my power to have led a life of happiness on Earth by loving God, and to have acquired boundless happiness for eternity; but, in consequence of having loved my vices, I must remain in this place of torments as long as God shall be God. She will then exclaim in the words of Job: "Who will grant me that I might be according to the months past, according to the days in which God kept me?"—*Job*, xxix. 2. Oh! that I were allowed to go back to the time I lived on Earth, when God watched over me, that I might not fall into this fire! I did not live among the savages, the Indians, or the Chinese. I was not left without the sacraments, sermons, or masters to instruct me. I was born in the bosom of the true Church, and have been well instructed and frequently admonished by preachers and confessors. To this prison I have not been dragged by the devils; I have come of my own accord. The chains by which I am bound and kept at a distance from God, I have forged with my own will. How often has God spoken to my heart, and said to me: Amend and return to me. Beware lest the time should come when thou shalt not be able to prevent thy destruction. Alas! this time has come; the sentence has been already passed; I am damned; and for my damnation there neither is, nor shall be any remedy, for all eternity. But, if the damned soul has lost God, and shall never see him, perhaps she can at least love him? No; she has been abandoned by grace, and thus she is made the slave of her sins, and compelled to hate him. The damned see that God is their adversary on account of their contempt for him during life, and are therefore always in despair. "Why hast thou set me opposite to thee, and I am become burdensome to myself"—*Job*, vii. 20. Hence, because the damned see that they are enemies of God, whom they at the same time know to be worthy of infinite love, they are to themselves objects of the greatest horror. The greatest of all the punishments which God shall inflict on them, will consist in seeing that God is so amiable, and that they are so deformed, and the enemies of this God. "I will set *thee* before thy face"—*Ps.*, xlix. 21.

10. The sight of all that God has done for the damned shall above all increase their torture. "The wicked shall see and shall be angry"—*Ps.*, cxi. 10. They shall see all the benefits which God bestowed upon them,—all the lights and calls which he gave

them,—and the patience with which he waited for them. They shall, above all, see how much Jesus Christ has loved them, and how much he has suffered for the love of them; and after all his love and all his sufferings, they shall see that they are now objects of his hatred, and shall be no longer objects of his love. According to St. Chrysostom, a thousand Hells are nothing, compared with the thought of being hateful to Christ. "Si mille quis ponat, gehennas, nihil tale dicturus est, quale est exosum esse Christo"—*hom.* xxiv., *in Matt.* Then the damned shall say: My Redeemer, who, through compassion for me, sweated blood, suffered an agony in the garden, and died on the cross bereft of all consolation, has now no pity on me! I weep, I cry out; but he no longer hears or looks to me. He is utterly forgetful of me. He once loved me; but now he hates and justly hates me; for I have ungratefully refused to love him. David says, that the reprobate are thrown into the pit of death. "Thou shalt bring them down into the pit of destruction"—*Ps.*, liv. 24. Hence St. Augustine has said: "The pit shall be closed on top, it shall be opened at the bottom, it shall be expanded downwards; and they who refused to know God, shall be no longer known by him". "Puteus claudetur sursum, aperietur deorsum, dilatatibur in profundum: et ultra nescientur a Deo qui Deum scire noluerunt"—*hom.* xvi., *cap.* 50.

11. Thus the damned see that God deserves infinite love, and that they cannot love him. St. Catherine of Genoa being one day assailed by the Devil, asked him who he was. He answered with tears: *I am that wicked one who is deprived of the love of God.* I am that miserable being that can never more love God. They not only cannot love God, but, abandoned in their sins, they are forced to hate him: their Hell consists in hating God whom they at the same time know to be infinitely amiable. They love him intensely as their sovereign good, and hate him as the avenger of their sins. "Res miserrima", says a learned author, "amare vehementer, et amatum simul odisse"—*Magnotius Medit.* Their natural love draws them continually to God; but their hatred drags them away from him. These two contrary passions, like two ferocious wild beasts, incessantly tear in pieces the hearts of the damned, and cause, and shall for all eternity cause them to live in a continual death. The reprobate then shall hate and curse all the benefits which God has bestowed upon them. The shall hate the benefits

of creation, of redemption, and the sacraments. But they shall hate in a particular manner the sacrament of baptism, by which they have, on account of their sins, been made more guilty in the sight of God; the sacrament of penance, by which, if they wished, they could have so easily saved their souls; and above all, the most holy sacrament of the altar, in which God had given himself entirely to them. They shall consequently hate all the other means which have been helps to their salvation. Hence, they shall hate and curse all the angels and saints. But they shall curse particularly their guardian-angels,—their special advocates; and, above all, the divine mother Mary. They shall curse the Three Divine Persons,—the Father, the Son, and the Holy Ghost; but particularly Jesus Christ, the Incarnate Word, who suffered so much and died for their salvation. They shall curse the wounds of Jesus Christ, the blood of Jesus Christ, and the death of Jesus Christ. Behold the end to which accursed sin leads the souls which Jesus Christ has so dearly bought.

SERMON XLIX.

FOR THE TWENTIETH SUNDAY AFTER PENTECOST.

On the predominant passion.

"For he was at the point of death..Lord, come down before that my son die"—*John*, iv. 47, 49.

OUR passions are not of themselves bad nor hurtful. When regulated according to the dictates of reason and prudence, they do us no injury, but are, on the contrary, profitable to the soul; but, when disorderly, they are productive of irreparable mischief to those who obey them; for, when any passion takes possession of the heart, it obscures the truth, and makes the soul incapable of distinguishing between good and evil. Ecclesiasticus implored the Lord to deliver him from a mind under the sway of passion. "Give me not over to a shameless and foolish mind"—*Eccl.*, xxiii. 6. Let us, then, be careful not to allow any bad passion to rule over us. In this day's gospel it is related, that a certain ruler, whose son was at the point of death (incipiebat enim mori), knowing that Jesus Christ had come into Galilee, went in search of him, and entreated him to come and cure his son. "Come down before that my son die". The same may be said of him who begins to submit to the tyranny of any passion. *He is at the point of the death* of the soul, which should be dreaded far more than the death of the body. Hence, if he wishes to preserve spiritual life, he ought to ask the Lord to deliver him as soon as possible from that passion—*Lord, come down before my soul die:* if he do not, he shall be miserably lost. I intend to-day to show the great danger of damnation to which all who submit to the domination of any bad passion, are exposed.

1. "Only this", said Solomon, "I found, that God made man right, and he hath entangled himself with an infinity of questions"—*Eccl.*, vii. 30. *God created man right,*—that is, in

the state of justice; but, by giving ear to the serpent, man exposed himself to temptation, and was conquered. He rebelled against God, and his passions rebelled against himself. These are the passions which, according to St. Paul, cause a continual war between the flesh and the spirit. "For the flesh lusteth against the spirit, and the spirit against the flesh"—*Gal.*, v. 17. However, with the aid of divine grace, it is in man's power to resist these passions, and not to allow them to rule over him. It is, as the Lord told Cain, even in the power of man to rule over them, and to bring them into subjection to reason. "But the lust thereof shall be under thee, and thou shalt have dominion over it"—*Gen.*, iv. 7. Let the assaults of the flesh and of the Devil to make us abandon the way of God, be ever so violent, Jesus Christ has said: "Lo! the kingdom of God is within you" —*Luke*, xvii. 21. Within us he has established a kingdom, in which the will is the queen that ought to rule over all the senses and passions. And what greater honour or glory can a man have, than to be the master of his passions?

2. The proper regulation of the motions of the mind constitutes the interior mortification so much recommended by spiritual masters, and secures the salvation of the soul. The health of the body depends on the regulation of the humours:—if one of them predominate to excess, it causes death. But the health of the soul consists in the proper control of the passions by reason. But, when any passion rules over reason, it first enslaves, and then kills the soul.

3. Many pay great attention to their external conduct: they endeavour to appear modest and respectful; but, at the same time, they cherish in their hearts sinful affections against justice, charity, humility, and chastity. For them is prepared the chastisement with which the Saviour threatened the Scribes and Pharisees, who were careful to have their cups and dishes clean, but nourished within unjust and unclean thoughts. "Wo to you, Scribes and Pharisees,—hypocrites; because you make clean the outside of the cup and of the dish; but, within, you are full of rapine and uncleanness"—*Matt.*, xxiii. 25. The Royal Prophet says, that all the beauty of a soul that is the true daughter of God, consists in an interior good will. "All the glory of the king's daughter is within"—*Ps.*, xliv. 14. Of what use, then, says St. Jerome, is it

to abstain from food, and, at the same time to allow the mind to swell with pride? or, to abstain from wine, and to indulge in the drunkenness of anger? "Quid prodest tenuari abstinentia, si animus superbia intumescit? quid vinum non bibere, et odio inebriari?" Christians who act in this manner, do not lay aside their vices; they only cover them with the mantle of devotion. A man, then, must divest himself of all bad passions; otherwise he will not be the king, but the slave of his affections, and in opposition to the command of the Apostle, sin shall reign in his heart: "Let not sin, therefore, reign in your mortal body, so as to obey the lusts thereof"—*Rom.*, vi. 12. Man, then, is, as St. Thomas says, the king of himself when he regulates his body and his carnal affections according to reason. "Rex est homo per rationem, quia per eam regit totum corpus et affectus ejus"—*in Joan.*, iv. But according to St. Jerome, "when the soul serves vice, she loses the honour of a kingdom"—*in Thren.*, ii. 7. She loses the honour of a queen, and becomes, as St. John teaches, the slave of sin. "Whosoever committeth sin, is the servant of sin"—*John*, viii. 34.

4. St. James exhorts us to treat the body and its lusts as we treat a horse. We put a bridle in the mouth of a horse, and we bring him wherever we please. "We put bits into the mouths of horses, that they may obey us, and we turn about their whole body"—*St. James*, iii. 3. Hence, as soon as we feel the cravings of any bad passion, we must restrain it with the bridle of reason; for, if we yield to its demands, it will bring us to the level of brute animals, that obey not the dictates of reason, but the impulse of their beastly appetites. "And man, when he was in honour, did not understand: he is compared to senseless beasts, and is become like to them"—*Ps.*, xlviii 13. "It is worse", says St. John Chrysostom, "to become like, than to be born, a senseless beast; for, to be naturally without reason is tolerable". The saint says, that to want reason by nature is not disgraceful; but, to be born with the gift of reason, and afterwards to live like a beast, obeying the lusts of the flesh, is degrading to man, and makes him worse than a senseless brute. What would you say, if you saw a man who would, of his own accord, live in a stable with horses, feed with them on hay and oats, and sleep, as they do, on dung? The man who

submits to the tyranny of any passion, does what is far worse in the eyes of God.

5. It was thus the Gentiles lived, who, because the darkness of their understanding prevented them from discerning between good and evil, went wherever their sensual appetite led them. "That you walk not", says St. Paul, "as also the Gentiles walk, in the vanity of their mind, having their understanding darkened"—*Ephes.*, iv. 17, 18. Hence they were abandoned to their vices,—to impurity and avarice; and blindly obeyed the commands of their passions. "Who, despairing, have given themselves up to lasciviousness, unto the working of all uncleanness, unto covetousness"—*verse* 19. To this miserable state are reduced all Christians who, despising reason and God, follow the dictates of passion. In punishment of their sins, God abandons them as he abandoned the Gentiles, to their own wicked desires. "Wherefore God gave them up to the desires of their own heart"—*Rom.*, i. 24. This is the greatest of all chastisements.

6. St. Augustine writes, that two cities may be built up in the heart of a Christian; one by the love of God, the other by self-love. "Cœlestem *(civetatim)* ædificat amor Dei usque ad contemptum sui; terrestrem ædificat amor sui usque ad contemptum Dei"—*lib.* XIV. *de Civ.*, *cap.* xxviii. Thus, if the love of God reign within us, we will despise ourselves: if self-love reign, we will despise God. But, in conquering self-love consists the victory to which shall be given a crown of eternal glory. This was the great maxim which St. Francis Xavier always inculcated to his disciples,—*Conquer yourself; conquer yourself.* All the thoughts and feelings of man, says the Scripture, are inclined to evil from his boyhood. "The imagination and thought of man's heart are prone to evil from his youth"—*Gen.*, viii. 21. Hence we must, during our whole life, zealously combat and conquer the evil inclinations which continually rise up within us, as noxious weeds spring up in our gardens. Some will ask how they can free themselves from bad passions, and how they can prevent them from starting up within them. St. Gregory gives the answer:—"It is one thing to look at these beasts, and another to keep them within the den of the heart"—*Mor.*, *lib.* VI., *cap.* xvi. It is one thing, says the saint, to look at these beasts, or bad passions, when they are

outside, and another to harbour them in the heart. As long as they are outside, they can do us no harm; but if we admit them into the soul, they devour us.

7. All bad passions spring from self-love. This is, as Jesus Christ teaches all who wish to follow him, the principal enemy which we have to contend with; and this enemy we must conquer by self-denial. "If any one shall come after me, let him deny himself"—*Mat.*, xvi. 24. "Non intrat in te, amor Dei", says Thomas a Kempis, "nisi exulet amor tui". Unless we banish self-love from the heart, the love of God cannot enter. Blessed Angela of Foligno used to say, that she was more afraid of self-love than of the Devil; because self-love has greater power than the Devil to draw us into sin. St. Mary Magdalene de Pazzi used to say the same, as we read in her life. "Self-love is the greatest traitor we have to guard against. Like Judas, it betrays us with a kiss. He who conquers it, conquers all enemies; he who does not conquer it, is lost". The saint then adds: "If you cannot kill it with a single stroke, give it poison". She meant, that since we are not able to destroy this accursed enemy, which, according to St. Francis de Sales, dies only with our last breath, we must at least labour to weaken it as much as possible; for, when strong, it kills us. Death, says St. Basil, is the reward which self-love gives to its followers. The wages of self-love is death; it is the beginning of every evil. "Stipendium amoris proprii mors est, initium omnis mali"—*S. Bas. Apud Lyreum, lib.* II. Self-love seeks not what is just and honourable, but what is agreeable to the senses. Hence Jesus Christ has said: "*He that loveth this life*"—that is, his sensual appetite or self-will—"*shall lose it*"—*John*, xii. 25. He who truly loves himself, and wishes to save his soul, should refuse to the senses whatever God has forbidden; otherwise he shall lose God and himself.

8. There are two principal passions which reign within us:—the concupiscible and irascible appetites—that is, love and hatred. I have said, *two principal passions;* for each of them, when vicious, draws in its train many other bad passions. The concupiscible appetite brings with it temerity, ambition, greediness, avarice, jealousy, scandal. The irascible brings with it revenge, injustice, slander, envy. St. Augustine advises us, in our combat with the passions, not to endeavour to beat them all down

in a single conflict. "Calca jacentem, conflige cum resistente"—*in cap.* viii. *Rom.* We must trample on the passion which we have cast to the ground, so that it may be no longer able to contend with us; and then we must endeavour to subdue the other passions which resist our efforts.

9. But we must endeavour above all to find out our predominant passion. He who conquers this, conquers all his passions; he who allows himself to be overcome by it, is lost. God commanded Saul to destroy all the Amalecites, along with all their animals, and all their property. He destroyed everything that was vile, but spared the life of King Agag, and preserved all that was valuable and beautiful. "And Saul and the people spared Agag, and the rest of the flocks of sheep,......and all that was beautiful, and would not destroy them; but everything that was vile, and good for nothing, that they destroyed"—I. *Kings*, xv. 9. In this Saul was afterwards imitated by the Scribes and Pharisees, to whom our Lord said: "Wo to you Scribes and Pharisees, because you tithe mint, and anise, and cummin, and have left the weightier things of the law, judgment, and mercy, and faith"—*Mat.*, xxiii. 23. They were careful to pay the tithe of things of least value, and neglected the more important things of the law, such as justice, charity to their neighbour, and faith in God. Some persons act in a similar manner; they abstain from certain defects of minor importance, and, at the same time, allow themselves to be ruled by their predominant passion; but, if they do not destroy this passion, they never shall gain the victory of salvation. The King of Syria commanded the captains of his cavalry to kill the King of Israel only, and not to mind the others. "Fight ye not with small or great, but with the King of Israel only"—II. *Paral.*, xviii. 30. They obeyed the order, slew King Achab, and gained the victory.

10. We must imitate the captains of Syria: unless we kill the king—that is, the predominant passion—we shall never be able to obtain salvation. The passion which brings man under its sway, first blinds him and prevents him from seeing his danger. Now, how can a blind man, led by a blind guide, such as passion, which follows not reason, but sensual pleasures, possibly avoid falling into some abyss? "If the blind lead the blind, both fall into the pit"—*Mat.*, xv. 14. St. Gregory says, that it is a

common artifice of the Devil, to inflame daily more and more our predominant passion, and thus he brings us into many horrible excesses. Through passion for a kingdom, Herod spilled the blood of so many innocent infants. Through love for a woman, Henry the Eighth was the cause of so many frightful spiritual evils, put to death several most worthy individuals, and, in the end, lost the faith. No wonder; for he who is under the domination of any passion, no longer sees what he does. Therefore he disregards corrections, excommunications, and even his own damnation: he seeks only his own pleasures, and says: Come what will, I must satisfy this passion. And, as eminent virtue is accompanied by other virtues, so an enormous vice brings in its train other vices. "In catena iniquitatis", says St. Lawrence Justinian, "fœderata sunt vitia".

11. It is necessary, then, as soon as we perceive any passion beginning to reign within us, to beat it down instantly, before it acquires strength. "Lest cupidity gain strength", says St. Augustine, "strike it down while it is small"—*in Ps.*, cxxxvi. St. Ephrem gives the same advice: "Unless you quickly destroy passions, they cause an ulcer"—*de Perfect.* A wound, if it be not closed up, will soon become an incurable ulcer. To illustrate this by an example, a certain monk, as St. Dorotheus relates (*serm.* xi.), commanded one of his disciples to pluck up a small cypress. The disciple obeyed, and drew it up with a slight effort. The monk then ordered him to pull up another tree, which was somewhat larger. He succeeded in the task; but not without a good deal of labour. The disciple was then told to pluck up a tree which had taken deep root; but all his efforts were ineffectual. The monk then said to him: Thus it is, my son, with our passions; when they have taken deep root in the heart, we shall not be able to extirpate them. Dearly beloved brethren, keep always before your eyes this maxim—that either the spirit must trample on the flesh, or the flesh shall trample on the spirit.

12. Cassian has laid down an excellent rule for conquering our passions. Let us endeavour, he says, to change the object of our passions; and thus from being vicious, they shall become holy. Some are prone to anger against all who treat them with disrespect. Such persons ought to change the object of their

passions, and turn their indignation into a hatred of sin, which is more injurious to them than all the devils in Hell. Others are inclined to love every one who possesses amiable qualities: they should fix all their affections on God, who is infinitely amiable. But, to recommend ourselves to God, and to beg of him to deliver us from our passions, is the best remedy against them. And, when any passion becomes very violent, we must multiply prayers. Reasonings and reflections are then of little use; for passion obscures our faculties; and the more we reflect, the more delightful the object of passion appears. Hence, there is no other remedy than to have recourse to Jesus and to most holy Mary, saying with tears and sighs: *Lord, save us, or we perish: do not permit us to be ever separated from thee. We fly to thy protection, O holy mother of God.* O souls created to love God, let us raise ourselves above the Earth; let us cease to fix our thoughts and affections on the miserable things of this world; let us cease to love dross and smoke and dung; and let us endeavour with all our strength to love the Supreme Infinite Good, our most amiable God, who has made us for himself, and expects us in Heaven to make us happy, and to make us enjoy the very glory which he enjoys for eternity.

SERMON L.

FOR THE TWENTY-FIRST SUNDAY AFTER PENTECOST.

On the eternity of Hell.

"And his lord, being angry, delivered him to the torture until he paid all the debt"—*Mat.*, xviii. 34.

In this day's gospel we find, that a certain servant having badly administered the affairs of his master, was found to owe him a debt of ten thousand talents. The master demanded payment; but the servant falling down, said: "Have patience, and I will pay thee all". The master took pity on him, and forgave the entire debt. One of his fellow-servants who owed him a hundred pence, besought him to have patience, and promised to pay him the last farthing: but the wicked servant cast him into prison. Hearing of this act of cruelty to his fellow-servant, the master sent for him, and said to him: Wicked servant, I have forgiven thee ten thousand talents, and for a debt of a hundred pence thou hast refused to show compassion to thy fellow-servant. He then delivered him to the torturers till he paid all the debt. Behold, dearly beloved brethren, in these last words, a description of the sentence of the eternal death which is prepared for sinners. By dying in sin, they die debtors to God for all their iniquities; and, being unable to make any satisfaction in the other life for their past sins, they remain for ever debtors to the divine justice, and must suffer for eternity in Hell. Of this miserable eternity I will speak to-day: listen to me with attention.

1. The thought of eternity is a great thought: so it was called by St. Augustine—*Magna cogitatio*. According to the holy doctor, God has made us Christians, and instructed us in the maxims of faith, that we may think of eternity. "We are Christians, that we may always think of the world to come". This thought has driven from the world so many of the nobles of the Earth, has made them renounce all their riches, and shut themselves up in the cloister, there to live in poverty and penance. This thought has sent so many young men into caves and deserts, and has animated so many martyrs to embrace torments and death, in order to save their souls for eternity. "For", exclaims St. Paul, "we have not here a lasting city; but we seek one that is to come"—*Heb.*, xiii. 14. This Earth, dearly beloved Christians, is not our country; it is for us a place of passage, through which we must soon pass to the house of eternity. "Man shall go into the house of his eternity"—*Eccl.*, xii. 5. In this eternity the house of the just, which is a palace of delights, is very different from the house of sinners, which is a dungeon of torments. Into one of these two houses each of us must certainly go. "In hanc vel illam æternitatem", says St. Ambrose, "cadam, necesse est"—*S. Amb. in Ps.*, cxviii. "Into this or that eternity I must fall".

2. And where the soul shall first go, there she shall remain for ever. "If the tree fall to the south or to the north, in what place soever it shall fall, there shall it lie"—*Eccl.*, xi. 3. On

what side does a tree fall when it is cut down? It falls on the side to which it inclines. On what side, brethren, will you fall when death shall cut down the tree of your life? You will fall on the side to which you incline. If you shall be found inclining to the south—that is, in favour with God—you shall be for ever happy; but, if you shall fall to the north, you must be for ever miserable. There is no middle place: you must be for ever happy in Heaven, or overwhelmed with despair in Hell. We must all die, says St. Bernard, or some other author *(de quat. Noviss.)*; but we know not which of the two eternities shall be our lot after death. "Necesse mori, post hæc autem dubia æternitas".

3. This uncertainty about his lot for eternity was the constant subject of the thoughts of David: it deprived his eyes of sleep, and kept him always in terror. "My eyes prevented the watches: I was troubled, and I spoke not: I thought upon the days of old, and I had in my mind the eternal years"—*Ps.*, lxxvi. 5, 6. What, says St. Cyprian, has encouraged the saints to lead a life, which, on account of their continual austerities, was an uninterrupted martyrdom? It was, he answers, the thought of eternity that inspired them with courage to submit to such unceasing rigours. A certain monk shut himself in a cave, and did nothing else than constantly exclaim: *O eternity! O eternity!* The famous sinner converted by the Abbot Paphnutius, kept eternity always before her eyes, and was accustomed to say: *Who can assure me of a happy eternity, and that I will not fall into a miserable eternity?* The same uncertainty kept St. Andrew Avellino in continual terrors and tears till his last breath. Hence he used to ask every one he met, *What do you say? shall I be saved or damned for eternity?*

4. Oh! that we too had eternity always before our eyes! We certainly should not be so much attached to the world. "Quisquis in æternitatis desiderio figitur, nec prosperitate attollitur, nec adversitate quassatur: et dum nihil habet in mundo quod appetat, nihil est quod de mundo pertimescat". He who fixes his thoughts on eternity, is not elated by prosperity, nor dejected by adversity; because, having nothing to desire in this world, he has nothing to fear: he desires only a happy eternity, and fears only a miserable eternity. A certain lady, who was greatly attached to the world, went one day to confession to Father M. D'Avila. He

bid her go home, and reflect on these two words—*always* and *never*. She obeyed, took away her affections from the world, and consecrated them to God. St. Augustine says, that the man who thinks on eternity, and is not converted to God, either has no faith, or has lost his reason. "O æternitas! qui te cogitat, nec pœnitet, aut certo fidem non habet, aut si habet, cor non habet"—*in soliloq.* O eternity! he who thinks on thee, and does not repent, has certainly no faith, or has lost his heart. Hence St. Chrysostom relates, that the pagans upbraided the Christians with being liars or fools: liars, if they said they believed what they did not believe; fools, if they believed in eternity and committed sin. "Exprobabant gentiles aut mendaces, aut stultos esse Christianos; mendaces si non crederent quod credere dicebant; stultos si credebant et peccabant".

5. Wo to sinners, says St. Cesarius of Arles; they enter into eternity without having known it; but their woes shall be doubled when they shall have entered into eternity, and shall never be able to leave it. "Væ peccatoribus, incognitam ingrediuntur". To those who enter Hell, the door opens for their admission, but never opens for their departure. "I have the keys of death and of Hell"—*Apoc.*, i. 18. God himself keeps the keys of Hell, to show us that whosoever enters, has no hope of ever escaping from it. St. John Chrysostom writes, that the condemnation of the reprobate is engraved on the pillar of eternity, so that it never shall be revoked. In Hell there is no calendar; there the years are not counted. St. Antonine says, that if a damned soul heard that she was to be released from Hell after so many millions of years as there are drops of water in the sea, or grains of sand in the Earth, she would feel greater joy than a criminal condemned to death would experience, at hearing that he was reprieved, and was to be made the monarch of the whole world. But no; as many millions of years shall pass away, as there are drops of water in the ocean, or grains of dust in the Earth, and the Hell of the damned shall be at its commencement. All these millions of years shall be multiplied an infinite number of times, and Hell will begin again. But of what use is it, says St. Hilary, to count years in eternity? Where you expect the end, there it commences. "Ubi putas finem invenire, ibi incipit". And St. Augustine says, that "things which have an

end, cannot be compared with eternity"—*in Ps.*, xxxvi. Each of the damned would be content to make this compact with God—Lord, increase my torments as much as thou pleasest; assign a term for them as distant as thou pleasest: provided thou fix a time at which they shall cease, I am satisfied. But no; this time shall never arrive. "My end", the damned shall say, "is perished"—*Lamen.*, iii. 18. Then, is there no end to the torments of the damned? No; the trumpet of divine justice sounds in the caverns of Hell, and continually reminds the reprobate, that their Hell shall be eternal, and shall never have an end.

6. If Hell were not eternal, it would not be so frightful a chastisement. Thomas a Kempis says, that "everything which passes with time is trifling and short". Any pain which has an end is not very appalling. The man who labours under an imposthume or cancer, must submit to the knife or the cautery: the pain is severe; but, because it is soon over, it can be borne. But a toothache which lasts for three months without interruption, is insupportable. Were a person obliged to lie in the same posture for six months on a soft bed, or even to hear the same music or the same comedy night and day for one year, he would fall into melancholy and despondency. Poor blind sinners! When threatened with Hell, they say: *If I go there, I must have patience.* But they shall not say so when they will have entered that region of woes, where they must suffer, not by listening to the same music or the same comedy, nor by lying in the same posture, or by toothache, but by enduring all torments and all evils. "I will heap evils upon them"—*Deut.*, xxxii. 23. And all these torments shall never end.

7. They shall never end, and shall never be diminished in the smallest degree. The damned must for ever suffer the same fire, the same privation of God, the same sadness, the same despair. Yes, says St. Cyprian, in eternity there is no change, because the decree is immutable. This thought shall immensely increase their sufferings, by making them feel beforehand, and at each moment, all that they shall have to suffer for eternity. In his description of the happiness of the saints, and the misery of the reprobate, the Prophet Daniel says: "They shall awake, some unto life everlasting, and some unto reproach to see it always"—*Dan.*, xii. 2. They shall always see their unhappy

eternity. *Ut videant semper.* Thus eternity tortures each of the damned not only by his present pains, but with all his future sufferings, which are eternal.

8. These are not opinions controverted among theologians; they are dogmas of faith clearly revealed in the sacred Scriptures. "Depart from me, you cursed, into everlasting fire"—*Matt.*, xxv. 41. Some will say: The fire, but not the punishment, of the damned is everlasting. Such the language of the incredulous, but it is folly. For what other purpose would God make this fire eternal, than to chastise the reprobate, who are immortal? But, to take away every shadow of doubt, the Scriptures, in many other places, say, that not only the fire, but the punishment, of the damned is eternal. "And these", says Jesus Christ, "shall go into everlasting punishment"—*Matt.*, xxv. 46. Again we read in St. Mark, "Where the worm dieth not, and the fire is not extinguished"—ix. 43. St. John says: "And the smoke of their torments shall ascend up for ever and ever"—*Apoc.*, xiv. 11. "Who", says St. Paul, "shall suffer eternal punishment in destruction"—II. *Thess.*, i 9.

9. Another infidel will ask: How can God justly punish with eternal torments, a sin that lasts but a moment? I answer, that the grievousness of a crime is measured not by its duration, but by the enormity of its malice. The malice of mortal sin is, as St. Thomas says, infinite (1, 2, *q.* 87, *art.* 4). Hence, the damned deserve infinite punishment; and, because a creature is not capable of suffering pains infinite in point of intensity, God, as the holy doctor says, renders the punishment of the damned infinite in extension by making it eternal. Moreover, it is just that as long as the sinner remains in his sin, the punishment which he deserves should continue. And therefore, as the virtue of the saints is rewarded in Heaven, because it lasts for ever; so also the guilt of the damned in Hell, because it is everlasting, shall be chastised with everlasting torments. "Quia non recipit causæ remedium", says Eusebius Emissenus, "carebit fine supplicium". The cause of their perverse will continues: therefore their chastisement shall never have an end. The damned are so obstinate in their sins, that even if God offered pardon, their hatred for him would make them refuse it. The Prophet Jeremias, speaking in the name of the reprobate, says: "Why is my sorrow become perpetual and my wound desperate,

so as to refuse to be healed?"—*Jer.*, xv. 18. My wound, they say, is incurable, because I do not wish it to be healed. Now, how can God heal the wound of their perverse will, when they would refuse the remedy, were it offered to them? Hence, the punishment of the reprobate is called a sword, a vengeance which is irrevocable. "I, the Lord, have drawn my sword out of its sheath, not to be turned back"—*Ezech.*, xxi. 5.

10. Death, which is so terrible in this life, is desired in Hell by the damned; but they never shall find it. "And in these days men shall seek death, and shall not find it: and they shall desire to die, and death shall fly from them"—*Apoc.*, xi. 6. They would wish, as a remedy for their eternal ruin, to be exterminated and destroyed. But, "there is no poison of destruction in them"—*Wis.*, i. 14. If a man, condemned to die, be not deprived of life by the first stroke of the axe, his torture moves the people to pity. Miserable damned souls! They live in continual death in the midst of the pains of Hell: death excites in them all the agony of death, but does not give them a remedy by taking away life. "Prima mors", says St. Augustine, "animam nolentem pellit de corpore, secunda mors nolentem tenet in corpore". The first death expels from the body the soul of a sinner who is unwilling to die: but the second death—that is, eternal death—retains in the body a soul that wishes to die. "They are laid in Hell like sheep; death shall feed upon them"—*Ps.*, xlviii. 15. In feeding, sheep eat the blades of grass, but leave the root untouched; hence the grass dies not, but grows up again. It is thus that death treats the damned; it torments them with pain, but spares their life, which may be called the root of suffering.

11. But, if these miserable souls have no chance of release from Hell, perhaps they can at least deceive or flatter themselves with the hope, that God may one day be moved to pity, and free them from their torments? No; in Hell there is no delusion, no flattery, no perhaps; the damned are as certain as they are of God's existence, that their Hell shall have no end. "Thou thoughtest unjustly that I shall be like to thee; *but* I will reprove thee, and set before thy face"—*Ps.*, xlix. 21. They shall for ever see before their eyes their sins and the sentence of their eternal condemnation. "And I will set before thy face"

12. Let us conclude. Thus, most beloved brethren, the affair

of our eternal salvation should be the sole object of all our concerns. "The business for which we struggle", says St. Eucherius, "is eternity". There is question of eternity: there is question whether we will be saved, and be for ever happy in a city of delights; or be damned, and confined for eternity in a pit of fire. This is not an affair of little importance; it is of the utmost and of eternal importance to us. When Thomas More was condemned to death by Henry the Eighth, his wife Louisa went to him for the purpose of tempting him to obey the royal command. Tell me, Louisa, replied the holy man, how many years can I, who am now so old, expect to live? You might, said she, live for twenty years. O foolish woman! he exclaimed, do you want me to condemn my soul to an eternity of torments, for twenty years of life?

13. O God! Christians believe in the existence of Hell, and commit sin! Dearly beloved brethren, let not us also be fools, like so many who are now weeping in Hell. Miserable beings! What benefit do they now derive from all the pleasures which they enjoyed in this life? Speaking of the rich and of the poor, St. John Chrysostom said: "O unhappy felicity, which has drawn the rich to eternal infelicity! O happy infelicity, which has brought the poor to the felicity of eternity!" The saints have buried themselves alive in this life, that, after death, they may not find themselves buried in Hell for all eternity. If eternity were a doubtful matter, we ought even then to make every effort in our power to escape an eternity of torments; but no; it is not a matter of doubt; it is a truth of faith, that after this life each of us must go into eternity, to be for ever in glory, or for ever in despair. St. Teresa says, that it is through a want of faith that so many Christians are lost. As often as we say the words of the Creed *life everlasting*, let us enliven our faith, and remember that there is another life, which never ends; and let us adopt all the means necessary to secure a happy eternity. Let us do all, and give up all; if necessary, let us leave the world, in order to secure eternal happiness. When eternity is at stake, no security can be too great. "Nulla nimia securitas", says St. Bernard, "ubi periclitatur æternitas".

SERMON LI.

FOR THE TWENTY-SECOND SUNDAY AFTER PENTECOST.

Straits and anguish of dying Christians who have been negligent during life about the duties of religion.

"Render, therefore, to Cesar the things that are Cesar's, and to God the things that are God's"—*Matt.*, xxii. 21.

ONE day the Pharisees, with the malignant intention of ensnaring him in his speech, that they might afterwards accuse him before the ministers of Cesar, sent their disciples to ask Jesus Christ, if it were lawful to pay tribute to Cesar. In answer the Redeemer, after looking at the coin of the tribute, asked: "Whose image and inscription is this?" Being told that it was Cesar's, he said: "Render then to Cesar the things that are Cesar's, and to God the things that are God's". By these words Jesus Christ wishes to teach us, that it is our duty to give to men what is due to them; and to reserve for him all the affections of our heart, since he created us to love him, and afterwards imposed upon us a precept of loving him. "Thou shalt love the Lord thy God with thy whole heart". Miserable the man who, at the hour of death, shall see that he has loved creatures, that he has loved his pleasures, and has not loved God. "When distress cometh upon them, they will seek peace, and there will be none"—*Ezech.*, vii. 25. They will then seek peace, but shall not find it; for many causes of distress and trouble shall assail them. What shall these causes be? Behold, the unhappy man shall then say, first: O God! I could have become a saint, but have not become one. Secondly, he shall say: Oh! that I now had time to repair the evil I have done! but time is at an end. Thirdly: Oh! that at least, in the short time which remains, I could remedy the past! but, alas! this time is not fit for repairing past evils.

First point. O God! I could have, but have not, become a saint.

1. Because, during their whole life, they thought only of pleasing God and sanctifying themselves, the saints go with great confidence to meet death, which delivers them from the miseries and dangers of the present life, and unites them perfectly with God. But the man who has thought only of his pleasures and of his own ease, and has neglected to recommend himself to God, or to reflect on the account which he must one day render, cannot meet death with confidence. Poor sinners! they banish the thought of death whenever it presents itself to them, and think only of living in pleasures and amusements, as if they were never to die. But, for each of them, the end must one day come. "The end is come; the end is come"—*Ezech.*, vii. 2. And when this end is come, every one must gather the fruit which he has sown during his life. "For what things a man shall sow, those also shall he reap"—*Gal.*, vi. 8. If he has sown works of holiness, he shall receive rewards and eternal life; but if he has sown evil works, he shall reap chastisements and eternal death.

2. The scene of his past life is the first thing which shall rush on the mind of the dying man, when the news of death will be announced to him. He shall then see things in a light very different from that in which he viewed them during life. The acts of revenge which appeared to him lawful—the scandals which he disregarded—the liberty of speaking obscenely and injuriously to the character of his neighbour—the pleasures which were regarded as innocent—the acts of injustice which he held to be allowable, shall then appear what they really were—grievous sins and offences against God, each of which merited Hell. Alas! those blind sinners, who voluntarily blind themselves during life, by shutting their eyes to the light, shall, at death, involuntarily see all the evil they have done. "Then shall the eyes of the blind be opened"—*Isa.*, xxxv. 5. At the light of the candle which lights him to death, "the wicked shall see and shall be angry"—*Ps.*, cxi. 10. He shall see all the irregularities of his past life—his frequent abuse of the sacraments, confessions made without sorrow or purpose of amendment, contracts completed with remorse of conscience, injury done to the property and reputation of others, immodest jests, rancours, and

vindictive thoughts. He shall then see the bad examples which he gave to young persons who feared God, and whom he treated with contempt and turned into derision, by calling them hypocrites and other reproachful names. He shall see so many lights and calls received from God, so many admonitions of spiritual fathers, and so many resolutions and promises made, but afterwards neglected.

3. He shall see particularly the bad maxims by which he regulated his conduct during life. *It is necessary to seek the esteem of the world, and to preserve honour.* But, is it necessary for a man to preserve his honour by trampling on the honour due to God? *We ought to indulge in amusements as often as we can.* But is it lawful to indulge in amusements by insulting God? *Of what use to the world is the man who lives in poverty and has no money?* But, will you, for the sake of money, lose your soul? In answer to these questions, the sinner says: *No matter. What can be done? If we do not make a fortune in the world, we cannot appear among our equals.* Such the maxims of the worldling during life; but, at death, he shall change his language. He shall then see the truth of that maxim of Jesus Christ, "What doth it profit a man, if he gain the whole world, and suffer the loss of his own soul?"—*Mat.*, xvi. 26. Unhappy me! the worldling shall exclaim on the bed of death, I have had so much time to tranquillize my conscience, and behold, I am now at the point of death, and I find my soul burdened with so many sins! What would it have cost me to have broken off such a friendship, to have gone to confession every week, to have avoided certain occasions of sin? Ah! very little; but, though it should have cost me a great deal of pain and labour, I ought to have submitted to every inconvenience in order to save my soul. Salvation is of greater importance to me than the dominion of the entire world. But, alas! the sentiments of negligent Christans at death, are as fruitless as the sorrows of the damned, who mourn in Hell over their sins as the cause of their perdition, but mourn in vain.

4. At that time they derive no consolation from their past amusements or pomps, from their exalted dignities, or from the humiliation of their rivals. On the contrary, at the hour of death, these things, like so many swords, shall pierce their hearts. "Evils shall catch the unjust man unto destruction"—*Ps.*, cxxxix. 12.

At present the lovers of the world seek after banquets, dances, games, and scenes of laughter and joy; but, at the time of death this laughter and joy, as St. James says, shall be turned into mourning and affliction. "Let your laughter be turned into mourning, and your joy into sorrow"—*St. James*, iv. 9. Of this we see frequent examples. A young man, who entertained his companions by sallies of wit and by immodest jests, is seized with a severe illness. His friends come to see him, and find him overwhelmed with grief and melancholy. He indulges no more in jests, or laughter, or conversation. If he speaks at all, his words are words of terror or despair. His friends ask why he speaks so despondingly—why he is so melancholy? Have courage, they say; your illness is not dangerous. They endeavour to inspire hope and cheerfulness: but he is silent. And how can he be cheerful when he feels his conscience burdened with many sins, sees that he must soon appear before Jesus Christ to give an account of his entire life, and that he has much reason to fear that he shall receive the sentence of eternal death? He will then say: O fool that I have been! Oh! that I had loved God! Had I loved him, I should not now find myself in these straits, in this anguish. Oh! that I had time to tranquillize the troubles of my conscience! Let us pass to the second point.

Second point. Oh! that I had time to repair the evil I have done! but now time is at an end.

5. *Oh! that I had time*, he will say, *to repair the past!* But, when will he say this? When the oil in the lamp is consumed: when he is on the point of entering into eternity. One of the greatest causes of the distress and anguish of the careless Christian, at the hour of death, is the remembrance of the bad use he has made of the time in which he ought to have acquired merits for Heaven, and in which he has accumulated merits for Hell. *Oh! that I had time!* Do you seek for time? You have lost so many nights in gaming, and so many years in indulging the senses, without ever thinking of your soul; and now you seek for time; but time is now no more. "Time shall be no longer"—*Apoc.*, x. 6. Were you not already admonished by preachers to be prepared for death? were you not told that it would come upon you when you least expected it? "Be you ready", says

Jesus Christ; "for at what hour you think not, the Son of Man will come"—*Luke*, xii. 40. You have despised my admonitions, and have voluntarily squandered the time which my goodness bestowed upon you in spite of your demerits; but now time is at an end. Listen to the words in which the priest that assists you shall tell you to depart from this world:—Proficiscere anima Christiana de hoc mundo. Go forth, Christian soul, from this world. And where shall you go? To eternity, to eternity. Death respects neither parents nor monarchs; when it comes, it does not wait even for a moment. "Thou hast appointed his bounds, which cannot be passed"—*Job*, xiv. 5.

6. Oh! what terror shall the dying man feel at hearing the assisting priest tell him to depart from this world! What dismay shall he experience in saying within himself: *This morning I am living, and this evening I shall be dead! To-day I am in this house; to-morrow I shall be in the grave: and where shall my soul be found?* His terror shall be increased when he sees the death-candle lighted, and when he hears the confesssor order the relatives to withdraw from his chamber, and to return to it no more. It shall be still more increased when the confessor gives him the crucifix, and tells him to embrace it, saying: *Embrace Jesus Christ, and think no more of this world.* He takes the crucifix and kisses it; but, in kissing it, he trembles at the remembrance of the many injuries which he has offered to Jesus Christ. He would now wish to repent sincerely of all his injuries to his Saviour; but he sees that his repentance is forced by the necessity of his approaching death. "He", says St. Augustine, "who is abandoned by sin before he abandons it, condemns it not freely but through necessity".

7. The common delusion of worldlings is, that Earthly things appear great, and that the things of Heaven, as being distant and uncertain, appear to be of little value. They regard tribulations as insupportable, and grievous sins as unimportant. The miserable beings are as if they were shut up in a room filled with smoke, which hinders them from seeing objects before their eyes. But, at the hour of death this darkness shall vanish, and the soul shall begin to see things in their real colours. At that hour, all temporal things appear to be what they really are, vanity, lies, and deception; and the things of eternity assume their true value.

Oh! how important shall judgment, Hell, and eternity, which are so much disregarded during life, appear at the time of death. According as these shall begin to put on their true colours, the fears of the dying man shall increase. "In morte", says St Gregory, "tanto timor fit acrior, quanto retributio vicinior; et quanto vicinius judicium tangitur, tanto vehementius formidator"—*Mor.* 24. The nearer the sentence of the Judge approaches, the more sensible the fear of condemnation becomes. Hence the sick man will say: *Oh! in what anguish do I die! Unhappy me! Oh! that I knew that so unhappy a death awaited me!* You have not known it; but you ought to have foreseen it; for you knew that a good death could not be expected after a wicked life. But, since I must soon die, oh! that I could at least, in the little time that remains, tranquillize my conscience! Let us pass to the third point.

Third point. Oh! that I could, in the little time that remains, repair the past! But, alas! this time is not fit for repairing past evils.

8. The time allowed to careless Christians at the hour of death, is, for two reasons, unfit for tranquillizing the troubles of their conscience. First, because this time will be very short; for at the commencement, and for some days during the progress of the disease, the sick man thinks only of physicians, of remedies, and of making his last will. During that time, his relatives, friends, and even the physicians, deceive him, by holding out hopes of recovery. Hence, deluded by these hopes, he will not be able for some time, to persuade himself that his death is at hand. When shall he begin to persuade himself that death is near? Only when he shall be at the very point of death. This is the second reason why that time is unfit for repairing the evils of the soul. At that time the dying man is sick in mind, as well as in body. He shall be assailed by pains in the chest, spasms in the head, debility, and delirium. These shall render him unable to make any effort to excite a true detestation of his past sins or to apply to the disorders of his past life a remedy which will calm the terrors of his conscience. The news of his approaching death will astound him to such a degree, that he shall be scarcely half alive.

9. A person labouring under a severe headache, which deprives him of sleep for two or three nights, will not even attempt

to dictate a letter of ceremony. And at death, when he feels but little, understands but little, and sees only a confusion of things which fill him with terror, the careless Christian adjusts a conscience burdened with the sins of thirty or forty years. Then are verified the words of the gospel,—"The night cometh when no man worketh"—*John*, ix. 4. Then his conscience will say to him: "Now thou canst be steward no longer"—*Luke*, xvi. 2. There is no more time for negociation; what has been done, is done. "When distress cometh upon them, they will seek for peace, and there shall be none. Trouble shall come upon trouble"—*Ezech.*, vii. 25, 26.

10. It is often said of a person, that he led a bad life, but afterwards died a good death; that by his sighs and tears, he gave proofs of sincere repentance. "Morientes non delicti pœnitentia", says St. Augustine, "sed mortis urgentis admonitio compellit"—*serm.* xxxvi. The wailing of such persons proceeds not from sorsow for their sins, but from the fear of imminent death. He was not afraid of sinning, says the holy doctor, but of burning. "Non metuit peccare, sed ardere"—*epis.* cxiv. Till this moment the dying man has loved sinful objects: will he now detest them? Perhaps he will then love them with more tenderness; for the objects of our affection become more dear to us when we are afraid of losing them. The celebrated master of St. Bruno died with signs of repentance; but when laid in the coffin, he said that he was damned. If, at the hour of death, even the saints complain that, on account of the state of the head, they can think but little of God, or make but little effort to excite good acts, how can the negligent Christian make these acts at death, when he was not in the habit of making them during life? It may be said that he appeared to have a sincere sorrow for the wickedness of his past life. But, was his sorrow true sorrow? The Devil persuades him that the wish to have sorrow is true sorrow; but he deceives him. The dying man will say: *I am sorry from the bottom of my heart*, &c.; but these words shall come from a heart of stone. "From the midst of the rocks they shall give forth their voices"—*Ps.*, ciii. 12. But he has frequently been at confession, and has received all the sacraments; he has died in perfect resignation. Ah! the criminal who goes to be executed, appears to be perfectly resigned; but why? Because he cannot escape from the officers of justice, who bring him in chains to the place of execution.

11. O moment on which eternity depends! This moment made the saints tremble at the hour of death, and made them exclaim: *O God! where shall I be in a few hours?* "Sometimes", says St. Gregory, "the soul even of the just man is disturbed by the terror of vengeance"—*Mor.*, xxiv. What, then, shall the careless Christian, who has disregarded God, feel, when he sees the scaffold prepared on which he must die? "His eyes shall see his own destruction, and he shall drink of the wrath of the Almighty"—*Job*, xxi. 20. He shall see with his own eyes death prepared for his soul, and shall from that moment begin to feel the anger of the Lord. The viaticum which he must receive, the extreme unction which will be administered to him, the crucifix which is placed in his hands, the recommendation of the soul which is read by the assisting priest, the lighting of the blessed candle,—all these shall form the scaffold of divine justice. The poor sick man perceives that he is already in a cold sweat, that he can no longer move or speak, that his respiration has begun to fail,—in a word, he sees that the moment of death is at hand, he sees his soul defiled with sins, the Judge waiting for him; Hell burning under his feet; and in this confusion of darkness and terror, he shall enter into eternity.

12. "O that they would be wise, and would understand, and would provide for their last end"—*Deut.*, xxxii. 29. Behold, dearly beloved brethren, how the Holy Ghost exhorts us to provide now for the terrible straits and distress by which we shall be encompassed at death, and to adjust at present the accounts which we must render to God; for it will be then impossible to settle these accounts so as to save our souls. My crucified Jesus, I will not wait till death to embrace thee; I embrace thee at this moment. I love thee above all things; and because I love thee, I repent with my whole heart of all the offences and insults I have offered to thee, who art infinite goodness; and I purpose and hope, with thy grace, to love thee always, and never more to offend thee. Through the merits of thy passion I ask thee to assist me.

SERMON LII.

FOR THE TWENTY-THIRD SUNDAY AFTER PENTECOST.

On impenitence.

"Lord, my daughter is even now dead"— *Matt.*, ix. 18.

How great is God's goodness! How difficult is it to obtain pardon from a man whom we have offended! When sinners cast themselves at the feet of the Lord with humility and with sorrow for having offended him, he instantly pardons and embraces them. "Turn to me, saith the Lord of Hosts, and I will turn to you"—*Zach.*, i. 3. Sinners, says the Lord, I have turned my back on you, because you first turned your back on me: return to me, and I will return to you, and will embrace you. When rebuked by the Prophet Nathan, David repented, and said: *I have sinned against the Lord;* I have offended my God. David was instantly pardoned; for at the very moment that he confessed his guilt, Nathan said to him: "The Lord also hath taken away thy sin"—II. *Kings*, xii. 13. But, let us come to the gospel of the day, in which we find that a certain ruler, whose daughter was dead, went immediately to Jesus Christ, and asked him to restore her to life: "Lord, my daughter is even now dead; but come, lay thy hand upon her, and she shall live". In explaining this passage, St. Bonaventure turns to the sinner, and says: "Your daughter is your soul; she even now is dead by sin; hasten your conversion". Brother, your soul is your daughter, that has just died by committing sin. Return immediately to God. Hasten; if you delay, and defer your conversion from day to day, the wrath of God shall suddenly come upon you, and you shall be cast into Hell. "Delay not to be converted to the Lord, and defer it not from day to day"—*Eccl.*, v. 8, 9. Behold the sermon for this day, in which I will show, first, the danger to which he who is in the state of sin, and defers his conversion, is exposed; and secondly, the remedy to be adopted by him who is in sin, and wishes to save his soul.

First point. The danger to which a person in sin, who defers his conversion, is exposed.

1. St. Augustine considers three states of Christians. The first is the state of those who have always preserved their baptismal innocence; the second is the state of those who have fallen into sin, and have afterwards returned to God, and persevered in grace; the third is of those who have fallen and have always relapsed into sin, and are found in that unhappy state at death. Speaking of the first and second class, he pronounces them secure of salvation; but, speaking of the third, he says: "Non dico, non præsumo, non promitto"—*hom.* xli., *int.* 50. *I do not say; I do not presume; I do not promise.* He neither says, nor presumes, nor promises, that such sinners are saved. From these words, it appears, that, in his opinion, it is very improbable that they obtain eternal life. St. Thomas teaches (2, 2, *qu.* 109, *a.* 8), that he who is in the state of mortal sin, cannot long abstain from the commission of some new sin. And St. Gregory says: "A sin which is not blotted out by repentance, by its weight, soon draws to another sin; hence it is not only a sin, but the cause of sin"—*l.* 3, *Mor.*, *c.* ix. One sin is the cause of another, because, in the sinner, reason is disordered, and inclines him to evil; and therefore he cannot long resist temptation. "Quando", says St. Anselm, "quis manet in peccato, ratio jam est deordinata et ideo veniente tentatione faciet id quod est facilius agere". Hence, according to the holy doctor, though they understand the great advantage of sanctifying grace, sinners, because, they are deprived of grace, always relapse, in spite of all their efforts to avoid sin. "Per peccatum non potest prosequi bonum quod cognoscit, conatur et labitur". But how can the branch that is cut off from the vine produce fruit? "As", says Jesus Christ, "the branch cannot bear fruit of itself, unless it abide in the vine, so neither can you, unless you abide in me"—*John*, xv. 4.

2. But some young persons may say: *I will hereafter give myself to God.* Behold the false hope of sinners, which leads them to remain in sin till death, and from death conducts them to Hell. Who are you that say, you will hereafter give your-

self to God? But who, I ask, promises you that you shall have time to give yourself to God, and that you shall not meet with a sudden death, which will take you out of this world before you give yourself to him? "He", says St. Gregory, "who has promised pardon to penitents, has not promised to-morrow to sinners"—*hom.* xii. *in Ev.* The Lord has promised pardon to all who repent of their sins; but to those who wish to continue in sin, he has not promised time for repentance. Do you say *hereafter?* But Jesus Christ tells you that time is in the hand of God, and not under your control. "It is not for you to know the times or moments which the Father has put in his own power"—*Acts*, i. 7. We read in the Gospel of St. Luke, that Jesus Christ, seeing a fig-tree which was fruitless for three years, ordered it to be cut down. "He said to the dresser of the vineyard: Behold, for these three years I come seeking fruit on this fig-tree, and I find none. Cut it down therefore. Why cumbereth it the ground?"—*Luke*, xiii. 7. Tell me, you who say that you will hereafter give yourself to God, for what purpose does he preserve your life? Is it that you may continue to insult him by sin? No; he gives you life, that you may renounce sin, and change your conduct. "Knowest thou not that the benignity of God leadeth thee to penance?"—*Rom.*, ii. 4. But you are resolved not to amend; and if you wish to give yourself to God only hereafter, he will say of your soul to the dresser of his vineyard: "Cut it down. Why cumbereth it the ground?" Why should such a sinner be allowed to remain on Earth? Is it to continue to offend me? Cut down this fruitless tree, and cast it into the fire. "Every tree, therefore, that doth not yield good fruit, shall be cut down, and cast into the fire"—*Matt.*, iii. 10.

3. But, should God hereafter give you time for repentance, will you, if you do not now repent, return to him hereafter? Sins, like so many chains, keep the sinner in bondage. "He is first bound with the ropes of his own sins"—*Prov.*, v. 22. My brother, if you cannot now break the cords by which you are at present bound, will you be able to break them hereafter, when they shall be doubled by the commission of new sins? To give him an idea of the degree of folly which impenitent sinners reach our Lord showed, one day, to the Abbot Arsenius, an Ethiopian, who, not being able to raise a load of faggots, added to their weight, and

thus became less able to raise it. Sinners, said the Saviour to the holy abbot, act in a similar manner. They wish to get rid of their past sins, and, at the same time, commit new ones. These new sins shall lead them into others more numerous and more enormous. Cain sinned against his brother, first, by envy; then, by hatred; and afterwards, by murder: finally, he despaired of the divine mercy, saying: "My iniquity is greater than that I may obtain pardon"—*Gen.*, iv. 13. Judas also was first guilty of the sin of avarice; he then betrayed Jesus Christ, and afterwards hanged himself. Sins chain the sinner, and make him their slave, so that he knowingly brings himself to destruction. "His own iniquities catch the wicked"—*Prov.*, v. 22.

4. Moreover, his sins weigh down the sinner to such a degree, that he no longer regards Heaven nor his own salvation. "My iniquities", said David with tears, "are growing over my head, and, as a heavy burden, are become heavy upon me"—*Ps.*, xxxvii. 5. Hence the miserable man loses reason, thinks only of Earthly goods, and thus forgets the divine judgments. "And they perverted their own minds, and turned away their eyes, that they might not look unto Heaven, nor remember just judgments"—*Dan.*, xiii. 9. He even hates the light, because he fears that it will interrupt his criminal pleasures. "Every one that doth evil hateth the light"—*John*, iii. 20. Hence, he becomes miserably blind, and goes round about continually from sin to sin. "The wicked walk round about"—*Ps.*, xi. 9. He then despises admonitions, divine calls, Hell, Heaven, and God. "The wicked, when he is come into the depth of sins, contemneth"—*Prov.*, xviii. 3.

5. "He hath", says Job, "torn me with wound upon wound; he hath rushed in upon me like a giant"—*Job*, xvi. 15. By conquering one temptation, a man acquires not only additional strength to repel future assaults, but also diminishes the power of the Devil. And, on the other hand, when we yield to any temptation, the Devil becomes like a giant, and we become so weak, that we have scarcely strength to resist him any longer. If you receive a wound from an enemy, you lose strength. If to this, new wounds be added, you shall be exhausted, and rendered unable to defend yourself. This is what happens to the fools who say: *I will hereafter give myself to God.* How can they resist the attacks of the Devil, after they have lost their

strength, and after their wounds have mortified? "My sores are putrefied and corrupted, because of my foolishness"—*Ps.*, xxxvii. 6. At its commencement, a wound is easily healed; but, when it becomes gangrenous, the cure is most difficult. Recourse must be had to the cautery; but even this remedy is in many cases ineffectual.

6. But, Father, St. Paul teaches, that God "*will have all men to be saved*"—I. *Tim.*, ii. 4; and that Jesus Christ came on Earth for the salvation of sinners. "Jesus Christ came into this world to save sinners"—I. *Tim.*, i. 15. God certainly wills the salvation of all who desire it: he wills the salvation of those who wish to save their souls; but not of those who labour for their own damnation. Jesus Christ has come to save sinners. To save our souls, two things are necessary;—first, the grace of God; and secondly, our own coöperation. "Behold, I stand at the gate and knock: if any man shall hear my voice, and open to me the door, I will come unto him"—*Apoc.*, iii. 20. Then, in order that God may enter into us by his grace, we must, on our part, obey his calls, and open our hearts to him. Likewise, St. Paul says, "with fear and trembling work out your salvation"—*Phil.*, ii. 12. He says, *work out.* Then we too must coöperate to our salvation by good works; otherwise, the Lord will only give us sufficient grace by which we shall be able to save our souls, but by which we certainly will not save them. Behold the reason: he who is in the state of sin, and continues to commit sin, is daily more and more attached to the flesh, and more removed from God. Now, how can God, by his grace, approach to us, when we withdraw farther from him? He then retires from us, and becomes less liberal of his favours. "And I will make it desolate,...and I will command the clouds to rain no rain upon it"—*Isa.*, v. 6. When the soul continues to offend God, he abandons her, and withdraws his helps. Hence she shall cease to feel remorse of conscience; she shall be left without light; and the blindness of her understanding and the hardness of her heart shall be increased. The shall become utterly insensible to the calls of God, to the maxims of faith, and to the melancholy examples of other rebellious souls that have closed their career in Hell.

But who knows, the obstinate sinner will say, *but God will show to me the same mercy which he has shown to certain great sinners?* In answer to this, St. Chrysostom says: "Fortasse dabit, inquis; cur dicis fortasse? Contigit aliquando; sed cogita quod de anima deliberas?"—*hom.* xxii., *in* II. *Cor.* You say: *Perhaps God will give me the grace of salvation.* But why do you say *perhaps?* Is it because he has sometimes given to great sinners the grace of eternal life? But remember, says the holy doctor, that there is question of your soul, which if once lost, is lost for ever. I, too, take you up, and admit, that God has, by certain extraordinary graces, saved some enormous sinners. But these cases are very rare; they are prodigies and miracles of grace, by which God wished to show the boundlessness of his mercy. But, ordinarily, sinners who wish to continue in sin, are, in the end, cast into Hell. On them are executed the threats of the Lord against obstinate sinners. "You have despised my counsels, and neglected my reprehensions. I also will laugh in your destruction......Then they will call on me, and I will not hear"—*Prov.*, i. 25, 26, 28. I, says the Lord, have called on them again and again, but they have refused to hear me. "But they did not hear nor incline their ears; but hardened their neck, that they might not hear me"—*Jer.*, xvii. 23. Now they call upon me, it is but just that I refuse to listen to their cries. God bears, but he does not bear for ever; when the time of vengeance arrives, he punishes past and present iniquities. "For the Most High is a patient rewarder"—*Eccl.*, v. 4. And according to St. Augustine, the longer God has waited for negligent sinners, the more severely he will chastise them. "Quanto diutius expectat Deus, ut emenderis; tanto gravius judicabit, si neglexeris"—*lib. de util. ag. pœn.* He who promises to amend, and wilfully neglects to return to God, is unworthy of the grace of true repentance.

8. *But God is full of mercy.* He is full of mercy; but he is not so stupid as to act without reason: to show mercy to those who continue to insult him, would be stupidity, and not goodness. "Is thy eye evil because I am good?"—*Matt.*, xx. 15. Will you persevere in wickedness because I am bountiful? God is good, but he is also just, and exhorts us all to observe his law, if we wish to save our souls. "If thou wilt enter into life, keep the commandments"—*Matt.*, xix. 17. Were God to show mercy to the wicked as well as to the just, and to give to

all the grace of conversion before death, he would hold out a strong temptation even to the saints to commit sin: but no; when his mercies have reached their term, he punishes, and pardons no more. "And my eye shall not spare thee, and I will show thee no pity"—*Ezec.*, vii. 4. Hence he says: "Pray that your flight may not be in the winter or on the Sabbath"—*Matt.*, xxiv. 20. We are prevented from working in the winter by the cold, and on the Sabbath by the law. In this passage, the Redeemer gives us to understand that, for impenitent sinners, a time shall come when they would wish to give themselves to God, but shall find themselves prevented by their bad habits from returning to him. Of this there are numberless melancholy examples. In his sermons on a happy death, Cataneus relates, that a dissolute young man, when admonished to give up his wickedness, said: I have a saint who is omnipotent, and this is the mercy of God. Death came; the unhappy man sent for a confessor; but while he was preparing for confession, the Devil wrote down before his eyes all his sins. He was seized with terror, and exclaimed: Alas! what a long catalogue of sins! And before he was able to make his confession, he expired. In his sermons for Sundays, Campadelli relates that a young nobleman addicted to sins of the flesh, was warned by God and by men to amend his life; but he despised all their admonitions. He afterwards fell into a severe illness, confessed his sins, and promised to change his life; but, after his recovery, he returned to the vomit. Behold the vengeance of God! Being one day in a field during the vintage, he took fever, went home, and feeling that the disease was far advanced, he sent in haste for a priest who lived near the house. The priest comes, enters the house, salutes the sick man, but sees a frightful spectacle, the eyes and mouth open, the face black as jet. He calls the sick man, but finds that he is dead. Dearly beloved brethren, take care that you too be not miserable examples of the justice of God. Give up sin; but give it up from this moment; for, if you continue to commit sin, the same vengeance which has fallen on so many others, shall also fall on you. Let us come to the remedy.

Second point. The remedy for those who find themselves in sin, and wish to save their souls.

9. Jesus Christ was one day asked, if the number of the elect is small. "Lord, are they few that are saved? But he said to them: Strive to enter by the narrow gate; for many, I say to you, shall seek to enter, and shall not be able"—*Luke*, xiii. 23, 24. He says, that many seek to enter Heaven, but do not enter; and why? Because they wish to gain eternal life without inconvenience, and without making strong efforts to abstain from forbidden pleasures. Therefore, he said: "Strive to enter at the narrow gate". The gate of Heaven is narrow: to enter it we must labour, and must do violence to ourselves. And we ought to be persuaded that what we can do to-day, we shall not be always able to do hereafter. The delay of conversion sends many Christians to Hell: the weakness, darkness, and obduracy of the soul, are, as we have already said, daily increased, and the divine helps are diminished. Thus, the soul shall die in her sins. You say: *I will hereafter return to God.* Then you know that, to save your soul, you must renounce sin;—why do you not give it up now that God calls you to repentance? *If at some time*, says St. Augustine, *why not now?* The time which you now have to repair the past, shall not be given to you hereafter; and the mercy which God shows you at present, will not be extended to you at a future time. If, then, you wish to save your soul, do immediately what you must one day do. Go to confession as soon as possible, and tremble lest every delay may be the eternal ruin of your soul.

10. "Nullus", says St. Fulgentius, "sub spe misericordiæ debet diutius in peccatis remanere, cum nolit in corpore sub spe salutis diutius ægrotare"—*S. Fulg. ad Petr. Diac.* Were a physician, says the saint, to offer you a remedy for sickness, would you say: I do not wish to be cured at present, because I hope to recover hereafter? And when there is question of the salvation of your soul, you say: I will remain in sin, because I hope that God will be merciful to me at a future time. But if, according to his just judgments, the Lord should not show you mercy hereafter, what shall become of you?—shall you not be damned? Let us, says the Apostle, do good while we have time to do it. "Therefore, whilst we have time, let us work good to all men"—*Gal.*, vi. 10. For time may not be given to us to do good hereafter. Hence the Lord exhorts us to guard our souls with great care;

because we know not the hour when he will come to demand an account of our life. "Watch, ye, therefore; because you know not the day nor the hour"—*Matt.*, xxv. 13.

11. "My soul is continually in my hands"—*Ps.*, cxviii. 109. He who wears on his finger a ring containing a diamond of great value, looks frequently at the ring to see if the diamond be secure: it is thus we ought to watch over our souls. And should we see that it has been lost by sin, we ought instantly to adopt every means in our power to recover it. We ought to turn immediately to Jesus, our Saviour, like Magdalene, who, as soon as she knew that he sat at meat, ran to him, cast herself at his feet, and by her tears obtained pardon (*Luke*, vii. 37). "Now the axe is laid to the root of the trees"—*Luke*, iii. 9. For all who are found in sin, the axe of divine justice is at hand to take away their life as soon as the time of vengeance arrives. Arise, then, Christian souls, and if you are bound by any bad habit, burst your chains, and remain no longer the slaves of Satan. "Loose the bonds from off thy neck, O captive daughter of Sion"—*Isa.*, lii. 2. "Posuisti vestigium", says St. Ambrose, "supra voraginem culpæ, cito aufer pedem". You have placed your foot on the mouth of a vortex—that is, on sin, which is the mouth of Hell: take away your foot, and retire; otherwise you shall fall into an unfathomable abyss.

12. *I find myself subject to an evil habit.* But, if you wish to give up sin, who can force you to commit it? All bad habits and all the temptations of Hell are overcome by the grace of God. Recommend yourself to the heart of Jesus Christ, and he will give you grace to conquer all enemies. But should you be in any proximate occasion of sin, you must immediately take it away; otherwise you shall relapse. "Potius præscinde", says St. Jerome, "quam solve". Do not wait to loose your bonds gradually; cut them by a single stroke. The Devil seeks to make you slow in shaking off your fetters. Look for a good confessor; he will tell you what to do. And should you have the misfortune of falling hereafter into any mortal sin, go immediately to confession, even on the same day or the same night, if you can. Finally, listen to what I now say to you: God is ready to assist you: If you wish, it is in your power to save your souls. Tremble, brethren, lest these words of mine, if you despise them, should be for you so many swords in Hell for all eternity.

SERMON LIII.

FOR THE TWENTY-FOURTH SUNDAY AFTER PENTECOST.

On blasphemy.

"When, therefore, you shall see the abomination of desolation"—*Matt.*, xxiv. 15.

All sins are hateful in the sight of God; but the sin of blasphemy ought more properly to be called an abomination to the Lord. Every mortal sin, as the Apostle says, dishonours God. "By transgression of the law, thou dishonourest God"—*Rom.*, ii. 23. Other sins dishonour God indirectly by the violation of his law; but blasphemy dishonours him directly by the profanation of his most holy name. Hence St. Chrysostom teaches, that no sin exasperates the Lord so much as the sin of blasphemy against his adorable name. "Nihil ita exacerbat Deum, sicut quando nomen ejus blasphematur". Dearly beloved Christians, allow me, then, this day, to show you, first, the great enormity of the sin of blasphemy; and secondly, the great rigour with which God punishes it.

First point. On the great enormity of the sin of blasphemy.

1. What is blasphemy? It is the uttering of language injurious to God; it is, according to the definition of theologians, *contumeliosa, in Deum locutio;* or, contumely against God. O God! whom does man assail when he blasphemes? He directly attacks the Lord. "He hath strengthened himself against the Almighty"—*Job*, xv. 25. Are you not afraid, O blasphemer, says St. Ephrem, that fire will come down from Heaven and devour you? or that the Earth shall open and swallow you up? "Non metuis ne forte ignis de cœlo descendat et devoret te, qui sic os adversus omnipotentem aperis? Neque vereris, ne terra te absorbeat?"—*Paren.* 2. The devils, says

St. Gregory Nazianzen, tremble at the name of Jesus; and we are not afraid to profane it. "Demones ad Christi nomen exhorrescunt, nos vero nomen adeo venerandum contumelia afficere non veremur"—*Orat.* xxi. The vindictive assail a man who is their own equal; but by their blasphemies, blasphemers appear to seek revenge against God, who does or permits what is displeasing to them. There is a great difference between an act of contempt towards the portrait of a king, and an insult offered to his person. Man is the image of God; but the blasphemer offends God himself. "He who blasphemes", says St. Athanasius, "acts against the very Deity itself". The man who violates the law is guilty of a crime; but he who attacks the person of his sovereign, commits an act of treason; therefore he receives no mercy, but is chastised with the utmost severity. What then shall we say of the man who blasphemes and insults the majesty of God? "If", said the high-priest Heli, "one man shall sin against another, God may be appeased in his behalf; but if a man shall sin against the Lord, who shall pray for him?"—I. *Kings*, ii. 25. The sin of blasphemy, then, is so enormous, that the saints themselves appear not to have courage to pray for a blasphemer.

2. Some sacrilegious tongues blaspheme the God who preserves their existence! "Tu Deo benefacienti tibi", says St. Chrysostom, "et tui curam agenti maledicis". O God! you stand with one foot at the gate of Hell; and if God, in his mercy, did not preserve your life, you should be damned for ever: and, instead of thanking him for his goodness, you, at the very time that he bestows his favours upon you, blaspheme his holy name. "If", says the Lord, "my enemy hath reviled me, I would verily have borne with it"—*Ps.*, liv. 13. Had you treated me with contumely and insult at the time that I chastised you, I would be more willing to bear with your impiety; but you revile me at the time that I confer my favours upon you. O diabolical tongue! exclaims St. Bernardine of Sienna, what could have induced you to blaspheme your God, who has created you, and redeemed you with his blood? "O lingua diabolica, quid, potest te inducere ad blasphemandum Deum tuum qui te plasmavit, qui te pretioso sanguine redemit?"—*serm.* xxxiii. Some expressly blaspheme the name of Jesus Christ—of that God who died on a cross for the love of them. O God!

if we were not subject to death, we should be glad to die for Jesus Christ, in order to make some little return of gratitude to a God who gave his life for us. I say, *a little return of gratitude:* for there is no comparison between the death of a miserable creature, and the death of a God. But, instead of loving and blessing this God, you, as St. Augustine says, revile and curse him. "Christ was scourged by the lash of the Jews; but he is not less scourged by the blasphemies of false Christians"—*S. Aug. in Joan.* Some have blasphemed and insulted the Virgin Mary, that good mother, who loves us so tenderly, and prays continually for us. Some of these blasphemers have received a horrible chastisement from God. Surius relates, in the 7th of August, that a certain impious Christian blasphemed the Blessed Virgin, and pierced her image with a dagger. As soon as he went out of the church to which the image belonged, he was struck by a thunder-bolt, and reduced to ashes. The infamous Nestorius blasphemed, and induced others to blaspheme, most holy Mary, by asserting that she was not the mother of God. But, before death, his impious tongue was eaten away by worms, and he died in despair.

3. "Who is this who speaketh blasphemies?"—*Luke*, v. 21. He is a Christian who has received the holy sacrament of baptism, in which his tongue has been in a certain manner consecrated to God. A learned author says, that on the tongue of all who are baptized, is placed blessed salt, "that the tongues of Christians may be made, as it were, sacred, and may be accustomed to bless God"—*Clericat., tom.* 1, *Dec. Tract.* 52. And the blasphemer afterwards makes this tongue, as St. Bernardine says, a sword to pierce the heart of God. "Lingua blasphemantis efficitur quasi gladius cor Dei penetrans"—*tom.* 4, *serm.* xxxiii. Hence the saint adds that no sin contains in itself so much malice as the sin of blasphemy. "Nullum est peccatum quod habet in se tantem iniquitatem sicut blasphemia". St. Chrysostom says, that "there is no sin worse than blasphemy; for in it is the accumulation of all evils, and every punishment". St. Jerome teaches the same doctrine. "Nothing", says the holy doctor, "is more horrible than blasphemy; for every sin, compared with blasphemy, is small"—*in Isa.*, cxviii. And here it is necessary to observe, that blasphemies against the saints, against holy things, or holidays,—such as the sacraments, the Mass, Easter Sunday, Christmas Day,

Holy Saturday,—are of the same species as blasphemies against God; for St. Thomas teaches, that, as the honour paid to the saints, to holy things, and holidays, is referred to God; so an insult offered to the saints is injurious to God, who is the fountain of sanctity. "Sicut Deus in sanctis suis laudatur", *as we read in the* 150*th Psalm*, "laudate Dominum in sanctis ejus, ita et blasphemia in sanctos in Deum redundat"—*S. Thom., qu.* 13, *a.* 13, *a.* 1, *ad.* 2. The saint adds, that blasphemy is one of the greatest of the sins against religion (*ibid. a.* 3).

4. Thus, from the words of St. Jerome we may infer, that blasphemy is more grievous than theft, than adultery, or murder. All other sins, says St. Bernardine, proceed from frailty or ignorance; but the sin of blasphemy proceeds from malice. "Omnia alia peccata videntur procedere partim ex fragilitate, partim ex ignorantia, sed peccatum blasphemiæ procedit ex propria malitia" —*Cic. serm.* xxxiii. For it proceeds from a bad will, and from a certain hatred conceived against God. Hence the blasphemer renders himself like the damned, who, as St. Thomas says, do not now blaspheme with the mouth—for they have no body,—but with the heart, cursing the divine justice which punishes them. "The detestation of the divine justice is in them an interior blasphemy of the heart"—*S. Thom.*, 2, 2, *qu.* 13, *a.* 4. The saint adds, that we may believe that as the saints in Heaven, after the resurrection, shall praise God with the tongue, so the reprobates in Hell shall also blaspheme him with the tongue. "Et credibile est quod post resurrectionem erit in eis etiam vocalis blasphemia sicut in sanctis vocalis laus Dei". Justly, then, has a learned author called blasphemy the language of Hell; because, as God speaks by the mouth of the saints, so the Devil speaks by the mouth of blasphemers. "Blasphemia est peccatum diabolicum, loquela infernalis: sicut enim Spiritus Sanctus loquitur per bonos, ita et diabolus per blasphemos"—*Mansi. Discors.* 7, *num.* 2. When St. Peter denied Christ in the palace of Pilate, and swore that he did not know him, the Jews said, that his language showed that he was a disciple of Jesus, because he spoke the language of his Master. "Surely", they said, "thou also art one of them; for even thy speech doth discover thee"—*Matt.*, xxvi. 73. Thus we may say to every blasphemer: You are from Hell; you are a true disciple of Lucifer; for you speak the language of the damned.

St. Antonine writes, that the entire occupation of the damned in Hell consists in blaspheming and cursing God. "Non aliud opus in inferno exercent nisi blasphemare Deum et maledicere"—*part* 2, *tit.* 7, *cap.* iii. In proof of this doctrine, the saint adduces the following text of the Apocalypse—"And they gnawed their tongues for pain: and they blasphemed the God of Heaven"—*Apoc.*, xvi. 10, 11. The holy doctor afterwards adds, that he who indulges in the vice of blasphemy, already belongs to the number of the damned, because he practises their art. "Qui ergo hoc vitio detinetur ostendit se pertinere ad statum damnatorum, ex quo exercet artem eorum"—*ibid.*

5. To the malice of blasphemy is added the malice of scandal, which generally accompanies blasphemy; for this sin is ordinarily committed externally, and in presence of others. St. Paul reproved the Jews, because by their sins they caused the Gentiles to blaspheme our God and to laugh at his law. "For the name of God, through you, is blasphemed by the Gentiles"—*Rom.*, ii. 24. But how much more criminal are Christians, who by their blasphemies induce other Christians to imitate their example? How does it happen, that in certain provinces blasphemies are never, or, at least, very seldom heard, and that in other places, this horrible vice is so prevalent, that the Lord may say of them: "My name is continually blasphemed, all the day long"—*Isa.*, lii. 5. In the squares, houses, cities, villas, nothing is heard but blasphemies. How does this happen? Some of the inhabitants learn to blaspheme from others: children from their parents, servants from their masters, the young from the old. In some families particularly the vice of blasphemy seems to be transmitted as an inheritance. The father is a blasphemer; hence, the sons and nephews blaspheme: to this inheritance their descendants succeed. O accursed father! Instead of instructing your children to bless the name of God, you teach them to blaspheme him and his saints. *But I reprove them when they blaspheme in my presence.* Of what use are these reproofs, when with your own mouth you give them bad example? For God's sake, for God's sake, O fathers of families, never blaspheme; but be particularly on your guard never to blaspheme in presence of your children. This is a crime which God can no longer bear in you. And whenever you hear any of your children utter a blasphemy, reprove them severely, and, in

obedience to the advice of St. Chrysostom, strike him on the mouth, and you shall thus sanctify your hand. "Contere os ipsius, manum tuam percussione sanctifica"—*hom.* i., *ad pop.* Certain fathers unmercifully beat a child for the neglect of some temporal business; but if he blaspheme the saints, they either laugh at his blasphemies, or listen to them in silence. St. Gregory relates (*Dial.* IV., *cap.* xviii.), that a child of five years, the son of a Roman nobleman, was in the habit of profaning the name of God. The father neglected to correct him; but he one day saw his son pursued by certain black men. The child ran to embrace his father; but they, who were so many devils, killed him in the father's arms, and carried him with them to Hell.

Second point. On the great rigour with which God punishes the sin of blasphemy.

6. "Wo to the sinful nation......they have blasphemed the Holy One of Israel"—*Isa.*, i. 4. Wo to blasphemers, eternal wo to them: for, according to Tobias, they shall be all condemned. "They shall be condemned that shall blaspheme thee"—*Tob.*, xiii. 16. The Lord has said by the mouth of Job, "Thou imitatest the tongue of blasphemers; thy own mouth shall condemn, and not I"—*Job*, xv. 5, 6. In pronouncing the sentence of their condemnation, God will say: It is not I that condemn you to Hell; it is your own mouth, with which you have dared to revile me and my saints, that condemns you. Poor miserable blasphemers! They shall continue to blaspheme in Hell for their greater torment: their very blasphemies in Hell shall always remind them that they are damned for ever in punishment of their blasphemies on Earth.

7. But blasphemers are punished not only in Hell, but even on this Earth. In the Old Law, they were stoned by the people. "And he that blasphemeth the name of the Lord, dying let him die; all the multitude shall stone him"—*Lev.*, xxiv. 16. In the New Law, they were condemned to death by the Emperor Justinian. St. Louis, King of France, ordered them to be punished by perforating their tongue, and by branding their forehead with a red hot iron; and when they afterwards relapsed into blasphemy, he ordained that they should die on the scaffold (*Homo Bon. de cas. res.*, *p.* 2, *c.* i.). Another author says, that the law renders blasphemers (as being infamous) incapable of giving testimony

(Navarr., cons. 11, *de offic. ord.).* By the constitution of Gregory the Fourteenth, they were deprived of Christian burial. In the *Authentica ut non. luxur. hom.*, it is said that blasphemies bring on famine, earthquakes, and pestilence. "Propter blasphemias, et fames, et terræmotus, et pestilentia fiunt". You, O blasphemer, complain that though you labour and submit to fatigue, you are always in poverty. You say: *I know not why I am always in misery: some malediction must have fallen on my family.* No; the blasphemies which you utter are the cause of your wretchedness, and make you always an object of God's malediction.

8. Oh! how many melancholy examples could I mention of blasphemers who have died a bad death. Father Segneri relates *(tom.* I., *Rag.* 8), that, in Gascony, two men who had blasphemed the blood of Jesus Christ, were soon after killed in a quarrel, and torn to pieces by dogs. In Mexico, a blasphemer being once reproved, answered: *I will hereafter blaspheme more than I have hitherto done.* During the night he found his tongue sewed under the palate, and died in that miserable state, without giving the least sign of repentance. Dresselius relates, that a certain person was struck blind in the very act of blaspheming. Another, in uttering a blasphemy against St. Antony, was seized by a flame which issued from the image of the saint, and was burnt alive. In his book against blasphemy, Sarnelli relates, that in Constantinople, a man called Simon Tornaco, who had blasphemed God, began like a mad dog to lacerate his own flesh, and died in his madness. Cantapratensis states *(cap.* xlviii.), that a person who had been guilty of blasphemy, had his eyes distorted, and that falling on the ground he bellowed like an ox, and continued to roar aloud until he expired. In the *Gallican Mercury (lib.* X.), we read that a man named Michael, who had been condemned to be hanged, when he felt the pain of the halter, burst out into blasphemies, and died instantly. After death his head fell from the body, and the tongue remained hanging out from the neck, as black as a coal. I abstain from fatiguing you with other terrible examples: you can find a great many of them in the work of Father Sarnelli against blasphemy.

9. But to conclude. Tell me, O blasphemers, if there be any of you present, what benefit do you derive from your accursed blasphemies? You do not receive pleasure from them. Bellar-

mine says, that blasphemy is a sin which produces no pleasure. You derive no profit from them; for, as I have already said, your blasphemies are the cause of your poverty and wretchedness. You derive no honour from them; your fellow blasphemers have a horror of your blasphemies, and call you *a mouth of Hell.* Tell me, then, why you blaspheme. *Father, the habit which I have contracted is the cause of my blasphemies.* But, can this habit excuse you before God? If a son beat his father, and say to him: *My father, have compassion on me; for I have contracted a habit of beating you;* would the father take pity on him? You say, that you blaspheme through the anger caused by your children, your wife, or your master. Your wife or your master put you into a passion, and you take revenge on the saints. What injury have the saints done you? They intercede before God in your behalf, and you blaspheme them. But *the Devil tempts me at that time.* If the Devil tempts you, follow the example of a certain young man, who, when tempted to blaspheme, went for advice to the Abbot Pemene. The abbot told him, that as often as the Devil tempted him to this sin, his answer should be: Why should I blaspheme that God who has created me, and bestowed so many benefits upon me? I will for ever praise and bless him. The young man followed the advice, and Satan ceased to tempt him. When you are excited to anger, can you speak nothing but blasphemies? Say on such occasions: *Accursed sin, I hate thee; Lord assist me; Mary, obtain for me the gift of patience.* And if you have hitherto contracted the abominable habit of blaspheming, renew every morning, as soon as you rise, the resolution of doing violence to yourself to abstain from all blasphemies during the day: and then say three *Aves* to most holy Mary, that she may obtain for you the grace to resist every temptation by which you shall be assailed.

www.ingramcontent.com/pod-product-compliance
Ingram Content Group UK Ltd.
Pitfield, Milton Keynes, MK11 3LW, UK
UKHW020647160625
6407UKWH00044B/905

9 781635 619805